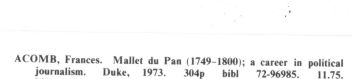

**ACOMB, Frances. Mallet du Pan (1749–1800); a career in political
journalism.   Duke,   1973.   304p   bibl   72-96985.   11.75.
ISBN 0-8223-0295-0**
A detailed study of one of the key journalistic figures of late 18th-
century France, this volume is useful primarily for its view of the mas-
sive upheavals of that period as seen through the eyes of a practical
and professional observer. Mallet du Pan has often been discussed as
the counter-revolutionary editor of revolutionary France who had to
live the last years of his life in exile. Acomb, making use of Mallet's
own papers and other primary sources, has written a full-length biography of the man, his politics, and his journalistic role — and frustrations. Acomb's writing is clear and extremely well documented. She
provides a well-balanced account of Mallet's unique position and his
contemporaries' views of his ideas and counter-revolutionary role. The
author, who is on the history faculty at Duke, has a previous book on
this period to her credit. As an in-depth study of a participant in
critical times, this volume is suitable for advanced students of French
history, but it is likely too specialized for most general collections.

Mallet Du Pan

Frances Acomb

MALLET DU PAN

(1749-1800)

A career in

political journalism

Duke University Press
Durham, N.C.
1973

Printed in the United States of
America by Heritage Printers

*To my sister
Evelyn Acomb Walker
and my brother
Edward Gray Acomb*

Acknowledgments

In my research for this study and in the writing I have incurred numerous obligations which it is a pleasure to acknowledge.

First, the Duke University Research Council made possible the initial indispensable research in Europe, it accorded numerous grants subsequently for continuing the work on this side of the water, and it has made the publication of the book possible.

I spent many weeks in Geneva working in the splendid collection of both manuscript and printed sources at the Bibliothèque Publique et Universitaire and am most grateful for the help afforded me by the staff, particularly M. Bernard Gagnebin, now Professor at the University of Geneva, who was then Conservateur des Manuscrits. At that time, too, the librarian of the Bibliothèque Publique de Neuchâtel obliged me by sending to the Library at Geneva, for microfilming, the important manuscript collection of Mallet Du Pan's letters to the Société Typographique de Neuchâtel (that is, principally to the publisher Osterwald), MS 1178, fo 22–121. It was the late M. Edouard Chapuisat, of Geneva, who called my attention to the existence of this collection. I am much indebted more recently to another Genevan, M. J.-D. Candaux, of the Société d'Histoire et d'Archéologie de Genève, for assistance in establishing certain biographical information about Mallet Du Pan.

M. Jacques Pons, librarian of the Bibliothèque de la Ville de Reims, informed me of an important letter in the collection there and arranged to send me a photographic copy. I am also indebted to the staffs of the Bibliothèque Nationale, the Archives Nationales, the Archives du Ministère des Affaires Etrangères, and the Bibliothèque de l'Institut de France, all in Paris; of the British Museum and the Public Record Office in London; and, in this country, the staffs of the Library of Congress, the New York Public Library, and the libraries of Vassar College and of Yale, Princeton, and Harvard universities, the University of North Carolina, and last but not least, Duke University, where the Interlibrary Loan Department in particular, under Mr. Emerson Ford, has afforded me invaluable assistance. Mrs. Ernest C. Hassold, Art History Librarian, was most helpful in the selection of a jacket illustration.

Especially, I must record my obligation to the late Sir Victor Alexander Louis Mallet, G.C.M.G., Mallet Du Pan's descendant, who with great liberality gave me access to the papers of Mallet Du Pan in London and permitted me to have such microfilm copies made as I desired, and I herewith thank his widow Lady Mallet, of Wittersham House, Wittersham, near Tenterden, Kent, and his son P. L. V. Mallet, Esq., for their permission to publish from these papers.

At one stage of my research, when I was unable to go to Paris, I was fortunate to secure the assistance of my colleague Mr. Pierre Aubery, now professor at the State University of New York at Buffalo, who located for me the correspondence of Mallet Du Pan with the comte de Vergennes and P.-M. Hennin in the Archives du Ministère des Affaires Etrangères and the Bibliothèque de l'Institut, respectively, so that subsequently I could procure microfilm copies. He also secured for me the assistance of M. Emile Danoën. I am grateful to both of them for such capable help at that juncture.

May I say here also that a number of other colleagues and friends have from time to time given me various sorts of references and assistance that have been much appreciated.

Mr. William N. Hicks, assistant editor, Duke University Press, and other members of the Press staff have been most helpful to me throughout the process of publication.

All quotations from documents in the Public Record Office are published by permission of the Controller of H.M. Stationery Office. Quotations from the Correspondance politique de Genève in the Archives des Affaires Etrangères are published by permission of the Ministre plénipotentiaire, chef du Service des Archives. For authorization to publish from the manuscripts concerning Mallet Du Pan in their keeping I am indebted to the Conservateur des Manuscrits de la Bibliothèque Publique et Universitaire de Genève, the Conservateur en chef de la Bibliothèque de l'Institut de France, le Directeur de la Bibliothèque de la Ville de Neuchâtel, and the Bibliothécaire de la Bibliothèque Municipale de Reims.

Contents

Introduction

Mallet Du Pan is most widely known as a counter-revolutionary publicist of the 1790's, frequently mentioned along with Friedrich Gentz and Edmund Burke. That part of Mallet's career which spanned the two decades prior to the French Revolution is much less well or widely known. Yet his reactions to the Revolution in France were along lines that he had already developed during those two preceding decades. He did not, in short, become a counter-revolutionary solely or even mainly on account of events beginning in 1789; in a sense, he already was one. On the other hand, the mature political observer of 1790 was not the same as the young man of 1770, even admitting that a certain complex of attitudes apparent at the beginning persisted. Mallet Du Pan's political and social views had in the interval undergone a development conditioned by both personal and political events and fortified by a good deal of reading and reflection which were incidental to his occupation. This study proposes to examine the nature of Mallet's thinking both before and after 1789.

Mallet's occupation was that of journalist. He was a professional who made his living, a good one, at journalism. A terse and incisive reporter, a sharp analyst, an indefatigable researcher and writer, specializing in political affairs but sensitive also to a wide range of the intellectual currents of the time, Mallet Du Pan described and interpreted the world around him, the world of the Enlightenment and the Democratic Revolution (to borrow the phrase of R. R. Palmer), in the periodicals he edited, and for the most part wrote, between 1781 and 1792: the *Annales politiques, civiles et littéraires du dix-huitième siècle . . . pour servir de suite aux Annales de M. Linguet* (with its continuation entitled *Mémoires historiques . . .*) and the political section of the *Mercure de France* (to the literary section of which he contributed on occasion also). Obliged to abandon journalism in 1792, when he joined the Emigration, he transferred his talents and applied his professional resources to the gathering and interpretation of intelligence on behalf of the Coalition against France. He turned again to journalism in 1798, with the *Mercure britannique*, to earn his livelihood in England.

Mallet Du Pan's main objective was, necessarily, to be a success at the business of journalism, which on the whole he was. How he became so is part of our purpose to relate. There were all sorts of difficulties, of course, including some of political origin. For the French revolutionary period the question of the relation between Mallet's journalism and his politics presents no problem to the historian; Mallet Du Pan then simply put out an opposition journal with superb disregard for political criticism. Before the Revolution, the matter appears somewhat more complicated. In Geneva, Mallet always protested that he was "impartial" (i.e., that he was not the man of a party), but his political line was such that he could not avoid the imputation of certain critics that his journalism was interested, as in his account of the events of the Genevan revolution of 1782. On the other hand, he incurred the hostility of the French ministry at the same time and later as being too outspoken. As Mallet's career shows, the pathway of the political journalist was beset with vexations if not outright perils, in a country like France at least. Inevitably, Mallet Du Pan's political opinions were colored by his experiences as a writer, both before and during the French Revolution.

Mallet Du Pan thought of himself, and wished to be thought of, as a contemporary historian. He was always referring to the primary importance of establishing the authenticity of information and he craved the freedom to interpret it in a historical context. No doubt his desire for recognition, for deference, lay behind this, but in any case the concept of the journalist as contemporary historian set a high standard of professional performance. Moreover, from his own general reflections on the nature of historical writing and the historical process and his own preoccupation with what he perceived as a European revolution, Mallet Du Pan developed a view of history as social evolution and a view of revolutionary dynamics that have their place in the study of eighteenth century historiography.

Mallet Du Pan

One

VOLTAIREAN AUSPICES

Jacques Mallet Du Pan, *citoyen de Genève*, was the elder son and first of two children of Etienne Mallet, pastor of the Church of Geneva at the village of Céligny, and of Eve-Michée-Elisabeth Du Pan, daughter of the syndic Jacob Du Pan. When Jacques was born, November 5, 1749, his father was forty, his mother thirty-two. According to report Etienne was an amiable and cultivated individual with an interest in natural science. It is said that he did not seek a more conspicuous post closer to the city because of poor health, and the two boys therefore spent their childhood at Céligny. In 1761 Etienne Mallet died,[1] leaving the supervision of his sons' upbringing to his widow and a formidable array of relatives. Madame Mallet lived until 1798, and made her home with her second son, Jean-Louis-

Note on spelling.—The reader will observe that there are variants in the spelling of the name Mallet Du Pan. Mallet's contemporaries sometimes wrote "Mallet du Pan," as did also A. Sayous, author and editor of the *Mémoires et correspondance*, and Mallet's descendant and biographer Sir Bernard Mallet; and the practice still persists. But the name of Mallet's mother's family, when not used in conjunction with another name, was normally written "Du Pan" or "Dupan." Mallet himself, signing his correspondence, used the form "Mallet Du Pan." The "D" is not always in the shape of a capital letter but it is always written large. He sometimes also signed a letter with the two initials "M D." I have chosen therefore to use the form "Du Pan" rather than "du Pan."

There is also a considerable present tendency to hyphenate the two names "Mallet" and "Du Pan," which indeed form a double surname. I have, however, chosen to follow the practice, which was Mallet's, of not using a hyphen.

1. Albert Choisy, *Notice généalogique et historique sur la famille Mallet de Genève, originaire de Rouen* (Geneva, 1930), pp. 31-32, 93, 97–98. A. Sayous, ed., *Mémoires et correspondance de Mallet du Pan, pour servir à l'histoire de la Révolution française*, 2 vols. (Paris, 1851), I, 2. Hereinafter cited as "Sayous."

Etienne.[2] Although Jacques respected his mother, one may wonder how close he was to her. In the record of his youth she appears simply as part of the family connection against which he rebelled after his fashion, without however breaking with them. According to the Genevan custom both sons added their mother's name, Du Pan, to their father's, Mallet. Jacques might have dropped the "Du Pan" when he married, taking his wife's name of Vallier instead.[3] Presumably for professional reasons, to distinguish himself from others named Mallet, and probably from pride of family, too, he continued usually (except with intimates) to call himself Mallet Du Pan, often adding "l'aîné," lest he be confused with his brother, who also went by that name.

The Du Pan belonged to the patriciate,[4] the untitled aristocracy, not landed but commercial, that controlled the government of Geneva. The Mallet family connection, which was large and came down in several branches, was patrician likewise, although the branch to which Pastor Etienne Mallet belonged was not the most illustrious in the city's social hierarchy.[5] Nevertheless, the lesser Mallet were touched by the luster of the greater and certainly shared in their attitudes. Madame Gallatin, who also was a patrician, was at pains to point out to the landgrave of Hesse-Cassel, when recommending Jacques Mallet Du Pan for a position at the court of Cassel: "He is a close relative of M. Mallet your Resident [the representative of the landgrave at Geneva]. He is not so nearly related to those [the Mallet family] of St. Peter's Court, but it is all the same family."[6] Mallet Du Pan said at a later time, speaking of the party of the patriciate: "I was born into that faction."[7]

2. Choisy, *La famille Mallet*, p. 98.

3. Bernard Mallet, *Mallet du Pan and the French Revolution* (London, 1902), p. 5n.

4. This appears incontrovertibly from all kinds of sources.

5. Choisy, *La famille Mallet*, pp. 57, 72, 93.

6. Louise-Suzanne Gallatin to Frederick II, landgrave of Hesse-Cassel, January 11, 1772, *Voltaire's Correspondence*, ed. Theodore Besterman, 107 vols. (Geneva, 1953–1965), LXXXI, 13. My translation. All subsequent quotations from the Besterman edition of the *Correspondence* are, when given in English, my translations. In quoting more than a phrase or two from any French source I have, as a rule, translated.

7. Mallet Du Pan to S. F. Osterwald, Geneva, September 21, 1779, Bibliothèque Publique de la Ville de Neuchâtel, MS 1178, fo 22–121.

Sent to school first to the College of Geneva, founded by Calvin, Mallet entered the Academy of Geneva, or the *Auditoires*, in 1764, when he was fifteen, and there pursued his formal education until about 1768 or 1769. He studied philosophy and law[8] but finally opted for a career in "letters," because he wanted most of all to write and because he had catholic intellectual interests. Belles lettres, history, public law, politics and political economy, science, philosophy—all commanded his attention. One might suppose that the variety and range of his reading implied a certain dilettantism, but Mallet Du Pan was then and always a hard worker and serious student.

The material rewards of authorship in the eighteenth century could be substantial, as Mallet's own career was to show, but they would certainly not be realized immediately. Yet the young Mallet Du Pan did not expect to be poor—he never saw himself, from first to last, as a dedicated starveling. For some years he counted on family assistance to sustain a comfortable if modest style of living. Etienne Mallet had had only his pastoral salary and his wife's dowry, which was not large, to support his family,[9] yet after his death they clearly did not suffer deprivation, and it furthermore appears that Jacques was never, in the years before he established himself professionally, without an allowance sufficient for a bachelor ménage with servant and books.[10] It was even enough to get married on—at least, one cannot see what other funds he had when he married. (He did begin soon thereafter, though, to feel the pinch.) The money may have come principally, if not entirely, from the Du Pan connection. In 1775, hoping to begin a career in Paris, Mallet was counting on the influence of a maternal uncle, who had long been a resident of the capital and was connected with the household of the duc d'Orléans.[11]

8. Sayous, I, 3; Choisy, *La famille Mallet*, p. 98.

9. B. Mallet, *Mallet du Pan*, p. 5. Mme Gallatin said Mallet Du Pan had "point de fortune." See her letter to the landgrave of Hesse-Cassel, March 11, 1772, in Voltaire, *Correspondence*, LXXXI, 110n. This title will always indicate the Besterman edition of the correspondence.

10. This is abundantly apparent from Mallet's correspondence. See especially his letter to Osterwald, Frankfort, July 17, 1772, Bibl. Neuch., MS 1178, fo 22–121.

11. Mallet Du Pan to Osterwald, Aubonne, August 30, 1775, ibid. The uncle must have been Jacob Du Pan, "négociant et joaillier de Mgr le Duc d'Orleans," who was also closely associated with the Mallet banking interest in Paris. See Herbert Lüthy, *La banque protestante en France de la révocation*

Two years later he wrote of an uncle, recently deceased, as "my bene-
factor, my second father, in possession at Paris of a fortune of which
we were the proprietors as well as he."¹² Mallet's situation in short
was such that, while sooner or later he must think in terms of re-
munerative occupation, he could at first afford to reject uncongenial
work. Whereas his younger brother became, like generations of his
forbears, *marchand drapier*, then *négociant*,¹³ Jacques was an intellectual who never considered commerce (except for investments)
and who was choosy in his own line, too.

The Geneva of Mallet's childhood and youth was Geneva in the
full tide of the Enlightenment, the Geneva of Voltaire's *chers Calvinistes*, where even the pastorate was responsive to rationalist influences, where a great breadth of secular culture was prized, where
the quarrel between Rousseau and Voltaire over the value of the
theater was at the same time an issue among the Genevans.¹⁴ Mallet,

---

de l'Edit de Nantes à la Révolution, Vol. II: *De la banque aux finances*
(1730–1794) (Paris, 1961), pp. 256–57, and notes.

12. Mallet Du Pan to Osterwald, Aubonne, December 11, 1778 [1777],
Bibl. Neuch., MS 1178, fo 22–121. The letter has been dated 1778, but in
what appears to be another hand than Mallet's. The evidence of the contents, including a reference to Mallet's forthcoming journey to London to
join Linguet, is against the dating December, 1778, whereas December, 1777,
is a likely date. However, the assumption that the uncle mentioned here was
the same Jacob Du Pan identified in the preceding note encounters a difficulty in the fact that, according to Lüthy, Jacob Du Pan did not die until
January 29, 1778 (*La banque protestante*, p. 389n.). Likewise Albert Choisy,
*Généalogies genevoises. Familles admises à la bourgeoisie avant la Réforma-
tion* (Geneva, 1947), p. 78, gives the date of this Jacob Du Pan's death as
January, 1778. Even supposing one disregarded the evidence about Mallet's
trip to London and assumed that the letter *had* been written in December,
1778, the identification would be no more certain, for Mallet writes of his
uncle as having only recently died. One is inclined to suppose an error in the
source from which Lüthy (and probably also Choisy) took his information,
the notarial register in the Archives d'Etat de Genève. Or possibly Mallet's
letter was written in February, 1778, and misdated "xᵇʳᵉ"—for the "xᵇʳᵉ"
is almost illegible, whereas Mallet's hand is in general quite legible. All translations into English of quotations from the Neuchâtel or any other MSS are
mine.

13. Choisy, *La famille Mallet*, pp. 31, 98. Jacques Mallet Du Pan used
to refer to his brother as "négociant." See his letter to Osterwald, June 6,
1778, Bibl. Neuch., MS 1178, fo 22–121.

14. Paul Chaponnière, *Voltaire chez les Calvinistes* (Paris, 1936), passim; Peter Gay, *Voltaire's Politics* (Princeton, N.J., 1959), chap. 4; R. R.

like the patriciate in general, followed Voltaire and not Rousseau, favoring the theater. Mallet Du Pan began early to cultivate an association with his neighbor, Voltaire. He became a frequenter "assez assidu" (his own words)[15] of the poet's house. He was aware, of course, of the professional advantages in such an association with Ferney, but it was more than this that drew him there, more too than his great admiration for Voltaire's art. He was dazzled by the philosophe and by his many-sided virtuosity. Voltaire was the greatest philosophe influence in the life of Mallet Du Pan.

Since Voltaire's friends were mainly patricians, and Mallet therefore knew people Voltaire knew, it must not have been difficult to secure entrée to Ferney. Our earliest record of the acquaintance dates from 1769, when Mallet Du Pan, not yet twenty, was given a letter of introduction from Voltaire to the reformer-jurist J.-M.-A. Servan at Grenoble. "This is a young man," Voltaire writes, "whom I envy . . . because he will have the honor of paying his respects to you: He is of an old family of the magistracy of Geneva. He knows that it is to Grenoble that one has to go to see the honor of the magistracy: he is one of those who most respect true virtue and eloquence."[16] To which Servan replied: "Monsieur, I have seen M. Mallet with the greatest pleasure, and I receive him as a mistress receives the bearer of a love letter."[17]

Voltaire's note suggests that about the personalities and questions of the day Mallet was already a knowledgeable young man. Indeed, if "letters" were Mallet's chosen vocation, politics were already, as with so many Genevans, his avocation. He aspired to make his mark in politics and perhaps also, in good time, a career. He made his début as a publicist on February 15, 1771, with a fiery tract of a hundred and sixty pages entitled *Compte rendu de la défense des citoyens-*

Palmer, *The Age of the Democratic Revolution*, 2 vols. (Princeton, N.J., 1959–1964), I, chap. 5.

15. Mallet refers to "une fréquentation assez assidue à Ferney," in a letter to Linguet, December 2, 1779, published in *Annales politiques, civiles et littéraires du dix-huitième siècle, ouvrage périodique, par M. Linguet,* VII, no. 54 (Dec., 1779), 385 (journal hereinafter referred to as *Annales de Linguet*).

16. Voltaire to Servan, Ferney, August 26, [1769], in Voltaire, *Correspondence,* LXXII, 281.

17. Servan to Voltaire, September 15, 1769, *ibid.,* LXXIII, 49.

bourgeois de Genève, adressé aux Commissaires des Représentans,
par un citoyen natif. Though it was published anonymously, the
author's identity was no secret. On February 22 the Petit Conseil
condemned it to be burned.[18] This pamphlet contains the germ of
much of the later publicist, and for this reason, and because Mallet's
relations with Voltaire were so much involved, the episode of the
Compte rendu requires careful attention.

   In order to appreciate Mallet's contentions, it is first necessary to
review briefly certain facts about Genevan politics and history in the
eighteenth century and the main lines of the bitter and involved constitutional controversy that wracked this town of some twenty-five
thousand souls even while it was advancing notably in prosperity and
opulence. Indeed, not only the views of the *Compte rendu* but the
subsequent development of Mallet's political thought were conditioned very largely by his experience of Genevan politics.

   Political power in Geneva was divided among several councils. The
largest was the Conseil Général, a body not elected but comprising
all adult males (some fourteen or fifteen hundred) who were *cito-*
yens or *bourgeois de Genève*, that is to say, all persons with political
rights. All *citoyens* were *bourgeois* but not all *bourgeois* were *cito-*
yens. The right of *bourgeoisie* could be acquired by purchase, citizenship belonging only to persons born in Geneva as the descendants of
bourgeois or *citoyens*; but as the right of *bourgeoisie* was not easily
acquired in the eighteenth century most members of the Conseil
Général were *citoyens*. The mere distinction between burgher and
citizen was not therefore very significant. The Conseil Général was
the law-making body, termed the Sovereign by those who wished to
increase its powers, and it also elected the Syndics. But the really active governing bodies were the Grand Conseil or Conseil des Deux
Cents, and the Petit Conseil of twenty-five members. These councils
not only wielded executive power, they had judicial functions, they
enacted ordinances, all legislative proposals for the Conseil Général
originated with them, they levied customary taxes from one year to
the next without referral to the Conseil Général, and down to 1768
they named from the Petit Conseil the list from which the Syndics
were elected. Moreover, all these powers were in the hands of the

   18. Isaac Cornuaud, *Mémoires de Isaac Cornuaud sur Genève et la Révolu-*
tion de 1770 à 1795, ed. Emilie Cherbuliez (Geneva, 1912), p. 13n.

patriciate, which was a hereditary oligarchy: for until 1768 the Small Council and the Council of Two Hundred each elected the members of the other. The patricians sat in the General Council, of course, but here they were a minority, some four or five hundred patricians and their supporters facing some thousand or eleven hundred citizens and burghers who were a middle class, less wealthy as a class than the patriciate, master craftsmen and merchants rather than bankers and *négociants* (though some of them were operating in a rather large way, too), less sophisticated than the patriciate and more tenacious of puritan tradition, but also highly literate and often cultivated, for both classes contributed to the liberal professions. They resented the patriciate's monopoly of government, and their antagonism had flared repeatedly into political action in the eighteenth century.[19] Those Genevans who were merely artisans, that is to say, the majority of Genevans, had, as will be explained presently, no political rights and many economic disabilities. They became a third force in Genevan politics after 1768; but the struggle between the burghers and the patriciate was primary. It was a socio-political rather than an economic contest, for economic grievances did not figure in it.

The condemnation of Rousseau's *Contrat social* and *Emile* in 1762 by the Small Council was the signal for a new round of controversy, the non-patricians championing Rousseau. Two parties formed, the party of the "sovereign" General Council with its middle class majority becoming known as Représentants because they claimed among other things that the Small Council was bound to consider petitions (*représentations*) presented by the citizens and bourgeois and in particular to accept petitions for referring to the General Council disputed questions of law; the patrician party of the

19. Definitions of terms and descriptions of the Genevan government from several points of view may be found in Jane Ceitac, *Voltaire et l'affaire des Natifs. Un aspect de la carrière humanitaire du patriarche de Ferney* (Geneva, 1956), chap. 1; Otto Karmin, *Sir Francis d'Ivernois (1757–1842). Sa vie, son oeuvre et son temps* (Geneva, 1920), pp. 6–7, 55; Henri Fazy, *Les constitutions de la République de Genève. Etude historique* (Geneva, Bâle, 1890), pp. 50–122; Palmer, *Age of the Democratic Revolution*, I, 127–28; Gay, *Voltaire's Politics*, pp. 190–95. Mallet Du Pan himself defined the terms for the foreign readers of his journal in 1782. See his *Annales politiques, civiles et littéraires du dix-huitième siècle; ouvrage périodique, pour servir de suite aux Annales de M. Linguet*, IV, no. 28 (Oct. 15, 1782), 202 (journal hereinafter referred to simply as *Annales*).

governing councils on the other hand becoming known as Négatifs, because they claimed for the Small Council the right to reject such petitions.[20] For political doctrine the Représentant party adopted the democratic concept of the will of the sovereign people as the source of law.[21]

Between 1765 and 1768 matters reached an impasse, for the General Council refused to elect as Syndics any of the persons presented from the Small Council. The patricians appealed to the mediation of the kingdom of France and the Swiss cantons of Berne and Zurich, all guarantors of a constitutional settlement made in 1738 that proved to have settled very little. The Republic of Geneva had long been a kind of client state of France, which tended to support the patriciate, which in its turn looked to France as the last line of defense against the democratic forces within. The General Council with its Représentant majority turned down the terms of the mediation, they refused to be cowed by a boycott of Genevan exports set up by the French foreign minister, Choiseul, and the Représentants began to carry arms and threaten to seize the city. The Small Council retreated, a compromise was reached (the Edict of Conciliation enacted by the General Council on March 11, 1768), and the French this time went along with the result.[22]

Under the Edict of Conciliation the patrician monopoly of government was infringed. The General Council was given a voice in elections to the Two Hundred: whenever fifty seats become vacant, an election should occur and twenty-five incumbents might be chosen by the General Council.[23] It was thus possible that in time the patriciate would lose their control of this body, which in fact did happen on the eve of the French intervention in Genevan affairs in 1782.[24] Moreover, the Syndics might be chosen from the Council of Two Hundred as well as the Small Council and even the composition of the Small Council itself was made subject to some review by the Gen-

20. Fazy, *Constitutions*, pp. 127–29. See also Palmer, *Age of the Democratic Revolution*, I, 130–31.

21. So, for one, Jean-Louis Delolme in 1767, quoted by Palmer, *Age of the Democratic Revolution*, I, 135.

22. Fazy, *Constitutions*, pp. 134–38; Karmin, *D'Ivernois*, pp. 22–31.

23. Fazy, *Constitutions*, p. 138; Ceitac, *Voltaire et l'affaire des Natifs*, p. 141.

24. Karmin, *D'Ivernois*, p. 77.

eral Council by a procedure called *ré-élection*, a species of recall: that is, at the time of elections to the Small Council the General Council might designate four incumbents to be replaced.[25] Thus in time the Représentants might also hope to control the Small Council, but certainly not very soon. The Représentants were by no means satisfied with these gains, since legislative initiative remained with the governing councils and the *droit négatif* of the Small Council was not denied. There was furthermore no adequate guarantee of the liberties of individuals against arbitrary procedure by the government.[26] For their part, the more intransigent Négatifs denounced the Edict of Conciliation. Nevertheless, for nearly a decade there was a Négatif-Représentant rapprochement. This unlikely development was not the result of any great access of reasonableness and moderation on either side. It came rather from their feeling a common danger. For the Edict of Conciliation had bitterly disappointed the body of Genevans who were without political rights at all, numerically about two-thirds of the population, who now organized politically to compel attention to their wants.

These were the people called the Natifs and Habitants. Natifs were persons born in Geneva who had not, however, acquired the right of bourgeoisie (expensive and grudgingly accorded). They were an artisan class who suffered from numerous and vexatious economic disabilities. They were not permitted to sell their products where or to whom they wished. Their capacity to achieve the status of master in a craft was hemmed about with restrictions, and they might not enter all professions freely. There was furthermore no legal way for them to bring their grievances before the governing councils, for the right of petition was reserved for Citizens and Burghers. Yet Natif families had often been Genevan for generations, and they were by no means an illiterate mass. Habitants were immigrants who had permission to reside and work in the town. They had fewer rights even than the Natifs and their accession to the bourgeoisie was regarded even more unfavorably. About the same in number as the Natifs, they followed the lead of the latter, and the party of the artisans in general was called the Natif party.[27] In the controversy of

25. Ceitac, *Voltaire et l'affaire des Natifs*, p. 141.
26. Ibid., pp. 141–42.
27. See references for note 19. Ceitac, *Voltaire et l'affaire des Natifs*, pre-

the 1760's between the patricians and the middle class, the artisans demanded consideration, too. Their leaders were obscure men, hesitant at first to strike out boldly on their own, but they found a champion in M. de Voltaire.

Voltaire's involvement in the affairs of Geneva must be emphasized here because it is central to our story. Until 1762, Voltaire had no criticism of the patricians, and he was the confirmed enemy of Rousseau. Allusion has been made already to the altercation over the theater in Geneva between Voltaire and the patricians on the one hand and Rousseau, the non-patricians, and the clergy as a body on the other, an issue Voltaire had himself in part created by presenting theater at Les Délices, his residence. But when the Small Council condemned Rousseau's books, Voltaire's viewpoint changed. He took up with Rousseau's supporters, who were Représentants, and began to find merit in the Représentants' attempts to break the control of the oligarchy that had proven itself so illiberal. Not that he repudiated his old friends completely. Characteristically, he tried in 1765 to effect a compromise between the parties on the issue of petitions. Neither the Négatifs nor the Représentants accepted it, and he dropped this line of action, moving on to a more radical position.[28] In the spring of 1766, while the mediation of the guarantor states was in progress, Voltaire was appealed to by Natif leaders to help them present *their* case to the mediators since, as non-bourgeois, they could not legally do so themselves. He came out for full civil equality for the Natifs together with some measure (rather indeterminate) of participation in the political life of Geneva.[29] Of course, the mediators did not recognize this interference. Voltaire continued nevertheless to give comfort and counsel to Natif leaders. In 1767, at the time of Choiseul's boycott against Geneva, he and Choiseul inaugurated a plan to build a new town nearby at Versoix in French territory which would be a refuge for artisan watchmakers from Geneva and—so Choiseul hoped—a source of profit to France.

During the crisis of 1768 the majority of Natifs supported the Représentants in preference to the Négatifs,[30] feeling that the patriciate,

sents the most complete analysis of the situation of the Natifs and the development of the Natif movement.
28. Gay, *Voltaire's Politics*, pp. 202–20.
29. Ibid., pp. 220–31; Ceitac, *Voltaire et l'affaire des Natifs*, pp. 43–62.
30. Karmin, *D'Ivernois*, p. 47.

though disposed to sponsor some concessions, had offered too little. But the Edict of Conciliation did not include civil equality for the Natifs. True, it facilitated their accession to the *maîtrise*, somewhat enlarged their commercial liberties, opened the liberal professions to them, and provided that twenty Natifs and Habitants in the current year would be permitted to purchase the right of bourgeoisie with five to be permitted to do so annually in the next five years.[31] But the Natifs were bitterly disappointed that economic and social disabilities had not been abolished. The cry went up now for political rights, which had not hitherto been emphasized. Pamphleteers claimed that the Natifs had once had political rights but had been done out of them, that once centuries ago they had participated in the General Council and should sit there again. This was a distortion of constitutional history, but the claim did have a certain plausibility.[32]

Négatifs and Représentants stiffened and even tried to take back what they had given. For instance, in July, 1769, the Small Council, urged by the Représentants, materially restricted by proclamation such small measure of liberty of trade as had been ostensibly granted in 1768 by the Edict of Conciliation.[33] There were other proceedings that inflamed Natif resentment, expressed at the time in pamphlets, political banquets, meetings, and demonstrations. These developments culminated, February 15, 1770, in a great riot that started as a demonstration on behalf of a Natif who, having sung derisive songs in public about the Représentants, was arrested and sentenced to prison. In the circumstances, the Small Council called the citizenry to arms. It did so with some hesitation, pressed by the Représentant party chieftains. Before the day was over, three Natifs had been killed.[34]

The upshot of the affair was the Edict of February 22, 1770, which, enacted overwhelmingly by the General Council, dissolved the Natif political "circles," exiled *without trial* eight Natif leaders, and declared that whoever demanded rights beyond the privileges granted to the Natifs in the Edict of 1768 (privileges which it now confirmed) would be punished as an enemy of the state. This proceeding was justified by the allegation that the riot had been plotted by the

31. Ceitac, *Voltaire et l'affaire des Natifs*, pp. 141–42.
32. Ibid., pp. 77–97, 143–54.
33. Ibid., p. 149.   34. Ibid., pp. 155–67.

Natif leaders. Naturally, the fact that the leaders had not been brought to trial but were simply banished without a hearing was regarded by critics as evidence that the government did not feel it could prove its case. The leaders, notably Jean-Pierre Bérenger, the principal Natif publicist, replied from exile.[35] Several hundred embittered Natifs departed from Geneva for Versoix. The Versoix project was, alas, not ready to receive them; it fell through completely after Choiseul's dismissal from the ministry that same year. Hence a large proportion of the emigrants returned to Geneva (to the relief of their rulers and employers, who were worried by the loss of all this skill); but some hundred families were settled by Voltaire at Ferney, where they prospered.[36]

Mallet Du Pan's *Compte rendu,* appearing just one year after the repression of the Natif party, defends the Natif cause with ardor, maintaining that the Natifs have been the victims of the grossest injustice. It is a philippic against the Représentant party as the principal authors of this injustice and indeed of all the troubles of Geneva. To expose them, says Mallet, is his principal aim—"C'est-là le but principal de cet écrit."[37]

The publicist declaims against the economic and professional disabilities of the Natifs, by which correspondingly the middle class interest has been privileged, and upholds as constituting fundamental human rights the free use of property and legal equality among classes of persons. "To fetter the use of property in the arts, agriculture, and commerce, without its being required by the public interest, is criminally to attack the most basic right of human liberty; moreover, to give privileges to one part of a nation at the expense of another is to attack the compact on which society is founded (*le pacte essentiel de la société*)."[38] The General Council is termed "a hereditary aristocracy, that is to say, the worst of governments."[39]

Since the Natifs have been denied under penalty the right to voice their grievances, since they have been judged, imprisoned, and exiled without due process of law, Geneva, says Mallet Du Pan, is republican only in form; it has become a despotic state, none the less so

35. Ibid., pp. 168–83.
36. Ibid., pp. 184–97; Gay, *Voltaire's Politics,* pp. 232–33.
37. *Compte rendu,* p. 129n.   38. Ibid., p. 50.   39. Ibid., p. 45.

for being a *despotisme populaire*.[40] ("Hereditary aristocracy" and "popular despotism" as used here by Mallet come to much the same thing.) "You [the authors of the Edict of February 22, 1770] are called free, and you have piled up these acts of absolute authority; republican, and you have only the spirit of inequality. . . . Liberty is in the laws, and you have denied laws to an entire people; . . . you have preached tolerance and formed a people of inquisitors."[41]

Mallet subscribes to the thesis that the exclusive privilege of citizenship had been a usurpation, and demands that any one born in Geneva should be ipso facto a citizen of the Republic. "Que la naissance fasse le citoyen."[42] (Hence the term "Citoyen-Natif" in the title of the tract, where Mallet Du Pan is writing in the guise of a Natif who *ought* to be a citizen.) He associates the usurpation of citizenship by the minority with the growth of the power of money. "The rights of citizenship (*droits de cité*) were the prize of birth and of *virtu* so long as Geneva needed citizens and courage; they became the prize of wealth when money replaced patriotism and the virtues."[43]

Not all the Représentants are wicked men, our moralist concedes. Some of them are only misguided.[44] Afflicted by the spirit of party, "the most frightful of the passions after religious intolerance,"[45] they are the dupes of their leaders, who themselves are fanatics, and also, more than this, hypocrites, charlatans, demagogues, their sole aim being personal power which they are willing to achieve by fraud and force.[46] Mallet does not hesitate to name names, one of which is that of Etienne Clavière.[47] Mallet Du Pan's war against the Gironde goes indeed a long way back!

The political theory of the Représentant party, with its concept of the sovereignty of the popular will, is rejected totally. For *Vox populi, vox Dei* is a fiction, and it is a fiction useful only to demagogues. It breeds an atmosphere of agitation in which they flourish. When the will of the people is above the laws, says Mallet, liberty is always lost—lost to interest, greed, mistrust, and fear, which prevail over justice.[48] Mallet's conception of what liberty does imply should

40. Ibid., p. 134.
41. Ibid., p. 125.
42. Ibid., p. 40.
43. Ibid., p. 39.
44. Ibid., pp. x–xi.

45. Ibid., p. vii.
46. Ibid., pp. x–xi, 3–4, and passim.
47. Ibid., pp. 32, 73.
48. Ibid., pp. 3, with note, and 11.

be stated in his own words. "A people is free," he affirms, "when its condition is politically determinate, [when] these relationships form the fundamental laws that the Sovereign is everywhere obliged to respect; it is free when the civil laws restrict its natural liberty only for the needs of the State, and when the criminal laws are the expression of the legitimate defense of its members. . . ." [49] Individual liberty under a settled constitution, this is Mallet's doctrine, and in his mind it is incompatible with the doctrine of popular sovereignty.

For future reference it is well to state here that whenever Mallet Du Pan speaks of democracy, what he means is always popular sovereignty or, in more Rousseauist terms, the sovereignty of the general will. The concept may or may not connote also what we should call a democratic franchise. He thinks of democracy primarily as a revolutionary phenomenon, and characteristic in the first place of a middle class although it will most likely soon extend to the common people. Mallet's terminology is in line with the prevailing usage of his period, rather than the nineteenth century.

It may seem strange that rejection of the democratic dogma of the time is coupled in the *Compte rendu* with a demand for the democratization of the citizenship (i.e., extending political rights to the plebs). The truth is, however, that Mallet Du Pan's advocacy of political rights for the Natifs has a limitation. He wishes to admit the Natifs to the General Council but he does not propose to extend the powers of the General Council at the expense of those of the Small Council and the Two Hundred. He seems to have two sorts of feelings about the role of the Natifs in politics. On the one hand, he does not presently mistrust them. He assumes that the plebs wants justice rather than power; beyond questions of livelihood and personal liberty, its members will be satisfied to leave ruling to the upper classes. The view of the Natifs of Geneva that emerges anywhere from Mallet's writings of the 1770's and 1780's is that of a good people, virtuous in every sense, peaceable, and sufficiently intelligent. They are not the Parisian sans-culotte terrorists of his later, French revolutionary, writings. They are more virtuous than the upper classes of Geneva because as yet uncorrupted by money. It is well therefore to have these people in the General Council where they will outnumber the middle class. On the other hand times change, no people is im-

49. Ibid., p. 43.

mune entirely to corruption or the virus of political fanaticism; the present Natifs, become citizens or bourgeois, might be infected by the Représentants' thirst for power and try to imitate them. Mallet interprets the tyrannical actions of the government in February, 1770, as the outcome inevitably of the extension in 1768 of the powers of the "Sovereign" (the General Council), which he regrets.[50] The drift of the *Compte rendu* is that a strong and independent executive is necessary in Geneva to offset the weight of the General Council.

If the Natifs have been the heroes and the Représentants the villains in this drama, what are the Négatifs? It is conceded that the magistracy have not showed up very well, that they have abused their powers, that the majority of the Négatifs went along with the Représentants in the unfortunate affair of February, 1770. A point is made, though, of noting honorable and courageous Négatifs who refused so to go along, and it is asserted that many others who conformed did so because they had been "deceived" by the Représentant *commissaires* about the existence of a plot, and were now embarrassed by their own gullibility.[51] It is claimed, moreover, that in the long run and in the nature of things, the real interests of the Natifs, their economic advancement and professional status, will be regarded favorably by the Négatifs, who have after all too much status themselves to resent or fear the rise of an artisan class. "It will not be the men of the robe or the capitalists (*capitalistes*) who will try to distinguish themselves from us [the Natifs], by forbidding us to be merchants or officeholders."[52] It is otherwise with the middle class, who are "our equals by blood, connections, manner of life, wants, and work."[53] "It will be those who are morally our equals who will endeavor to be so no longer, by oppressing us."[54] Mallet more than once takes the opportunity of being snobbishly scornful of the non-patrician bourgeoisie who want a bigger share in ruling Geneva. "I do not congratulate myself that I shall destroy the prejudices and recall to justice the base interest of a merchant Sovereign."[55] Mallet thought it ridiculous for

---

50. Ibid., p. 12. Mallet inveighs particularly against *ré-élection* of the members of the Petit Conseil.

51. Ibid., pp. 18 n. 2, 79, 130–31, 135 n. 5, 136.

52. Ibid., p. 22n.

53. Ibid., p. 45.

54. Ibid., p. 22n.

55. Ibid., p. 122.

Genevans "to regard as our Princes those who used to sell us our clothes, our provisions, and our watches."[56]

From what has been said, it would certainly seem that one idea in our publicist's mind was a new alignment in Geneva, an alliance of Négatifs and Natifs against the Représentants. It may be objected that such an interpretation of the *Compte rendu* does not take account of those features of the work that would have antagonized the patriciate. For, after all, it *was* a frontal attack on the policy of the Négatifs, who are accused of stupidity at the least, and it *was* a justification of popular opposition.[57] Even though the justification invoked is the defense of basic human rights and not the principle of popular sovereignty, which is rejected, the Négatifs might well regard this as a distinction without a difference. The idea of a Négatif-Natif alliance against the Représentants was not inherently improbable, however, for some Natifs had favored it and the Natif leader Isaac Cornuaud was just about to take it up and promote it with some success.[58] Mallet's trouble was that he overshot the mark. He was surprised, and genuinely hurt, by the unanimity of disapproval in the patriciate. He had meant to write a shocker, no doubt; but also he had hoped for more in Geneva than a *succès de scandale*, more than the approval of the Natifs, who acclaimed the *Compte rendu*, said Cornuaud, as a gospel.[59]

This is not to deny the reality of Mallet's sympathy for the Natifs. The objective reader may be put off by the intricacy and even speciousness of the arguments used in the *Compte rendu* to damn the Représentants while exonerating the Négatifs, he may be repelled by Mallet's snobbery toward the majority of Citizens and Bourgeois of Geneva, he may think therefore that Mallet is more against the overdog than for the underdog (a suspicion that arises more than once later about this champion of a long list of underdogs), yet he will have to realize that Mallet's sympathy for the Natifs and his interest in their cause are genuine. The question is, how did he come by such an attitude?

56. Ibid., p. 31.
57. This is implicit in the whole work, but Mallet has his Citoyen-Natif say explicitly that it is only natural to have revolted against the state of things in Geneva. Ibid., p. 47.
58. Karmin, *D'Ivernois*, pp. 53–54, 69–70.
59. Cornuaud, *Mémoires*, p. 133.

From the memoirs of Cornuaud, again, we learn that Mallet Du Pan was frequenting Natif circles and attending Natif political banquets some time between the summer of 1769 and February of 1770. Cornuaud attributed his interest in the Natif cause to an amorous intrigue that, according to the memoirist, Mallet was carrying on with a Natif married woman whom he saw on these occasions.[60] There may indeed have been such an affair, and the young man's political sympathies may have been influenced by it, but some skepticism seems justified, for during the rest of his life, certainly, women influenced Mallet Du Pan very little, and at this point much greater weight should probably be given to other factors. One of these was his friendship with J.-P. Bérenger, which began probably about this time. Bérenger was a Natif, an orphan of humble birth but well educated by a foster father. Like Mallet Du Pan, he had chosen a career in letters with a special leaning toward history. Nine years Mallet's senior, just of an age to be admired in an elder-brother role, he was the principal Natif publicist in the turbulent period 1768–1770 and was one of the eight Natif leaders exiled by the decree of February, 1770.[61] Several pages of the *Compte rendu* are given to a warm defense of Bérenger's role in 1770.[62] Mallet Du Pan and Bérenger were to remain over many years, as Mallet's correspondence shows, in friendly contact, though their political views were not to remain identical.

But Mallet Du Pan's association with Voltaire had also begun in the summer of 1769, as we have seen, and the language of Voltaire's letter to Servan ("Il sait que c'est à Grenoble qu'il faut aller pour voir l'honneur de la magistrature") indicates that Mallet and Voltaire had already talked about public affairs in sympathetic agreement. It seems quite possible that Mallet first came to the Natif cause through Voltaire. In any case, it is certain that Voltaire (or Mallet's idea of Voltaire) had much to do with the young man's action subsequently. In the *Compte rendu* Voltaire's authority is confidently invoked. The promoters of the Versoix project are "the

60. Ibid., pp. 95, 110.
61. Sayous, I, 14; *Dictionnaire historique et biographique de la Suisse* (Neuchâtel, 1920–), II, 64; Albert de Montet, *Dictionnaire biographique des Genevois et des Vaudois*, 2 vols. (Lausanne, 1877–1878), I, 42; Jean Senebier, *Histoire littéraire de Genève*, 3 vols. (Geneva, 1786), III, 295.
62. *Compte rendu*, pp. 112–16.

great men [Choiseul and Voltaire] who have concerned themselves with our [the Natifs'] misfortunes."[63] A remark of Voltaire relating to an occurrence unflattering to the Représentants is familiarly reported. "The Sieur Deluc senior," says Mallet, "said after the massacre of three Natifs, striking blows with his cane, *good, good, there are three killed already.* M. de Voltaire, against whom he wrote a thick book, very diffuse and very tiresome, said jokingly *that he resembles the Apostles before the descent of the Holy Spirit.*"[64] To be sure, Voltaire would never have written the *Compte rendu.* It was not in his style and manner; he was suave where Mallet was rude and belligerent, and he was not so unsympathetic as Mallet to the political ambitions of the Représentants. But on the whole Mallet's view of the Natif affair is Voltaire's view, and we must deduce that he published the *Compte rendu* anticipating Voltaire's approval. Because of the availability of his illustrious patron's credit, his *démarche* seems rather less reckless than it might otherwise appear. For if Voltaire's own involvement with the Natifs had thoroughly exasperated important people in Geneva, he had still not lost their good will entirely. They still appreciated the luster he had shed on the town, he was still the man of Calas (for which Genevans of all classes admired him), and he knew how to retrieve a position. He retrieved his own, and in Mallet's case, the Patriarch was glad to recognize his obligation to a disciple.

The young publicist's standing in Geneva had certainly not been advanced and his future was in doubt. One may imagine the anxious consultations of relatives eager for him to settle down, and, so Mallet Du Pan believed afterward, preferably somewhere else.[65] In the course of the year a promising situation opened up. It chanced that the Landgrave Frederick II of Hesse-Cassel wanted a professor of history and belles-lettres for his academy at Cassel. Jacques Mallet's relative Paul-Henri Mallet, sometime Royal Professor of Belles-Lettres at Copenhagen, member of the Genevan Council of Two Hundred and married to a Du Pan, was now, as we have already noted, the landgrave's resident at Geneva, and he was furthermore

63. Ibid., p. 82.
64. Ibid., pp. 117–18n. Mallet's italics.
65. Mallet Du Pan to Osterwald, July 17, 1772, Bibl. Neuch., MS 1178, fo 22–121; Mallet Du Pan to Rieu, November 11, 1772, Bibliothèque Publique et Universitaire de Genève, MS Supp. 150.

engaged in writing a *History of the House of Hesse* of which the first volume had already appeared.[66] Perhaps this was the channel through which word of the vacancy passed. But the landgrave, who had been educated in Geneva,[67] also was in contact with other people there. One of them was, as is well known, Voltaire, whose correspondence with the landgrave was always profuse in expressions of admiration for that prince's qualities. The initial solicitation on Jacques Mallet's behalf would seem to have come from a friend of the family who was also the friend of both the landgrave and Voltaire, Madame Gallatin (Suzanne Louise Gallatin). (There is a story that a member of the Pictet family also approached Voltaire on Mallet's behalf.)[68] "A M. Mallet," wrote Madame Gallatin, "a M. Mallet of Geneva, of good character (*de bonnes moeurs*), 24 years of age [she was wrong here; Mallet Du Pan was then twenty-two], of much intelligence and learning, has entreated me to ask Your Serene Highness to give him a place in your Academy." She coupled with her request that of Voltaire, to whom she habitually referred as "notre ami," who was asking for the favor "because of the lively interest he takes in this person."[69] Within the month Mallet had secured the position at a salary of five hundred écus, or fifteen hundred livres.

Expressing her thanks, Madame Gallatin thought fit to caution the landgrave that the new appointee was not, despite his patrician connections, a man of society. "He is very well informed," she said, "very shy. Having been always devoted to study, he is not at ease in society as someone else would be." But, she hastened to add, "he has too much intelligence not to succeed," and she asserted that

66. Senebier, *Histoire littéraire*, III, 290; Eugène Haag, *La France protestante; ou, Vie des protestants français qui se sont fait un nom dans l'histoire*, 10 vols. (Paris, Geneva, 1846–1859), VII, 192–93; *Nouvelle biographie générale depuis les temps les plus reculés jusqu'a nos jours . . .*, 46 vols. (Paris, 1853–1866), XXXIII, 72–74.

67. So Mallet indicates in his *Quelle est l'influence de la philosophie sur les belles lettres? Discours inaugural prononcé à Cassel le 8 avril 1772* [Cassel, 1772], pp. 3–4.

68. Gustave Desnoiresterres, *Voltaire et la société française au XVIIIᵉ siècle*, 8 vols. (Paris, 1867–1876), VII, 157, n. 1, citing Constant MSS, Bibl. Genève; Paul Chaponnière, *Voltaire chez les Calvinistes*, pp. 246–47, also citing the Constant MSS.

69. Mme Gallatin to the Landgrave Frederick of Hesse-Cassel, December 11, 1771, in Voltaire, *Correspondence*, LXXX, 193.

Voltaire had a high opinion of him: "Our friend values him highly."[70] When Voltaire himself wrote to thank the landgrave for Mallet's appointment he expressed no reservations. "This is a young man," he said, "who is indeed worthy to serve a philosopher prince. I envy him," he added, "as much as I thank you for your benevolence to him."[71] His advice to the young professor did on the other hand contain a note of warning. "Live happy, my dear philosopher, with a prince who is full of merit and of justice, whereas your compatriots have experienced some trouble. The labor that you are going to undertake is in every way agreeable. You will have more than one occasion to show in your work that prudent and tolerant spirit so necessary to society. . . ." Then he concluded kindly: "Good night: if I am still alive when you return, come talk reason at Ferney."[72]

Arriving at Cassel toward the end of February, 1772, Mallet Du Pan seems to have made a good first impression on the landgrave.[73] Alas, his own almost immediate reaction to Cassel was violently negative, and within a month he had in very emphatic terms let Voltaire know his feelings. It is apparent from his letter that he was homesick and felt out of his element. The library was very large and there were many books, but nobody wanted culture, least of all French culture (and Mallet at this point did not think there was any German culture). "The French books especially are chosen with a very distressing Germanic barbarism; in general one would learn more in an hour with you than in a year here, where the court is military and not at all curious about literary masterpieces." One senses how much he had come to depend on Voltaire. Having no father of his own, he addresses the poet-philosopher as "mon cher papa," calls himself "your pupil" and "one of your apostles," and begs him not to forget "that I have nothing but your books and the remembrance of you in these deserts; that I should be inconsolable to spend my young days in letters far from you if I did not have all

70. Mme Gallatin to Frederick of Hesse-Cassel, January 11, 1772, ibid., LXXXI, 12.

71. Voltaire to the Landgrave Frederick of Hesse-Cassel, January 25, 1772, ibid., p. 37.

72. Voltaire to Mallet Du Pan [January 25, 1772], ibid., p. 38. The dating, which is Besterman's, differs from that of previous editors who erroneously placed it in May, 1774.

73. Frederick, landgrave of Hesse-Cassel, to Voltaire, February 28, [1772], ibid., p. 89.

the new instruction you will give to philosophy and to letters." Would "mon bon papa" please have sent to him, through Cailler, *marchand libraire* at Geneva, the latest volumes of the *Questions sur l'Encyclopédie?* Of the landgrave, Mallet writes that he "is good to me" and he praises the tolerant attitude of that prince, who has removed priestly censorship from Hesse-Cassel, where Holbach's *Système de la nature* and Voltaire's "refutation" of it are sold side by side. But, adds Mallet:

> There is an immense work to be done here; the Calvinist atrocity still dominates the universities, the ministers, and even the priests. They are fanatic and orthodox; in a word I shall exhaust all the feeble enlightenment that I owe to you in eradicating the work of St. Boniface.[74]

Gently but firmly the master repeated the admonition his disciple had not understood and enlarged upon the opportunity the post afforded to a philosopher of tact:

> My dear and amiable professor, who will never profess anything but the truth and the noble scorn of impostors, how fortunate you are to be with a just, good, enlightened prince, who tramples infamous superstition under-foot, and who places religion in virtue, who is neither Papist, nor Calvinist, but man. . . . You have a fine career before you; teaching history in a new fashion, and destroying the absurd lies that disfigure all the histories, you can attract to Cassel a great number of foreigners who will learn the French language and the truth at the same time.[75]

When Voltaire wrote, however, Mallet had already (on April 8, 1772) delivered his inaugural professorial address before an audience that included "the Landgrave, six princes of the Empire, and a most numerous gathering,"[76] and his performance was in accord with his aforementioned statement of purpose to do all in his power to uproot the work of St. Boniface in Germany. The address, entitled *Quelle est l'influence de la philosophie sur les belles lettres?* is in praise of the Enlightenment. The eighteenth century is not indeed

74. Mallet Du Pan to Voltaire, Cassel, March 21, 1772, ibid., pp. 132–34.
75. Voltaire to Mallet Du Pan, April 24, [1772], ibid., pp. 205–6.
76. Voltaire to D'Alembert, July 1, [1772], ibid., LXXXII, 97–98.

held to be in all respects the greatest age, for it is inferior to the age of Louis XIV in that the latter produced greater works of the imagination and the intellect, but it is superior in philosophic character, it is the century (though fifth century Athens was indeed such another) when philosophy has taken over belles lettres.[77] Mallet singles out half a dozen names for special mention: Fénelon, who seems to him more of the eighteenth than the seventeenth century; Fontenelle; Lamotte; Montesquieu; Diderot and D'Alembert, editors of the *Encyclopédie*, "monument digne du siècle"; and above all "the eagle" Voltaire, to whom several pages full of praise and gratitude are devoted.[78] It should be noted, in view of Mallet's later opinions, that at this time Rousseau and Linguet are not given a very high rating, though they are conceded to be interesting writers.[79] They are not true philosophes. Various English names are included, but with no sense of a comprehensive coverage;[80] and we observe that for Mallet the Enlightenment is French and English almost exclusively. It is certainly not at all German. While such a view is not surprising for the time with a person of French culture, one would think that in a German city Mallet would have gone out of his way to find some German to praise beside the landgrave. The Enlightenment is of course only the more or less happy outcome of a long dismal tale. Mallet accepts the Enlightenment periodization of history (the great and constructive ages being those of Pericles, of Augustus, of the Renaissance, of Louis XIV, of the eighteenth century), together with the Voltairean view of the history of Christianity. From the time when Christianity triumphed over ancient religions to the time of Calas, it was nothing but *fanatisme, ergoterie théologique, esprit convertisseur*; and the history of the Protestant Reformation was no exception.[81] The struggle, moreover, is held to be not yet over. The philosopher must continue to fight fanaticism of religion where it still remains; he must define the rights of society and defend them; he must seek to reform the laws and "create" a criminal jurisprudence; he must propagate among the uninformed the knowledge of science and of history.[82] Mallet is a little pessimistic, subscribing to some sort of cyclical theory of cultural history.[83]

77. *Quelle est l'influence de la philosophie?*, p. 8 and passim.
78. Ibid., pp. 6, 80–87.
79. Ibid., pp. 86, 89–90 and n., 124–28.
80. Ibid., pp. 89–90.
81. Ibid., pp. 70–74.
82. Ibid., pp. 81–82.
83. Ibid., pp. 96–97.

Beside throwing down the glove to the theologians and the orthodox generally, Mallet also takes care to antagonize his colleagues of
the academy. He scornfully pronounces prevailing modes of education to be pedantic and scholastic, he would diminish the emphasis
on Latin studies and put it on modern language, literature, and
history.[84]

The whole address, which incidentally showed off considerable
learning, is couched in a high flown and tortuous style, and the
thought, as one reviewer complained, is not always clear.[85] But the
drift of the address is plain enough and the audience did not like it.
They proceeded to make life miserable for the speaker, or rather
more miserable. By the middle of July, 1772, less than six months
after arriving, Mallet Du Pan had resigned and had departed from
Cassel in disgust and wrath. He wrote at the time, in a white heat of
resentment:

> For six months I drank the lees of disgust, of military rudeness,
> of the total lack of books, correspondence, connections, men of
> letters. Depressed from having been deceived in a country where
> I had been promised prosperity and consideration, I was assailed
> by the most hateful persecution, by envy, the priestly *canaille*,
> the disdain of courtiers indignant to behold a republican who
> was not fashionable. Courtiers' bickerings between the minister
> of France and those of the Landgrave, in which I was involved as
> associate and client of the former, led me to give my resignation,
> justified by my uselessness in an academy where no student un-
> derstood or cared about French letters. The Prussian party,
> which was already agitated to see a Frenchman [so Mallet Du
> Pan thought of himself in Germany] in affairs, [together with]
> the confessors who do not love the authors of Voltairean ad-
> dresses, determined the Prince to accede to my request. I had
> against me at the same time Luther, Rome, and Calvin. So many
> annoyances and base maneuvers were altogether beyond my
> strength.[86]

84. Ibid., pp. 7–12.
85. *Journal helvétique, ou Annales littéraires et politiques de l'Europe,
et principalement de la Suisse,* Dec. 1772, pp. 20–23.
86. Mallet Du Pan to Osterwald, Frankfort, July 17, 1772, Bibl. Neuch.,
MS 1178, fo 22–121.

To a different correspondent a few months later Mallet said more of the tension between his colleagues and himself. "I found myself affiliated with the most terrible pedants who ever adorned the universities. Uttering among themselves the most frightful abuses in barbarous Latin, they did not forget that I was a foreigner, French, and especially that I did not Latinize invectives." Mallet said that the landgrave had originally supposed, on the authority of the *beaux esprits* of Cassel, and given the reluctance of German gentlemen to learn French, that he would teach French literature in Latin—a "burlesque idea."[87] He claimed furthermore that the director of the academy was a scoundrelly adventurer who had been made a minister because he had persuaded the landgrave he could make that prince king of Poland![88] He complained that militarism was ruining Germany. While Mallet Du Pan had indeed a sort of Voltairean antipathy to warfare, his point here was that in Germany, and particularly in Hesse, only the military positions were really prestigious. As to the precise circumstances of his leaving Cassel, he said he had requested either to be permitted to resign outright, or to be given an appointment as custodian of the prince's private library. That position, however, was presently confided to a *valet de chambre*, the landgrave having preferred to let him go.[89]

Of his own responsibility for the Cassel fiasco, the former professor admitted to "too much candor," then added, characteristically, "and I presume to say, honesty (*droiture*)."[90] It must be conceded to him, though, that Voltaire and Mallet's family had painted too rosy a picture of the opportunities at Cassel. Given his extreme unhappiness in the situation, it is hard to see what choice he had but to resign.

But what next? Mallet tells us that on leaving the landgrave's service he turned down two advantageous offers from the elector of Trèves and the prince of Darmstadt, respectively. Incidentally, if Mallet had these offers, and there is no reason to doubt him, he must have impressed some people at Cassel favorably in spite of everything. But he had concluded, quite rightly, that he was no man for

87. Mallet Du Pan to Henri Rieu, Neuchâtel, October 10, 1772, Bibl. Genève, MS Supp. 150.

88. Mallet Du Pan to Rieu, Neuchâtel, November 11, 1772, ibid.

89. Mallet Du Pan to Rieu, Neuchâtel, October 10, 1772, ibid.

90. Mallet Du Pan to Osterwald, Frankfort, July 17, 1772, Bibl. Neuch., MS 1178, fo 22–121.

the court of any petty eighteenth century principality. "A man of letters, a republican, I will never be the slave of a master's base courtiers. I renounce forever these degrading grandeurs other people had caused me to think of."[91] It would be necessary to find something else.

He was precluded from returning to Geneva by the attitude of his family and their friends, who had no doubt hoped that he would turn into a replica of Paul-Henri, and who, he said, were "irritated to see me give up a place that, at a distance of 150 leagues, they judged profitable." Besides, he added, "it would not be in Geneva that the author of the *Compte rendu* would find tranquillity."[92] Madame Gallatin, who assured the landgrave that she was desolate to have recommended Mallet Du Pan, for surely he had been totally to blame, said that the whole affair was very unfortunate for his mother and his family, "which is generally well regarded and honored in our country."[93] She said that they had written to him not to return. (We should not understand by this that they broke with him completely.) Though very angry, she professed to pity him and wondered what would become of this "poor wretch."[94]

In such circumstances, Mallet Du Pan bethought himself of a man he had never seen but whom he knew well by reputation and with whom he had already corresponded—Samuel-Frédéric Osterwald, whose Société Typographique at Neuchâtel was one of the more famous publishing houses of the whole area. Together with his son-in-law, the ex-Pastor Bertrand, Osterwald edited the *Journal helvétique,* a respected and respectable periodical that illustrates to what degree "philosophy" had mellowed and secularized the outlook of French Swiss Protestant intellectuals. He also published a great many books, especially those of a censorable kind. From the Société Typographique, wrote the French revolutionary Brissot, who had visited Neuchâtel and been one of Osterwald's authors before the French Revolution, "came almost all the good political and philosophical books with which France at that time was inundated. They were brought in easily as contraband across the Jura Mountains, and

91. Ibid.   92. Ibid.
93. Mme Gallatin to Frederick, landgrave of Hesse-Cassel, August 12, 1772, in Voltaire, *Correspondence,* LXXXII, 151.
94. Mme Gallatin to Frederick, landgrave of Hesse-Cassel, August 26, 1772, ibid., pp. 179–81.

Lyon then offered facilities for distributing them throughout France. Neuchâtel had succeeded Holland in this [kind of enterprise]."⁹⁵

Now the Principality of Neuchâtel was then a property of the king of Prussia, who was himself, of course, a philosophe. But the town was in a measure self-governing, and its citizens were clearly in certain matters more conservative than the king. When in 1771 Osterwald and Bertrand published Holbach's *Système de la nature*, so great was the outcry in Neuchâtel that Osterwald was forced to resign from his elective office of banneret and Bertrand was unfrocked by the local company of pastors.⁹⁶ No doubt Mallet Du Pan had heard the affair talked of at Ferney, whence also no doubt was derived his early acquaintance (by correspondence) with Osterwald. Voltaire, as is well known, professed to be alarmed by the materialistic tenor of the *Système* but he also fumed at the bigotry of the Neuchâtelois. He protested to his friend the king of Prussia. "He [Osterwald] belongs to your century," he said vigorously, "and the Neuchâtelois belong to the thirteenth or the fourteenth." He declared his admiration for the publisher: "This man is mild in temper, very conciliatory and very wise, and at the same time, possessed of an intrepid philosophy, capable of rendering service to reason and to yourself, and equally devoted to both."⁹⁷ One derives a similar impression from Mallet Du Pan's correspondence, wherein Osterwald, then about sixty years of age, appears as a personage benevolent and obliging, yet shrewd withal.

Mallet had approached Osterwald, first, while still at Cassel, to publish certain pieces of writing including his inaugural address, then wrote next from Frankfort, after he had left Cassel, asking asylum, as it were, in Neuchâtel. He appealed to Osterwald as one philosophe to another, on the ground of similar experiences of persecution, pouring out his story of the Cassel villainies, calling himself "a free disciple of Voltaire (*un élève de Voltaire libre*)" and, more bitterly, "abortive child of Voltaire (*avorton de Voltaire*)." Would Osterwald find him a house, a retreat, where he could study and write, re-

95. J.-P. Brissot [de Warville], *Mémoires*, ed. Cl. Perroud, 2 vols. (Paris, n.d.), I, 284–85. My translation.
96. *Dictionnaire historique et biographique de la Suisse*, II, 147, and V, 208.
97. Voltaire to Frederick II of Prussia, August 21, [1771], in Voltaire, *Correspondence*, LXXX, 20.

cover from the recent upsetting experiences, and enjoy the publisher's society from time to time?[98] Osterwald obliged, and Mallet lived some while in Neuchâtel, certainly during the following autumn and winter if not longer, in close association, both professional and personal, with Osterwald and Bertrand and the latter's family.

Osterwald took Voltaire's place as fatherly adviser, for the Cassel episode produced an alteration in the relations of Mallet with Voltaire.[99] Voltaire naturally was sent a copy of the inaugural address and he thought it so ridiculously impolitic that he wrote D'Alembert to this effect. The author, he remarked wryly, had been his gift to the landgrave! It was not unlikely Mallet would be ousted.[100] But his tone to Mallet was still kindly and gracious (after all, Voltaire was in a way the hero of the address) although the words nevertheless sound a little weary.

Lazy as I seem [wrote Voltaire], I have none the less been charmed with the wealth of erudition that you display in your discourse, and the noble hardihood with which you speak. You will go far, I assure you; you will be one of the firm supports of philosophy and of good style. I wish you all kinds of good fortune. If you stay where you are, work will sustain you; if you do not stay, you will inspire liking (*vous serez tres-aimable*) wherever you are. Rest assured that I am keenly interested in everything that can accord with your wishes, and that no one is more truly and sincerely attached to you than this old hermit of Ferney, who is very conscious of all that you are worth and will deserve.[101]

98. Mallet Du Pan to Osterwald, Cassel, June 13, and Frankfort, July 17, 1772, Bibl. Neuch., MS 1178, fo 22–121.

99. It was M. Edouard Chapuisat, of Geneva, who very kindly called my attention to the existence of the correspondence of Mallet Du Pan with Osterwald at the Bibliothèque de la Ville de Neuchâtel, and to its importance in demonstrating Mallet's feelings of hostility toward Voltaire. M. Chapuisat's article, "Voltaire et Mallet Du Pan," *Revue des travaux de l'Académie des Sciences Morales et Politiques et comptes rendus de ses séances*, 4e Série, 1952, pp. 152–64, is based on this correspondence, supplemented by certain other letters of Mallet Du Pan.

100. Voltaire to D'Alembert, July 1, 1772, in Voltaire, *Correspondence*, LXXXII, 97–98.

101. Voltaire to Mallet Du Pan, July 27, 1772, ibid., pp. 129–30.

Voltaire recognizes here the possibility of Mallet's leaving Cassel, but not, probably, as a voluntary act. When he learned of his protégé's resignation, his displeasure erupted. For he was in reality totally out of patience and, like Madame Gallatin, angry to have been put in the wrong, as he felt, with the landgrave. "Our friend," that lady wrote the prince, "is very angry that he [Mallet Du Pan] should not have applied himself in a way to please you. . . . Our friend does not know what to make of it. We both feel sorry for him and are resolved not to involve ourselves any more with him."[102] A letter from Mallet to the landgrave, written on his departure and sent on by the prince to Madame Gallatin, was shown by her to "our friend," who "evidenced an unheard of astonishment. The place where he [Mallet Du Pan] says that he is being given back to Ferney stopped him [Voltaire], he repeated, '*to Ferney*! But,' said he, 'he is mad, can one write to a prince like Monseigneur the Landgrave in this manner! There is no name to give such actions, they are beyond imagining.' "[103] Voltaire took care himself to let the landgrave know he did not approve of Mallet's behavior.[104] Unlike Madame Gallatin, he did not load the boy's name with imputations of disgrace, and his anger subsequently cooled, but at this point anyway he would not concern himself further about Mallet Du Pan.

Mallet was acutely aware of Voltaire's displeasure. It is not known whether he heard of it through informants. Certainly Madame Gallatin was not writing to him, from what she said to the landgrave. His own letters give the impression that he simply deduced Voltaire's reaction from his patron's refusal to see anything wrong in Cassel or any deficiency in the landgrave. Since Voltaire had not sympathized, he must be hostile. For his own part, Mallet was very angry with Voltaire. He felt that he had just experienced a sudden disillusioning insight into the philosopher's prejudices in favor of princes. He felt that all the people who had had anything to do with his going to Cassel, Voltaire included, had been thinking of their own interest, not that of the young man they were sponsoring, and he was bitterly

102. Mme Gallatin to Frederick, landgrave of Hesse-Cassel, August 12, 1772, ibid., p. 151.

103. Mme Gallatin to Frederick, landgrave of Hesse-Cassel, August 26, 1772, ibid., p. 179.

104. Voltaire to Frederick, landgrave of Hesse-Cassel, September 15, 1772, ibid., LXXXIII, 17–18; Voltaire to the same, October 28, 1772, ibid., p. 96.

resentful. He was not only angry but hurt, for he felt that Voltaire had rejected him. He did not feel, at least at this point, any regret for the disappointment of a patron to whom he was considerably indebted. *He* was the injured party.

Once established at Neuchâtel, however, he began to think again of Ferney, perhaps was encouraged to do so by Osterwald. He undertook to mend his fences, cautiously and indirectly. He wrote to Henri Rieu, a cultivated and kindly habitué of Ferney, one of Voltaire's intimate circle. He wanted, he said, to renew the friendship he had had formerly with Rieu, and to secure his esteem, hence as "the deserter from Cassel" he was presuming to justify himself. The letter is a long one, explaining all the circumstances of his leaving the landgrave's services. On the other hand, there is no apologizing. Then follows a request for Rieu's opinion about a work Mallet has begun—a history of the Polish struggle against the First Partition, commissioned by certain Polish refugees (Count Oginski, Prince Radziwill, and others) whom he had met at Cassel and Frankfort. Mallet is pro-Polish and highly critical of Catherine and Frederick. Voltaire, he says, "is too great a believer in St. Catherine and in the Cartouche of the Kings," hence of course nothing of this project can be breathed to him. But Mallet's implication is that if it were not for the nature of the subject, he would be happy to have "le Nestor" know of his doings. Yet still there is no explicit request that any part of the letter be repeated to Voltaire, let alone any recommending of himself to the lord of Ferney.[105]

Mallet was lucky in Henri Rieu, as he was lucky in Osterwald. On Rieu's advice he wrote Voltaire a letter (which unfortunately seems not to have survived) "in your manner, and in his, where I recommend my interests to him through your obliging mediation." A certain wariness remained with him, though (and remained permanently). "I have seen too clearly that the glass through which he looked at Cassel was not mine," he says to Rieu in the enclosing letter: "I tried out my blade on his prejudices; his response showed me that it was blunted. Without the courage you have given me I would have suppressed any supplication."[106] "Le Nestor," whose instincts

105. Mallet Du Pan to Rieu, Neuchâtel, October 10, 1772, Bibl. Genève, MS Supp. 150.
106. Mallet Du Pan to Rieu, November 11, 1772, ibid.

were to retain all his friends, responded with his former graciousness. The society of Ferney was once more open to Mallet Du Pan and remained so.

Voltaire's response certainly at first touched Mallet deeply. On learning not long afterward that the old man was unwell, he wrote to Henri Rieu:

> I learn, Monsieur, that you are not leaving le Nestor's side in his poor state of health. I am grieved for his enfeeblement and his sufferings, not on my own account but for mankind (*les hommes*) and good literature. In forty years of labor his eloquence has only sketched the outlines (*les rides*) of fanaticism. If le Nestor should die who will take over the scalpel? And what will happen to the theater, taste, and history when the deference that was paid to him universally is no longer an influence, and we shall behold only the lion dead, and not the fools he would have crushed in his jaws? I was expecting no more from his courteous old age than barren well-wishing; his pen is more indolent than his heart, and after all, how should I have deserved his services? Your friendship, more enlightened and more courageous than my situation [permitted me to be], benevolently importuned in my favor his last moments of health. I thank you, and I should wish, though it were forever of no advantage to me, to redeem the sick man's days with mine.[107]

The very awkwardness of his expression in this letter is an indication of the strength of his feeling.

107. "J'apprens, Monsieur, que vous ne quittez point le Nestor cacochisme. . . . Je pleure son affaiblissement et ses maux non pas pour moi, mais pour les hommes et la bonne littérature. Quarante ans de travaux éloquens n'ont fait qu'ébaucher les rides du fanatisme; si le Nestor vient à mourir qui prendra le scalpel? et que deviendront la scène, le goût, et l'histoire, quand le déférence universelle qu'on lui porte devenue inutile, on ne verra que le lion mort, et non les sots qu'il aura croqués? Je n'attendais plus de sa viellesse bienséante que des voeux stériles: sa plume est plus paresseuse [sic] que son coeur, et apres tout, pourquoi aurai je mérité ses services? Votre amitié plus éclairée et plus courageuse que ma situation, avait bien voulu solliciter les derniers momens de sa santé en ma faveur, je vous rends graces, et je voudrais dût-il m'être éternellement inutile, racheter des miens les jours du malade." Mallet Du Pan to Rieu, March 1, 1773, ibid.; also in Voltaire, *Correspondence*, LXXXIV, 139–40.

At what date Mallet Du Pan left his refuge among the mountains of Neuchâtel is not known, for the sources for the period from March, 1773, to May, 1775, are scanty. Neuchâtel was too isolated for him and in his mind only a temporary solution in view of the hostility he felt he would encounter in returning to Geneva. "I am far from willing . . . to conduct the funeral of my vocation in these mountains," he wrote in November of 1772. "But barren as they are, they are better than our den [Geneva] where I should not escape the critics, the reproaches, the givers of advice, and all the annoyances which would attend a deserter from the Landgrave of Hesse."[108] His letter to Rieu in March, 1773, written from Neuchâtel, gives no hint of his departing,[109] but the reconciliation with Voltaire must have strengthened the pull of Geneva and perhaps it gave him the sang-froid to face his family again.

It was the understanding of Mallet Du Pan's descendants that prior to his marriage, which occurred on August 4, 1774, at Allaman,[110] he was living in Geneva, whence he used to visit Aubonne, only a short distance away in the Pays de Vaud. It was there that he met his bride.[111] Now family tradition errs in certain respects, for it omits the residence at Neuchâtel and also a later residence in Aubonne, which lasted until the end of 1777. But there is no evidence that the family tradition is incorrect in holding that for some time before his marriage he was living in Geneva.

The lady, two or three years younger than her husband, was Mademoiselle Françoise Vallier, daughter of a minor official of Aubonne, the *capitaine et conseiller* François-Gédéon Vallier. They met while both were playing in amateur theatricals at the house of M. de Tscharner, *bailli* of Aubonne. Her part on the occasion is said

108. Mallet Du Pan to Rieu, Neuchâtel, November 11, 1772, Bibl. Genève, MS Supp. 150.

109. Mallet Du Pan to Rieu, Neuchâtel, March 1, 1773, Voltaire, *Correspondence,* LXXXIV, 139–40.

110. Choisy, *La famille Mallet,* pp. 32, 100.

111. B. Mallet, *Mallet du Pan,* pp. 12–13. This source relies on the recollections of Mallet Du Pan's son, John Lewis Mallet, *An Autobiographical Retrospect of the First Twenty-five years of His Life,* with a preface by Sir Louis Mallet and printed for private circulation (1890). This in turn was based, for his father's early life, largely on what Jean-Louis learned from his father's brother.

to have been that of the marquise de Clairville in Sedaine's *Gageure imprévue.*[112] From all the evidence, the marriage, which was for Mallet Du Pan certainly a love match, was one of great mutual devotion, though not one in which the wife shared her husband's intellectual interests. Mallet Du Pan would not have wanted that, anyway, for he did not like intellectual women and was very conservative about the role of women in society. Madame Mallet was not without character, but clearly deferred to her husband, and this was as it ought to be, in his view. From the viewpoint of his relatives in Geneva, Mallet had offended a third time: first the *Compte rendu,* then Cassel, and now this marriage! The bride was charming personally, yes, but she did not have the family position of a Mallet or a Du Pan nor did she bring a substantial dowry, and she was only somewhat grudgingly accepted.[113]

The family attitude may have been responsible for the young couple's decision at first to live in Aubonne rather than in Geneva. But in May of 1775 Mallet brought his wife to Geneva to be naturalized[114] and in the late fall of that year he was hoping to settle there for the winter at least, because he wanted his first child to be born within the city's walls.[115] Alas, Geneva was too expensive. The child, named Jean-Louis-Etienne, was born at Aubonne after all in early December, 1775.[116] Mallet decided to buy furniture and establish a domicile at Aubonne for the time being.[117] It is clear that the circumstances of the young couple were exceedingly modest, and Mallet, now *père de famille,* as he was wont to style himself, was very conscious of a need to augment his income.

He was active in one way and another. He remained in close contact with Osterwald and the Société Typographique de Neuchâtel, performing diverse services. He was enterprising and as the area of

112. Choisy, *La famille Mallet,* pp. 32, 100.
113. Ibid.; B. Mallet, *Mallet du Pan,* p. 13.
114. Mallet Du Pan to Osterwald, Aubonne, May 12, 1775, Bibl. Neuch., MS 1178, fo 22–121.
115. Mallet Du Pan to Osterwald, Aubonne, November 7, 1775, ibid.
116. Mallet Du Pan to Osterwald, Aubonne, December 9, 1775, ibid. This corrects Choisy, *La famille Mallet,* p. 108, where the birth date is given as December 26.
117. Mallet Du Pan to Osterwald, Aubonne, December 9, 1775, Bibl. Neuch., MS 1178, fo 22–121.

his contacts and correspondence broadened, the services became more varied. He criticized manuscripts; he put the publisher in touch with authors and booksellers and negotiated for him with booksellers in Geneva, Lyon, and Grenoble; he informed Osterwald of new books that appeared in Geneva; and he kept him up to date on Voltaire's activities, literary or otherwise, and did commissions for him at Ferney. When writing Osterwald of his idea of moving to Geneva at the close of the year 1775, Mallet said he hoped to be more useful to him there.

There is evidence in Mallet's correspondence that he sometimes contributed book reviews (*extraits*) to the *Journal helvétique*. These are hard to trace because reviews in this periodical were not signed and are of quite uniform style. They mingle quotation and comment skillfully, they are all intelligent, moderate in tone, brief, clear, and interesting. In the issue of March, 1775, Mallet had a fifteen-page signed article on Voltaire as dramatist, especially as a writer of historical tragedy. It is an enthusiastic essay, wherein the poet's excellence is found to consist in a combination of dramatic invention and historical imagination, unspoiled by "romantic insipidities."[118] The article conforms to the standard of writing of the *Journal helvétique*, and may possibly have been edited. Mallet Du Pan needed at this time the discipline of having to write to suit Osterwald and Bertrand. It was one of them who had criticized the style of his inaugural address at Cassel as high-flown and involved. That had been in 1772, but even now, in 1775, Bertrand was critical of a work Mallet did not write for them but published independently, his *Doutes sur l'éloquence et les systèmes politiques* (of which much more will be said presently). The author, wrote Bertrand, was one "whose conspicuous talents will make all his works pleasing and valuable, but who would make them still more useful by subjecting the ardor of his talent and his imagination to a more logical method."[119] Though a little put out, Mallet Du Pan remarked to Osterwald: "I have read with thanks and docility the review that M. Bertrand . . . has written of my little pamphlet of 184 [pages]. It is quite true that I write much too fast; and when I revise, imagination takes over and I add to the sense in-

118. *Journal helvétique*, March, 1775, p. 82.
119. Ibid., Oct. 1775, p. 23.

stead of changing it. . . . It is worth more at my age to have to cut down than to add."[120]

By the summer of 1775, Mallet had not succeeded in publishing very much (and he paid for the printing of the *Doutes*). He had made repeated efforts, indeed. There was his projected work on the partition of Poland, which he had while still at Cassel talked Count Oginski and Prince Radziwill into commissioning as an *ouvrage de commande*, and which he worked on at Neuchâtel. It will be remembered that he consulted Henri Rieu about this. Rieu dissuaded him from even trying to publish it, principally because the author was residing in territory of the king of Prussia, the "cartouche des rois," one of the partitioners.[121] Mallet returned to this subject in 1775, only to have his work refused by booksellers both at Lyon and at Paris for what he believed was prudence,[122] the subject being still so "hot" that an edition might run the risk of confiscation.

Mallet was interested in Poland not because he admired anything about the regime there before the Partition but because he was fascinated by that event, which he thought an act of international brigandage that at the same time gave the political analyst food for thought. Poland was to become Mallet's stock warning to Genevans and the denizens of other lesser powers to put their houses in order lest by the disorder they too invite the interference of their more powerful neighbors and in the end lose their independence. In 1775, however, the "lesson" of Poland may not have been foremost in his mind. He seems most of all to have been casting about for a good subject for a book.

He had no better luck with less controversial topics. The Académie de Marseille had rejected an "épitre philosophique" in its competition of 1772, and apparently Osterwald was not interested in it either.[123] Mallet continued to compose essays for the prizes offered by this or that academy, receipt of which would hasten the recognition

120. Mallet Du Pan to Osterwald, Aubonne, November 7, 1775, Bibl. Neuch., MS 1178, fo 22–121.

121. Mallet Du Pan to Rieu, Neuchâtel, October 10 and November 11, 1772, Bibl. Genève, MS Supp. 150.

122. Mallet Du Pan to Osterwald, Aubonne, [July] 9, 1775, Bibl. Neuch., MS 1178, fo 22–121.

123. Mallet Du Pan to Osterwald, Cassel, June 13, and Frankfort, July 17, 1772, ibid.

he so much desired. He did an "Eloge de Catinat" for a competition of the Académie Française in 1775, and went so far as to try to clear it in advance with the Sorbonne, to reduce the possibility of a setback from the censorship. His uncle who was attached to the household of the duc d'Orléans saw to this. However, so many changes were advised that the author withdrew his "Eloge" from the competition with the intention of publishing it independently.[124] It appears that Osterwald at one point offered to publish it along with the winning essays,[125] but as late as January, 1776, Mallet was uncertain whether he would actually do so,[126] and I have never seen it anywhere. At the same time, he hoped to compete at Toulouse with an *éloge* of L'Hôpital, and at Besançon with an essay on the subject: "Comment les moeurs servent-t-elles au bonheur des états?"[127] As far as I know, these efforts, too, were never published save as they may have been reworked later for his journal—for everything Mallet studied was ultimately utilized in that form. He was also eager to do an extensive critical study of contemporary French literature, taking as his point of departure the *Mémoires sur la littérature* of the anti-philosophe dramatist and critic Palissot, disputing it and adding to the discussion sixty to eighty authors of whom Palissot had said nothing. Rieu's opinion was solicited on this project, too. If Rieu did not approve of it, Mallet said, he would not proceed.[128] Perhaps Mallet was angling for Voltaire's reaction to the idea. Voltaire himself had been circumspect in dealing with Palissot, who was a formidable opponent and who had moreover had the protection of the minister

124. Mallet Du Pan to Osterwald, Aubonne, [July] 9, 1775, ibid.
125. Mallet Du Pan to Osterwald, September 23 and December 9, 1775, ibid.
126. Mallet Du Pan to Osterwald, Aubonne, January 23, 1775 [correctly 1776], ibid.
127. Mallet Du Pan to Osterwald, Aubonne, December 9, 1775, ibid.
128. Mallet Du Pan to Rieu, Aubonne, July 1, 1771 [1775], Bibl. Genève, MS Supp. 150. The cataloguer has read the date as 1771. However, the final digit looks as much like "5" as "1" and moreover the letter was written from Aubonne, where Mallet was living in 1775, and reads as though he had been there some time and did not expect to leave. There is every reason to think that in July of 1771 Mallet was still living with his family in Geneva. The main argument in support of the reading "1771" would be that this was the publication year of Palissot's *Mémoires sur la littérature* (*Nouvelle biographie générale*, XXXIX, 90). However, the interest in so controversial a work would not have died with the year 1771.

Choiseul.[129] Whatever Rieu answered (and this is not known), the project did not materialize.

In late April of 1775 Mallet Du Pan made a trip to Turin and in the spring of 1776 another to the vicinity of Lake Como, no doubt on some literary mission and very likely in search of literary material. They provided the subject for a romantic and sentimental reminiscence, of a genre in which this journalist was not accustomed to work, entitled "Le tombeau de l'Isle Jennings." But this was not published until 1785,[130] ten years later.

In Mallet's correspondence in 1775, the feeling of frustration is very pronounced. He complained to Henri Rieu that he was restless, that his peace of mind was disturbed, owing to "my situation that I would like to change without succeeding in doing so."[131]

Meanwhile, his whole philosophic viewpoint was changing. The attitude of deference and discipleship toward Voltaire, which had seemed renewed with the reconciliation, was turning into an increasingly critical reaction. Other influences were entering Mallet's thought, which began to assume an ambivalent and eclectic character that is not easy to describe. These new influences were anti-philosophe.

129. Desnoiresterres, *Voltaire et la société française*, V, 364–65; *Biographie universelle . . .*, XXXII, 421.

130. *Mercure de France*, 1785, no. 43 (Oct. 22), pp. 148–64.

131. Mallet Du Pan to Rieu, Aubonne, October 8, 1775, Bibl. Genève, MS Supp. 150.

Two

THE REVOLT AGAINST
PHILOSOPHY

Mallet Du Pan's revolt against philosophy was in the first place an assertion of personal autonomy, a repudiation of the authority of the ruling "sect," more a revolt against philosophes than against philosophy itself; and while it quickly became theoretical, and as such was a pretty considerable revolt, something of the personal element persisted. Frustrated, disaffected, disillusioned, critical, Mallet Du Pan was in a mood to sympathize with, identify himself with others who repudiated philosophe leadership.

The change is first noticeable in 1775, with the appearance of Mallet's interest in the brilliant and erratic lawyer and journalist Simon-Nicolas-Henri Linguet, who was then, at thirty-nine, the stormiest personality in the world of French letters. It was to be Mallet's journalistic collaboration with Linguet that lifted him from obscurity and first brought him fortune. That was later, however; the collaboration did not get under way until 1777, and was in fact productive, in its turn, of disillusionment. Linguet's mark on Mallet's intellectual development was not a consequence of their professional association, but rather, in part, a cause of it.

The singularity of Linguet's career was arresting. Well educated (a product of the College de Navarre in Paris), a man of various talents, great ambition, and a high opinion of himself, but without money, Linguet for a good many years did various things to make a living while he aspired to attain a career in letters. In Paris, where he resided for eight years during this early period, Linguet saw much of the society of the arch-anti-philosophe Fréron (he wrote occasionally for Fréron's *Année littéraire*) and the Jesuit Father Berthier, who had the privilege of the *Journal de Trévoux*. At the time of the dissolution of the Jesuit Order in France, in 1762, Linguet published pamphlets and verses in their behalf. He decided in 1764, in order to improve his fortunes, to enter the career of law, and practiced before the Parlement of Paris.[1] Here fame came to him, first as the principal counsel for the defense in the trial of the chevalier de la Barre, accused together with certain other youths of having mutilated a wayside cross at Abbeville under the influence of free-thinking ideas. Linguet could not save the chevalier but he did save the young man's friends.[2] His name was bracketed with that of Voltaire, who had recently brought about the Royal Council's posthumous exoneration of Jean Calas. In a succession of cases, both criminal and civil, Linguet became the most renowned trial lawyer in France, with a reputation for the rescuing of likely victims of a miscarriage of justice. He had earlier published a work entitled *Nécessité d'une réforme dans l'administration de la justice et dans les loix civiles en France* (Amsterdam, 1764).[3] Voltaire, who regarded him as a fellow-worker in the field of legal reform, declared: "For if this Linguet has otherwise some very great faults, it must be admitted that he has written some good works and done some fine acts."[4]

Yet Linguet finished his career as a lawyer with less honor than notoriety. He was egotistical, maladroit, seeming almost to crave trouble, to delight in antagonizing. He could have pleased by his wit and vivacity and in his earlier years had sustained pleasant friendships,[5] and he was never a bully. But in retaliation against injuries real or fancied he was *méchant* and formidable. His sense of persecution continually increased and with it his egoism to the point, finally, of megalomania. His colleagues of the bar in Paris were outraged beyond endurance because he dramatized himself flamboyantly, insulted them, and declined conforming to professional etiquette.[6] On their demand the Parlement of Paris expelled him from the legal order. This was in February of 1774. Linguet fought the ouster tooth and nail but it was sustained in March of 1775 by the "old" Parlement which had just been recalled, replacing the "Maupeou" Parle-

1. Jean Cruppi, *Un avocat journaliste au XVIIIe siècle. Linguet* (Paris, 1895), pp. 1–46.
2. Ibid., pp. 69–154.   3. Ibid., p. 43n.
4. Voltaire to Condorcet, November 23, 1774, in Voltaire, *Correspondence*, LXXXIX, 115.
5. Cruppi, *Linguet*, pp. 35–57.   6. Ibid., passim.

ment which originally rendered the decree.[7] The public was vastly entertained by the spectacle, which was further enlivened by a side issue, the lawyer's dispute with his former client, the duc d'Aiguillon, over the large fees Linguet charged him.[8] Financially, Linguet always thought in very large amounts.

Some months after his disbarment in 1774 from the practice of law, Linguet was taken on by that great entrepreneur in publishing, Charles Panckoucke, to be author-editor of the *Journal de politique et de littérature*,[9] for which Panckoucke had the privilege. The acquaintance of publisher and editor dated from an episode of Linguet's legal career when he had been lawyer for the plaintiff in a suit against Panckoucke but had succeeded in negotiating a settlement agreeable to both parties.[10] The publisher agreed to pay the former lawyer a basic salary of 10,000 livres,[11] a goodly figure (a decade later he was to bring Mallet Du Pan to the *Mercure de France* for 7,200),[12] but apparently Linguet's talents for attracting readers seemed worth the price. Voltaire himself said then that one of his greatest pleasures was to read Linguet's journal, "which becomes more interesting all the time."[13] The ex-lawyer's style was lively, pointed, without verbiage. It became repetitive when clouded by his egocentricity, but this fault was not at first very apparent. The political items of the *Journal* were written factually and without comment, owing to the censorship. The literary section, where the author had greater liberty, was much more spicy. Linguet's writing in general reflected a viewpoint sometimes sophistical but never trite, a wrongheadedness and

7. Ibid., pp. 342–45, 370–90.
8. Ibid., pp. 204–5, 355–64.
9. *Journal de politique et de littérature, contenant les principaux évènemens de toutes les cours; les nouvelles de la république des lettres, etc.* (Brussels [Paris], Oct. 25, 1774–[June, 1778]). In June, 1778, the journal was merged with the *Mercure de France*, to improve the latter's political coverage, as was explained to readers in the issue of June 25, 1778, p. 73.
10. Cruppi, *Linguet*, p. 366 and n. 2.
11. Ibid., pp. 366–67 n. 3. A bonus would be paid in the event of the subscriptions exceeding six thousand.
12. Contract between Mallet Du Pan and Charles Panckoucke, March 4, 1784, London, Mallet Papers.
13. Voltaire to Marin, August 11, [1775], Voltaire, *Correspondence*, XCI, 153–54. He wrote: "... je vous prie de dire à M. Linguet qu'un de nos plus grands plaisirs est de lire son journal, qui devient de jour en jour plus intéressant."

impulsiveness mixed with great shrewdness, intensity of feeling served by a calculating rationality.

Even while he won the praise of Voltaire and other reformers for his work in the La Barre and other cases, Linguet had been carrying on a resounding quarrel with certain philosophes over basic principles, public policies, and literary reputations. In 1767 he had published his most controversial work, the *Théorie des loix civiles, ou principes fondamentaux de la société*, wherein he challenged sharply every assumption of the meliorism of the Enlightenment. Linguet's pessimism was extreme. *Bienfaisance*, says Linguet, is an illusion, an invention, a hypocrisy. There is no such thing as natural law. There is no primitive social contract. Linguet's version of the origin of social organization and the institutions of property and of servitude runs as follows: The most primitive human organization must have resembled the wolf pack, without relations of gratitude, of submission, or permanence. Some of the hunters banded together to despoil the rest. Next, rules were set up and enforced to keep the despoilers from turning on each other and to prevent those who had nothing from turning on those who had everything. The origin and fundamental purpose of all laws is to protect the property of the rich against attack by the poor, who are three-quarters of the human race.[14] Servitude came into existence with society. And servitude, hard as it is, is the best possible existence for the propertyless, since by the very principle of the conservation of property the slave is accorded shelter and subsistence. The free laborer on the other hand is in the worst possible position, since no one has any interest in supporting him. Liberty is a fraud; it only multiplies the opportunities for exploitation.[15] Political liberty Linguet thinks of as something to increase the power of the vested interests, the *corps intermédiaires* of the old regime, who are the great exploiters. Therefore he takes exception to Montesquieu, for whom monarchy is founded on the *corps intermédiaires*. Linguet is far from advocating the radical redistribution of property or communism, since by his premises of human motivation the cycle of exploitation would only begin all over again. The laws must be based on property; but Linguet advocates

14. *Théorie des loix civiles*, new ed., 3 vols. (vols. III–V of *Œuvres de Linguet*, 6 vols., London, 1774), I, 235–67.
15. Ibid., III, 57–103, 300–1.

what he refers to rather vaguely as bringing the laws back to their primitive simplicity. He would abolish, for example, the distinction between land and other forms of wealth. He upholds the theory of a strong monarchy wherein the monarch's "right" to rule depends upon his vigilance to defend the property of the subjects, and not on any social contract.[16] The *Théorie des loix civiles* concludes with a scathing denunciation of the philosophes. They are hypocrites, or at best they assuage their sense of guilt (for they are not among the sufferers) with fair words, which are all their fine systems of rights and liberties amount to. Since the hopes thus raised cannot in the nature of things be realized, the philosophic doctrines are worse than useless. Why add the sense of injustice to the burden of slavery?[17] Naturally, the *Théorie des loix civiles* was ill received by the philosophe literati.

For years Linguet did battle specifically against the Economists, or Physiocrats, who were increasingly a power in the government, and their doctrine of economic liberty.[18] Simultaneously, he became involved in a long-drawn-out literary feud with La Harpe, of the *Mercure de France*,[19] the principal journal of literary criticism, and La Harpe's supporter D'Alembert, philosophe chieftain and influential secretary of the Académie Française. Lawyers, parlements, Economists, Encyclopedists, Academicians—they were all in Linguet's eyes simply *corps intermédiaires*, to be fought without quarter asked or given.

Linguet carried his literary feud into the pages of the *Journal de politique et de littérature*, where it brought him grief. In 1775, the first prize of the Académie for an *Eloge de Catinat* went to La Harpe. (It will be remembered that Mallet Du Pan had thought of participating in this competition, but had withdrawn.) Linguet criticized La Harpe's work severely in the *Journal*, La Harpe replied in the

16. Ibid., I, 1–113, 129–63.
17. Ibid., III, 300–14.
18. He fought them in pamphlets, in the *Journal de politique et de littérature*, and in the *Annales de Linguet*. See Henri Paris, "Rapport sur les concours," *Travaux de l'Académie Impériale de Reims*, XXX (1859), 494–503.
19. Cruppi, *Linguet*, pp. 177–78; Baron Grimm, entry of December, 1770, in *Correspondence littéraire, philosophique et critique par Grimm, Diderot, Raynal, Meister, etc.*, ed. Maurice Tourneux, 16 vols. (Paris, 1877–1882), IX, 197.

Mercure, and Linguet answered.[20] The affair was another public spectacle in which Linguet held the spotlight. Finally Linguet overplayed his hand. He made La Harpe's election to the Académie Française in July of 1776 the subject of a vitriolic report in the *Journal*,[21] and the Académie struck back. The ministry was approached, and the minister of Foreign Affairs, the comte de Vergennes, in whose jurisdiction lay the licensing of journals, required Panckoucke to dismiss his editor or lose his privilege for the *Journal*. Panckoucke not only complied, he agreed to accept La Harpe as editor in Linguet's place,[22] and La Harpe thereafter became more than ever an object of Linguet's enmity, which was implacable. The ex-editor was in a sense revenged by a decline in the *Journal*'s popularity. "The *Journal de littérature* . . . has been much less successful than it deserves to be," complained Condorcet to Voltaire. "People bought the Linguet [journal] while saying that it was detestable; they do not buy the new journal at all, because it is not absolutely perfect."[23] "Linguet was not endowed with an inimitable genius," remarked Brissot de Warville, who had been one of Linguet's secretaries on the publication, "but he had a superior talent for polemics, and he put more verve and wit into one page than La Harpe and Suard together into an entire volume."[24] When he wrote this, Brissot had long been disillusioned with Linguet, but at the period to which he was referring he was a devoted admirer of the journalist.[25] It is curious that Brissot de Warville and Mallet Du Pan, who were otherwise so different and who came within a decade to detest each other utterly, should both have been at this time, each at the beginning of his career, partisans of the unfortunate but formidable Linguet.

20. *Journal de politique et de littérature*, Sept. 25, 1775, pp. 110–25, and Oct. 25, 1775, pp. 252–58.
21. Ibid., July 25, 1776, pp. 404–12.
22. [Louis Petit de Bachaumont et al.], *Mémoires secrets pour servir à l'histoire de la république des lettres en France, depuis MDCCLXVII jusqu'à nos jours; ou Journal d'un observateur* (hereinafter cited as "Bachaumont"), 36 vols. (London, 1784–1789), IX, 178 (Aug. 2, 1776), 183–84 (Aug. 8, 1776), 206–7 (Sept. 6, 1776), 237 (Oct. 14, 1776); Linguet to J.-P. Brissot, [July, 1776], in J.-P. Brissot, *Correspondance et papiers*, ed. Claude Perroud (Paris, [1911]), p. 2; H. Paris, "Rapport sur les concours," p. 498.
23. Condorcet to Voltaire, January 1, 1777, in Voltaire, *Correspondence*, XCVI, 6.
24. Brissot, *Mémoires*, I, 87, my translation.
25. Ibid., pp. 82, 93–94.

We learn from Mallet's letters to Osterwald that his interest in Linguet was first aroused while he was carrying on a correspondence with a certain Prussian nobleman, one Baron von Boden, chamberlain to Prince Henry of Prussia, on the subject of Linguet's exclusion from the bar.[26] How Mallet came to make this acquaintance is not known—perhaps it dated from Cassel days. In any case, the result was that he put his ideas together in a small book that he called *Doutes sur l'éloquence, et les systèmes politiques, adressés à M. le Baron de B*****, publication of which, he understood, the baron would subsidize. Presumably the baron ultimately paid up, though this is not quite clear; there was no business arrangement, and Mallet was late in settling his account with his publisher, who was Osterwald. He had five hundred copies printed, including a few on fine paper for presentation purposes. The rest he undertook to distribute for sale by booksellers.[27] Naturally he hoped to improve his general literary reputation by the *Doutes sur l'éloquence*, which from all appearances did not happen, as the work, dashed off in a great hurry, appeared incoherent and people scarcely knew what to make of it.[28] But Mallet's principal object in this enterprise was much more specific and immediate—precisely, it was to recommend himself to Linguet, whom he did not know personally, as a possible collaborator on the *Journal de politique et de littérature*, where Linguet was still firmly in control and in the enjoyment of his striking success. The *Doutes sur l'éloquence* was an apology for the journalist. In the event that Linguet accepted him, Mallet would of course move to Paris, and he counted on being able, while establishing himself, to draw upon the credit of his uncle and on his uncle's influential contacts. Mallet was in a fever of impatience to rush the printing through, for it chanced that the uncle was just then visiting Geneva, but would leave soon, and in imagination Mallet saw himself making an impression in the personal presentation of a copy of his book, on which occasion he would ask for his uncle's assistance. Probably he also wanted his uncle to see that Linguet's copy reached him. Osterwald was obliging, but alas, the presentation copy failed to arrive from Neuchâtel before the

26. Mallet Du Pan to Osterwald, Aubonne, August 23, 1775, Bibl. Neuch., MS 1178, fo 22–121.

27. Mallet Du Pan to Osterwald, Aubonne, August 23 and 30, 1775, and December 9, 1775, ibid.

28. Mallet Du Pan to Osterwald, Aubonne, November 7, 1775, ibid.

uncle's departure. Mallet's disappointment overflowed in reproach
to the publisher, who however failed to take offense. In due course,
Linguet's copy was dispatched to him, together with a letter, by another private hand—not by public conveyance, lest it be held up
somewhere by the authorities.[29] This was about the beginning of
October, and Mallet congratulated himself that the action came
very much a propos, following hard upon Linguet's altercation with
La Harpe over the latter's *Eloge de Catinat.* "Linguet at this moment
cannot or ought not to be but little affected by an apology written by
a foreigner," he wrote hopefully to Osterwald.[30]

How Linguet did in fact react to this overture is not known. Mallet
did not go to Paris at this time, and I have seen no evidence (despite
the assertion of Sayous[31]) that he contributed in any way to the
Journal de politique et de littérature. If any real connection was
formed with Linguet prior to the latter's dismissal from the *Journal,*
in July of 1776, I do not know of it. Mallet Du Pan and Linguet appear to have met first in the late summer or early fall of that year,
when Linguet, wandering and irresolute, wanting to start a journal of
his own but uncertain where to pitch camp, appeared at Ferney.[32]
Voltaire, who called him "this devil of a Linguet" and "madman,"[33]
still admired both the talent of the writer and the courage of the
man, and was perhaps besides somewhat afraid of him. He tried to
give him good advice. " 'You are maladroit,' said to him the very
adroit Hermit of Ferney [it is Mallet Du Pan reporting]; 'You should
imitate the Romans; they took good care not to have two wars on
their hands at the same time, and you have ten.' "[34] Linguet decided
to publish in London, where he announced his forthcoming journal
in terms calculated to attract the maximum attention, attacking the
Parlement, the Académie Française, the royal council in general and
the comte de Vergennes in particular—only the king, said a French

29. Mallet Du Pan to Osterwald, Aubonne, August 30, September 8,
September 23, September 29, November 7, and December 9, 1775, ibid.
   30. Mallet Du Pan to Osterwald, November 7, 1775, ibid.
   31. Sayous, I, 29.
   32. Voltaire to Marin, January 24, [1777], Voltaire, *Correspondence,*
XCVI, 42; Mallet Du Pan, *Annales,* IV, no. 28 (Oct. 15, 1782), 221.
   33. Voltaire to Condorcet and D'Alembert, January 21, 1775, *Correspondence,* XC, 27; Voltaire to D'Alembert, April 8, [1777], ibid., XCVI, 139–40.
   34. *Annales,* IV, no. 28 (Aug. 15, 1782), 221.

news source, was spared![35] The first number of the famed *Annales politiques, civiles et littéraires du 18e siècle* appeared as of March 30, 1777.

Mallet declared later that at the time Linguet left France, they discussed a collaboration,[36] and this was certainly under way by the spring of 1777. The history of that collaboration will be related in another chapter.[37] For the purposes of the present one, only a few facts need be noted. After a year in London, where Mallet joined him briefly in February and March, 1778, Linguet moved his publication to the vicinity of Brussels. He divided the subscriptions territorially with Mallet, who supervised the distribution (and kept the proceeds) in his own area, operating from Lausanne first, then Geneva. For the content of the *Annales* Mallet Du Pan contributed raw material and wrote a number of articles, but essentially this journal as written was Linguet's work and bears his stamp. The collaboration ended in September, 1780, when Linguet, visiting Paris, was arrested suddenly and imprisoned in the Bastille, not to be freed until May, 1782. In April, 1781, Linguet being silenced, Mallet Du Pan began to publish in Geneva his own journal, which he called *Annales . . . pour servir de suite aux Annales M. Linguet.* In 1783 the title became *Mémoires historiques, politiques, et littéraires sur l'état present de l'Europe,* because Linguet, now out of prison, wished to resume publication of the *Annales politiques, civiles, et littéraires.* He broke furiously with Mallet when the latter refused to renew his former professional association. It was in his own *Annales,* published in Geneva, that Mallet Du Pan first showed his stature as a journalist of mature talent and distinction, although there had been some forecast of this talent in the scattered contributions that are identifiable as his in Linguet's *Annales.* In 1784, at the solicitation of Charles Panckoucke, he abandoned his *Mémoires historiques* and went to Paris as author-editor of the political section of the *Mercure de France* and occasional contributor to the literary section, remaining in this capacity until his emigration in 1792.

The *Doutes sur l'éloquence,* which in 1775 introduced Mallet Du

35. Bachaumont, X, 57 (March 3, 1777).
36. Mallet Du Pan to [Des Franches], January 18, 1781, AAE, Correspondance politique de Genève, LXXXVII, fol. 80–81.
37. See below, chapter 4, passim.

Pan to Linguet, shows that a considerable change had taken place both in Mallet's estimation of that writer and in his view of philosophy and the philosophes since the delivery of his inaugural address at Cassel three years before. Then, he had commented on the *Théorie des loix civiles* as "an eloquent book, made for humanity," but marred by "atrocious singularities written in cold blood." "What a pity," he had exclaimed, "that a virile philosopher, gifted with great talents, who has spoken many truths, should have sacrificed decency to the point of wanting to be successful with these sorry Asiatic jests!"[38] It is essentially Voltaire's verdict; Linguet is fundamentally on the right side insofar as he fights injustice and especially the iniquities of the *corps*; and he is a gifted writer. But his paradoxical paeans to slavery, his scourging of liberty, are bizarre ways of making his point, while his denunciations of the party of humanity are outrageous and intolerable.

Mallet's reaction as seen in the *Doutes sur l'éloquence* is very different. There was a chord in him that responded to Linguet's harsh pessimism. He felt a realism and toughmindedness that appealed to him in the theses of the *Théorie des loix civiles*, which, in his words, "reduces itself to showing society in a state of violence."[39] In this connection he devotes several paragraphs of the *Doutes* to praising another great realist, Machiavelli, who he says should be regarded not as theorist but as historian, the analyst of things as they are.[40] Mallet supports Linguet against all the social thinkers who start with natural law and the social contract.[41] He also supports him against Montesquieu.[42] Yet, at the same time, he lets the reader see that he cannot himself be quite so pessimistic as Linguet, who "sometimes gives metaphors for reasons, exaggerates our moral sicknesses, and leaves them without remedy."[43] Mallet turns from Linguet's version of *monarchie simplifiée* to the work of a more notable and constructive exponent of monarchical absolutism and enemy of the *corps intermédiaires*, the marquis d'Argenson, and it is obvious that D'Argenson, rather than Linguet, is Mallet's most admired political

38. *Quelle est l'influence de la philosophie?*, p. 128.
39. *Doutes sur l'éloquence, et les systêmes politiques, adressés à M. le baron de B****, chambellan de S. A. R. le prince H. de P. Par M. M. citoyen de Genève* (London [Neuchâtel], 1775), p. 165.
40. Ibid., pp. 169–72.   42. Ibid., pp. 113–14, 146.
41. Ibid., pp. 72, 82–83, 93–94.   43. Ibid., p. 166.

master.[44] But, he avers (since the *Doutes* must of course praise Linguet), there is a perfect agreement between the monarchy of the *Théorie des loix civiles* and that of the *Considérations sur le gouvernement de la France*.[45]

Adverting to Linguet's expulsion from the bar, Mallet is guarded, not feeling quite sure of his ground, but he tends to attribute it to professional jealousy.[46] With relish he takes up Linguet's controversy with the Economists, who sacrifice the weak to the strong while crying liberty, and who, posing as rationalists, are simply "mystagogues" (a reference no doubt to the Physiocratic doctrine of self-evident truths), and absolutely intolerant and sectarian, a species of fanatics: "Hors de leur école, point de salut."[47] Finally, though not least of all, Mallet upholds Linguet against the other philosophical-literary forces with whom the latter is at war. Linguet is a first-rate writer, he claims, whose qualities of imagination, learning, and "facility of ideas and of work," rank him in these respects with Bayle and Voltaire.[48] He has been the victim of the hostility of inferior talents who cannot appreciate views that are unusual, bold, and unfashionable. The world of letters is no longer free.[49] Put it another way—"Letters are no longer a republic; they are an aristocratic monarchy, where political considerations confer the rank; where complaisance and circumspection secure friends."[50]

Mallet was exaggerating his own private opinion when he compared Linguet with Voltaire; he really thought Voltaire was in a class by himself. But he was not exaggerating when he denounced the philosophic world of letters as prejudiced and unfree, as is evident from his correspondence. "Now there is La Harpe doubly victorious, a second time," he wrote Osterwald, referring to La Harpe's having been awarded the first prize by the Académie Française for his *Eloge de Catinat*. "He has supporters in the Académie who will always see that he wins. It is no matter that he is cold and affected; [but] I doubt that the public will subscribe to the verdict of this senate of literary cabalists."[51] In the "shocking quarrel" between Linguet and "this

44. Ibid., pp. 147–51. See below, chapter 3, pp. 74–77.
45. Ibid., p. 149.
46. Ibid., p. 39.
47. Ibid., pp. 64–72.
48. Ibid., pp. 29–30.
49. Ibid., pp. 49–61.
50. Ibid., p. 175.
51. Mallet Du Pan to Osterwald, Aubonne, September 8, 1775, Bibl. Neuch., MS 1178, fo 22–121.

knave of a La Harpe" the latter, said Mallet, "seems to me to be much in the wrong."[52]

Had it been only a question of Linguet's influence at this time the intellectual history of Mallet Du Pan might have been much different. But a greater victim of the philosophic literati now also engaged his interest: Jean-Jacques Rousseau. Mallet had of course long been aware of *the* great quarrel of the century in the French world of letters, the quarrel between Voltaire and the Encyclopedists on the one hand and Rousseau on the other. He had been on Voltaire's side, not aggressively, not with positive criticism of Rousseau's conduct and point of view, but as a matter of course. But by the close of the year 1776, if not earlier, he was expressing indignation at what he felt to be unjust and malevolent treatment of Rousseau by the philosophic Academicians and their friends. Writing to an acquaintance in Geneva who had known Rousseau personally (as Mallet Du Pan himself had not), he burst out:

> This bastard of a M. Asselin [La Harpe] who made himself Linguet's successor [on the *Journal de politique et de littérature*], . . . who has sold himself, his little cold pen, his interested and jealous soul, and his talents, for he has some, to D'Alembert and to Voltaire, has slandered Rousseau in the last number of his journal. . . . Remember [Mallet went on at white heat] the letter of D'Alembert under the name of Valpole [sic], and all the jests made by him and his crowd about Rousseau's pride on receiving a pension, on being a protégé, set all the aspersions cast on him by D'Alembert besides the impertinent phrase of the little serpent who is his [D'Alembert's] protégé, [and] you will see there a hypocritical irony more detestable, in my opinion, and more injurious than a formal outrage. I know well enough the language of those gentlemen, when speaking of Rousseau, to appreciate the malice of the satirical style. The journals appear to have no other aim but to affront all the reputations and to disparage the men of letters who have not been able to attain the Académie.[53]

52. Mallet Du Pan to Osterwald, Aubonne, November 7, 1775, ibid.
53. Mallet Du Pan to Beauchâteau, Aubonne, December 1, 1776, Bibl. Genève, MS Supp. 363, Collection Coindet, fol. 71.

Mallet Du Pan was on Rousseau's side now, no doubt about it.

The more Rousseau attracted Mallet's sympathy, the more Voltaire, one of "those gentlemen," repelled it. Mallet's sympathy for Rousseau was in fact a symptom of his hostility to Voltaire, which had roots that were both philosophical and quite personal to himself. By 1775 the mood of admiring devotion that had followed on Mallet's reconciliation with "le Nestor" had passed. The disenchantment he had experienced in consequence of the Cassel episode returned. Cassel stuck in his memory. "I saw too well," Mallet Du Pan had said, "that he looked at Cassel through other glasses than mine."[54] These glasses (*lunette*) of Voltaire's, his vanity and love of adulation which led him to flatter princes like the landgrave in order to receive their flattering attentions in return, came to seem to Mallet Du Pan Voltaire's most conspicuous trait.

Mallet continued to visit Ferney often, but chiefly because to do so seemed professionally advantageous. Not only were there contacts to be made through Ferney, and news items to be reported to Osterwald at Neuchâtel, there was the opportunity of accumulating data for future use by an enterprising literary historian. He was frank about this to Osterwald. After describing to the publisher on one occasion how Voltaire was being lionized socially, how among other attentions he had been invited to the wedding at Chambéry of the prince of Piedmont, and how the French king's brother had sent his *grand écuyer*, the marquis de Montesquiou, to convey the message, he exclaimed, "What an old age!" "What a succession of prosperities! What a life! What a fine field for the historian!"[55] When somewhat later, in the fall of 1775, he perceived that the old man was unwell, and thought that he might not live out the winter, he advised Osterwald, as a publisher, to cultivate Father Adam, the former Jesuit whom Voltaire had sheltered at Ferney. "A witness to twenty years of the life, the weaknesses, the passions of Voltaire, one who will survive him, is not a man to be regarded indifferently," he remarked.[56] After the lord of Ferney's death, Mallet wrote to Pastor Jacob Ver-

54. Mallet Du Pan to Rieu, Neuchâtel, November 11, 1772, Bibl. Genève, MS Supp. 150.

55. Mallet Du Pan to Osterwald, September 23, 1775, Bibl. Neuch., MS 1178, fo 22–121.

56. Mallet Du Pan to Osterwald, Aubonne, December 9, 1775, ibid.

nes, his friend and confidant: "Having during seven years of association with M. de Voltaire collected much material on the illustrious
dead, I am putting it in order." [57]

Mallet's correspondence with Osterwald shows how his reserved
and critical attitude could flare into outright hostility. It chanced
that Osterwald was the intermediary for certain Venetian admirers
of Voltaire who wished to honor the poet by presenting him with a
print, a portrait of himself, and Mallet Du Pan undertook, as a favor
to Osterwald, to be the bearer of the gift. The portrait was not, alas,
flattering, and the old man, "our eighty-year-old Narcissus," who was
exceedingly sensitive about his ugliness and in fact hated portraits of
himself, flew into an uncontrollable rage. He railed at the bearer as
well as the donors. "I am assured that he is furious with me," Mallet
wrote Osterwald, "and with all those who have participated in so
abominable a plot." Mallet did not dream of mollifying the Patriarch
by apologizing, for "nothing equals the contempt I have conceived
for this idol of the century, whose philosophical charlatanism is more
than proven by this fantastic action. This man has never, at Paris, at
Berlin, at Ferney, known any but petty passions; the beauty of his
works is only the microscope for his faults." [58]

Voltaire calmed down, Mallet swallowed his resentment, and it
was at Ferney later that same year that, as has been noted, Mallet Du
Pan met Linguet. In the following year, when he was planning to
join Linguet in London, he received from Voltaire a bon voyage letter expressing cordial good wishes for the success of the *Annales*. [59]

57. Mallet Du Pan to Jacob Vernes, Lausanne, December 3, 1778, in
Louis Dufour-Vernes, *Recherches sur J.-J. Rousseau et sa parenté, accompagnés de lettres inédites de Mallet-du-Pan, J.-J. Rousseau et Jacob Vernes*
(Geneva, 1878), p. 42. My translation.
58. Mallet Du Pan to Osterwald, Aubonne, January 23, 1775 [1776],
Bibl. Neuch., MS 1178, fo 22–121. The contents of the letter clearly place
it in January 1776 rather than January 1775.
59. Voltaire to Mallet Du Pan [c. June, 1777], in Voltaire, *Correspondence*, XCVI, 209–10. The letter was first published by Mallet Du Pan from
the manuscript, which no longer exists (as does not, apparently, any copy),
in a communication to Linguet of December 2, 1779, for the *Annales de
Linguet*, VII, no. 54 ([Dec.], 1779), 385–86. The letter is undated. Beuchot
put it in 1775, which is of course wrong. Moland put it in 1777. Besterman
fixes on June, 1777, probably because the *Supplément aux Nouvelles de
divers endroits* for May 28, 1777, advertised that subscriptions for the *An-*

Mallet's trip to London in February and March, 1778, coincided with Voltaire's triumphal journey to Paris and subsequent death there and burial under the macabre circumstances that are well known. The news, details of which he learned from the Tronchins, Voltaire's friends in Geneva, and from Wagnière, Voltaire's secretary,[60] filled Mallet with fascinated horror. He saw the visit to Paris, which was arduous for one of Voltaire's age, as having been conceived by the philosophes, his supposed friends, notably D'Alembert, to exploit him for their own advantage. With utter disregard for his health they had persuaded him to undertake the journey by appealing to his vanity. Dr. Cabanis had assured Mallet that Voltaire, had he but stayed at home, might have lived ten years longer. Probably, Mallet speculated to Osterwald, D'Alembert, "this base and hypocritical geometer," was even secretly pleased to have Voltaire out of the way, since now *he* moved up from second to first place among "the sect"![61]

The relations of Voltaire with the other philosophes, D'Alembert in particular, appeared to Mallet Du Pan in much the same light as the relations of the poet with princes, that is to say, as relations of reciprocal interested adulation. Mallet Du Pan says in one of the extremely few articles in Linguet's *Annales* that he signed: "He [Voltaire] regarded them as the support of the pedestal on which he was mounted; and in order to subordinate to himself all the subaltern trumpets of the orchestra, he took the greatest pains to humor its director: there was never among men of letters a more curious bargain than that which bound M. de Voltaire to M. d'Alembert. By an agreement tacitly settled on between them, the Poet never failed to go into raptures over the literary talents of the Geometer; and the Geometer over the profound philosophy of the Poet. . . ." The poet

---

nales de Linguet would be received by "M. Mallet . . . à Genève, ou à Aubonne" up to July 1. Though he notes that Mallet was still at Aubonne in November (in fact, he was probably there in December), he thinks Voltaire might have been expecting him to leave about July 1. Actually, on June 18 Mallet wrote Osterwald that he was expecting to leave at the end of August or beginning of September (Bib. Neuch., MS 1178, fo 22–121).

60. Mallet Du Pan to Osterwald, Geneva, June 13, 1778, and Lausanne, September 5, 1778, ibid.

61. Mallet Du Pan to Osterwald, Geneva, June 13, 1778, ibid.

(Mallet goes on) did not always really believe what he said to please D'Alembert and company. It had been alleged in the *Mercure* that Voltaire on one occasion, to the knowledge of all his friends, had called Linguet "the first writer of the charnel-houses, without a doubt." If this was the case, says Mallet, and it is just possible, it was not the opinion *I* heard him express about Linguet many a time; and Mallet forthwith produces the letter Voltaire wrote him when he was going to London, a document in which Linguet is highly spoken of.[62] The immediate purpose of this article by Mallet Du Pan was to defend Linguet by invoking a favorable judgment of him on Voltaire's part; yet Mallet did so in such a way as in effect to dispraise Voltaire.

Mallet's censure of Voltaire was not restricted to a criticism of the Patriarch's vanity and his interested literary maneuvers. It went much deeper, being also a matter of philosophic viewpoint. As early as the year 1775 Mallet was showing irritation at Voltaire's polemic against Christianity. Informing Osterwald that Madame Denis, Voltaire's niece, was recovering from a recent serious illness that had much alarmed her uncle, Mallet wrote ironically: "Le Nestor . . . is hard at work thanking God by the composition of his history of Christianity. . . ."[63] In Mallet's view now, Voltaire, the champion of toleration, had become fanatic himself, a *convertisseur*. Mallet liked neither the fanaticism nor the anti-Christian bias. At the time of Voltaire's death he wrote to Osterwald that "the great man we mourn" was at the same time one "whom posterity will eternally reproach for a disregard of all morality and for a weakness of character that is besides, and always will be, the hallmark of philosophy."[64] The judgment he expressed at this time to Pastor Jacob Vernes, who was already the confidant of Mallet Du Pan that he was to be for many years, was as severe as anything Mallet ever wrote about Voltaire. The occasion for his letter to Vernes was an article in the *Annales* by his associate Linguet, wherein Voltaire and Rousseau (dead in the same year) are bracketed together as enemies of religion. This Mallet protests vehemently. Voltaire, he says, was the prince of mockers at all things sacred,

62. Mallet Du Pan to Linguet, December 2, 1779, *Annales de Linguet*, VII, no. 54, 387–88.
63. Mallet Du Pan to Osterwald, Aubonne, May 12, 1775, Bibl. Neuch., MS 1178, fo 22–121.
64. Mallet Du Pan to Osterwald, Geneva, June 13, 1778, ibid.

the skeptical buffoon and mountebank who for twenty-five years inundated Europe with his sorry jests. It is not Christianity alone of which Voltaire made a farce as disgusting as it was childish; it is also moral conduct (*les moeurs*), conjugal fidelity, disinterestness, all the domestic virtues; he never clearly articulated the dogma of a future life, and a thousand times he made it seem ridiculous. Is it permissible to confound such a man with a writer who, on every page, burns with the love of decency (*honneteté*) and of virtues? Rousseau will only be read, will only be appreciated, by souls still pure. The evil that the Confession of the Vicar and his apologies can do to the spirit of some individuals carries with it the remedy in the saintliness of his [Rousseau's] morality preached with that eloquence of sentiment that he alone has and that he takes with him to the grave. Whatever may have been his weaknesses, his caprices, his actual faults, he will always be a man and writer worthy of respect.

Linguet had missed a great opportunity of striking a mortal blow at "our philosophers." Instead of portraying Rousseau as their standard bearer he should have shown how Rousseau became the object of their hatred because he refused to follow their doctrines. "By contrasting their scandalous theories on remorse, shame, personal interest, the materiality of all our feelings, and consequently of our duties, with Jean-Jacques' hymns on these matters ceaselessly profaned and degraded by our wise men, he would have rendered homage to the truth and service to human kind."[65]

There is an autobiographical allusion in this letter. Mallet says he has a purer respect for religion than Linguet, who is merely paying court to the archbishop of Paris, whereas "I have for religion a respect founded on resipiscence, on perilous experiences where the enfeeblement of moral ideas and their principles all but overthrew me twenty times." In connection with this confession he comments that, while Rousseau's heterodoxy may indeed be unsettling to some minds, and it is therefore not useful to publicize it, still Rousseau's very heresies are marked by a tone of decency and sincerity, and Mallet underscores Rousseau's "attachment to the purest theism, his

65. Mallet Du Pan to Jacob Vernes, Lausanne, December 3, 1778, in Dufour-Vernes, *Recherches sur J.-J. Rousseau*, pp. 41–42.

penetrating warmth [effective] in bringing minds back to the fundamental dogmas [that is, belief in God and a future life] and hearts
back to the virtues."[66]

What the perilous experiences might have been which Mallet
said nearly were his undoing a number of times we do not know. One
thinks of Cornuaud's tale of an intrigue with a Natif woman or wom-
en, but there is no further evidence along this line. One recollects
that Mallet's marriage occurred (1774) about the time that he was
becoming disenchanted with Voltaire, whom he was accusing of
mocking conjugal fidelity. Possibly his marriage was a factor in the
conversion he was undergoing. In any case, it is Rousseau above all
who justifies the anti-philosophe in Mallet Du Pan, Rousseau the
great contemporary prophet of anti-hedonism, of conscience, of a
theistic religion, the Rousseau of the *Vicaire Savoyard*.

Mallet Du Pan pursued thenceforth his personal war against the
philosophes. Still, there was a residuum of "philosophy" in his
thought and feeling, a considerable one, rather specifically Voltairean, too, and it must be given due place in this account. It included a sensitiveness to social distress and a certain commitment to
the cause of humanitarian reform. He said of his own journal in
1782: "If these *Annales* can have some utility, it is by providing us
with the occasion sometimes of debating the interests of reason and
of humanity against the interests of force and against the despotism
of custom in legislative actions."[67] There is in his published writing
a frequently expressed sympathy with the *bas peuple* of town and
countryside, "poor and unhappy everywhere":[68] there are many references for example to the iniquities of serfdom and the manorial
system and praise for governments that attack the problem;[69] hostility to the exclusiveness of the guilds, which prevents the workers of

66. Ibid.
67. *Annales*, IV, no. 31 (Nov. 30, 1782), 423.
68. *Mémoires historiques, politiques et littéraires sur l'état présent de l'Europe* [continuation of the *Annales*, without break in pagination or numbering
of volumes and issues], V, no. 38 (March 30, 1783), 322.
69. *Doutes sur l'éloquence*, pp. 107, 165–66; *Mémoires historiques*, V,
no. 37 (March 15, 1783), 319; ibid., VI, no. 47 (August 15, 1783), 411–19;
Mercure de France, 1787, no. 4 (Jan. 27), pp. 163–64; ibid., no. 26 (July
14), pp. 60–62. (The title *Mercure de France*, or, as hereinafter cited, *Mercure*, refers to the literary section of this journal. The political section will
be given its own title in the documentation.)

the towns from improving their status;[70] concern lest trade policy and taxation discriminate in favor of the wealthy and against the poor[71] (one trouble with the Economists in Mallet's view is that their policy of liberty is all in favor of the capitalists); interest in the improvement of the wretched conditions in the Hôtel-Dieu in Paris, the great charity hospital;[72] advocacy of the abolition of the slave trade and the emancipation of the children of slaves, i.e., gradual emancipation;[73] strong articles on the emancipation of the Jews from social as well as religious discriminations, praising the Emperor Joseph II especially for his actions in this regard. In his passage through Frankfort after leaving Cassel, Mallet had seen the Frankfort ghetto, which he described as a pestilential slum. Mallet does not like the Jews, whom he characterizes as fanatical, sordid, and cowardly, but these qualities, he holds, are only the consequence of centuries of Christian persecution. "Liberate them then from ignominy, give them back the free use of their faculties, banish these odious distinctions and you will elevate their soul and they will assume again the dignity of mankind."[74] Mallet harps insistently on the reform of codes of law and judicial procedure, especially criminal procedure, wherein he praises Leopold of Tuscany and Frederick of Prussia. Like Voltaire, he argues for the introduction of jury trial on the basis of English experience,[75] and like Voltaire, too, he makes a point of reporting cases involving the tragic miscarriage of justice in the courts.[76]

Like Voltaire, Mallet laments war. The interest of governments and parties may be served by war, but seldom that of peoples. How, he asks, have ambitious princes in modern times got their subjects

70. *Annales*, IV, no. 25 (Aug. 30, 1782), 17.
71. *Doutes sur l'éloquence*, pp. 67–73; *Annales*, II, no. 10 (Sept. 15, 1781), 90–105.
72. *Mercure*, 1786, no. 6 (Feb. 11), pp. 54–68.
73. *Journal politique de Bruxelles* [the political section of the *Mercure de France*], 1788, no. 7 (Feb. 16), p. 108.
74. *Annales*, I, no. 7 (July 30, 1781), 407–18; *Mercure*, 1784, no. 9 (Feb. 28), pp. 149–55; ibid., 1786, no. 5 (Feb. 4), pp. 31–38. The quotation is from the first reference.
75. *Annales*, III, no. 19 (Feb. 15, 1782), 152–90; ibid., IV, no. 31 (Nov. 30, 1782), 423–35; *Mémoires historiques*, VI, no. 42 (May 30, 1783), 99–101; *Journal politique de Bruxelles*, 1784, no. 40 (Oct. 2), p. 3; *Mercure*, 1784, no. 14 (April 3), p. 24; ibid., 1785, no. 42 (Oct. 15), pp. 101–9.
76. *Mémoires historiques*, VI, no. 41 (May 15, 1783), 45–59; ibid., no. 42 (May 30, 1783), pp. 65–78.

to go to war solely to wrest territory from their neighbors? He answers: "It is by making them take for heroism and duty [what is] the lowest of the cowardly acts of servitude, bringing one's blood and one's money as tribute to the fields of battle." "Doubtless the citizen ought to die on the frontiers of his country when it is threatened, and the subject ought to defend the sceptre that protects him and to which he has sworn allegiance; but what has this devotion to the defense of the Prince and of homes in common with the caprices of ambition, these errors of Councils, these petty interests of calculation and mistrust where the Powers put their skill and their resources to the test?"[77] Trade wars are called by Mallet "this monster with two heads peculiar to our customs, our times, and our climates."[78] He has, however, no solution for the problem of war between states. By this time he was far too expert in international politics, and too pessimistic, to proffer remedies. As for internal violence, which is usually to be attributed to the spirit of the *corps* and the spirit of *convertisseurs*, there is a remedy; it lies in monarchy that concentrates in itself all the force of the state, but a force that will be, naturally, the servant of reason and not of despotism.[79]

Mallet has much to say against religious bigotry, or "fanaticism," among Christians, and supports the movement for the toleration of dissenters and their acquisition of civil rights. He argues that intolerance is against the spirit of the Gospel,[80] a view that would be acceptable to some of his many Catholic subscribers. He has himself a certain ecumenical-Protestant conception of plural forms of belief. Moreover, he believes in toleration because he is a rationalist, and intolerance is fanatical and obscurantist.

A persistent rationalism is continually cropping up. It appears in a pervasive interest in natural science. It may be seen in an insistence on skepticism in the writing of history and journalism, on *la critique*, to which he devoted several essays,[81] and which in general he practised. It appears in his raillery at all forms of credulity. How he relishes exposing miracles, messiahs, and charlatans, in the manner of

77. *Annales*, I, no. 2 (May 15, 1781), 84–88.
78. Ibid., pp. 100–1.
79. See below, chapter 3, *passim*.
80. *Annales*, I, no. 5 (June 30, 1781), 305.
81. Ibid., V, no. 36 (Feb. 15, 1783), 204–5; *Mémoires historiques*, V, no. 37 (March 15, 1783), 301; *Mercure*, 1785, no. 24 (June 11), pp. 73–83.

Fontenelle and Voltaire! He quotes Fontenelle on the subject of credulity: "Give me four persons who believe I can turn day into night, and I will demonstrate it to two million."[82] This comment was in reference to animal magnetism, which was all the rage in Paris when Mallet went to the *Mercure* in 1784. In the latter journal he tells his readers that danger lies this way, with the destruction of the distinction between fantasy and reason.[83] He was genuinely scandalized, writing Pastor Vernes: "We shall be returned to barbarism."[84]

Animal magnetism, or mesmerism, was in the first instance a therapy that rested on the postulate of a universal fluid surrounding and permeating all bodies and explaining alike the phenomena of gravity, electricity, and magnetism (conceived as both mineral and animal), and of health and disease. Animal magnetism, as therapy, referred to the induction of the proper circulation of this fluid by physical contacts with a mesmerized apparatus and other human bodies, usually in group séances where patients experienced "crises." Health was a question of the harmony between man and nature, and of social harmony. There was a strong humanitarian impulse in mesmerism as philosophy. Mesmerists often went on at the same time to involve themselves with the frankly occult, including communication with spirits. In 1784 animal magnetism was declared to be pseudoscience and charlatanism by a royal commission of medical men and members of the Académie des Sciences. Mesmerists, organized in many places as Societies of Harmony, vigorously defended their doctrine.[85] Furthermore, certain mesmerists meeting at the house of the banker Kornmann in Paris comprised a group of political activists, a somewhat undifferentiated assortment of future revolutionaries at this point united by a common discontent with "despotism," for example Bergasse, Duval d'Eprémesnil, Duport, Lafayette, Carra, and Brissot.[86] In so far as we know, Mallet was unaware or unsuspecting of any such political dimension to animal magnetism. His reaction was simply that of the rationalist who is put

82. *Journal politique de Bruxelles*, 1784, no. 50 (Dec. 11), pp. 76–77.
83. Ibid., 1785, no. 24 (June 11), p. 76.
84. Mallet Du Pan to Vernes, Paris, October 28, 1784, Bibl. Genève, MS D.O.
85. Robert Darnton, *Mesmerism and the End of the Enlightenment in France* (Cambridge, Mass., 1968), chaps. 1 and 2, passim.
86. Ibid., chap. 3

off by pseudoscience, by the craze for the occult, by theatricality in method, by *sensiblerie*.

In a somewhat different vein, Mallet as a rationalist is hostile still to the theology of the schools. The devotion of the Belgian clergy, opposing the Emperor Joseph II, to "the scholastic theology of Louvain, such as was taught in Europe three centuries ago," he calls "this overflowing of enthusiasm.[87] Unlearned Protestant sects and their vagaries fare no better in his opinion. "One may see these ephemeral successes of charlatanism with fanaticism and ignorance only in the countries, like Protestant Germany, where religion is not superstitious enough to close the understanding to every heterodox belief, nor the people enlightened enough to reject foolish opinions."[88]

And yet, all the same, for all his rationalism, the erstwhile apostle of Voltaire to the Germans, who undertook at Cassel to undo the work of St. Boniface, has become a tremendous defender of religion. This is on the score of its social utility (rather than its truth). The established religion is preferred, whatever it may be, and dissident cults take an inferior position. For dissidents need to be subordinated, since it is in the nature of sectaries to be a politically and socially disturbing element; justice is satisfied if they are not compelled to live by other rites but may follow their own, "sans éclat," and if they have the same social and economic opportunities as other citizens. This was essentially the policy decreed by Joseph II in 1781 and the French monarchy in 1787, both reported by Mallet Du Pan with approbation.[89] As for the religion of the state, it would, Mallet naturally assumed, be the dominant religion of the people, in order that religion might the more effectively support society and the state. But the sects, too, if they are docile and their morality unimpeachable, are useful. They too are dikes against indifferentism, an argument used by Mallet Du Pan to persuade Catholics to accept religious toleration.[90] The greatest danger today lies not in fanati-

87. *Journal politique de Bruxelles*, 1787, no. 43 (Oct. 27), pp. 189–90; ibid., 1788, no. 7 (Feb. 16), p. 140.

88. *Mémoires historiques*, V, no. 38 (March 30, 1783), 341.

89. *Annales*, II, no. 14 (Nov. 15, 1781), 336–53; *Mercure*, 1787, no. 25 (June 23), pp. 157–60; *Journal politique de Bruxelles*, 1788, no. 1 (Jan. 5), p. 3; ibid., 1789, no. 36 (Sept. 5), pp. 66–79.

90. *Annales*, II, no. 14 (Nov. 15, 1781), 354–55.

cism of religion but in an indifferentism that points to atheism. And so we find Mallet ardently supporting traditional, institutional Christianity as the most effective means of inculcating belief in a God of judgment and a future life of rewards and punishments. As for "natural" religion, a deistic or theistic belief, it never occurred to him to suggest that *it* might be the religion of the state on the score of possessing elements common to all faiths; the idea would have struck him as chimerical. On the other hand, he defended the theistic writings of Rousseau, as we have seen, and even on occasion of Voltaire,[91] on the score that some souls might be won thus to the basic tenets of religion who would otherwise remain indifferent, or even atheist. And he vigorously defended the "deistic" Abrahamites of Bohemia who, refusing to call themselves either Christians or Jews and not fitting the tolerated categories of Joseph's Edict of 1781, were deported to the Turkish frontiers of Hungary.[92]

Mallet, always reticent about defining publicly or even privately his own personal religious convictions, was at one point forced into a statement. Subscribers to his *Annales*, who had been Linguet's subscribers and who clearly included many Catholics, objected when he advertised in his *Annales . . . pour servir de suite aux Annales de M. Linguet* the publication of the works of Voltaire. Was he a freethinker? What were his religious principles anyway? His principles, answered the journalist, were those "of a Citizen of Geneva, brought up in the Calvinist Religion, that of his ancestors and his Sovereign [i.e., the Republic of Geneva], having learned from the excellent education that one receives in his country and by the example of the most virtuous and most enlightened clergy, to worship the Divine Hand in Its works and in the Benefit of Revelation, to be religious without superstition and tolerant without impiety."[93] Mallet Du Pan could be as casuistical as the next person and the phrase "benefit of Revelation" permits a *double entendre*. Does this mean acceptance of the *truth* of Revelation, or simply recognition of the utility of its being believed in by whoever believes in it? From all the evidence I know, one must conclude that Mallet's own most private

91. See below, pp. 65–66.
92. *Annales*, V, no. 34 (June 15, 1783), 85–88; *Mémoires historiques*, V, no. 39 (April 15, 1783), 412–17; ibid., VI, no. 46 (July 30, 1783), 344–49.
93. *Annales*, II, no. 15 (Nov. 30, 1781), 435–44.

belief was a deism, or theism. But at the same time he objected vehemently to the philosophic attack upon traditional Christianity.

His criticism is most forcibly stated in an early number of his
Annales, when he reviewed the new edition that appeared in 1781 of
Raynal's famous best seller, the *Histoire philosophique et politique
des établissemens et du commerce des Européens dans des deux In-
des.* Never, he says, does Raynal encounter anywhere a superstition or
an absurd opinion but he recapitulates with bitter wrath the history
of Christianity. He does not know such words as reform or correct.
"He breaks indiscriminately all the altars, all the doctrines." What is
the usefulness of this? Would he want his family, his servants, his
debtors, his rulers, not to believe in the immortality of the soul or in
Providence? Let the philosophes reflect on the way of life (*moeurs*)
of our era and ask themselves if this is the time to go about destroying the religious sanction of virtuous behavior. For:

> What will replace these motives? The laws; your [Raynal's] ten
> volumes protest against their tyranny and their absurdity. Gov-
> ernments? They are all corrupt. Education? Perverted by the
> influence of our *moeurs,* feeble motive force soon weakened by
> the education of the world and destroyed by the passions of
> youth. Interest? And you compose the history of its crimes.
> What is left for us? To cause truth to penetrate into councils,
> professional posts, and consciences? I pose you then the ques-
> tion of Festus to Saint Paul: What is the truth? Until the unani-
> mous voice of all the sages and the whole universe has answered
> me, let Paradise remain for unhappy men, and remorse for wick-
> edness.[94]

But it is not only religion, it is virtue itself that the philosophes
destroy, with their hedonistic theory of human behavior. "Some
modern philosophers, at whose head one must put Helvétius, have
founded states on the vices, and public happiness on corruption.
They entitled this combination, *Union of private interest with the
general interest.* This doctrine of the Mandevilles, of the La Métries,
and other writers of metaphysical discourses can be called the hand-
book of the eighteenth century, it is the code of egoism; it is likewise
the most false as it is the most pernicious of theories. There exists

94. Ibid., I, no. 4 (June 15, 1781), 252–55.

but one way to tie the public welfare to that of individuals, it is to inculcate upright feelings in the latter, and to make good *moeurs* guarantors of probity."[95] Mallet Du Pan does not believe that social utility is the sum of private utilities. He does not believe in enlightened self-interest. Self-interest is simply self-interest and self-indulgence.

It is curious to trace the appearances of Rousseau and of Voltaire in the pages of Mallet Du Pan's *Annales* and his articles in the *Mercure de France*, as well as in his correspondence, after the letter to Vernes in 1778.

Rousseau, alas, was only too human, and on the basis of the *Confessions*, which he reviewed, Mallet publicly admits serious shortcomings in his hero. Rousseau has a repellent vanity, though it is different from Voltaire's. Rousseau is self-deceived and self-righteous. "Through his frankness, one perceives a studied effort always to cover his blameworthy inclinations with virtues. . . . He has spoken well of the greater number of the persons he has mentioned, but of no one as well as he speaks of himself." And it is not possible to accept Rousseau's portrait of Madame de Warens, described by Mallet as "a shameless pedant," whose promiscuity would be shocking enough without Rousseau's excuse (that she was entirely indifferent), which only makes it more unnatural. What a pity that he should have put his authority behind the notion of Madame de Warens' essential virtue, thus encouraging other women to imitate her! Moreover, how could "a just and honorable man" ever have dreamed of making public such conduct in his benefactress? However, for this as for his strange behavior on many other occasions, his general failure to come to terms with his environment, Mallet finds extenuating explanations in Rousseau's undisciplined and aimless youth, when he lived so completely in a world of fantasy and imagination that any adjustment to the real world became impossible.[96] There is further extenuation, moreover, in the insanity of his later years.[97] Mallet insists that, both by his eloquence and by his doctrine, Rousseau is a bulwark of "the first truths, of every religion, morality (*les moeurs*), domestic duty, public and private virtues," and that all who con-

95. Ibid., V, no. 35 (Jan. 30, 1783), 175.
96. Ibid., III, no. 22 (March 30, 1782), 370–79.
97. *Mémoires historiques*, V, no. 38 (March 30, 1783), 343–46.

tinue to class him with the sophists "who destroy the roots of every moral obligation" are wrong.[98] He waxes indignant again in thinking of the famous and bitter quarrel between Rousseau on the one hand and Voltaire, D'Alembert, and the Encyclopedists on the other. "Have you read the correspondence of Voltaire that has just come out?" he inquired in 1789 of his friend Etienne Dumont. "One sees exposed there the infernal underhand dealings, the intolerance, the intrigues, of the philosophic sect. . . . Ah, churlish charlatans, how well Rousseau knew you!"[99]

On the subject of Voltaire, Mallet's feelings appear more complicated. Fortunately for him, no such strong censure as was contained in his comments to Vernes in the year of Voltaire's death found its way at that time into print, or he would have been embarrased to adopt the line he took up soon after beginning publication of his *Annales*, where he tried to detach Voltaire from the philosophe "sect" in order to defend him (and himself) against the anathemas of the churchmen. The occasion of the effort was the objection of a number of readers, principally of the clergy, to Mallet's promotion of projected new editions of Voltaire's works. (It was in this connection that he made the statement of his religious beliefs already quoted.) In point of fact, Mallet was himself interested in one of these projects, though he did not see fit to tell his readers so.[100] He declares that he holds no brief for Voltaire's rage against revealed religion, but that as "a real illness, a fever of his mind," it was explainable. Voltaire's mind had been seduced in youth by "the excessive liberty" of the Regency—that was one factor. Beyond that, however, he was revolted by the troubles in the Cévennes and the wretched controversies over the doctrine of grace among Catholics and by the general atmosphere of intolerance and fanaticism that hung over the latter

98. *Mercure*, 1787, no. 34 (Aug. 25), p. 165.

99. Mallet Du Pan to Étienne Dumont, Paris, March 11, 1789, in A. Blondel, ed., "Lettres inédites de Mallet du Pan à Etienne Dumont (1787–1789)," *Revue historique*, XCVII (Jan.–April, 1908), 121. This and all other quotations in English from these letters published by Blondel are my translation.

100. Mallet Du Pan to Osterwald, Geneva, December 17, 1781, Bibl. Neuch., MS 1178, fo 22–121. Later, in 1784, Mallet was to be found soliciting friends of Voltaire in and around Geneva, on behalf of "the publishers of Voltaire at Paris," for Voltaire's correspondence. See Mallet Du Pan to Rieu, Geneva, April 20, 1784, Bibl. Genève, MS Supp. 150.

years of the reign of Louis XIV. There was also his own experience in
the Bastille, where he wrote the *Henriade* against the oppression of
consciences. "The persecutions by which he was beset redoubled that
influence [of the atmosphere of his youth]. His sojourn in Germany,
the murder of Calas, and the execution of the Chevalier de la Barre,
ended by depriving him of all restraint." In everything he did and
wrote against the Church and its doctrines, he was, however, entirely
disinterested. "Into this perseverance in unbelief there entered
neither self-interest, nor vanity of forming a sect, nor intent to excuse
his vices, as has been too ridiculously alleged against him; a hardworking old man, spending twelve hours daily in his study, was assuredly not a frightened libertine. Only his hatred for a doctrine that
his reason distorted, and that he imagined was made to stain the
earth with blood, prejudices strengthened by sentiment, such were
the only causes of his delirium."[101]

Voltaire, he says, was assuredly no atheist, as these correspondents
assert. Where is the page on which he denies the existence of God
and a future life of rewards and punishments, or subscribes to any
tenets of philosophical materialism? What of the *Poëme sur la loi
naturelle* to refute the materialistic La Mettrie, or the attack of Voltaire, alone among the philosophes, on the materialistic *Système de
la nature* of Holbach? No, Voltaire hated both atheism and fanaticism. He held them to be the twin poles of a world of confusion and
horror, and he never privately denied what he published in this matter. Mallet here tells the story, which has often been repeated, of how
he heard Voltaire, one day at table, stop his guests in a conversation
where the existence of God was brought in question and send the
servants from the room, explaining that he wanted these same servants to believe in conscience and in the Divinity.[102] In retelling the
story, nearly twenty years later, in his *Mercure britannique*, Mallet
Du Pan identified the guests as D'Alembert and Condorcet, who in
fact visited Voltaire together in 1770.[103] This would have been one
of Mallet's earliest memories of the Sage of Ferney. (The story has
sometimes been treated as though it were apocryphal, perhaps without real knowledge of its provenance. I see no reason to doubt its

101. *Annales*, I, no. 5 (June 30, 1781), 294–96, 307.
102. Ibid., pp. 299–303.
103. *The British Mercury*, II, no. 14 (March 15, 1799), 342.

historicity, for I do not believe Mallet Du Pan would have invented an incident out of whole cloth, and passed it out as genuine truth or claimed to have witnessed what he did not see.)

The moral tone and implications of Voltaire's writings are also defended by Mallet against charges of obscenity and libertinism, which he asserts to be baseless, save for one canto of the *Pucelle*. In all the *contes, poésies fugitives,* and *romans*, literary forms in which, says Mallet, moral scruples are least likely to be found, "you will see the author always blithe, never erotic; gallant rather than sensual; and never exceeding the liberty that is permitted every day in the conversations of good society." And, almost incidentally, dissociating Voltaire from philosophical materialism, he dissociates him from a hedonistic ethic: where, he asks, is the page on which Voltaire reduces virtue to self-love?[104]

Voltaire's manner of life, his benefactions, are praised in warmest terms. "Fortune was prodigal of its gifts to him; he ennobled the employment of them by assuring himself a new sort of glory, and new pleasures; his retreat was embellished with useful establishments; they prospered under his eyes, by his counsel as much as by his aid. His tireless ambition to excel extended itself to care for the welfare of the Province; there people gave thanks for the enjoyment of his influence; his existence was peaceful like his household."[105]

When subscribers persisted in being outraged by his attitude on the subject of Voltaire, Mallet said to them that they were wrong to confound all the philosophes in one anathema. "You . . . and all the adversaries of the Philosophes, you have been deficient in statecraft," he objected. He told them they should have shown the philosophes at odds with each other, they should have accepted the help of Rousseau and of Voltaire against the others.[106]

It was of course only three years since Mallet Du Pan had himself condemned Voltaire along with the other philosophes, described Rousseau to Vernes as Voltaire's opposite, philosophically speaking, and complained that Linguet had done wrong to denounce Rousseau along with Voltaire. In this time Mallet's point of view had shifted. He was now the judicious historian rather than the bitter

104. *Annales*, I, no. 5 (June 30, 1781), 295–96, 300.
105. Ibid., p. 282.
106. Ibid., II, no. 15 (Nov. 30, 1781), 443.

moralist. He had remembered his own debt to "le Nestor," and was in a way repaying it. He had known Voltaire well in his home for eight consecutive years, he told his readers. Voltaire had done him services and taught him lessons, and he would keep for Voltaire's abilities and his person an esteem all the greater for not being based on conformity of opinion.[107] Besides, Mallet was reacting in a characteristic way against anybody who attempted to impose a point of view on his writing, and the Voltairean still in him reacted particularly against clerical interference.

And yet, the portrait of Voltaire changes once again, and we are again acutely conscious of Mallet's ambivalence. This time, Voltaire is described as the historian of magnificent princes, of a Leo X or Louis XIV, whose culture or whose lavish enterprises evoke only the historian's (Voltaire's) admiration, while their immoral actions, the burdens laid on their subjects, are explicitly or implicitly excused. "This lack of regard for morality, for seemly behavior, for public utility, could be supported by many citations. One might see in them the Historian, now Courtier, now Republican, changing maxims like an accomplished flatterer, after having shown himself hitherto an austere avenger of the rights of humanity."[108] It is again Voltaire the egotist, the flatter of the landgrave of Hesse-Cassel, who cannot be forgiven! There is, of course, a great deal more to Mallet Du Pan's appreciation of Voltaire as historian than is suggested in the foregoing quotation, but rather than discuss the subject here, it seems more appropriate to consider it later in relation to Mallet's profession as journalist.

Mallet Du Pan might be in several minds about Voltaire, but he was constant in his antipathy toward D'Alembert, secretary of the Académie Française, the kingmaker philosophe. D'Alembert was the Number One enemy. After him came Condorcet, who in turn rose to Number One upon D'Alembert's death in 1785. When Mallet writes of Condorcet his pen is dipped in vitriol.

Two articles of Mallet's *Annales* in February and April of 1782 are devoted to the election of Condorcet, already secretary of the Académie des Sciences, to the Académie Française. "For a month now, M. de Condorcet has been one of the Princes spiritual of the Church

107. Ibid., I, no. 5 (June 30, 1781), 294.
108. Ibid., V, no. 36 (Feb. 13, 1783), 211–13.

of which M. d'Alembert is the St. Peter," Condorcet "his faithful disciple, his confrere in Geometry, in encomiums in little works with great pretentions." Condorcet's rival for the seat, the astronomer Bailly, who missed election by one vote, is regarded by Mallet Du Pan as the better candidate, both as scientist and man of letters, all the more in that he had had the support of Buffon, whom Mallet admires as much as he dislikes D'Alembert. "M. de Buffon, greatly superior to malicious gossip and the shallow pride of lording it in an Academy, had the candor to prefer him and the courage to serve him." But in vain. "This recommendation and the wish of the men of letters"—who have protested—"have not prevented M. d'Alembert from being once again the sponsor of the member-elect, and of placing on the head of M. de Condorcet the wretched crown of M. Bailly." [109] It was, in short, a repetition of the case of La Harpe: in both instances, men who did not deserve the honor received it because D'Alembert pushed them.

But the matter means much more for Mallet than did the case of La Harpe; the issues now much transcend those of a literary quarrel. The second of the two articles in the *Annales* about Condorcet's election concerns Condorcet's address to the Académie at the time of his reception into it on February 21, 1782. In form an *éloge* of Condorcet's predecessor, Saurin, the address is primarily a statement of that theory of progress which was to be much more fully elaborated in the famous *Esquisse d'un tableau historique des progrès de l'esprit humain* of 1793. Mallet reports it at some length, with commentary. Condorcet writes of the eighteenth century as "this century when, for the first time, the general system of the principles of our knowledge has been developed, when reason has at last discovered the road it is to follow," and Mallet scornfully exclaims: "Since reading M. de C., it is worth the pain of living in the eighteenth century." Condorcet says: "In the proportion that enlightenment increases, the methods of instruction are perfected; the human mind seems to grow larger, and its limits draw back. A young man, on coming out of our schools, possesses more actual knowledge than the greatest geniuses, I do not say of antiquity, but even of the seventeenth century, were able to acquire by long labors." This, retorts Mallet, is "naïve," sheer conceit of intellect. What! our schoolboys wiser than Cicero, Pliny,

109. Ibid., III, no. 19 (Feb. 15, 1782), 201–5.

Bacon, Galileo, Descartes, Leibnitz, Machiavelli, Bayle! Condorcet goes on to say that the moral sciences, following the same method as the physical, will attain the same degree of certitude. Progress will be slower, but already in the present century, owing to the efforts of enlightened men, the evils of human society are fewer than they were formerly. The progress of knowledge is the most important condition of moral advancement: "In all men, ignorance is the most fecund source of their vices."

No, answers Mallet, ignorance is not the chief source of vice, nor is knowledge the chief source of virtue. Indeed, "intellectual achievements, multiplying themselves, have become the arm of the wicked as of the just, of the impostor as of the philosopher." Virtue consists in following "principles consecrated by a universal conscience." Here, in a way, is the Rousseauist speaking. Though conscience is not for Mallet Du Pan the mystical intuition of the *Vicaire Savoyard*, but rather, wisdom and right attitudes inculcated by training and by habit, still Rousseau and Mallet would both deny that virtue flows directly from knowledge. Insofar as knowledge has anything to do with the matter, it is understanding that is the fruit of the experience of all times and antedates our age.[110]

It is the cardinal fault of Condorcet to be the example par excellence of *goût de système*—the passion for abstract argument, imposing patterns on experiential material in accordance with certain prejudices or preconceptions. This is, alas, a distinguishing feature of the century, which "has given to everyone who speculates the right to fabricate his own [conceptions of morality], and to render problematical principles consecrated by a universal conscience, and now become the plaything of opinion." For forty years argument has been going on about law, economics, education, and many other matters, says Mallet Du Pan, and the only result is "a confusion of ideas, an anarchy of opinions, a universal skepticism based on this crowd of new doctrines; ephemeral products of the fashion, of libertinism of the mind, and of the *goût de système* that has fled from the sciences into philosophy. It has substituted its own prejudices for those of

110. Ibid., no. 23 (April 15, 1782), pp. 409–24. The text of the address upon which Mallet is commenting is contained in *Œuvres de Condorcet*, ed. A. Condorcet O'Connor and M. F. Arago, 12 vols. (Paris, 1847–1849), I, 391–401. My translation.

preceding centuries and its own errors for those of ignorance. . . ."
The new truth which philosophy is so confident of discovering has
yet to be found. Philosophy is "the alchemy of the moral sciences,"[111]
and Condorcet is "the new Nostradamus."[112]

We are living in a time, in short, thinks Mallet, when men have
lost their moral and intellectual roots, and are at once too skeptical
and too credulous. In the view of Mallet Du Pan, the vogue for animal magnetism and other occult doctrines is basically the same phenomenon as the vogue for the doctrine of enlightened self-interest or
the idea of progress. These things are all symptoms of the intellectual
superficiality of the era. To Pastor Vernes he writes, from Paris:
"Knowledge has generalized a skepticism of prejudice that is quite as
blind as the former superstitions and that hands opinion over to a
thousand different follies."[113] He made a little satire on virtue and
hypocrisy, in his *Annales,* out of the story of a prize of money being
offered to whatever individual should, in the judgment of some
academy, have performed the most meritorius action in all Paris.
"Since pretention to wit and verbosity have become a universal fad,"
he writes,

> people have become infatuated, in verse and in prose, with some
> philosophic being or other, the subject of brochures and conver-
> sations. The controversies concerning deism were the fashion at
> one moment; then people were fascinated with sensibility: a
> certain metaphysical tenderness, insipid and nauseous, abounds,
> having addled all brains: toleration followed; then the *produit
> net,* succeeded by liberty: today it is nothing else [than] the
> question of Jeannot and virtue. . . . We are at the carnival of
> humanity; even the hangman begins to talk of it; every one wants
> a part in this masquerade. . . . To make virtue the object of such
> twaddle is to have destroyed the very idea of it. . . . Besides, what
> does it matter to a villager of the outskirts of Paris to be shown
> in an Academy, with his ridiculous virtue, like an exotic animal?
> It is at home, among his like, that it is sweet for him to hear his
> name spoken with praise. By naming him at Mass, as a fine citi-

111. *Annales,* III, no. 23 (April 15, 1782), 416.
112. Ibid., pp. 411–12.
113. Mallet Du Pan to Vernes, Paris, Nov. 9, 1785, Bibl. Genève, MS
D.O.

zen, his *curé* would reward him with as much satisfaction for his pride and with less danger for his innocence.[114]

Mallet laments what he describes as the contemporary decadence of French literature and learning, which is not exactly sudden but is suddenly evident with the disappearance of Voltaire and Rousseau, "the two Atlases of literature." He complains of a general passion for novelties, for sensational discoveries. "There are so many amateurs that the adepts have lost credit, so many judges that one no longer is afraid of the judgments." Hence "this crowd of charlatans of every sort, who have replaced the geniuses of the last century and the first half of this one."[115] Philosophy has become a kind of anti-intellectualism, in the guise of rationality.

Some exception must be made to this judgment, Mallet thinks, in regard to the development of natural science. Mallet particularly excepts the naturalist Buffon, whose *Histoire naturelle des oiseaux* was reviewed by him in the *Mercure de France*. In his estimation Buffon is the epitome of the careful, empirical scientist, and the universal pattern, the general ladder of being, that appears from his work is a valid conception because of the evidence on which it rests. Buffon is free of *esprit de système*. "Everything is tied together in this work by the generalizations that result from particular details. The writer never fails to seize and present these universal laws; they cause to emerge from the parts of this vast picture the plan and the unity of the designs of the great Architect. Describing penguins or birds without wings, M. le Comte de Buffon causes one to observe the progressive difference and the points of continuity (*prolongement*) which, while distinguishing the great families of the quadrupeds from the birds and the fish, nevertheless bring them together and attach them to the general ladder [of being]."[116] It should be noted that Mallet thinks of Buffon's science as supporting a deistic cosmology. It apparently did not occur to him to ask whether this was a scientific conclusion.

The Abbé Gabriel Bonnot de Mably is cited also as an exception to the general decadence of letters, though not for the same reason. Rather, he is compared with Rousseau as a beneficent moral influ-

114. *Annales*, III, no. 23 (April 15, 1782), 427–30.
115. Ibid., VI, no. 48 (Aug. 30, 1783), 454–59.
116. *Mercure*, 1784, no. 22 (May 29), pp. 217–19.

ence. "All nations had honored this writer with an esteem that is accorded to talent alone, and that M. de Mably as well as J.-J. Rousseau merited for the constant sobriety (*sagesse*) of their principles." It is true, says Mallet, that Mably is too exclusively the moralist, too unrealistic, to be a first-rate historian or political analyst, but in his way all his works are concerned with "the primary interests of man as a social being and the defence of his rights"—the *Entretiens de Phocion* are especially valuable. Moreover, Mably writes soberly about society and politics, unlike "a rout of modern ranters, who never write on liberty but with delirium." In his personal life Mably was equally admirable, holding aloof from other men of letters and all their wretched intrigues. "M. de Mably lived long apart from the literature of Paris, to which the nature of his activities made him a stranger; no academy could honor itself with having received him, and he left behind a fine example for men of letters in his conduct and in his labors."[117] Mably and Buffon, however, were both holdovers from an earlier generation, and their example scarcely affected Mallet's judgment of the period when he was writing.

For all the emphasis he laid upon empiricism, Mallet Du Pan was not himself entirely unaffected by *esprit de système*. This may be seen notably in his acceptance of a cyclical theory of culture about which there was something doctrinaire and even deterministic. The cycle develops whether we will or no. He subscribed to the theory in 1772 when he was a philosophe and in 1787 when he was not. He thought that French culture, after about 1750, was on the downswing.[118] The notion of course reinforced his pessimism, given that the culture was deteriorating as seemed obvious to him in the 1780's. He never speculated about when the upswing might be expected.

Mallet raised the theoretical question of the relation between men's behavior on the one hand and their concepts of moral values and of truth on the other. The terms in which the question presented itself to him were: which is antecedent, the decline of *moeurs* or the corruption of philosophy, that is of *la saine philosophie*, by materialism, hedonism, and the general intellectual license of the age, *goût*

117. *Journal politique de Bruxelles*, 1785, no. 19 (May 7), pp. 30–31; *Mercure*, 1788, no. 15 (April 12), p. 61.
118. *Quelle est l'influence de la philosophie?*, pp. 96–98; *Mercure*, 1787, no. 34 (Aug. 25), pp. 154–55.

de système? His answers are not, on the face of it, consistent. The philosophes may be excoriated, for example, and Rousseau upheld, as moral teachers, as though it made a difference in men's behavior what they said. On the other hand, however, we find Mallet explicitly affirming that it is *moeurs* that are primary.[119] But if one looks at the way in which Mallet writes history, describes historical phenomena, these divergent viewpoints may be reconciled, for here conceptual factors and factors of external condition and development are mutually interacting, so that one cannot say always what is cause and what is effect. As special pleader Mallet will single out whatever factor it suits him to single out at the moment. Often he emphasizes the ideas of the intelligentsia so that they seem primary; yet he is far from believing these to be the whole story.

As an assessment of Mallet's anti-philosophism before the French Revolution, the present chapter is incomplete, for it omits any consideration of his hostility to the democratic dogma, and this hostility was basic. The democratic ideology was a form of philosophism, no less so in that it was associated with the name of Rousseau. But this subject should be considered in the general context of Mallet's politics, and hence has been put into the following chapter.

---

119. For example, in the *Mercure*, 1787, no. 34 (Aug. 25), pp. 153–59.

Three

MALLET DU PAN'S POLITICS

(1775-1783)

Those twin fiascos, the *Compte rendu* and the Cassel episode, left young Jacques Mallet with feelings of personal resentment against the social system. He was contemptuous of caste-ridden Germany, "the fatherland of the wretched vanities of grandeur . . . where one must have a title to be a man; where . . . men's lives are judged by their distinctions, and these distinctions never derive from themselves."[1] But the Genevan patriciate, though a different kind of ruling class from the German, seemed to him at this time but little better. Mallet became quite vehemently antiaristocratic in his sociopolitical opinions. So far as Geneva was concerned, he abstracted himself for the nonce from the politics of his city, where indeed for several years he did not reside, and transferred his attention from the problems of republics, which seemed bound to be aristocracies, in fact if not in theory, to the more interesting phenomenon of the struggle between aristocracy and monarchy.

He privately avowed a predilection for monarchical government: "I do not know whether you will take my monarchical complaisances in good part," he wrote to Henri Rieu when sending him a copy of his tract, *Doutes sur l'éloquence*, "but it is the government meditation always brings the philosopher back to."[2] In this work he presented himself to the public (and to Linguet) as an admirer of *la monarchie simplifiée* and enemy of the *corps intermédiaires*, citing in support of his position the *Considérations sur le gouvernement de*

1. *Doutes sur l'éloquence*, p. 11.
2. Mallet Du Pan to Rieu, Aubonne, October 8, 1775, Bibl. Genève, MS Supp. 150.

la France of the marquis d'Argenson, first published, posthumously, in 1764.

It will be recalled that D'Argenson, himself a *grand seigneur*, had proposed to free the French monarchy from *grands seigneurs* and all *corps intermédiaires*. He would abolish property in office,[3] all exemptions from taxation,[4] all privileges save honorific ones.[5] He would even reform, though he would not abolish, the manorial obligations.[6] Against the favorite project of the eighteenth century feudal reaction, the revival of provincial estates wherein the nobility would naturally predominate, D'Argenson would establish in all localities and provinces elected assemblies representing, not orders, but property owners.[7] This would be "true democracy in the midst of monarchy." It would be the best means of reconciling liberty with authority, for D'Argenson repudiated the extreme centralizing tendencies of the seventeenth century administrative monarchy, which he called "la monarchie simple et absolue," and maintained that in all affairs that concerned them locally the property owners should have, through representatives, consultative and administrative powers.[8] At the same time, for D'Argenson the authority of the crown must be final and overriding. All legislative and taxing authority, all policies affecting the nation as a whole, all ultimate decisions, must belong to the crown, the only so to speak impartial institution, the only one with a pure conception of the national welfare. Intendants (*commissaires*), paid not by the provinces but by the crown, would supervise the provincial administration, and the parlements, though permitted to comment on royal decrees, must promptly register and execute what the royal council should decide.[9] D'Argenson did not think it would be easy to carry through his reforms, but they should be adopted in principle and gradually worked out. He believed the crown had in the third estate a vast reservoir of support. Only the privileged orders would be affronted by his propo-

3. Marquis d'Argenson, *Considérations sur le gouvernement ancien et présent de la France, comparé avec celui des autres états; suivies d'un nouveau plan d'administration* (Amsterdam, 1784), pp. 149–53, 226–28, 234.
4. Ibid., p. 198. 6. Ibid., pp. 220–21, 223–24.
5. Ibid., p. 237. 7. Ibid., pp. 196–204, 271–72.
8. Ibid., pp. 11, 248–49, 254–57, 273; pp. 28–34, 209–12, 271–72.
9. Ibid., pp. 196, 205, 207–10, 213–14, 225.

sitions, and even the privileged would in time be won over. His ideas, he maintained, were compatible with the traditions of French history.[10] D'Argenson's appeal was both to history and to utility, while eschewing all the abstractions of contemporary political theory—and herein undoubtedly lay much of its attraction for Mallet Du Pan.

> All Europe [avers Mallet in his *Doutes sur l'éloquence*] groans under aristocracy, more or less modified. It is filled with *corps,* orders, nobles, tribunals, all privileged, all jealous of their exemptions, all tyrants over the classes at whose expense they are exempted. If one opposes them, they sound the tocsin; if one restrains them, they cry oppression; if one leaves them alone, some commit usurpations on the others, and all together on the body of the nation. . . . But at last, one begins to tire of these baneful prejudices, to feel the necessity of a simplified regime that assimilates men and conditions . . . and that keeps the sword of justice lifted over titled malefactors who insolently make sport of human miseries. . . . A régime that makes all men equal before the laws and freely puts them into effect; that is not alarmed by the resistant solidarity of *corps* or of popular bodies (*départemens populaires*); and whose plenitude of power can successfully dissolve all these excrescences of hereditary consulates, irremovable senates, patrimonial *noblesse.* A régime that would prevent the enormous inequality of fortunes in controlling the officers of the sovereign through the fear of their becoming redoubtable to the prince and the nation. A régime, in fine, which, breaking all the barriers raised between the monarch and people, causes their wills and their interests to coincide. . . .[11]

Such, says Mallet, is the new régime proposed by the marquis d'Argenson in his work which is to be regarded as the answer to the *Esprit des loix* of Montesquieu. "This *Esprit des loix,*" declares Mallet, "is a plea for aristocracy, for all the courts of justice, for the *noblesse,* the clergy, all those who have one foot on the throne and are trying to put two there." Montesquieu "everywhere confounds the liberty of the *corps* with the liberty of the people. His monarchy is a chimera, whose image he takes from feudal government." On the other

10. Ibid., pp. 35–36, 175, 244, 270–73, 296–97.
11. *Doutes sur l'éloquence,* pp. 142–45.

hand, "the Marquis d'Argenson has come to contest all these [feu-dal] notions rejuvenated under the epigrammatic style of the Bor-deaux président." Unfortunately, Mallet observes, the credit of D'Argenson is much less than that of Montesquieu.[12]

Mallet Du Pan does not extend his hand to *all* the proponents of *monarchie simplifiée*.[13] It will be remembered that in the *Doutes sur l'éloquence* he denounces the Economists, or Physiocrats. He ob-jects to them partly because, as it seems to him, their policies are in reality all for the men of property and not for the common people, the poor. In the principal economic issue of the moment, the ques-tion of the freedom or regulation of the grain trade, Mallet sided against the Economists and with those who contended that govern-ment regulation of the trade in grain was essential to ensure an abun-dant and cheap supply of bread.[14] Yet there were other specific issues on which Mallet might have commended the Economists because his views and theirs were similar. He criticized for example the ex-clusiveness of the guilds, and in the *Doutes* he refers with obvious hostility to "these legal knaveries of masterships, of exclusive con-cessions, of municipal rights."[15] However, I have not discovered anywhere his ever allowing the Economists credit for attacking these things, too, then or later. Basically, Mallet disliked the Economists because they were philosophes and among the most doctrinaire.[16] Voltaire, who admired D'Argenson, too,[17] who had just recently fought for the monarchy and against the parlements in the attempt of Maupeou to destroy their political power, and who was also no doctrinaire, was supporting the freedom of the grain trade,[18] as he

12. Ibid., pp. 145–47.
13. This is Mallet's term, not D'Argenson's. But D'Argenson does say that the true object of "the science called politics (*la politique*)" is to reduce matters from the complex to the simple (*Considérations*, p. 22), and his view of the contemporary situation in France was indubitably that it was chaotic.
14. *Doutes sur l'éloquence*, pp. 63–67.
15. Ibid., p. 128.
16. Ibid., pp. 63–67. See also the preceding chapter of the present study, p. 49.
17. Peter Gay, *Voltaire's Politics: The Poet as Realist* (Princeton, 1959), p. 104, quoting a letter of Voltaire to D'Argenson, May 8, 1739.
18. *Petit écrit sur l'arrêt du Conseil du 13 septembre 1774 qui permet le libre commerce des blés dans le royaume* (1775), *Œuvres complètes de Voltaire*, new ed., 52 vols. (Paris, 1877–1885), XXIX, 344; Voltaire to

supported in everything the then controller general, Turgot. Here the *Doutes sur l'éloquence* provides further evidence of the growing divergence of Mallet's views from Voltaire's.

Turgot, the least doctrinaire of those who professed Physiocratic principles, is described later in Mallet's *Annales* as noteworthy "if not for prudence, at least for the integrity of his views." But Turgot was not to his mind a great controller general, not to be compared with Colbert or Necker. He had not improved the condition of the finances, and he philosophized too much, for he presented his edicts with too much *raisonnement* (which was bad, because in an age when everyone systematized, this only called into question the utility of the best of laws.)[19]

Mallet was to become in the 1780's a great admirer of Adam Smith. His remarks in praise of the "free-trade" Eden Treaty of 1786 are reminiscent of the *Wealth of Nations*. He is not here for free trade under all circumstances, and thinks that it is poor policy for a great nation that is capable of industry to be industrially dependent on a foreign country, but nevertheless, when two great states are so nearly equal in economic strength as France and England, and neither is industrially dependent, they can but benefit industrially, he says, if protection is withdrawn and each makes that which it can make best.[20] Although the Eden Treaty happened to be largely the work of the Economist Dupont de Nemours, Mallet still had no time for his like, whereas he was full of praise for the Scot. "I adopt the greater part of Smith's fundamental ideas," he wrote a friend in 1788, "but, in no way, those of the French economists, whom I regard as the vainest and the most dangerous of theorists in respect to administration."[21] Unlike the Economists, Smith did not seem to him a systematizer, a doctrinaire.[22]

D'Alembert and Condorcet, January 16, 1775, *Correspondence*, XC, 16–17; Voltaire to D'Alembert and Condorcet, January 21, 1775, ibid., XC, 27.

19. *Annales*, II, no. 9 (Aug. 30, 1781), 53–55.

20. *Journal politique de Bruxelles*, 1787, no. 1 (Jan. 6), pp. 16–17.

21. Mallet Du Pan to Etienne Dumont, June 19, 1788, in A. Blondel, ed., "Lettres inédites," p. 111.

22. For other indications of Mallet's esteem see: *Journal politique de Bruxelles*, 1785, no. 30 (July 23), p. 161; *Mercure*, 1785, no. 53 (Dec. 31), p. 204; ibid., 1787, no. 26 (July 14), p. 58n.; *Mercure historique et politique* (title of the political section of the *Mercure de France* at this date), 1790, no. 33 (Aug. 14), p. 106.

If D'Argenson was the principal literary source of Mallet's enthusiasm for reforming monarchy, this enthusiasm, which pervaded his political writing throughout the 1780's and inspired some articles written during the French Revolution, was sustained by close observation of contemporary actualities, namely, the personalities and the activities of the monarchs conventionally termed the "enlightened despots." First in his *Annales*, then afterward in the *Mercure de France* with its political section called the *Journal politique de Bruxelles*, he published many an article, short and long, relating to the policies of the Emperor Joseph II, of Leopold, grand duke of Tuscany, later Emperor Leopold II, and of Frederick the Great, not to mention lesser lights. (There is but little on Catherine of Russia, whom Mallet considered a fraud.) [23] They are informed and informative, discerning articles, politically sophisticated, Mallet Du Pan the political commentator at his best.

The activities of reforming absolutism here appealed to Mallet Du Pan as the implementation of what he liked to call, by analogy with natural science, *la politique expérimentale*. Eschewing a priori reasoning, ignoring and hostile to grand subversive principles like the general will, the rights of man, or the "natural and essential order" (Mallet was quick to reject the suggestion that Leopold of Tuscany or the margrave of Baden owed anything to the Economists),[24] *la politique expérimentale*[25] drew data from history, from the realities of constitutional law, from statistics, from the needs of subjects, from the art of government (here some practitioners fell short, like Joseph, whose sense of the art of government was defi-

23. On Russia, see *Annales*, I, no. 4 (June 15, 1781), 236–37; ibid., IV, no. 27 (Sept. 30, 1782), 178; *Mercure*, 1787, no. 4 (Jan. 27), pp. 163–65.

24. *Mémoires historiques*, VI, no. 47 (Aug. 15, 1783), 413.

25. Both the idea and the term itself appear frequently in Mallet's writing. In the *Doutes sur l'éloquence* he says he is convinced that "metaphysical" definitions and treatises must be eschewed in favor of *la politique expérimentale*, which is founded on the study of history (p. iv). And again, political truth is to be read "in the facts and not in our intelligence" (pp. 133–34). Eight years afterward he uses similar words: "In the study of government, as in physics, it is better to observe with one's eyes than with one's intelligence"—and this is termed *la politique expérimentale* (*Mémoires historiques*, VI, no. 41, May 15, 1783, 13). In 1789 he wrote to Vernes: "Of all the sciences, legislation ought to be the most empirical (*expérimentale*)." See Mallet Du Pan to Vernes, Paris, March 18, 1789. Bibl. Genève, MS D.O.

cient)—and it proceeded pragmatically to the reformation of concrete abuses, to arrive thus at an impressive totality of reforms.
"From one end of Europe to the other," wrote Mallet in 1783, "the
Cabinets are in labor. . . . If this zeal continues," he went on, "the end
of the eighteenth century will show a revolution in laws, in religions,
in practices, like that already effected in *moeurs* and in opinions."
The emperor and the king of Prussia were the great artisans (*grands
ouvriers*), he said.[26]

Mallet never (or almost never) expressed reservations about the
nature of the reforms of these monarchs, about the justifiability of
the *kind* of changes. The reforming monarchs were doing what
needed to be done. However, his first admiration for Joseph—"this
prince [who] ascended the throne with the operations of his reign in
his portfolio . . . prime minister of his own authority, sole author of
his plans . . . master of his opinions, which is not often the case with
Kings, all his reforms linked one to another and developed under the
firm hand that holds the chain"[27]—this admiration was early modi-
fied by reservations concerning the emperor's power to execute his
projects. There was too much to carry out all at once, the reformer
"strikes everything and at the same time—the church, discipline,
canon law, the monks, the fortresses, the administration, the economy civil and military, luxury, legislation. It is an encyclopedia of
new institutions."[28] The implementation of the edicts on religious
toleration fell short of the emperor's intention, because people's
minds were not prepared for the spirit of his measures—witness the
unfortunate deportation of the sect of Abrahamites to the frontiers
because they were neither Catholics, Protestants, nor Jews.[29] The
reforms relating to the manorial system set in train a jacquerie in
Hungary, which the government had to suppress with troops because
the peasants were excited by the emperor's promises and by the hostility of the landlords.[30] Mallet criticized the emperor's *lourderie*, as
he called it, in imposing his administrative and ecclesiastical reforms
in Brabant. All Brabant, he observed in 1787 to his friend Vernes,

26. *Mémoires historiques*, V, no. 39 (April 15, 1783), 424.
27. *Annales*, III, no. 18. (Jan. 30, 1782), 109–10.
28. *Mémoires historiques*, V, no. 39 (April 15, 1783), 424.
29. Ibid., VI, no. 46 (July 30, 1783), 344–49.
30. *Journal politique de Bruxelles*, 1785, no. 1 (Jan. 1), pp. 17–18.

was aflame, and he added: "It is not enough to effect useful reforms, they must be effected seasonably and legally."[31] In his obituary article on Joseph in the *Mercure*, in March of 1790, Mallet summed up his estimate of the reign. An impartial posterity, he said, would find much more to praise than to condemn in Joseph. "Joseph II was prodigal of ordinances to the point of abuse; but the immensity of the disorders they attacked is astonishing. The edict on toleration, firmly upheld, the law on marriages, the reform of the criminal code, the equality of protection and of opportunities among the various classes of subjects toward which several preparatory rulings tended, the unrelenting struggle against an excess of feudal privileges, the improvement of education, the praiseworthy and uniform severity in the enforcement of the laws, will forever do honor to this reign of ten years, so shortened and so full." Joseph's personal behavior as a ruler, moreover—his simplicity, beneficence, respect for merit, and hardworking devotion to his tasks—was exemplary. But on the other hand, Joseph was impatient and arbitrary. "Without a doubt, it is a fault, even with an absolute power, to permit oneself great innovations, without having prepared public opinion for them"—as in the case of the ecclesiastical reforms in Belgium. Too often, Joseph paid too little attention to local traditions and national prejudices, even national historic rights (*droits*). He was fascinated by the idea that an empire should be symmetrical and governed by uniform laws, "but one does not remake men like decrees."[32] Tradition then sets limits to *monarchie simplifiée* (as indeed D'Argenson would have said, too).

This criticism of the attempt to assimilate Belgium and Hungary into a uniform, highly centralized system was Mallet's principal criticism of the content of Joseph's reforms, as distinguished from the manner. Although the Hungarian nobility resisted Joseph's reform of the manorial system as well as his attempt to destroy the autonomy of Hungary, although indeed the autonomy of Hungary was in part a bulwark of the manorial system there, Mallet Du Pan does not take Joseph to task for his attacks upon that system. Indeed, in this same obituary article he praises him for doing so. In another article written just before Joseph's death, remarking on "the feudal

31. Mallet Du Pan to Vernes, Paris, July 1, 1787, Bibl. Genève, MS D.O.
32. *Mercure historique et politique*, 1790, no. 11 (March 13), pp. 88–95.

oppression under which the Hungarian peasants vegetate," he describes the Hungarian magnates as "a species of sovereigns." Although at the same time he observes that one could not expect to
attack old rights or even ancient abuses with impunity, he goes no
further in his criticism.[33]

Mallet Du Pan was of course well aware that Joseph and Frederick, like Catherine, were territorial expansionists and he did not
find this admirable, but it did not, to his thinking, vitiate the credit
they deserved for internal administration.

In respect to Joseph's brother Leopold, Mallet had no reservations
at all but only praise. For if Leopold was not so spectacular as Joseph,
if he was more cautious and realistic, he was the more to be admired.
Mallet understood perfectly that Leopold, as grand duke of Tuscany,
where he made his name as an enlightened monarch, did not face
problems of the same magnitude as Joseph's. Nevertheless, his
achievement was not for all that to be depreciated, for he carried
through successfully important reforms of a sort on which Mallet
placed a high valuation, where other princes less committed to the
public welfare would have let things be. Mallet said in his *Annales* in
1782: "There are few sovereignties in Europe where the supreme
power decrees more legislative measures than in Tuscany, or as important ones."[34] (There could be just a touch of flattery here, for
Mallet set much store by his Italian circulation, but that was not
what determined his point of view.) He proceeded to discuss, that
same year, Leopold's reform of criminal jurisprudence, his abolition
of imprisonment for debt, and suppression of the Inquisition.[35] In
1792, in his obituary article on Leopold in the *Mercure historique et
politique*, Mallet writes:

> Leopold brought about the disappearance of a great part of the
> privileges of the capital, burdensome to the rest of the Grand
> Duchy. The abolition of seigneurial jurisdictions, his criminal
> code, his reform of the prisons, his laws on the imprisonment of
> debtors, his encouragement of the clearing of the land, and sev-
> eral other acts of his administration, merited this sovereign en-

33. Ibid., no. 5 (Jan. 30), pp. 322–23.
34. *Annales*, IV, no. 26 (Sept. 15, 1782), 129.
35. Ibid., III, no. 19 (Feb. 15, 1782), 152–81; ibid., IV, no. 26 (Sept.
15, 1782), 129–31; ibid., no. 31 (Nov. 30, 1782), 423–35.

thusiastic praise. . . . He was reproached for too great an economy, [for] the passion for governing in every detail, a passion
common to all the princes of his house. . . . These faults were
compensated for by the spirit of order and of application, by
knowledge, by aversion for war, by the love of justice, by a constant solicitude for the needs of his subjects.

For Leopold as successor to Joseph, Mallet has the highest praise:

In two years from his accession to the Imperial throne, Leopold
had given his government a brilliance that few reigns have offered us: an honorable peace, the Netherlands recovered, the
diverse branches of the Monarchy made strong again, a difficult
alliance concluded.[36]

This is to be sure a polemical article reflecting Mallet's war at the
time upon the Jacobins, the Brissotins in particular, but it also re-
flects quite simply Mallet's admiration for Leopold as a more skillful
practitioner of *la politique expérimentale* than Joseph. Previously,
at the time of Joseph's death, there was an article in the *Mercure
historique et politique* publishing a rescript of Leopold that repudiated Joseph's changes in Belgium. The announcement purported to
come from Belgium but there can be no doubt that it reflected Mallet Du Pan's own opinion. The rescript, says the *Mercure*, removes
all causes of complaints and cannot be disdained, "coming from a
Prince without reproach, covered with the universal esteem of Europe, [a prince] whose desire was always opposed to the innovations
so unfortunately essayed in our provinces."[37]

The king of Prussia appears, in Mallet's obituary article in the
Journal politique de Bruxelles, early in 1787, as a superb figure. He
had many kinds of ability, says the notice—ability as soldier, legislator, administrator, and "academician." He was the administrator
par excellence. Mallet calls him "supreme inspector of the state,"
noting that he supervised everything in such detail as to make mere
clerks of his subordinates, but offers no adverse comment on that
fact, presumably regarding it as being at most a defect of the virtue
of Frederick's marvelous comprehension. His projects are said to

36. *Mercure historique et politique*, 1792, no. 12 (March 24), 219–20.
37. Ibid., 1790, no. 12 (March 20), p. 225.

have been always mature, carefully prepared, and followed through. He developed the prosperity of his states, reformed judicial procedure, and put before the country in 1784 the project of a uniform civil code for Prussia. In all things "the great machine of the State operated without shocks, obeying a fixed and gradual movement."[38] There is no feeling in this article that Frederick ought to have considered problems he did not take up. As is well known, Frederick did not even think of touching the seigneurial system on the estates of the Prussian nobility. Mallet Du Pan, as we have seen, considered the seigneurial system in Europe to be a proper subject for reform, and he commended other princes for their actions in this field. He even went so far as to admonish the government of Naples that it ought to destroy the seigneurial courts and put a limit upon "usurious" feudal dues (*redevances*).[39] It might be remarked that the obituary on Frederick appeared in the *Mercure* under French censorship, whereas Mallet's frankest discussions had appeared in his own *Annales*, which were not censored, or appeared in the *Mercure* when the censorship had been lifted, which was in August of 1789. In 1787, Mallet would not have been free to criticize a foreign government in the *Mercure* on such a matter as the seigneurial system, had he wanted to. But did he want to? He had said in the *Annales* in 1783 that the emperor and the king of Prussia were the great fashioners (*grands ouvriers*) of the developing European social revolution, but had added that whereas the emperor was attacking everything at once, in Prussia things were going more slowly, "and perhaps with greater maturity."[40] All in good time. And in so many ways the rule of Frederick had been so solid and so brilliant that it required to be presented as an illustration par excellence of *la politique expérimentale*, no less than Leopold's.

Meantime, while following and reporting so assiduously the activities of enlightened monarchs, Mallet Du Pan had again become involved with republican politics and the revolutionary movements of the 1770's and 1780's that seemed largely, if not entirely, a phenomenon peculiar to republics. "A wind of revolution and of revolt seems

38. *Journal politique de Bruxelles*, 1787, no. 1 (Jan. 6), pp. 6–11.
39. *Mémoires historiques*, V, no. 37 (March 15, 1783), 319–20.
40. Ibid., no. 39 (April 15, 1783), p. 425.

to blow from all quarters of the horizon," observed Mallet's *Annales.* "In whatever direction one turns, one breathes its exhalations."[41] As reform promoted by governments was a major subject of Mallet's journalism, so was popular revolution. They appear together in his writing in a kind of contrapuntal theme.

In 1779 Mallet Du Pan returned to Geneva, having lived away at least since his marriage in 1774. Until 1778 he had resided at Aubonne. In that year, when the *Annales de Linguet* were moved by their author from London to a location near Brussels, Mallet had wanted to set up in Geneva the *réimpression* to which he had the rights, but he located it in Lausanne instead, one reason being "the stupid cowardliness of the government of Geneva which threatened to declare war on my edition."[42] The next year, however, Mallet, his family, and his edition were at last located in Geneva.[43] It is not entirely clear what had happened meantime, if anything, to make him feel more welcome there. Probably the Genevan government was sufficiently assured that Linguet's journal, which was officially tolerated in France, would not embarrass the relations of Geneva with the French minister of Foreign Affairs. Mallet had wanted to return to the city not only because it was more advantageous professionally to work there, but also because his attachment to Geneva had revived, and he wanted again to become part of its life. "I am getting to the age where the need for a country makes itself felt," he said to Osterwald.[44] He even aspired, once established, to public office, "to fulfill my vocation as citizen in the posts for which I may be judged worthy."[45] (Mallet never achieved public office,[46] and it may be

41. *Annales,* IV, no. 27 (Sept. 30, 1782), 173.
42. Mallet Du Pan to Osterwald, Aubonne, July 21, 1778, Bibl. Neuch., MS 1178, fo 22–121.
43. Mallet Du Pan to Osterwald, Lausanne, June 5, 1779, ibid.
44. Ibid.
45. Mallet Du Pan to Osterwald, Geneva, September 21, 1779, ibid.
46. In the first edition of *Notices généalogiques sur les familles genevoises,* II (Geneva, 1831), ed. J.-A. Galiffe, it is stated (p. 434) that Mallet Du Pan was a member of the Council of Two Hundred; but in the second edition of this volume (Geneva, 1895), edited by J.-B.-G. and Aymon Galiffe, this statement has disappeared from the notice on Mallet Du Pan (pp. 664–65). It was patently erroneous, and I am indebted to M. Jean-Daniel Candaux, of the Société d'Histoire et d'Archéologie de Genève, for informing me of the difference between the two editions of Galiffe, a standard reference.

doubted that, once back in the thick of things, he continued to think of his doing so as an immediate possibility, since he never consistently identified himself with a party. On the other hand, there is no doubt that he aspired to be a political influence.)

The move coincided with the onset of a new political crisis in Geneva. The accord of 1770 between Négatifs and Représentants for the repression of the Natifs, which had provoked Mallet's *Compte rendu*, had proven fragile, and broke over a project to codify the laws. This the Représentants, led by Clavière and Du Roveray, were promoting, whereas many Négatifs were opposed to it. For the project was highly political: it involved not only a civil and criminal code, but a constitutional one as well. That meant taking up the question of the disputed right of representation and other matters that in turn involved the question whether political supremacy belonged to the General Council of Citizens and Bourgeois, as the Représentants claimed, or to the governing councils (the Small Council and Council of Two Hundred), the stronghold of the patriciate. It will be remembered that the General Council had in 1768 obtained some share in elections to the Council of Two Hundred and the right to unseat four members of the Small Council (right of *ré-élection*) on the occasion of elections to that body;[47] but that otherwise tenure was permanent and these councils predominated in choosing each the members of the other. The Négatifs now took the name of Constitutionnaires, signifying their hostility to any further constitutional change in a democratic direction,[48] and some of them wanted to undo what had been done in 1768. At least, so said Francis d'Ivernois, a leading Représentant, in his history of the Genevan crisis,[49] and Mallet Du Pan accused them of bad faith.[50] In 1777 the General Council, with its Représentant majority, had removed by *ré-élection* four opponents of a code within the Small Council, whereupon the governing councils consented to a committee of their members, made up half of Négatifs and half of Représentants, being empowered to draw up a code. About the first of

47. See above, chapter 1, pp. 10–11.
48. Karmin, *D'Ivernois*, p. 52.
49. [Sir Francis d'Ivernois], *Tableau historique et politique des deux dernières révolutions de Genève*, 2 vols. (London, 1789), I, 143–44.
50. Mallet Du Pan to Osterwald, Geneva, September 21, 1779, Bibl. Neuch., MS 1178, fo 22–121.

September, 1779, this committee produced and published a draft project and requested that it be allowed further time. Abruptly, it was dissolved (September 3) by the Council of Two Hundred, the majority of whom found the draft unacceptable.[51]

The Constitutionnaires had preceded this *démarche* in the Council by soliciting, secretly, the support of the French foreign minister, Vergennes, who forthwith announced in the strongest possible terms that he would give it to them. A letter from him to the French resident in Geneva, dated September, 1779, and made public, stated that His Majesty could not tolerate any revision of the constitution of Geneva such as was indicated in the project for a code, nor any violence in Geneva, should violence arise over the issue.[52] (The legal basis of Vergennes' action, just as in the 1760's, was the fact that France, together with Zurich and Berne, was a guarantor of the settlement of 1738 that had terminated an earlier episode of strife in Geneva.)

Mallet Du Pan reacted angrily against the Négatifs. Nothing had transpired in the immediately preceding years to destroy the resentments he had acquired, as we have seen, against the Genevan patriciate; rather the contrary, one would surmise, in view of his difficulty in getting his edition of the *Annales de Linguet* located in Geneva. Now these same people were willing to put Genevan independence in jeopardy, just to avoid talking with their rivals. Mallet had his own reservations about the project for a code, which he described as a Pandora's box;[53] but the great thing was for the Genevans to settle their quarrels among themselves, to avoid at any cost bringing in the French. Now Mallet, as a Genevan, was proud of his heritage of French culture, and like other Genevans he considered close relations of many sorts between them and the French to be natural. But also he cherished the uniqueness of Geneva, which was a great city, not in territory or number of inhabitants but in its traditions, its economic importance and cultural eminence; and its quality had come from its freedom to manage its own internal affairs. Mallet had a clear appreciation of Geneva's historic dependence on France

51. D'Ivernois, *Tableau historique*, I, 82, 84, 100.
52. Karmin, *D'Ivernois*, p. 51; Fazy, *Constitutions*, p. 147.
53. Mallet Du Pan to Osterwald, Geneva, September 21, 1779, Bibl. Neuch., MS 1178, fo 22–121.

in external affairs and the present weakness of her position as a small city-state in a great-power European polity. By the same token, he had no time for those who would exploit this weakness for partisan aims. In all Mallet Du Pan's political twists and turns this attitude about Geneva was to remain pretty constant.

His wrath exploded in a letter to Osterwald:

> An aristocratic phalanx that dominates the Great Council [the Two Hundred] has just reduced us to the last extremity by the most dangerous, the most illegal resistance. . . . I see nothing but bad faith, insolence, despotic pride, haughty extravagance, fanatical party spirit in this band of 2 or 300 Patricians for whom the *Patrie* is only a word, and who, at the first revolt against their pretentions, are always prepared to call the Foreigner inside our walls. I was born in that faction, I have all kinds of ties with it, but I see in it only a thousand faults which I detest.[54]

And again:

> There we are then in the lion's clutches—where since 1768 the defeated party [the Négatifs, obliged to make concessions to the Représentants in 1768] has been trying to put us. . . . Do they think the citizens will not be indignant to see their government, their city, their independence given over to foreign influences by Genevese hands! I confess to you, neutral enough in the discord of opinions, I cannot see with indifference this conspiracy to deliver us up to a sovereign legislator of 30,000 square leagues. —And when one thinks that the basic reason is the humiliation of seeing Messieurs Du Roveray and Clavière taking the lead in the composition of the Code, instead of M. Saladin and Company, one may indeed say that
>
> > This universal alarm
> > Is the work of a gnat.[55]

At this point it is only the Négatifs, and not at all the Représentants, who are the objects of Mallet's wrath. It was just the reverse of his

---

54. Ibid.
55. Mallet Du Pan to Osterwald, Geneva, October 1, 1779, ibid.

attitude in the affair of the *Compte rendu.* The Représentants, who were the majority of citizens referred to, appear not as disturbers of the peace but only as the upholders of Geneva's independence.

These were privately expressed judgments, but Mallet also took a public stand, to which he was at the outset forced by Linguet. In October the *Annales de Linguet* carried a copy of Vergennes' aforesaid letter to the French resident, together with a commentary by Linguet supporting Vergennes' stand and expressing supreme contempt for those Genevans, citizens of such a petty state—"République imperceptible"—who would so much as imagine disputing the policy of a great power like France.[56] Mallet was aghast. He decided that his duty as Linguet's agent required him to distribute the issue as it stood, but he circulated with it in Geneva a disclaimer of the views expressed in Linguet's article, declaring that he had absolutely no part in furnishing the author the material to compose it.[57] The disclaimer drew the unfavorable attention of the resident, who reported it to Versailles.[58] Mallet's protest to Linguet must have been pretty strong, for the following number of the *Annales de Linguet* carried a long letter written from the Représentant point of view. This article says that the French minister in effect threatens the independence of the city, calls the Négatifs who invoked his help "the faction [that is] an enemy of the Republic," and says the party that is represented to the mediators (France, Berne, and Zurich) as the most suspect is the one most deserving of confidence.[59] The letter is not in Mallet's style; it was, presumably, solicited. Mallet told Osterwald with obvious satisfaction that the issue containing it had caused a sensation in Geneva.[60]

How far did Mallet Du Pan's new commitment to the Représentant point of view extend? In December, 1780,[61] he published his

56. *Annales de Linguet,* VII, no. 49 (Oct. 1779), 43–48.

57. Note of Mallet Du Pan, distributed with no. 49 of the *Annales de Linguet* and dated at Geneva, October 27, 1779. AAE, Correspondance politique de Genève, LXXXIV, fol. 371.

58. Gabard de Vaux, French resident at Geneva, to Vergennes, October 31, 1779, ibid., fol. 368–69.

59. *Annales de Linguet,* VII, no. 50 [c. Nov. 1779], 65–85.

60. Mallet Du Pan to Osterwald, Geneva, December 14, 1779, Bibl. Neuch., MS 1178, fo 22–121.

61. The date is taken from the citation in E. Rivoire, *Bibliographie historique de Genève au dix-huitième siècle,* 2 vols. (Geneva, 1897), no. 2021,

views on the situation in a pamphlet entitled *Idées soumises à l'examen de tous les conciliateurs. Par un médiatur sans consé-quence.* He had already in October participated in a *représentation*. (This is the assertion of Brissot de Warville,[62] whose statement might be considered open to some question; but Mallet Du Pan did not deny it when he denied other assertions Brissot made about him.) Mallet agrees, in his *Idées soumises*, that the intransigence of the government is to be deplored. The present system in Geneva shows the vices of aristocracy. "A spirit becomes naturalized there that is composed of *esprit de corps* and the spirit of family, as well as the love of power, against which the reason of a Magistrate of the greatest integrity finds trouble defending itself."[63] Insensibly the public interest becomes subordinated to that of the association (*compagnie*). "Behold, then, in a tribe of twenty-four thousand souls a considerable number of families who have a spirit, opinions, an interest, very different from those of the rest of the citizens."[64] The root of the trouble is cooptation of offices, with permanent tenure, which hardens the aristocratic spirit and gives it tenacity— "as may be judged by the course pursued unintermittently for sixty years by the Parlements of France."[65] The solution, then, is *amovi-bilité*, or election of the Small Council for a term of years (by, pre-sumably, the General Council; but Mallet is concerned here not with the question of the franchise but simply with that of election). He adduces the example of many contemporary republics and ap-peals to various authorities, notably D'Argenson.[66]

Amovibilité, Mallet is convinced, will destroy *esprit de corps* and will require the magistrates to be responsible in the exercise of their powers; it will be much more effective than *ré-élection*, in reality, recall, and it will not carry the invidious connotation of *ré-élection*

as quoted by Otto Karmin, ed., in *Un mémoire inédit de Francis d'Ivernois sur la situation politique à Genève au début de 1791 et sur les moyens d'y établir un gouvernement stable* (Geneva, 1915), p. 13n.

62. [J. P. Brissot de Warville], *Le Philadelphien à Genève, ou Lettre d'un Américain sur la dernière révolution de Genève, sa constitution nouvelle, l'émigration en Irlande, etc., pouvant servir de tableau politique de Genève jusqu'en 1784* [sic] (Dublin, 1783), p. 84.

63. *Idées soumises à l'examen de tous les conciliateurs par un médiateur sans consequence* (Geneva, [1780]), p. 19.

64. Ibid., pp. 20–21.   65. Ibid., p. 21.   66. Ibid., pp. 10–16.

for the magistrate.[67] However, his plan does not envisage reducing the extent of the magistrates' powers (except for some restriction in the use of the *droit négatif*)[68] or their subordination to the General Council. He holds still, as he did in 1771, to the idea of a strong executive, as the Small Council was.[69] He wants to keep the Small Council strong because he thinks that any great change in the structure of government is to be feared,[70] and especially so in the case of eighteenth century Geneva. The large power of the Small Council is no bad thing, he says, "under an aristo-democratic form of government, the most fragile of all owing to jealousy of prerogatives and the rivalry of competencies. The political bond being there more relaxed, especially today when education, paternal authority, Religion and *moeurs* serve but feebly to tighten it, too great a division of the executive power would bring us soon to Anarchy."[71] He rejects a widely advocated Représentant proposition for a special tribunal to judge of representations because such a body would in effect be endowed with supreme authority and this would constitute too great a change in the structure of the republic.[72] Besides, all attempts to settle the question of sovereignty are in the existing agitation of opinions chimerical. The enthusiastic dreamers of such projects do no good. What is needed is a pragmatic approach[73]—in a word, *la politique expérimentale*. His own proposal seems to him, of course, to fall in this category, since it does not touch the disputed question of sovereignty.

The strictures of the *Idées soumises* on aristocracy relate not only to the patriciate, an aristocracy of old families, but also to "wealth of recent creation," which is also a form of aristocracy and quite as dangerous to the health of the body politic because it is scornful of republican proprieties (*bienséances républicaines*). Whereas rank and birth show a pride tempered by *politesse* and manners considerate of the people (*popularité des manières*), it is not so with "wealth of recent creation." "The vanity of the newly rich does not condescend in this way." Nothing is more calculated to generate popular discontent.[74] This "wealth of recent creation" was of course

67. Ibid., pp. 15–17, 24–26, 34–36, 48.   68. Ibid., p. 33.
69. Ibid., pp. 18–19.   72. Ibid., pp. 6–9.
70. Ibid., pp. 5–6, 9.   73. Ibid., pp. 5, 9, 15, 31, and passim.
71. Ibid., pp. 18–19.   74. Ibid., pp. 28–31.

to be found primarily among the Représentants. Mallet Du Pan was, in short, as Cornuaud described him, only a Représentant "mal converti."[75]

The *Idées soumises* had been intended as a work of compromise,[76] but as such had no effect. The situation in Geneva only deteriorated, rapidly. And in the civil violence of 1781–1782 Mallet's Représentant sympathies vanished entirely.

A new element was introduced into the disputes by the reappearance of the Natifs on the stage. The resentments of the artisan class following the repression of 1770 had been concentrated against the Représentants to such a degree that the Négatifs felt it possible, when the Négatif-Représentant rivalry was resumed, to build a party among the Natifs. They held out the promise of equality of civil and economic rights. Their instrument was Isaac Cornuaud, who also became the instrument of Versailles.[77] During the year 1780 the Représentants themselves sought, by direct negotiation with Versailles, to win Vergennes over to a neutral viewpoint.[78] That failing, they began to bid against the Négatifs for Natif support, going so far as to hold out the bait of political rights as well as civil equality— a complete reversal of the stand they had taken in 1770. In January, 1781, occurred another brush between the Représentants and the Négatifs: the Représentant procurator general, Du Roveray, was deprived of office by the Small Council because he had remonstrated publicly against the influence of Versailles with the government and the activities of Cornuaud.[79] On February 5 the Représentants, with Natif assistance, seized the strong points of the city and on the 10th the Représentant majority in the General Council enacted a great democratic edict which, among other things, conferred full equality of civil rights upon the artisan class, admitted Natifs of the third generation to the bourgeoisie, and recalled the Natif exiles of 1770.[80]

The Edict of February 10 remained however a dead letter, since the Small Council, backed by Vergennes, would not enforce it.[81] In September Vergennes announced the dissolution of the joint asso-

75. Cornuaud, *Mémoires*, p. 328.
76. Mallet Du Pan to Osterwald, Geneva, December 13, 1780, Bibl. Neuch., MS 1178, fo 22–121.
77. Karmin, *D'Ivernois*, pp. 52–54.
78. Ibid., pp. 59–61.   80. Ibid., p. 69; Fazy, *Constitutions*, p. 152.
79. Ibid., pp. 66–68.   81. Karmin, *D'Ivernois*, p. 70.

ciation of mediation of France, Berne, and Zurich (the Swiss having shown themselves rather reluctant to follow the French lead); France would act alone, and Vergennes proceeded to concentrate troops in Franche-Comté and Gex.[82]

Meantime Mallet had begun to publish, as he had long ardently wished, his own journal, of which he was both author and publisher and not merely publisher and reportorial assistant. The first number of the *Annales . . . pour servir de suite aux Annales de M. Linguet* is dated April 30, 1781, following by about three months the Représentant *coup d'état* and edict to admit the Natifs to the Bourgeoisie. The *Annales* and their successor, the *Mémoires historiques*, have much to say about Genevan affairs.

The first important article appeared October 15, 1781, occasioned by Vergennes' declaration that the triple guarantee of 1738 was ended. It is of course unreasonable, it is said here, to suppose that the foreign minister has any designs upon the independence of the Republic; the subject is raised only because it is commonly talked of not only in Geneva but elsewhere. But the outcome actually is up to the Genevese themselves. They will only have themselves to blame if violence or extreme contention are followed by intervention.[83] The rest of the article is a lament on the theme of republican factions, which are likened to *corps*. Once men are formed into political "battalions," they behave like *corps*, "they permit themselves everything and never depart from their principles or their mode of action." There is no distinction in this article between Négatifs and Représentants; both are held to be consumed by the love of power and the spirit of faction. "Never did any people take so much trouble to avoid coming to an agreement."[84] It is impossible, said Mallet in the next issue, to imagine one party or the other now carrying off a complete victory. Refusal to think of conciliation is a crime against the *Patrie*; let the Genevans remember Poland![85]

The climax came in six months. About the beginning of the year 1782 the Représentants gained control of the Two Hundred in the election held by the General Council, but the Small Council re-

82. Ibid., p. 77.
83. *Annales*, II, no. 12 (Oct. 15, 1781), 239.
84. Ibid., pp. 241–44.
85. Ibid., II, no. 13 (Oct. 30, 1781), 263–64.

mained Négatif[86] and on April 7 rejected a last petition of the Représentants on behalf of the Natifs.[87] The latter had been growing ever more restive at the nonimplementation of the Edict of February, 1781, and on April 8 they poured through the streets. The uprising was primarily a Natif action, but the Représentant chieftans quickly assumed the leadership because they could not afford not to do so.[88] There was little bloodshed. During the following three months a revolutionary Commission de Sûreté kept order. The leading Négatifs were held as hostages pending negotiations.[89] Throughout the month of June Geneva was besieged by the forces of France, Berne, and Sardinia. Although the Natif populace wanted to fight, the Représentant leaders finally rejected a course so hopeless. Failing to secure some sort of not unfavorable terms by negotiation, they settled in the end for outright capitulation. On the night of July 1–2 the hostages were released and the Représentant leaders, who knew themselves to be proscribed anyway by the victors, fled the city as some of their partisans cried treason.[90]

Under the French occupation that followed, the power of the patriciate was reestablished. On November 21, 1782, the General Council, with most of the Représentants excluded, adopted an edict that regularized the Négatif victory. The great majority of Natifs who had recently been admitted to the bourgeoisie lost that status, and the Représentants, whose leaders were moreover formally banished, lost the political advantages they had reaped in 1768. The "circles" were suppressed, and the liberty of the press was restricted.[91]

Publication of Mallet's *Annales* had been suspended during the crisis, but was resumed in mid-July. The issues of August 30 and September 15 carried two long articles on the revolution in Geneva.[92] Mallet entitles his account "Réflexions générales," stating that he cannot now provide a detailed relation of events. No Genevans are cited by name. Concerning his own role he is silent. Something about

---

86. Karmin, *D'Ivernois*, pp. 77–78.
87. Ibid., p. 86.
88. Ibid., pp. 87ff.; Fazy, *Constitutions*, p. 155.
89. Karmin, *D'Ivernois*, p. 89.
90. Ibid., pp. 97–101; Fazy, *Constitutions*, pp. 156–61.
91. Fazy, *Constitutions*, pp. 161–69; Karmin, *D'Ivernois*, pp. 103–7.
92. *Annales*, IV, no. 25 (Aug. 30, 1782), 5–48; ibid., no. 26 (Sept. 15, 1782), pp. 69–128.

that can be gleaned, however, from a few subsequent bits of evidence. He visited the Sardinian commander Marmora, with the knowledge of the Commission de Sûreté, he said later, to intercede for more favorable terms of surrender than were actually granted; he had had a long talk with Flournoy, one of the subsequently proscribed Représentants, about this mission.[93] Cornuaud, moreover, says that Mallet Du Pan was of some influence in persuading the majority of the bourgeoisie to capitulate rather than to resist further.[94] The articles in the *Annales* are, as their title suggests, an interpretative historical sketch. Mallet says his aims are to unravel the complexities of Genevan politics for foreign readers who are baffled by them, and to provide all readers with an objective account such as they will obtain nowhere else. He claims to be above party: "I do not owe an accounting of my opinions to any party or any authority, but to the conscience of those who contributed [even] less than I to our public misfortunes."[95] He does not pretend not to pass judgment, but only not to be beholden, not to be *factieux*. At the same time, his point of view is unmistakably slanted in regard to party. It is the Représentants now who bear almost all the onus for what has happened. The Négatifs to be sure are not exactly exonerated, for it was they who sought a foreign intervention to begin with, they contributed to the corruption of the populace by bidding against the Représentants for Natif support, and they had been quite inflexible. But there is a certain understatement about Mallet's relation of these facts concerning the Négatifs, whereas the accusations against the Représentants are sharp and clear.

The Edict of February 10, 1781, giving to the Natifs not only civil equality (a just concession, Mallet says, on which all parties were agreed) but admitting a large number to the bourgeoisie, was, he holds, founded upon a specious idea of a unified political community.[96] Mallet no longer accepts the thesis he had accepted in 1771, that the people had been deprived of political rights once theirs, that birth should make the citizen. He now does not admit that the Natifs have any historic claim to such rights; indeed, he accepts the thesis

93. *Mémoires historiques*, VI, no. 45 (July 15, 1783), 283–84.
94. Cornuaud, *Mémoires*, p. 383.
95. *Annales*, IV, no. 25 (Aug. 30, 1782), 11–12.
96. Ibid., p. 24.

that they had voluntarily despoiled themselves of political rights,[97] hence they have no constitutional title to them. Geneva is a polity with historic political distinctions, and one cannot all at once destroy such distinctions in a state without grave risk. The Edict of February 10 proposed to alter the existing political relations of the classes in Geneva, it proposed to alter the relation of the executive and legislative powers, weakening the former by enlarging the majority of its opponents in the General Council, and it was enacted in violation of the proper legal forms. For the edict did not have the prior sanction of the governing councils but was the product of an armed insurrection. The Small Council, in refusing to enforce the edict, was on perfectly constitutional ground.[98]

While Mallet Du Pan is prepared sometimes to admit at least in theory that there is a right of insurrection to secure personal liberty, property, and livelihood, he does not see such a situation in this case, where the issue is simply a question of political power. Here, the obligation to be conciliatory rests principally on the "outs," not on the "ins." The Small Council was in the right because it was the established authority no matter how few it represented or how illiberal their views, and was acting legally. Besides, he thinks that time was working for the Représentants and against the Négatifs, within Geneva; and had the former let the quarrel die down, Versailles would have turned its attention away.[99]

To be sure, the uprising of April, 1782, was in the first place a Natif rather than a Représentant revolt and only the "dregs" of the bourgeoisie were at that time involved in it. The rest of them were taken by surprise and there was considerable dismay. But they joined in. "But the baneful ascendancy of party fanaticism, the tyrannical and absurd point of honor to follow, even into crime, the banner one is linked with, the praiseworthy desire to control, as it must be believed, the excesses of an unruly multitude, decided the generality of the Citizens to become their [the Natifs'] accomplices."[100]

The fact that the period of revolutionary government was not marked by bloodshed was proof that "the Genevese was factious rather than wicked, and inclined to bad actions more by party doctrines than by corruption of the heart."[101] This was intended of

97. Ibid., p. 46.   98. Ibid., pp. 24–26.   99. Ibid., p. 15.
100. Ibid., p. 33.   101. Ibid., no. 26 (Sept. 15, 1782), p. 123.

course as a compliment to the Genevese, but also one notes that for Mallet Du Pan the observation serves to underline the dire potency of partisanship and of wrongheaded doctrine. The articles are peppered with sarcastic references to "political visionaries" and to the anarchical reasonings of "metaphysical chatterers." Even the author of the *Contrat social*, avers Mallet, allows that the community may dissolve the government only by legal means, never by force[102] (reference to chapter xviii [in Book III] of Rousseau, *Contrat social*). He flings out this pronouncement: "Republican factions come to an end sooner or later by tyranny. So, let the Prices, the Raynals, and other enthusiasts who are called by giddy brains the defenders of the peoples but whom I call their poisoners—let them come stir up to effervescence the dregs of states; let them nourish restlessness and disquiet in legitimizing insurrections by the inalienable right to revolt; let us oppose them, not by argumentation, but experience. . . . The history of Geneva before our eyes, we shall see liberty destroying itself continually by its attempted self-aggrandizement. Twenty happy nations have received chains while looking for a government without abuses, and not one has found it."[103] Although Mallet uses "faction" in the plural, his words were naturally taken to be an attack upon one party, the Représentants.

In article after article, with regard to any polity where the revolutionary spirit was at work, Mallet's journal pursued this same theme.

Without precisely denouncing the Anglo-American insurgents for their struggle against Britain, Mallet is not sympathetic, and indeed sides with the Loyalists, who he says are a much larger fraction of the population than is generally supposed.[104] The British are taken to task for having too feebly championed the interests of the Loyalists at the peace.[105] The new American regime moreover is described as unstable, anarchical.[106] The worst of the American Revolution is that it has spawned a "swarm of fanatics" in Europe.[107] Mallet's distaste for this phenomenon is displayed in a review of a French work

102. Ibid., no. 25 (Aug. 30, 1782), p. 46.
103. Ibid., no. 26 (Sept. 15, 1782), p. 125.
104. Ibid., no. 29 (Oct. 30, 1782), pp. 274–80; *Mémoires historiques*, V, no. 39 (April 15, 1783), 391–92.
105. *Mémoires historiques*, V, no. 39 (April 15, 1783), 389–407.
106. Ibid., VI, no. 47 (Aug. 15, 1783), 430–34.
107. Ibid., p. 425.

entitled *Essais historiques et politiques sur la révolution de l'Amérique septentrionale,* by Hilliard d'Auberteuil. In style and dogma,
writes Mallet, this is a new edition of Raynal. He proceeds to show,
by citations and confrontations, that the picture painted by the author is one of extravagant stereotypes.[108] (The book does indeed belong to the category of utopian and propagandistic literature on
America that flourished in the 1780's.) Mallet comments that one
has only to note that the book was published in Paris, and under the
author's own name, to mistrust its point of view and to suspect the
probable relations of the author with the government.[109] That European governments, i.e., France, should have championed the American insurgents appears to Mallet Du Pan to have been a great folly.
"While legalizing this uprising with subsidies, alliances, and even
manifestoes, the Sovereigns of Europe consequently legitimated the
principles of their [the Americans] insurrection. There is not any
[ruler] to whom the peoples of his states, dissatisfied with authority,
cannot say, like the sectaries of the [American] Congress: 'You
hold your authority only by our consent. All power emanates from
us; you are our mandatory and our servant: consequently, we have
the inalienable right to reform the government, to change it or to
abolish it.' "[110] For Mallet at this point, the doctrine of the rights of
man in the Declaration of Independence is but a step removed from
that of the sovereignty of the people. "The point where the Government ceases to be legitimate and becomes tyrannical being inappre-
ciable, the result is that ambition, scorn for the laws, the desire to
shake off the yoke can determine a revolt, like fear or the burden of
oppression. In this respect everything depends on the circumstances
and the opportunity."[111] The American insurgents are the Genevan
Représentants all over again.

Politics in the Dutch Netherlands were the object of numerous
articles. Here was the perfect example of the pernicious effect of partisan rivalry, for the century-long conflict between the stadholder and
the municipal aristocracy had reduced the parties representing these
forces to agencies of foreign powers, Britain and France.[112] Mallet

108. *Annales,* IV, no. 27 (Sept. 30, 1782), 133–72.
109. Ibid., p. 140.   110. Ibid., p. 169.   111. Ibid., pp. 169–70.
112. Ibid., I, no. 6 (July 15, 1781), 335–36.

Du Pan is not a neutral observer here, any more than in the case of the Americans. Of all the constituted authorities in Europe, he declares, none is more legitimate than the stadholderate, sanctioned in 1748 by the public will and serving as a defense against "confederative anarchy" and "aristocratic despotism."[113] Yes, Mallet Du Pan himself can invoke the concept of the general will, when the general will seems to him to be on the side of political cohesiveness and monarchical authority, when, he would say, it represents a true consensus and not partisanship and is in favor of political stability. Mallet's criticism of the municipal aristocracy and endorsement of the stadholderate does not extend here to an idea that the Dutch should not have stood up against the British. He claims that they need not have been so thoroughly worsted by the British, had they but collaborated before the war with the squadrons of the Armed Neutrality; but, he says, the spirit of commerce, incompatible in the long run with the patriotic spirit, prevented this, while the pro-French, anti-British alignment of the aristocratic party ultimately involved it in the war that had just ended so disastrously for Holland.[114]

At this juncture in Dutch affairs the democratic or Patriot movement against not only the stadholder but the aristocracy, the regent families who resembled the Genevan patriciate, was not sharply differentiated from the older conflict between stadholder and aristocracy, and when Mallet Du Pan was writing his *Annales* and its sequel the *Mémoires historiques,* he treated the struggle in Holland not only as a particularly reprehensible manifestation of republican factionalism, but as something analogous to the conflict elsewhere between aristocracy and monarchy, without stressing the democratic element he had denounced in the case of Geneva. But he also prophesied, no doubt by an analogy with Genevan history, that matters would get "worse," coming to a popular revolt, before they got "better."[115] In any case the independence of the Dutch was at stake. "If the feeble voice of a foreigner familiar with the spectacle of republican storms . . . might be heard, I would invite Holland to cast

113. Ibid., V, no. 35 (Jan. 30, 1783), 147.
114. Ibid., I, no. 6 (July 15, 1781), 326–29.
115. Ibid., pp. 352, 356.

her eyes about her, on the powers that are her neighbors, on the fate of modern republics [read Geneva, Poland]. . . ."[116]

The drift of all these articles was clear enough, but Mallet stated it explicitly, on the occasion of announcing his change of title in 1783 from *Annales . . . pour faire suite aux Annales de M. Linguet* to *Mémoires historiques*. "In this universal effervescence, the result of the progress of enlightenment (*lumières*) and of the anarchy of opinions," he declared, "it is useful in all things to bring minds back to moderation, the governments to justice, and dispositions (*les têtes*) to tranquility."[117] In the same number he published some remarks critical of Mirabeau's *Des lettres de cachet & des prisons d'état*, which had recently appeared. For however bad the use of *lettres de cachet* might be, the book seemed to him irresponsibly seditious. "To warn authority of abuses is the duty of a citizen. To overthrow governments in order to correct them is an act of madness."[118]

Mallet's articles on the revolution in Geneva drew a stinging rejoinder, in this same spring of 1783, from the pen of Brissot de Warville, entitled *Le Philadelphien à Genève*. It was published anonymously. Brissot had been in Geneva briefly around the middle of June, 1782, while the allied forces of France, Berne, and Sardinia were encamped outside the city, and here he had met leading Représentants. He proceeded thence to Neuchâtel, where he planned to interest Osterwald in a journalistic project, and stayed about a month,[119] during which interval most of the Représentant leaders who had fled the city turned up there also. From this time dated Brissot's close association with Clavière, who furnished him with funds.[120] It would appear that Brissot nourished a personal grudge against Mallet Du Pan, who had in his journal described Brissot's *Théorie des lois criminelles* as vague and pointless theorizing,[121] and had refused to announce "avec éloge"[122] Brissot's *Correspondance universelle, ou ce qui intéresse le bonheur de l'homme et de la so-*

116. Ibid., V, no. 35 (Jan. 30, 1783), 167.
117. *Mémoires historiques*, V, no. 37 (March 15, 1783), 264.
118. Ibid., p. 298n.
119. Brissot, *Correspondance et papiers*, pp. xxii–xxiii.
120. Ibid.
121. *Annales*, III, no. 19 (Feb. 15, 1782), 183.
122. *Mémoires historiques*, VI, no. 45 (July 15, 1783), 260.

ciété, which began to appear in December of 1782. According to the memoirs of Brissot, Pastor Jacob Vernes, Mallet's good friend and also a Représentant, had invited the two journalists to supper together while Brissot was in Geneva, on which occasion Mallet for some reason—"whether mistrust, whether indifference"—failed to show up.[123] Whatever was the reason, and whatever Vernes thought about it, clearly it made no difference in his friendship with Mallet Du Pan, who for years was wont to turn to Vernes, although they were of different political persuasions, whenever he felt the need of saying exactly what he thought on controversial subjects. The episode stuck in Brissot's memory, however, as a slight to himself.

The *Philadelphien* was written to preach a revolutionary ideology, to advertise the cause of the banished Représentant chieftains, and to denigrate a journalistic rival who happened to be also a political opponent. Mallet's reply appeared in his *Mémoires historiques* for July 15, 1783, and was distributed also to booksellers as a separate publication. Osterwald was sent twenty-five copies, along with a copy for Flournoy, one of the Représentants who was still, evidently, at Neuchâtel. "I count on your friendship and your impartiality," Mallet Du Pan wrote the publisher, "to cooperate in distributing this defense (*ce préservatif*): 2500 copies of it are circulating at this moment."[124] Thus began a decade-long literary and political enmity.

In his *Philadelphien* Brissot celebrated resistance to the "aggressiveness" of the executive powers in Geneva by the "other powers," and says of the ensuing "tempest," i.e., the uprising: "M. Mallet thinks it disastrous, but I think it salutary. . . . I shall always prefer this state of agitation to the deadly calm of unlimited monarchies; in these dissensions, great talents arise and are manifested. . . ."[125] Brissot calls Mallet the apologist of despotism.[126] *You* are the true promoter of despotism, Mallet flings back, for despotism is the usual result of civil strife in republican governments. "Revolt is legitimate when the infractions of the laws put in question justice, liberty and property in regard to individuals. . . . Beyond that, an uprising of

123. Brissot, *Mémoires*, I, 280.
124. Mallet Du Pan to Osterwald, September 2, 1783, Bibl. Neuch., MS 1178, fo 22–121.
125. Brissot, *Le Philadelphien à Genève*, p. 123.
126. Ibid., p. 122.

factions, prompted by pride, by party jealousy, by restlessness, even by minor wrongs . . . is a demonstrated madness."[127]

Brissot's version of what had happened in Geneva since 1768 is not pro-Natif; it is simply pro-Représentant. The Natif demands of 1770 had been excessive and the fact that Mallet Du Pan supported them then against the Représentants is a count against him. In 1782, the Représentants joined the Natif uprising solely to hold it in check, and therefore they did not deserve to be banished.[128]

What, asks Brissot, is to be thought of the principles of any one who has changed parties as often as Mallet Du Pan, "who, devoted at first to the Natifs, exhaled in his shocking writings all his spite against the Représentants and the aristocrats; who, reconciled there-after with the partisans of popular liberty, supported their efforts," then however when the party was crushed proceeded to attack it while withholding criticism of the victorious Négatifs![129] Brissot claims that Mallet Du Pan had personal resentments against some of the proscribed Représentants because his comments had not been heeded.[130] He also claims, by innuendo, that Mallet's interest is in writing to please those who triumphed in Geneva. Mallet, he says, pretends to write impartially, but, he queries: "Is it not true in effect that a full and entire security regarding your person and your pecuniary interests would be absolutely indispensable to carry through the project that you advertise [i.e., publication of the *Mémoires historiques*]?"[131] Finally, Brissot chooses to interpret Mallet's analysis of the French view of the intervention as an ex-tended justification.[132] What Mallet had said was simply that the French monarchy had an economic and political interest in the sta-bility of Geneva and a natural antipathy to democratic government. He had also remarked that the law of nations could not be counted on to defend Geneva against a great power.[133]

Mallet Du Pan retorts that, as for the history of his party affilia-tion, the whole city is his witness that he has never belonged to a party. Ask it to name any he was enrolled in, any political formula he

127. *Mémoires historiques*, VI, no. 45 (July 15, 1783), 293–94.
128. *Le Philadelphien à Genève*, pp. 36, 42, 59–62.
129. Ibid., pp. 5, 36, and passim.   131. Ibid., pp. 76–77, 130.
130. Ibid., p. 112.   132. Ibid., pp. 123–24.
133. *Annales*, IV, no. 26 (Sept. 15, 1782), 83–85.

adhered to, committees of which he was a member, deliberations he voted in, "the Circle, in a word, that received my signature." Never having belonged to any party, how could he have gone from one to another? To his dying day he would honor himself for independence of party; let a man who could not think for himself go join a club! His principles, moreover, have been constant.[134]

It is of course true that Mallet Du Pan's theoretical position was always an individual, even a maverick, one, and it is true that there was a basic consistency about his theoretical viewpoint over the years. But the answer does not dispose of the fact that his sympathies and antipathies in politics did change from time to time. As to why they did, why in particular he ceased to support the Représentants in the recent crisis, he says that it was because it was important to avoid an abrupt political transition in Geneva during the struggle between aristocracy and democracy (a view wherein he differed of course from the Représentants), and that the interest of the Représentant party was not the interest of the Republic.[135] He denies any personal resentments and calls on Brissot to name any of the proscribed persons with whom he has ceased to practice "the social consideration (*les egards de société*) owing even to those from whom one differs in opinion."[136] Actually, Mallet Du Pan was to have continuing friendly contacts with various Représentants, including exiles, as subsequent correspondence makes clear. As for his alleged justification of the intervention, Mallet with reason denied the charge: the most he had said was that the law of nations is inadequate to defend the independence of small states.[137]

Brissot was an unscrupulous and vindictive fighter, he took Mallet Du Pan's phrases out of context and combined them to produce a distorted impression of Mallet's outlook. Yet it must be conceded that Mallet's involutions, his ambiguities, his taste for paradox, laid him open to such treatment. Brissot was right, moreover, not to take at face value Mallet's assertion of independence and impartiality. It seems quite true that Mallet Du Pan was persuaded that he had no axe to grind, since he reserved to himself the liberty of antagonizing even those whose favor he desired, and he certainly wore no party's

134. *Mémoires historiques*, VI, no. 45 (July 15, 1783), 264–69.
135. Ibid., p. 267.
136. Ibid., p. 274.   137. Ibid., p. 286.

livery. It is not easy to assess his motivation in the Genevan crisis, but certain matters are fairly clear. On the one hand, he never had accepted the Représentant political philosophy, hence the authoritarian viewpoint in his account of the Genevan revolution of 1782 is consistent with his earlier ideas. But still this does not explain things entirely. Just as one sees in the period of tactical rapprochement with the Représentants certain personal factors—the reaction against the patriciate, the influence perhaps of a view of society associated with Rousseau rather than Voltaire, which is to say, with the majority of the bourgeoisie rather than the patriciate—so one may also look for personal factors in the rejection of the Représentants.

The central fact of this period of Mallet's career is that he achieved an ambition, cherished for some years, to publish a journal of his own. On Linguet's journal he had been an associate publisher and a reportorial assistant. Now he was both author and publisher. In this situation his professional interest required that he dissociate himself from any Représentant connection. To his way of thinking, it was possible, nay even professionally necessary, to do this without going over to the Négatifs. But the regime in Geneva was Négatif and the press was under surveillance; and moreover if Mallet were to keep Linguet's subscription list in France, as he hoped to do, he must obtain at least a tacit toleration from the French foreign minister to distribute his journal in that country. In his agonizing efforts to secure this, he would point out to the minister that the political message of his journal was all against the democratic dogma and in favor of established authority.[138] This is a subject that will be dealt with in the following chapter.

Here it may be pointed out, however, that although Mallet Du Pan was criticized in the course of his career by Genevans of every stripe, they cast no slurs on his patriotism or his integrity. Only Brissot did this, and Brissot was French, not Genevan. Mallet Du Pan may be regarded as behaving as a Genevan entrepreneur ordinarily would in dealing on his own account with Vergennes, even under the conditions of a French intervention, and even though that inter-

138. Mallet Du Pan to Vergennes, Geneva, November 4, 1782, AAE, Correspondance politique de Genève, XCIII, fol. 467; Mallet Du Pan to Vergennes, Geneva, February 25, 1783, ibid., XCIV, fol. 66.

vention was an event he deplored. The economy of Geneva was dependent on foreign trade, whether in watches, for example, or in books, and it was a matter of course that a Genevan in his business should seek to make arrangements with a foreign government. Mallet was moreover not promising to write only what the foreign minister would want to read, and he made no effort to soften his already published criticisms of Vergennes' policy with regard to the American Revolution.

It may incidentally be observed that, as for French interference in the political affairs of Geneva, it was not only the Négatifs who sought it. The Représentants were to welcome it in their turn, when the circumstances should seem to favor their party. Mallet Du Pan, who wanted always to keep the French out and who always contended that the best way to do this was for the Genevans to settle their differences among themselves, was as much a Genevan patriot as any.

Four

THE GENEVAN JOURNALIST

When Linguet came to the vicinity of Geneva in the late summer or early fall of 1776, he was probably attracted mainly by the general reputation of the area as a center of the book trade, a region where there was a certain specialty in the printing and distribution of controversial literature. Looking toward the resumption of a journalistic career, he perhaps thought of Osterwald at Neuchâtel, as he was to do two years later. No doubt the author of the *Doutes sur l'éloquence* had come to mind, too, and, although Mallet Du Pan could hardly have seemed to Linguet at the time a prospect of the first importance, the two soon met—at Ferney as we have seen.[1] It appears that Mallet for his part was still eager to become Linguet's associate; but he understood also that he was now in a position to negotiate, and he was obviously unwilling to commit himself very far in an enterprise not yet established. Linguet was slow in making up his mind where to settle, in hopes possibly of being able to return to Paris. First he was rumored to be in Brussels, then at Maastricht.[2] Then early in 1777 he set up in London, where the first number of the famed *Annales politiques, civiles et littéraires* appeared, dated March 30, 1777. It was scheduled to come out on the 15th and 30th of each month.

Mallet Du Pan's close association with this journalist who was also a kind of public personality lasted nearly four years. It was his principal schooling in the conditions of a demanding and often risky profession. Here he learned, beside the craft of journalism, what the odds in the profession were—what the profits might be, where the

1. See above, chapter 2, p. 46.
2. Bachaumont, IX, 236 (Oct. 13, 1776); Voltaire to Marin, January 24, [1777], *Correspondence*, XCVI, 42.

pitfalls lay, what one might expect of censorship. He learned both by watching and by doing, for from the start he had considerable responsibility. The association was also, to change the metaphor, a springboard from which Mallet Du Pan vaulted to an independent success in a way that Linguet bitterly resented, charging Mallet with appropriating what was not his to take. Mallet, persuaded of his own right in the matter, protested the accusation, or innuendo. What actually happened, or at least what the evidence permits us to think was the case, will be related in due course.

The partnership began briskly. Mallet declared that he and Linguet discussed the plan of the *Annales* before Linguet went to London.[3] It seems to have been then agreed that he would gather and forward news for Linguet to work up. As early as November, 1776, while living at Aubonne, he was soliciting a regular correspondence on Genevan affairs from a friend who lived in the city, to be exchanged, he said, with "a friend I left in Germany."[4] Very likely the substance of such news letters (and Mallet began a regular practice of cultivating numerous *correspondances*) was intended to find its way to Linguet's *Annales*.

Mallet's job was also to gather subscriptions. In May, 1777, Osterwald's *Journal helvétique* carried an advertisement for the *Annales de Linguet* that was doubtless written by Mallet Du Pan.

These *Annales* [it said], which are composed and printed at London, will present in succession the picture of the times, in the three divisions that the title comprises [*Annales politiques, civiles et littéraires*]. The example of a journal that is truly free, solely devoted to the defense of peoples and the truth, will at last be realized here. Examining the present and the future situation in affairs of state, in legislation, military affairs, finance, commerce, religion, letters, and social behavior (*moeurs*), it will, the author is pleased to think, dispel some erroneous ideas and win some victories for virtue and for liberty. This enterprise, the only useful one of its kind to have been projected, could only

3. Mallet Du Pan to Des Franches, January 18, 1781, AAE, Correspondance politique de Genève, LXXXVII, fol. 80–81.
4. Mallet Du Pan to Beauchâteau, Aubonne, November 14, 1776, Bibl. Genève, MS Supp. 363, Collection Coindet, Autographes Genevois, fol. 69.

be conceived and carried out by a writer who combines with reason and talent the courage that so rarely accompanies them.[5]

This was to promise a good deal, more indeed than Mallet Du Pan was later to think Linguet had delivered. But at this time he was all enthusiasm. Prospective subscribers in Switzerland and Italy were apprised that they might address the booksellers of Geneva or Lausanne, or "Mr. Mallet, former professor (*professeur honoraire*) of the Academy of Cassel [that unfortunate affair was at least good for a title!]," who could be reached at Geneva or Aubonne and would also be glad to take subscriptions for an edition of Linguet's collected works.[6] (Linguet was always promoting the continuing sale of his previously published works, counting on the curiosity his journal sustained to create a demand.)

There was no question at this point of an edition of the *Annales* printed, or reprinted, in Switzerland. All subscribers with whom Mallet Du Pan dealt would receive the original edition published by Linguet at London, and Linguet was pressing Mallet to join him there.[7] In June of 1777 Mallet expected to go in August or September. He had just negotiated a contract with his associate by which Linguet and his London booksellers would pay him, Mallet Du Pan, an annual salary for eight years, guaranteed, even if they were to dismiss him after a year. Mallet was certainly extremely pleased with this arrangement, though when he wrote to Osterwald about it he did not specify the amount of the salary. Perhaps it would be adjusted to profits, which he expected to soar.

> To give you a slight idea of the profits of these gentlemen [he wrote], you should know that they they are realizing at this day [after less than three months of operations, that is] more than 4000 livres on the undertaking. It will be much more when the journal is better known, communications better established, the ministerial inquisition less rigorous.

5. *Journal helvétique*, 1777, II, 71.
6. Ibid., pp. 71, 74.
7. Mallet Du Pan to [Des Franches], January 18, 1781, AAE, Correspondance politique de Genève, LXXXVII, fol. 80–81. (Written at a time when Mallet was soliciting the patronage of Des Franches, the Genevan minister at Paris, who turned the letter over to the Department of Foreign Affairs.)

As to the last point, he reported that a friend who had recently brought him letters from Linguet together with some numbers of the *Annales* had had a great deal of trouble at Calais; but even so, there were many subscriptions in France.[8]

Mallet Du Pan did not, however, go to London to join Linguet until some time in January of 1778. In one of his letters there is mention of the serious illness of his mother and the death of his uncle in Paris,[9] but it was not these family events, that would not seem to have antedated the late fall of 1777,[10] that caused the original postponement of his departure. That, it seems, was owing to the decision to put out a *réimpression* of the *Annales* at Lausanne, by contract between Linguet and the Société Typographique of Lausanne as printers and booksellers. Mallet Du Pan was active in setting up the project and looking after Linguet's (and of course at the same time his own) interest.

The reasons for a *réimpression* were to take advantage of a mushrooming market for the journal and to prevent its falling to pirates. For the *Annales de Linguet* were extensively pirated. Less than a year after the inception of the journal Linguet reported that he knew of four illegitimate reprintings, beside the two legitimate ones put out at Lausanne and The Hague respectively,[11] and in January of 1780 he declared that there were in France nineteen pirated editions.[12] What made the game so attractive for pirates was Linguet's price, which was steep: a year's subscription to the *Annales de Linguet* cost 48 livres de France, whereas the *Mercure de France*, for example, cost only 24.

A Swiss pirated edition was being published quite openly at Yverdon a month or so after Linguet had started in London, and it sold for 24 livres. Mallet's correspondence with Osterwald at the time is full of references to his efforts to drive the pirate out of business, chiefly by claiming that the Yverdon edition could not be more than

8. Mallet Du Pan to Osterwald, Aubonne, June 18, 1777, Bibl. Neuch., MS 1178, fo 22–121.
9. Mallet Du Pan to Osterwald, December 11, 1778 [1777], ibid. On the dating of this letter, see chapter 1, p. 6, n. 12.
10. See chapter 1, n. 12.
11. *Annales de Linguet*, II, no. 16 ([Nov.], 1777), 469.
12. Ibid., VII, no. 56 ([Jan.], 1780), 453–56.

a mutilated version of Linguet's journal. For the Canton of Berne, in whose jurisdiction Yverdon lay and which was always deferential to the French Foreign Office, would assume Linguet to be for the most part unacceptable to it.[13] The pirate fought back, printing in one issue a stinging libel against Linguet, together with a sarcastic reference to Mallet Du Pan as "a self-styled professor Mallet, agent plenipotentiary for M. Linguet in the region of Switzerland."[14] However, Mallet and Linguet were able to enlist the authorities of Berne on their side, then instituted proceedings—apparently a lawsuit— that ended with the flight and bankruptcy of the pirate, whose subscribers were coming over to him one by one, Mallet reported, by the time he left for London (which was also when publication started at Lausanne). In the course of this little war Linguet and Mallet were aided also by the French authorities, who undertook to exclude the Yverdon edition as contraband at the French frontier.[15]

At this point it becomes necessary to digress somewhat and consider the curious relationship of Linguet with French authority, especially with "the Minister," i.e., the minister of Foreign Affairs, who was Vergennes. It seems extraordinary that by January of 1778 the *Annales* should enjoy favor to such an extent that a special effort would be made at the frontier to exclude unauthorized versions. This was a far cry from the situation six months earlier, when Mallet had written of the trouble a courier had had in getting through the port of Calais with two issues of the London edition.[16]

Furthermore, at some point between the close of June and the beginning of November, 1777, the *Annales* received, not merely a permission to circulate in France, but the privilege of the post. Linguet went so far as to declare some years later that each number of

13. Mallet Du Pan to Osterwald, Aubonne, June 18, 1777, Bibl. Neuch., MS 1178, fo 22–121; *Annales de Linguet*, II, no. 12 [Sept. 15, 1777], 276; ibid., Yverdon pirated edition, II, no. 13 [Sept. 30, 1777], 342–43; *Annales de Linguet*, II, no. 16 [Nov., 1777], 471–72.

14. *Annales de Linguet*, Yverdon edition, II, no. 14 [Oct. 15, 1777], 408–15.

15. *Annales de Linguet*, III, no. 23 [March, 1778], 412; Mallet Du Pan to Osterwald, Aubonne, December 11, 1778 [1777], and January 2, 1778, Bibl. Neuch., MS 1178, fo 22–121; "Prospectus" for Mallet's Lausanne edition, *Journal helvétique*, September 1778, p. 83.

16. See above, p. 109. n. 8.

the *Annales* prior to their suppression in 1780 had been distributed by the post in France by "an express and formal order coming directly from the Minister."[17] That claim is certainly an exaggeration, but there is no doubt that the privilege of the post was received within a few months of the start of publication. This was an inestimable advantage, a basic factor in the success the journal enjoyed in France. Perhaps it was a factor in the decision to authorize a secondary edition at Lausanne,[18] for it was expected that the Lausanne edition would in part be subscribed for in France.

This favorable reversal of fortune took place in spite of what Linguet was doing to antagonize some of the most influential personages. He had for one thing heralded the publication of his *Annales* in London by publishing a *Lettre de M. Linguet à M. le comte de Vergennes*, wherein he claimed that he had left France because he had been denied justice there and because his person was in danger. He would, he added, know how to take vengeance![19] Then there was the resounding affair of the duc d'Aiguillon, who had formerly been a legal client of Linguet and who persisted in refusing to pay the fees his counsel had demanded. In April of 1777 D'Aiguillon received from London a copy of a hostile brochure, the *Aiguilloniana*, that was obviously from Linguet's pen. Copies went also to the ministers, including D'Aiguillon's uncle, the comte de Maurepas, and Linguet threatened to broadcast it over France. It was proposed to get Linguet back to Paris somehow to imprison him in the Bastille. However, his friend and Paris agent, a silk merchant named Lequesne, who had got wind of the plan and who seems to have had special access to Vergennes, interceded. The incipient scandal was quashed by Lequesne going to London, getting hold of all the copies of the *Aiguilloniana*, and having Linguet sign in the presence of the French ambassador a promise never to repeat what he had done.[20] But Maurepas himself was not immune from Linguet's pleasantries, and quite

17. From a separately paged "Avis aux souscripteurs," dated January 1, 1783, p. 16, in *Annales de Linguet*, X.

18. Mallet Du Pan to Osterwald, [Aubonne], January 2, 1778, Bibl. Neuch., MS 1178, fo 22–121.

19. Henri Martin, "Etude sur Linguet," *Travaux de l'Académie Impériale de Reims*, XXXI (1860), 87.

20. Ibid., p. 91; Cruppi, *Linguet*, pp. 204–5.

a little stir was created in Paris in the summer of 1777 by the appearance of a "méchant" *Lettre de Me. Linguet au comte de Maurepas.*[21]
All this while the *Annales* were yet new and still so to speak on
probation!

At the same time, Linguet also had powerful influences working
for him. First, there were the royal family. The old king, Louis XV,
had received Linguet at court at the time of one of his most striking
legal successes, the defense of the comte de Morangiès.[22] The present
king, Louis XVI, was well disposed. "This writer," he is reputed to
have said, "teaches me my catechism, and I did not yet know it; I
have never read with as much interest as when I read Linguet."[23] The
queen, too, was a partisan, the reason at this time being, it appears,
her hostility to D'Aiguillon.[24] Later she could observe that Linguet
was a friend to the Austrian alliance and the emperor, whose client
he ultimately became. In the successive crises of his career Paris certainly believed that Linguet had the king and queen for him, not to
mention Monsieur (the comte de Provence), and that they remained
well-disposed even when obliged to deprecate his conduct.[25] For his
part, Linguet consistently took a tone of adulation toward the king
and queen.[26] Beside royalty, Linguet's partisans included many of
the clergy and the "devout" party. For, while his political and social
theory had no basically Christian sanctions, it was anti-philosophe.
While he advocated civil marriage for Protestants and the improvement of their status in regard to property, still he said it was right for
King Louis XIV to have revoked the Edict of Nantes.[27] The Jesuit
Order had properly been suppressed (the pope, of course, had done
this in the end), and yet they had been, in France, more sinned

21. Bachaumont, X, 261 (Oct. 24, 1777).
22. Cruppi, *Linguet*, pp. 334–35.
23. Quoted, ibid., p. 353. My translation.
24. Ibid.
25. Bachaumont, IX, 193–94 (Aug. 19, 1776); XIII, 300 (March 6, 1779),
and 328 (March 29, 1779); XV, 230 (July 21, 1780). See also M. de Lescure,
ed., *Correspondance secrète, inédite, sur Louis XVI, Marie Antoinette, la cour
et la ville de 1777 à 1792*, 2 vols. (Paris, 1866), I, 44 (April 10, 1777) and
320 (Oct. 14, 1780).
26. *Annales de Linguet*, I, no. 3 [c. April 30, 1777], 108; ibid., IV [no. 25,
c. Aug. 15, 1778], 10–11.
27. Ibid., II, no. 10 ([Aug.], 1777), 122–23, and no. 16 ([Nov.], 1777),
494.

against than sinning,[28] the chief sinners being, of course, the philosophes and the Robe. Linguet was against religious intolerance and fanaticism, but where, he asked, did you find them nowadays? Not in the Church, but in the Robe. It was rumored that the archbishop of Paris kept a copy of the *Annales* on the mantelpiece beside his breviary.[29]

As for the ministry, Linguet no doubt struck a sympathetic chord even in those he otherwise irritated, because he was on the side of the monarchy against the *corps intermédiaires*. He had of course long since denounced any alliance with the Economists; but their hour of triumph, with Turgot, was past, leaving at the helm only those more conservative defenders of the monarchy to whom he might well make some intellectual appeal. There was for instance Sartine, formerly lieutenant-general of police in Paris, and minister of the navy from 1774 to 1780. Although one of Linguet's biographers says that it was Sartine who, in the affair of the libel *Aiguilloniana*, suggested that the best answer to Linguet would be to put him in the Bastille,[30] there is good evidence for questioning this, or at least for supposing Sartine may have had second thoughts. Mallet Du Pan remarked, on hearing the news of Sartine's fall in 1780, that Linguet "loses a warm friend in M. de Sartine,"[31] and Linguet had himself in 1778 referred publicly to Sartine in highly complimentary terms.[32]

Even Vergennes, "the Minister" to all journalists, must be accounted, up to a point, one of Linguet's well-wishers. To a professional diplomatist like Vergennes, experienced, absorbed in his *métier*, the railing of an eccentric publicist against himself personally might well have seemed a matter of indifference, if the man were potentially useful—and Vergennes had a good eye for the political uses of journalism. It is pretty clear that what ultimately turned him against Linguet is that the journalist proved not to be amenable in

28. Ibid., I, no. 3 ([May], 1777), 151–56.
29. Bachaumont, XI, 185–86 (April 8, 1778).
30. Martin, "Etude sur Linguet," *Travaux de l'Académie Impériale de Reims,* XXXI (1860), 91.
31. Mallet Du Pan to Osterwald, November 4, 1780, Bibl. Neuch., MS 1178, fo 22–121.
32. "Un ministre qui, ayant passé sa vie dans des départemens bien étranges à la marine, a sçu cependant tout-à-coup se concilier l'estime, l'amitié, et même la confiance de ce corps ombrageux, autant qu'illustre [i.e., the navy]." *Annales de Linguet,* III, no. 21 (Feb. 15, 1778), 304.

the discussion of *la politique,* where the Foreign Ministry was of course most sensitive. However, this was not immediately apparent. Although he established his journal in England, Linguet made sure that he would not be thought of as a defector. Immediately on arriving in London he made a point of assuring the French ambassador of his unalterable attachment to king and *patrie.*[33] These sentiments he indicated again in dedicating his *Annales* to the king of France, and his articles on England in the journal were certainly not Anglophile.

Mallet Du Pan was not in the least alarmed by any thought of the complications and risks that Linguet's past career and present situation might have foretold. Mallet was shrewd but not overly cautious. He had no capital to lose in the venture unless it were the cost of the trip to London; he stood to earn what was in his view a good deal of money; and he was confident of being able to turn any eventualities to his own advantage. He was still young (he only turned twenty-eight in November of 1777) and the future looked very promising.

The approach of war between France and Britain brought crisis to the affairs of the *Annales.* Linguet declared that he was assured by eminent English authority that he need not think of leaving England, that he would be quite secure personally should he continue publication there despite what he had written. But what interpretation would Frenchmen put upon his staying? No, he would leave. "At the first canon shot, I depart."[34] Shortly after he had said this, the Franco-American treaties of commerce and alliance were signed. The first was public information, the second was inferred. Whatever plans Mallet had concerted with Linguet for a collaboration in London—and it is not entirely clear whether he had intended to establish a domicile in England—these plans were now all shelved. The only question was, where on the Continent should the *Annales* be taken? It was decided to try Geneva, or failing that somehow, some town in Switzerland. Mallet, who had not been in London more than two months, left it about the end of March,[35] while Linguet remained

33. Martin, "Etude sur Linguet," *Travaux de l'Académie Impériale de Reims,* XXXI (1860), 81.

34. Linguet to Lequesne, February 10, 1778, quoted and paraphrased ibid., p. 93.

35. A letter of Mallet Du Pan to Osterwald, dated January 2, 1778, refers

behind to wind up his affairs and to publish the last number of the current year, which by good fortune was just expiring.

Although he subsequently told his readers he had supposed the presses printed as freely in Switzerland (which in his mind included Geneva) as in England,[36] this was not quite the truth, for he was actually quite nervous about the deference of Geneva and the Swiss cantons to Versailles. Hence he made sure of Versailles first, with the mediation of the invaluable Lequesne,[37] receiving from Vergennes the following statement, dated April 23, 1778: "I promise you as much on the word of M. le comte de Maurepas as on my own, a complete security for your person in the new domicile that you are proposing to take. I very willingly give you the assurance of this and that of leaving you master of your own actions, persuaded that neither religion, the King nor the State will be attacked in your writings."[38]

Linguet left London probably late in April and crossed France to Geneva, where, to Mallet's chagrin, the *Annales* were *not* welcome. Linguet tried Berne and Soleure, he negotiated with Osterwald at Neuchâtel, but without success.[39] Conditions unacceptable to him were stipulated. He then tried Brussels, counting on the good will of the emperor, who did not disappoint him. He was obliged, however, or felt obliged, to have the journal printed not in Brussels itself but in a small village near Ostend.[40] From Brussels he announced to the literary and political worlds of Paris, which continued to follow his movements with the most intense curiosity, that publication

---

to his imminent journey to London, which he calls "la Babylone enfumée qui m'ouvre *ses bras d'argent*." Bibl. Neuch., MS 1178, fo 22–121. Linguet, writing to Lequesne, April 3, 1778, states: "M. Mallet du Pan part d'ici." Quoted in Martin, "Etude sur Linguet," *Travaux de l'Académie Impériale de Reims*, XXXI (1860), 93.

36. *Annales de Linguet*, III, ([no. 24, c. March 30], 1778), 521–22; ibid., IV, no. 25 ([Aug.], 1778), 13.

37. Martin, "Etude sur Linguet," *Travaux de l'Académie Impériale de Reims*, XXXI (1860), 94.

38. Vergennes to Linguet, April 23, 1778, ibid. My translation.

39. Ibid., p. 95; Mallet Du Pan to Osterwald, Geneva, June 6, 1778, Bibl. Neuch., MS 1178, fo 22–121; Bachaumont, XII, 11–12 (June 12, 1778), and 96 (Aug. 29, 1778); *Annales de Linguet*, IV, no. 25 ([Aug.], 1778), 13–16.

40. *Annales de Linguet*, IV, no. 25 ([Aug.], 1778), 28; Bachaumont, XII, 96 (Aug. 29, 1778).

would be resumed on August 15.[41] Meanwhile, some time before he actually settled in Belgium, and perhaps more than once, Linguet had a personal interview with Vergennes which was more than satisfactory to him,[42] so that he boasted of "the most generous loyalty" shown him by the ministry. This was, characteristically, by way of fulminating against the governments of Geneva and Switzerland which had rejected his *Annales* lest they contain something to displease the government of France. Of course, his old enemies the *compagnies* (the bench, the bar, the Académie, the philosophes), who, as he thought, had successfully prevented his reestablishment in France, his ultimate desire, were also back of the fright that his presence seemed to inspire abroad.[43]

Mallet Du Pan and Linguet now had a new agreement superseding the contract of the preceding year by which Mallet was to have been paid a salary for eight years as collaborator. It was stipulated that if Linguet did not settle in Switzerland, he would leave Mallet there to be a collaborator "à discrétion," and Linguet's agent (*correspondant*) "for all our provinces," but receiving, instead of salary as before, all Linguet's rights in the Lausanne edition. A partition of the territory of the *Annales* was made, giving Mallet's edition exclusive rights in Switzerland, Italy, Germany, and the entire Midi, together with "our frontier areas"[44] (presumably the eastern provinces of France, for Mallet had, for example, a large order from Besançon).[45]

Mallet briefly had hopes of settling himself and his edition in Geneva, but they were dashed as we have seen by "the imbecile cowardliness of the government of Geneva, which threatened to declare war on my edition."[46] Besides, the Société Typographique of Lausanne considered that they still had rights in it. Though eminently dissatisfied with their work,[47] Mallet agreed to continue to employ them, but only as his printers, not his booksellers. He himself

41. Bachaumont, XII, 64 (Aug. 7, 1778).

42. Martin, "Etude sur Linguet," *Travaux de l'Académie Impériale de Reims*, XXXI (1860), 94–96; letter of Linguet to Lequesne, Brussels, July 22, 1778, ibid., p. 95; Bachaumont, XII, 49 (July 24, 1778).

43. *Annales de Linguet*, IV, no. 25 ([Aug.], 1778), 15–16.

44. Mallet Du Pan to Osterwald, Geneva, June 6, 1778, Bibl. Neuch., MS 1178, fo 22–121.

45. Mallet Du Pan to Osterwald, Lausanne, September 15, 1778, ibid.

46. Mallet Du Pan to Osterwald, Aubonne, July 21, 1778, ibid.

47. Mallet Du Pan to Osterwald, Geneva, June 6, 1778, ibid.

would handle that function beside overseeing the printing, and to do these things more efficiently he moved, in July, 1778, from Aubonne to Lausanne.[48]

The *Annales* were still plagued by pirates. One could try to under-cut them by reducing one's price, and Linguet permitted this to Gosse, bookseller at The Hague, who was putting out the other authorized reprinting, but he stoutly refused to come down for his own edition (except to subscribers in Brussels) or for the Lausanne edition before Mallet took it over. He asserted in 1780 that each subscription of 48 livres cost him 12, including paper, printing, post-age, and the booksellers' rate of 6 livres for any subscriptions taken through them.[49] (No collaborator's salary was included in this esti-mate, for Mallet Du Pan was no longer in Linguet's employ.) Still, Linguet's costs left him 36 livres clear, and great was the buzzing in the literary world concerning his profits. Gossip put them for the first year (when indeed he still had a salaried collaborator) at 50,000 livres.[50] Brissot recorded a few years later that Linguet was reputed to have made 100,000 livres from his *Annales*—surely, he added, an exaggeration, but just as surely each single number must have brought him more than J.-J. Rousseau made all told from the *Emile!*[51] Certainly Linguet was living in a rather ample fashion dur-ing the second year of the *Annales*, occupying a château near Brus-sels.[52] He resented the imputation of cupidity, denied that he was very rich, and as usual took the opportunity to refer to his grievances: he sought from the *Annales*, he said, simply a "suitable affluence (*aisance honnête*)," in order to keep in society the "honorable stand-ing (*rang honnête*)" he had won as a lawyer before his disbarment.[53] Linguet preferred other means of fighting competition to that of reducing his price. One expedient was the book dividend, consisting, of course, of some title taken from among his other works, or of previous years of the *Annales* offered at a reduced price.[54]

48. Mallet Du Pan to Osterwald, Aubonne, July 21, 1778, ibid.
49. *Annales de Linguet*, VII, no. 56 [Jan., 1780], 457–70.
50. Bachaumont, XII, 99 (Aug. 31, 1778).
51. Brissot, *Mémoires*, I, 99–100.
52. Ibid.; Brissot, *Correspondance et papiers*, p. 5n.
53. *Annales de Linguet*, VII, no. 56 [Nov., 1779], 459–65.
54. Ibid., II, no. 12 ([Sept.], 1777), 276; ibid., VI, no. 47 ([Sept.], 1779), 456–57; ibid., VII, no. 52 ([Nov.], 1779), 196; ibid., IX, no. 65 ([June,

As soon as Mallet Du Pan took over Linguet's rights in the Lausanne edition, he reduced the price to 30 livres, postpaid, everywhere except Switzerland, and there he put it down to 27 livres.[55] At this price he was confident he could beat the pirates. His edition, of course, continued to have the official franchise Linguet had obtained in France, including the privilege of the post, and there was "the most powerful protection of the Government" at the frontier, so that pirated editions could enter the kingdom "only by the cleverest contraband commerce." In Switzerland likewise he had the privilege exclusively, and in the Italian states of Sardinia, Milan, Venice, Tuscany, and the States of the Church. Only "lower Germany," said Mallet, would be abandoned to pirates;[56] but he reported about the same time a big order (*une forte affaire*) from the bookseller Virchaud of Hamburg.[57]

To Mallet's delight, his edition brought him suddenly a prosperity to which he was entirely unaccustomed. Subscriptions came in volume at the beginning of the second year of the Lausanne edition, Italy and the Midi being the great outlets—"It is only Switzerland that lags."[58] He exulted to Osterwald: "The *Annales* continue to multiply advantageously: I am not recovered from the surprise into which this success has thrown me."[59] Concerning the subscription year 1778–1779 he wrote: "Thank God, my edition . . . is indeed prospering, I have about eight hundred subscribers, and a profit of 7 to 8000 livres clear this year."[60]

1780]), 57–61; Mallet Du Pan to the Société Typographique de Neuchâtel, Geneva, May 17, 1780, Bibl. Neuch., MS 1178, fo 22–121.

55. Mallet Du Pan to Osterwald, Aubonne, July 21, 1778, Bibl. Neuch., MS 1178, fo 22–121.

56. Mallet Du Pan to Osterwald, Lausanne, September 5 and October 3, 1778, ibid.

57. Mallet Du Pan to Osterwald, Lausanne, September 15, 1778, ibid.

58. Mallet Du Pan to Osterwald, Lausanne, October 3, 1778, ibid.

59. Mallet Du Pan to Osterwald, Lausanne, October 23, 1778, ibid.

60. Mallet Du Pan to Osterwald, March 3, 1779, ibid. It seems certain that livres de France are meant, not livres de Genève. Not only were subscriptions always quoted in livres de France (as was the case with Mallet's own journal later), but the sum of 8000 Genevan livres would have been much out of line with what we know otherwise of the trend of Mallet's income as journalist, since the metallic equivalent of the Genevan livre was more than half again that of the French. Mallet would hardly have netted the equivalent of over 12,000 livres de France in 1779. For raising the question of which livre was

He was not without business irritations, however, being engaged in continuous skirmishing with his printers, the Société Typographique of Lausanne, whom he considered thoroughly dishonest. In the late spring of 1779 he was able to get rid of that connection[61] and shortly afterward to leave Lausanne, where he had also felt professionally disadvantaged.[62] It was then that he returned to Geneva, which was intellectually far more stimulating and incidentally offered more satisfactory business arrangements. Besides, he wanted also to return to Geneva, as we have already seen, to participate again in its civic affairs.[63] If he negotiated any agreement with the government of Geneva about the toleration of his edition, which a year earlier the government had threatened, no record of this is known. Very likely he was simply taking his chances on the ground that no vigorous objection was forthcoming.

Not long after returning to Geneva, Mallet was able to change significantly his arrangements with Linguet. There would now be no more reprinting, and therefore no more business or editorial supervision of production, no capital tied up in warehoused numbers. Mallet Du Pan would become simply a distributing agent for Linguet's edition, so far as his business function was concerned. He would buy the *Annales* from Linguet at 9 livres per subscription, printed and stitched (*brochés*) and sent postpaid to Lyon. The shipment would go from Brussels to Lyon directly by *diligence*, traversing the distance in ten days. Those copies destined for the Midi would be forwarded from Lyon; the remainder would be sent to Mallet Du Pan in Geneva by courier, which would take one day, and from Geneva they would be sent on to their destinations elsewhere. His own profit would be no less, said Mallet Du Pan.[64] Presumably Linguet thought the scheme worthwhile to him, too, although by the reckoning he published of his costs per subscription they would not be covered by the 9 livres Mallet would pay him. But with a larger

---

involved and furnishing me the exchange figure (168 to 100 as of 1781) I am obliged to Professor George V. Taylor of the University of North Carolina, Chapel Hill.

61. Mallet Du Pan to Osterwald, from Lausanne, March 3, March 8, and June 5, 1779, and from Geneva, September 21, 1779, ibid.

62. Mallet Du Pan to Osterwald, June 5, 1779, ibid.

63. Ibid.

64. Mallet Du Pan to Osterwald, Geneva, September 21, 1779, ibid.

edition costs might be reduced, or so he may have reasoned, or possibly he had padded the figure of his costs. The most obvious flaw in the scheme was the dual price system, for Linguet was still refusing to come down and his direct subscribers in Rouen or Paris might well feel aggrieved if they were to discover that Mallet's subscribers in Toulouse paid 30 livres while for the identical thing they had to pay 48. They were not supposed to know, of course, as Mallet indicated to Osterwald when telling him about the plan ("These details are for you. I reveal them to you incognito"),[65] but how long would it remain a secret? Linguet, whose entire career consisted of expedients, never calculated for the long run. Faced now with fifteen to twenty pirates eating into the profits that might be his, why not take what he could when he could?

Mallet Du Pan was, for his part, thinking that Linguet was likely to be out of business before too long,[66] and this probably explains his reluctance to go on tying up capital in a *réimpression*. As it turned out, Mallet's expectation was fulfilled within a year.

The expectation had been, actually, a hope as well. Mallet had soon come to find the association unbearably trying. The difficulty had nothing to do with money. On this score from the beginning Mallet could not have been happier. The most exasperating thing about Linguet from Mallet's viewpoint as a business manager was that he did not stick to a schedule. His issues frequently were late, sometimes weeks late, and while this bothered Linguet not at all, Mallet complained that it made trouble for *him*. "These intermittences tire me, vex me, cause me involuntarily not to keep my word," he said to Osterwald, "and the Proteus who holds the pen makes sport of complaints [from subscribers], then leaves them to his agents [to deal with]."[67]

But mostly the trouble had to do with the content of the *Annales*. Now the hallmark of Linguet's journalism was its highly personal quality. Linguet's journal, wrote the Bachaumont recorder, was truly his own, "for he speaks in it of hardly anything but himself or of

65. Ibid.
66. Mallet Du Pan to Osterwald, Lausanne, March 8, 1779, ibid.
67. Mallet Du Pan to Osterwald, Lausanne, November 21, 1778, Bibl. Neuch., MS 1178, fo 22–121.

things and people in relation to himself, bringing around to this point matters that would appear at first to have nothing to do with him."[68] As for his collaborator's role, Mallet Du Pan's principal and regular contribution to the *Annales* throughout the association with Linguet was in the form of political and literary information based partly on his immediate experience, as in the case of affairs in Geneva, partly on the network of *correspondances* he was establishing, and partly on the reading of a good many gazettes, not to mention, of course, books. This his letters of the period abundantly substantiate, both inferentially and explicitly. But the finished product in the *Annales* was, on the whole, Linguet's. There are indeed some entire articles that seem to have been written by Mallet Du Pan, resembling the writing later in his own journal, the *Annales . . . pour servir de suite aux Annales de M. Linguet*. Sometimes it seems that Linguet has reworked the style of what is basically Mallet's article. Sayous supposed that all the articles on "political economy," usually involving the Economists or Physiocrats, were left to Mallet Du Pan, who he says was more at home in this subject than Linguet.[69] On the contrary, the only article in this category that seems to the present writer to be unmistakably Mallet's is one which traces the history of French public finance from the Middle Ages to the ministry of Necker, and that, too, without so much as mentioning Turgot.[70] In point of fact, the Economists were a specialty of Linguet's; he had written philippics against them for years before he began publishing the *Annales*, and the tenor of the articles in that journal is the same as that of his writings that preceded it. The articles in the *Annales de Linguet* that do suggest Mallet Du Pan's authorship are not limited to "political economy," but have a considerable range, both political and literary.

Occasionally, Mallet intervened to modify Linguet's interpretations. One such intervention has already been discussed, namely, the countering of Linguet's expression of hostility to the Genevan Représentants in 1779 by the subsequent publication of an article sympathetic to them.[71] Again, Mallet objected to an article of Linguet's on

68. Bachaumont, X, 261 (Oct. 24, 1777).
69. Sayous, I, 32–33.
70. *Annales de Linguet*, I, no. 7 ([June], 1777), 440–46.
71. See above, p. 89.

the American war in which it is stated that the English are facing disaster,[72] and he wrote to Osterwald: "I am not at all of his way of thinking concerning the American war or that of France, you will see in [No.] XVIII or XIX my reply to this pleading."[73] Linguet began to veer about, and in several succeeding numbers there were references to the advantage held by the English in seaborne commerce.[74] On the question of Rousseau, too, the *Annales de Linguet* shifted ground. Of Linguet's bracketing Voltaire and Rousseau under a double anathema,[75] Mallet complained to Pastor Vernes: "M. Linguet has only read Jean-Jacques in passing, especially the *Emile*, which he regards as a piece of nonsense, as he told me, considering that Education itself is that; he promises to re-read it, but his judgment is made, he will read only what he has decided."[76] Mallet commented that he was not surprised that Linguet should pay no attention to his ideas on the subject, for "it is true that I was not paying court to the Archbishop of Paris."[77] (Linguet, of course, was.) Six months later, however, there appeared in the *Annales* an article which, though written in the style of Linguet, contains a reference to Rousseau in the vein of Mallet Du Pan: D'Alembert is said to have been wrong to attack Rousseau as he did in his *Eloge* of Milord Maréchal. "The candor and eloquence of this Philosophe will, in the centuries to come, earn him pardon for his errors." Rousseau, Linguet says, is in every way superior to the "philosophe flunkeys (*valetaille*)."[78]

The value set by Linguet on Mallet's contribution appears to have risen with the passage of time. He had been dissatisfied at first. After Mallet's departure from England in 1778 Linguet wrote to Lequesne in Paris that Mallet had turned out to be "inferior, lazy (*bas, paresseux*)," that "his work is of no account (*nul*)." Very likely he had complained to Mallet himself, too, for he recorded (and sadly at

72. *Annales de Linguet,* IV, no. 26 ([Sept.], 1778), 99–101.

73. Mallet Du Pan to Osterwald, Lausanne, October 3, 1778, Bibl. Neuch., MS 1178, fo 22–121.

74. *Annales de Linguet,* IV, no. 27 ([Oct.], 1778), 173–74; ibid., no. 29 ([Dec.], 1778), pp. 312–20.

75. Ibid., no. 28 ([Nov.], 1778), pp. 95–96.

76. Mallet Du Pan to Vernes, Lausanne, December 3, 1778, quoted in Dufour-Vernes, *Recherches,* pp. 41–42. My translation.

77. Ibid.

78. *Annales de Linguet,* VI, no. 41 ([July], 1779), 46–47.

that), that the cordiality between them had disappeared. All in all, he viewed with misgiving, he told Lequesne, the plan of joining Mallet Du Pan "in his country."[79] Now certainly laziness was not one of Mallet's shortcomings; he was on the contrary a hard worker. Very likely he did not produce much during the few short weeks he was in London, but hardly from laziness. It is more likely that the trouble arose from disputes over the use of Mallet's material. That Linguet came to depend on Mallet's contribution is evident from his effort to secure Mallet's collaboration again when he resumed publication after his release from the Bastille. However, he never published a word to admit that Mallet Du Pan was more than an agent concerned with circulation. It seems that Mallet was content to let it be so, lest he be identified too closely with the controversial Linguet. It was important to preserve his own identity. His disclaimer of any share in the composition of Linguet's contemptuous article on Geneva in October of 1779 will be recalled.[80]

Mallet's exasperation with the tenor of the *Annales* was kindled by the very first issue of the Brussels edition, No. 25, containing a *Lettre au roi* which, he said, "has singularly displeased me."[81] No. 26 was "more piquant" than No. 25, but Mallet disagreed with the view of the war therein expressed and disliked Linguet's apology for France. "I see there only a dishonest sophist," he told Osterwald, "who is pardoned for this abuse of talent by reason of his inventiveness of expression. He does not believe a word of his apology for France."[82] No. 27 was "mediocre, but no more [railing against the] philosophes. The King of Prussia is jeered at."[83] This last was a reference to an article on the War of the Bavarian Succession and the Frederician army.[84] No. 27 had been three weeks late, moreover, for no good reason. But exasperation was offset by the lure of profits, and not only that but, even more important, by the idea of obtaining some day the succession to the *Annales*, in the expectation that

79. Linguet to Lequesne, April 3, 1778, quoted in Martin, "Etude sur Linguet," *Travaux de l'Académie Impériale de Reims*, XXXI (1860), 93–94.
80. See above, p. 89.
81. Mallet Du Pan to Osterwald, Lausanne, September 5, 1778, Bibl. Neuch., MS 1178, fo 22–121.
82. Mallet Du Pan to Osterwald, Lausanne, October 23, 1778, ibid.
83. Mallet Du Pan to Osterwald, Lausanne, November 21, 1778, ibid.
84. *Annales de Linguet*, IV, no. 27 ([Oct.] 1778), pp. 148–56.

sooner or later Linguet would abandon the journal[85] by choice or by compulsion. To become a journalist himself, and not to remain merely a business manager and reportorial assistant, this was then Mallet's great ambition, and what could be a more propitious entry upon such a career than to succeed to Linguet's title and to fall heir to the subscriptions he had had as a distributor of the *Annales de Linguet!* "If I were not assured," he wrote to Osterwald in November of 1778, "that after the year is completed, he will abandon this labor, which will fall into hands less eloquent but more judicious, if I were not persuaded that one can do much better than he [though] without doing it as agreeably, that is to say, that one can gain in variety, promptitude, interesting news (*nouvelles de curiosité*), impartiality, what one would lose in style, that consequently your servant, moving to a suitable location with a good co-partner, and even losing half of the present subscribers, would make a very advantageous speculation, I would abandon, I would already have abandoned this one."[86] This dream was founded on an understanding with Linguet that Mallet asserted had been part of their agreement when they separated in 1778, Linguet to set up the Brussels edition, Mallet to take over the Lausanne *réimpression*. Whether it was written or oral he did not say,[87] and since no document containing it is known and since Linguet subsequently did not act as though one existed, it must be assumed to have been oral only. None the less, Mallet used it as a talking point with others and to convince himself. As for the question whether even an oral agreement existed, it may be confidently said that, insofar as we know anything about Mallet's character, we can believe he would not have invented it, though he doubtless took it more seriously than Linguet.

So Mallet Du Pan bided his time, and while he was waiting an unforeseen and quite different opening developed. Jean-Elie Bertrand, Osterwald's son-in-law and editor of Osterwald's *Journal helvétique*, died. In an affectionate letter of condolence which was also a business proposition, Mallet Du Pan said he thought it possible to

85. Mallet Du Pan to Osterwald, Lausanne, November 21, 1778, Bibl. Neuch., MS 1178, fo 22–121.
86. Ibid.
87. Mallet Du Pan to [Hennin], Geneva, February 8, 1781, Bibl. Reims, MS 1916, Lettre No. 183.

continue publication of the *Journal helvétique* in such a way that Bertrand's family might continue to receive some income from it. He knew of a good editor for the literary part, one Du Rey [Du Rey de Morsan], who merely wished to supplement an independent income, while he himself, Mallet Du Pan, could handle the political section in addition to his work with the *Annales de Linguet*. "I believe it would be easy to extend the success of this journal," he said confidently, "especially by strengthening the political part. I am myself very much in a position to contribute here, having acquired many useful *correspondances* as well as periodicals."[88] Osterwald accepted Mallet's proposal directly, somewhat to the latter's embarrassment; for no sooner had he offered his services than he learned of developments in Paris that opened up the prospect of his succession to Linguet's *Annales*.

Mallet's information was that Linguet would be permitted to finish out the current year of the journal, but not to begin another. He wrote eagerly of what he would do with the chance that seemed to be before him, assessing his qualifications. Although he could not hope to equal Linguet's style, which he thought accounted for half of Linguet's success, he would compensate for this inferiority by the substance of his work, which would be "an instructive and thoughtful history of the time substituted for mad diatribes against England and the parlements. I have basic knowledge of the resources of the enterprise," he added; "if it is left to me, I replant it at London [a citizen of Geneva, unlike a French subject, would find no problem in this choice of location]."[89] Thus he explained to Osterwald why he could not after all take over the post on the *Journal helvétique*, at least at present. That was in March, 1779.

Continually, during 1779 and 1780, Linguet ran into trouble with the authorities in France, and distribution was repeatedly suspended. Rumors circulated of his giving up the *Annales*, but Linguet persistently denied them,[90] while Mallet Du Pan cooled his heels in Ge-

88. Mallet Du Pan to Osterwald, Lausanne, March 3, 1779, Bibl. Neuch., MS 1178 fo 22–121.

89. Mallet Du Pan to Osterwald, Lausanne, March 8, 1779, ibid.

90. Bachaumont, XIII, 254–55 (Jan. 15, 1779), 300 (March 6, 1779), 327–28 (March 29, 1779); ibid., XIV, 148–49 (May 11, 1779), 161 (Aug. 24, 1779); ibid., XV, 292 (Sept. 14, 1780); *Annales de Linguet*, VI, no. 46 ([Aug.], 1779), 392; ibid., IX, no. 67 ([July or Aug.], 1780), 130.

neva. Finally, on September 27, 1780, Linguet was arrested in Paris and confined in the Bastille, whence he did not emerge until May 18, 1782.

Since the government did not announce its reasons, they were then and have been since much debated, but certain facts seem clear enough. In March, 1780, the government in France forbade the distribution of two numbers because, it seems, of a sustained drubbing in them of the Parlement of Paris and a malicious if not entirely unfounded thrust at the public integrity of the maréchal duc de Duras, a peer of France who happened to be one of the Academicians responsible for Linguet's dismissal from the *Journal de politique et de littérature* back in 1776.[91] From Brussels, Linguet wrote a letter to Le Noir, *lieutenant de police*, demanding the resumption of distribution. He also proceeded, according to his own statement later, to assert defiantly that he did not consider himself subject to the censorship!

> I never intended to subject myself to any sort of censorship [he said in this letter]: on the contrary, I have protested openly, I have several times put into print, that I would have no other censor than my own sense of propriety (*mon propre délicatesse*). I have not uttered a word it could disavow. . . . I can be punished for my love for France, for my devotion in every sense to my country; I can be forced to decide, out of disgust, to stop writing, [but] I will never be reduced to writing as a slave. Of all the indemnities that the Government of France owes me, the freedom of my pen is, it seems to me, the least expensive, and, I dare to say it, the most useful for itself.[92]

Here, Linguet believed, and not any personal attacks in the offending issues of his journal, was the cause of his arrest, for the *lettre de cachet* which authorized it had been issued shortly after the sending of the letter to Le Noir, while the duc de Duras was not that impor-

---

91. Martin, "Etude sur Linguet," *Travaux de l'Académie Impériale de Reims*, XXXI (1860), 97–98, 97n; Bachaumont, XV, 127 (April 21, 1780), 128–29 (April 23, 1780); *Annales de Linguet*, X (1783), 30–34; Mallet Du Pan to Osterwald, Geneva, October 13, 1780, Bibl. Genève, MS D.O.
92. *Annales de Linguet*, X (1783), 30–34.

tant![93] One cannot but think Linguet was probably right, provided one combines with the offending letter certain substantive grievances on the part of the ministry which were cumulative. Mallet Du Pan believed that Linguet had for one thing run afoul of a feud between Necker and Sartine that was to end, in October, 1780, with Sartine's dismissal, though he did not believe Linguet, who was of the Sartine faction, was the author of an anti-Necker pamphlet attributed to him. Mallet also thought a certain article in No. 71 of the *Annales* had probably antagonized the ministry.[94] This was an imaginary speech of the king of England to the American colonials in rebellion, written by an imaginary Swiss—a republican, forsooth, denouncing the cause of republicans. The Franco-American alliance is implicitly criticized. In all Europe only France had thought such an alliance a good course, adopting it basically out of jealousy of English trade.[95] Thus Linguet, who had previously upheld the American policy of Vergennes, now by implication at least reversed himself and moreover in effect cast doubt on the propaganda of a just war, a war against the oppression of peoples by the British, to which the ministry had lent itself.[96]

But this was only one item. It was rumored that Vergennes had offered Linguet 2000 écus of pension if he would refrain from writing of war or *la politique*, and that he had refused.[97] If this story was not fact, the point of it lay sufficiently close to the mark. From the foreign minister's point of view, this article on the American war must have been only the culmination of irritations. The reticences of Vergennes in the matter of the Austrian alliance were not supported in the *Annales*, where Linguet was anti-Prussian and pro-Austrian (since his patrons were the queen of France and the emperor). In the case of Geneva, he had, to be sure, supported Vergennes and the

93. Ibid.; Martin, "Etude sur Linguet," *Travaux de l'Académie Impériale de Reims*, XXXI (1860), 98–99.

94. Mallet Du Pan to Osterwald, Geneva, November 4, 1780, Bibl. Neuch., MS 1178, fo 22–121.

95. *Annales de Linguet*, IX, no. 71 ([Sept.], 1780), 441–48.

96. Frances Acomb, *Anglophobia in France 1763–1789: An Essay in the History of Constitutionalism and Nationalism* (Durham, N.C., 1950), pp. 83–85.

97. Bachaumont, XVI, 25 (Oct. 15, 1780).

French intervention, but he had done it in such terms as to put Vergennes in the worst possible light with the majority of Genevans.[98] As Hennin, a *premier commis* in the Department of Foreign Affairs, summed up the situation to Mallet Du Pan:

> The temerity not to say the impudence of his writings, at which people began by laughing, ended by arousing indignation. . . . Although M. le comte de Vergennes, who had forgiven him for his eccentricities (*ses écarts*), had no part in his punishment, it is very possible that a vexatious idea of the *Annales de Linguet* remains with him and that he would be happy to see them forgotten.[99]

If Vergennes had no share in Linguet's punishment, he did not lift a finger to prevent it, and Le Noir told Linguet that it was from Vergennes that he had learned of Linguet's visit to Paris,[100] for which the *lettre de cachet* had been held in readiness.

As for Mallet Du Pan's reaction at this juncture, he said that he was sorry for Linguet and that he thought it was a scurvy trick to seize the author while his work was still circulating freely by the post. He was also on the other hand relieved to be free of the association, feeling, as he did, that he had put up with a great deal from Linguet personally, and that Linguet's playing to the galleries and his personal warfare, "his periodic sorties against all the books, all the systems, all the projects, and all the *corps*,"[101] were a spurious sort of journalism.[102] At the same time, he had to think about his own future. The silencing of Linguet had of course dried up the source of Mallet's own income. More than ever now he wanted the succession to the *Annales* in order not to sacrifice the advantage his association with Linguet's journal had brought him.

Mallet went on the assumption that Linguet would regard the

98. See above, pp. 87–89.
99. Hennin to Mallet Du Pan, Versailles, [February] 26, [1781], Paris, Bibliothèque de l'Institut de France, Papiers et correspondance de Hennin, MS 1269, No. 30–31.
100. Martin, "Étude sur Linguet," *Travaux de l'Académie Impériale de Reims*, XXXI (1860), 99.
101. Mallet Du Pan to Osterwald, Geneva, October 13, 1780, Bibl. Genève, MS D.O.
102. Mallet Du Pan to Osterwald, Lausanne, October 23, 1778, Bibl. Neuch., MS 1178, fo 22–121.

agreement of 1778 about the succession as being in effect even though his relinquishment of the journal had not been voluntary. "It remained settled between us," Mallet stated, "that the succession of the work would belong to me, at the moment when its author should lay down the pen," and he asserted that Linguet would have remained faithful to the agreement had he had the time before his incarceration.[103] Mallet deferred taking any action because he at first believed that Linguet's imprisonment would be short. His information at the beginning of November was that the agent in Paris, Lequesne, had begun publicly to receive subscriptions for the next year.[104] (Luckily Linguet, at the time he was arrested, had just finished a subscription year.) By the middle of January, however, Mallet had made his decision to undertake a journal himself as Linguet's successor, in the belief that Linguet's release was after all not imminent, and also "on the strongest presumptions that he will never, or not for a long time, recover the liberty again to take up his work."[105] A letter Mallet received from the Department of Foreign Affairs in February tended to justify his presumptions, for it showed that Vergennes would be hostile to a toleration for Linguet.[106] There was the question whether Linguet might not decide to publish anyway without any sort of permission even if the lack of a legitimate market in France should greatly reduce the profits he was accustomed to look for. Might he not publish out of sheer defiance? This would not be out of character, and he might act thus despite his desire, which was also part of his character, to make a great deal of money out of his writing. In his communications with "the Department" relative to his securing a permission for his own journal, Mallet did not discuss the possibility. He wrote as though he thought Linguet would regard publication without permission to distribute in France as being out of the question.

Although in his own behalf he thus build up a case for Linguet's

103. Mallet Du Pan to [Des Franches], January 18, 1781, AAE, Correspondance politique de Genève, LXXXVII, fol. 80–81.

104. Mallet Du Pan to Osterwald, Geneva, November 4, 1780, Bibl. Neuch., MS 1178, fo 22–121.

105. Mallet Du Pan to [Des Franches], January 18, 1781, AAE, Correspondance politique de Genève, LXXXVII, fol. 80–81.

106. Hennin to Mallet Du Pan, Versailles, [February] 26, [1781], Bibl. de l'Institut, Papiers et correspondance de Hennin, MS 1269, No. 30–31.

withdrawal from journalism being considered permanent, he was careful to advertise that he was using Linguet's title only until the time, if ever, when Linguet should want to resume it.[107] In the last analysis, Mallet based his right to advertise his own journal as the successor to the *Annales de Linguet*, using Linguet's title, on a combination of considerations: the fact that Linguet's work *was* suspended and presumably for some considerable time if not permanently; the previous understanding that the succession would devolve on him; and the feeling that his own professional and financial interest in the journal and his contribution to it entitled him to exploit the association.

People like Osterwald, Rieu, and Des Franches, the Genevan minister at Paris, who knew the circumstances, evidently regarded Mallet's course as reasonable, since they went along with it. However, Lequesne, Linguet's Paris agent, objected. He was said to have approached the emperor to intercede for Linguet's release.[108] Similarly, Gosse, bookseller at The Hague, who had continued to put out an authorized *réimpression* of the *Annales de Linguet*, was hostile. According to the account given by Mallet Du Pan to Osterwald, Gosse had at first attempted to make a deal with him. His subscribers, learning from the announcement of Mallet Du Pan's *Annales . . . pour servir de suite aux Annales de M. Linguet* that Linguet would not be putting out his fourth year, asked for their money back. Gosse thought perhaps he could salvage some of these subscriptions by becoming Mallet's agent, but asked Mallet for his *Annales* gratis the first year simply for access to Gosse's subscription list, which Mallet might then have for the succeeding year. Mallet refused the proposition as disadvantageous, and he was sure also that Lequesne's opposition was owing to demands for reimbursements—he quoted a figure of three hundred subscribers as having already, by the first of June, withdrawn their 48 livres. This was the source, he was certain, of some current rumors about Linguet's imminent release.[109]

Mallet's assumption of Linguet's title also drew some criticism in the literary world that had been attentive to Linguet's movements.

107. *Annales*, I, no. 2 (May 15, 1781), 65.
108. Bachaumont, XVII, 336 (Aug. 20, 1781).
109. Mallet Du Pan to Osterwald, June 2, 1781, Bibl. Neuch., MS 1178, fo 22–121.

"There are always people clever at succeeding not only to the dead but even to the living," wrote the Bachaumont *nouvelliste*, "when they can do it with impunity and without objection. Thus it is that one sees at Geneva MM. Mallet and Durey de Morsan continuing the Annales of Me. Linguet."[110] This stung. To be accused of appropriating the literary rights of another, to be classified, in effect, with La Harpe! Mallet Du Pan was not slow to retaliate. His *Annales* for August 30, 1781, contained a ten-page blast against the *nouvelles à la main* in general and Bachaumont in particular. He called them gross and calumniating. He did not allude to his own case, but pointed out that Linguet among others had been cruelly treated by this same gossip-monger.[111] Mallet kept insisting to subscribers that his work was not a *continuation* of Linguet's *Annales*, which in any case his lesser talents would have made unthinkable, but a *supplement*.[112] He used Linguet's last number, the suspended No. 72, as his own No. 1, but took care to correct and enlarge it.[113] The necessity of answering the queries of Linguet's well-wishers among his subscribers led him to assume in his journal a general tone of grief and friendship that was far from being what he really felt about Linguet.

Linguet's release on May 18, 1782,[114] inaugurated a difficult and embarrassing period. At that time Mallet's *Annales* were suspended, owing to the Genevan revolution of April and the subsequent French occupation of the city. He reported in July, 1782, when his issue of April 30 actually came out, that he had been in correspondence with Linguet, who it seems had not as yet however indicated any intention of resuming publication of his journal.[115] Some time thereafter (how soon is not clear) Linguet did apprise him of such an intention, upon which, said Mallet in a later account, "I offered to M. Linguet, unconditionally, to terminate mine [that is, his own journal]."[116] What Mallet obviously meant, since this was what he did, was to

---

110. Bachaumont, XVII, 335–36 (Aug. 20, 1781).
111. *Annales*, II, no. 9 (Aug. 30, 1781), 36–46.
112. Ibid., no. 13 (Oct. 30, 1781), "Avis" on cover; *Journal helvétique*, Aug., 1782, p. 77, advertisement for the *Annales* of Mallet Du Pan.
113. *Annales*, I, no. 2 (May 15, 1781), 65.
114. Martin, "Etude sur Linguet," *Travaux de l'Académie Impériale de Reims*, XXXI (1860), 102.
115. *Annales*, III, no. 24 (April 30, 1782), "P.S. du 10 juillet," 536–40.
116. *Mémoires historiques*, V, no. 37 (March 15, 1783), 259.

give up the title he had been using, but not the publication of a journal under another name, a journal for which he would naturally hope to retain his present subscribers. This did not satisfy Linguet. "On December 17 last [December, 1782]," wrote Mallet in his renamed journal, now the *Mémoires historiques, politiques et littéraires sur l'état présent de l'Europe*, "he informs me of his withdrawal to London; he questions me about my intentions; he wants [to know] them, he says before publishing anything; he asks for material from me on the catastrophe of Geneva, of which he is going to make himself the judge; *he will in short concern himself with everything that can be the most advantageous to me* [Mallet's italics]."[117] Linguet in other words wanted again, probably felt the need of, Mallet's collaboration, and he proposed to take for his own uses what would otherwise be the substance of Mallet's journal.

Now Mallet Du Pan had clearly never had any intention of resuming his collaboration with Linguet; he had not been holding the fort against Linguet's return but establishing himself as a journalist of standing in his own right. Quite apart from any monetary consideration (and conceivably he might have done better as Linguet's associate than alone), he could not, having come into his own professionally, have agreed to Linguet's proposal. Linguet chose to think that he had been betrayed, and the quarrel was aired in the two journals. Linguet proclaimed from London, where he was now publishing his revived *Annales*, that he would fight "counterfeiters." "In order at the least to take every pretext from those among them who appropriated my flag . . . to steal from me, and who called themselves my representatives, my tributaries, so as to accredit their fraud," he wrote, "I declare that I approve no secondary edition. Without exception, I acknowledge only that of London, made under my eyes."[118]

Mallet felt that he could not be silent, he could not let Linguet's slurs pass. He had to justify himself to his subscribers (formerly, many of them, Linguet's subscribers); yet he was unwilling to publicize the specifics of his association with Linguet, which would have constituted his best justification. For one thing, his differences with Linguet might have thrown a strange light on the effusive expressions

117. Ibid.
118. *Annales de Linguet*, X (Jan., 1783), 23–24.

of friendliness to Linguet in all his hitherto published references to Linguet's imprisonment. For another, such an account would have shown how close had been the professional relationship between the two journalists, a fact which Mallet was anxious not to emphasize. Therefore his reply, published in the first issue of the journal to bear the new title *Mémoires historiques*, was simply a moralistic gloss upon his conduct, and has a disingenuousness that displeases. In tying up his reputation with Linguet's, he says, he had been imprudent and not sufficiently mindful of his own interest. (So? What about Linguet's subscriptions?) His own conduct had been motivated by "a considerateness (*délicatesse*) to which nothing obligated me," and he had looked for the same thing in Linguet, who on the contrary had turned upon him.[119] This is Mallet Du Pan at his worst.

Mallet's personal correspondence and papers contain a few references to Linguet in subsequent years, but so far as is known he had nothing further to do with his former associate.

While Linguet was in the Bastille Mallet's subscribers had importuned him with queries about the prisoner. Hence his effusively friendly references prior to the break between them. More difficult to deal with, in a way, was the fact that Mallet's *Annales* were expected to reflect Linguet's prejudices; particularly, they were expected to be as anti-philosophe as Linguet's *Annales*. Mallet Du Pan was anti-philosophe but not in the manner of Linguet or to the same degree, and the different tone of his journal was soon perceived. It was thought that he should have joined the campaign of denunciation that was being launched, about the time he began publication, against the several editions of Voltaire's works that were then being projected.[120] Mallet met the objection head on. He said he deprecated Voltaire's attacks upon the Church and the Scriptures but asserted that in all other respects the influence of Voltaire was beneficent and that his opponents had said many untrue things about him.[121] He told another subscriber that *la philosophie* was not after all a monolithic thing to be condemned in its entirety.[122] Such interchanges were infrequent, however. There is no way of knowing

119. *Mémoires historiques*, V, no. 37 (March 15, 1783), 258–59.
120. *Annales*, I, no. 5 (June 30, 1781), 290–92.
121. Ibid., pp. 294–309.
122. Ibid., II, no. 15 (Nov. 30, 1781), 435–44. See above, pp. 64–66.

whether Mallet lost subscribers because of his difference from Linguet in this matter.

Subscriptions came, indeed, in gratifying number, though not all at once. Mallet reported prior to the appearance of the first issue: "The receipt of subscriptions is reasonably good. The Prospectus will increase it, I hope."[123] He counted on Osterwald to announce his *Annales* in the *Journal helvétique*.[124]

The most serious impediment to Mallet's reaping the success he hoped for lay in the reluctance of "the Minister" to grant him entry into France, let alone the use of the post. Now Mallet understood well enough that Linguet's successor could hardly be *persona grata* to Vergennes, unless he could persuade him "that I succeed Linguet without imitating him."[125] He brought all his batteries carefully into position for this purpose. First, he did not attempt to approach Vergennes without intermediaries whom his family's position in Geneva and his former association with Voltaire made available to him. He solicited and secured the good offices of the Genevan minister in Paris, Des Franches. He was fortunate in the fact that the *premier commis* in charge of Franco-Genevan relations in the Département des Affaires Etrangères was P.-M. Hennin, formerly French resident in Geneva and a distant relative of Mallet Du Pan by marriage to a Mlle Mallet.[126] Hennin was also a friend of Henri Rieu, who consented to second Mallet's request for permission.[127]

In his memoranda to Des Franches and Hennin, Mallet Du Pan took credit for some of the success of Linguet's *Annales* (for one thing, he had conceived the plan of the journal, he said), and he referred to the agreement by which he was to become Linguet's successor in the event of Linguet's ceasing to publish the *Annales*. At the same time, he emphasized the trials he had suffered from Linguet's temperament and his own refusal to get involved in Linguet's feuds;

123. Mallet Du Pan to Osterwald, Geneva, March 20, 1781, Bibl. Neuch., MS 1178, fo 22–121.

124. Mallet Du Pan to Osterwald, June 2, 1781, ibid.

125. Mallet Du Pan to Rieu, Geneva, March 21, 1781, Bibl. Genève, MS D.O.

126. Louis Sordet, *Histoire des résidents de France à Genève* (Geneva, 1854), p. 101; Mallet Du Pan to Osterwald, Geneva, July 3, 1781, Bibl. Neuch., MS 1178, fo 22–121.

127. Mallet Du Pan to Henri Rieu, February 3, 1781, Bibl. Genève, MS Suppl. 150, and March 21, 1781, ibid., MS D.O.

hence the absence of any reason for expecting his behavior to resemble Linguet's: "I have neither enmities, nor quarrels, nor vengeances to give expression to; not having to complain of any one, I have no one to ridicule." So he promised: "The rule by which I will write is to be firm without rashness, veracious without licence, scrupulous and impartial with circumspection."[128] Furthermore his principles were such, he said to Hennin, that "I am not afraid to contract with you the solemn engagement never to alarm authority."[129] The sanction for this promise lay, he said, in his residing and publishing in Geneva and in belonging to a family of the patriciate. "No one, Monsieur, knows better than you that to compose a journal at Geneva or to compose it at Paris is almost the same thing for the French Government. . . . One would not tolerate very long there a known resident composing and printing outrages against everything we ought to respect. For immediate censors I have our Government, the family to which I belong, and my connections of every sort: these happy ties should reassure you, more particularly than any one else, as to the circumscribed limits that I would not go beyond with impunity." And Mallet offered, finally, to send to Paris every issue, every single copy destined to a subscriber in France, to be released only on the approval of the *lieutenant de police*.[130] At this point he asked not only toleration but circulation by the post. There was a hint that of course if necessary he would do what he could to get his work circulated illegally; but it was unreasonable that such a journal as his should not circulate with permission.[131]

Vergennes was not impressed, nor, really, was Hennin, despite the obliging tone of his replies. Linguet, too, had been censored, he too had always manifested devotion to the state, religion and *les moeurs*, and still he had been from the minister's viewpoint vastly annoying and embarrassing—and all the more just because he had the most august patronage in the realm and was difficult to get at. In Mallet's case, there was no such august patronage, there was rather a different sort of danger. Although Mallet invoked his relation to the Genevan patriciate as a sanction of his good behavior, it was well known

128. Mallet Du Pan to [Des Franches], January 18, 1781, AAE, Correspondance politique de Genève, LXXXVII, fol. 80–81.
129. Mallet Du Pan to [Hennin], February 8, 1781, Bibl. Reims, MS 1916, Lettre No. 183.
130. Ibid.   131. Ibid.

that he had never been politically orthodox. First there had been the *Compte rendu*, then he had become more pronouncedly anti-Négatif, though without quite becoming Représentant—and the French resident in Geneva had called Vergennes' attention to Mallet's disclaimer of any part in Linguet's article of October, 1779, on Geneva.[132] He was known as a maverick. Furthermore he had adopted a Cassandra-like tone, prophesying Geneva's loss of independence as the consequence, of course, of the next French intervention, which was already in the cards. Besides, it was not really the case that publishing in Geneva was just the same as publishing in Paris, as witness the very fact that the *Annales* of Mallet Du Pan were published there. "I have tried to explain your project and your promises to him again," wrote Hennin, referring to the plea Mallet had sent to Vergennes, via Des Franches, the minister of Geneva, "but he showed the greatest repugnance for it, observed that we had too many journals, and appeared to me especially to consider those that treat affairs of state (*qui traitent de politique*) as not very suitable to enter the Kingdom." Hennin frankly advised Mallet to give up the idea of following in Linguet's footsteps.[133]

Mallet Du Pan refused to be discouraged. He wrote Hennin that he could not give up the enterprise now, on account of "profitable engagements in Germany, in Holland, in Switzerland, in Italy." He hoped, he said, that his first issue would change M. de Vergennes' mind, and meanwhile he would solicit, not the use of the post, but only the grace not to be forbidden in the realm, and to be allowed to advertise freely in the public papers.[134] He was asking, that is, a tacit permission, a sort of limited approval that was not infrequently accorded publications at the time.[135] Hennin replied, in effect, that he could not say any more at that point to M. de Vergennes, but that if Mallet composed his journal in such a way as to overcome the min-

132. Gabard de Vaux, French resident in Geneva, to Vergennes, October 31, 1779, AAE, Correspondance politique de Genève, LXXXIV, fol. 368–69.
133. Hennin to Mallet Du Pan, [February] 26, [1781], Bibl. de l'Institut, Papiers et correspondance de Hennin, MS 1269, No. 30–31.
134. Mallet Du Pan to Hennin, Geneva, April 1, 1781, ibid., No. 32.
135. Nicole Hermann-Mascard, *La censure des livres à la fin de l'ancien régime (1760–1789)* (Paris, 1968), pp. 114–16. This work describes the *permission tacite* only for books, but it is evident that periodicals were accorded analogous favors.

ister's prejudices, he would try to find the right moment to get the interdiction lifted.[136]

Mallet succeeded in his purpose, briefly, on the basis of his first three numbers (April 30, May 15, and May 30, 1781). "The *Annales* are going to circulate by the post throughout the Kingdom," he wrote Osterwald jubilantly. "The Minister has done justice to my intentions, and was convinced by reading the first numbers that I would not be a mad firebrand like Linguet. He has written me, on this subject, a very civil letter,[137] and after many tribulations, I now regard the future of the *Annales* as decided."[138] Did this permission ever take effect? Two weeks later Mallet wrote Osterwald that he was still having some difficulty, though the worst was over.[139] According to Bachaumont in August, "the new journal enters France only furtively."[140] Bachaumont's news might have been, of course, behind the event, but if the interdiction *was* lifted, it was soon down again. The principal cause of the journal's loss of favor was Mallet's article in the issue of October 15, 1781, on the conflict in Geneva between Négatifs and Représentants and the possibility of a French intervention. Complaining that political factionalism was a disease of the times that was widespread, the article, it will be recalled, is critical of both parties. Of the French it is said that although "all intelligent minds see in the justice of Louis XVI and in the integrity of his Minister sure guarantees of the independence of the Republic," still people are questioning what might be the intentions of the foreign minister.[141] In the next issue Mallet recapitulated: refusal of the factions to think of conciliation is a crime against the *patrie*; let the Genevans remember what had happened to Poland.[142] For the reaction of Vergennes, it is best to let Hennin speak:

> I have several times tried to make M. le Comte de Vergennes give up his resolution not to permit entry of the *Annales poli-*

136. Hennin to Mallet Du Pan, Versailles, April 18, 1781, Bibl. de l'Institut, Papiers et correspondance de Hennin, MS 1269, No. 34.

137. I have seen no copy of this.

138. Mallet Du Pan to Osterwald, June 19, 1781, Bibl. Neuch., MS 1178, fo 22–121.

139. Mallet Du Pan to Osterwald, Geneva, July 3, 1781, ibid.

140. Bachaumont, XVII, 336 (Aug. 20, 1781).

141. *Annales*, II, no. 12 (Oct. 15, 1781), 239. See above, p. 93.

142. Ibid., No. 13 (Oct. 30, 1781), pp. 263–64.

tiques into the Kingdom [Hennin informed Mallet], but in vain. The minister is persuaded that there are objections to allowing the circulation of works written with a certain liberty in regard to political affairs because they become nourishment for *frondeurs* and fill hare-brained people with ill-considered ideas which can only make it harder to bring them around to being sensible. Your article [on] Geneva was very well done, Monsieur. You see what it has brought on you. Writing on politics in general or on some abuses in the principal states of Europe you will find Représentants everywhere. Governments are not at all anxious to promote a ferment of writings on questions relating to administration because they see the evil that results from them and expect no good. Moreover the [domestic] periodicals that are approved complain of being injured by toleration of those that are printed abroad. Therefore, Monsieur, I do not see hope of your obtaining very soon the free entry of your work into the Kingdom, and however valid may be the reasons you advance and the promises you make, I advise you not to speculate on the sale of it in France.[143]

The clear lesson of this letter was that Vergennes' objection had nothing to do with *licence* or *indécence*, for in neither respect had Mallet Du Pan offended. He had written soberly. He had however raised the most basic questions, he had discussed them critically, in short he had written "with a certain liberty," and this was what Vergennes would not tolerate. To Vergennes, an acceptable political journal was either a mere gazette like the *Gazette de France* or *Journal de Paris*, or else a mouthpiece for the policy of the foreign minister, as the *Affaires de l'Angleterre et de l'Amérique*, written in support of French intervention in the American Revolution, had been.

Such remained Vergennes' position. Nevertheless, Mallet Du Pan tried to shake it, to obtain at least a *tolérance tacite*. His new efforts were made against the background of the Genevan revolution of 1782 and the military intervention of France, Sardinia, and Berne. Because of the crisis the *Annales* appeared tardily. The first number of

143. Hennin to Mallet Du Pan, Versailles, November 24, 1781, Bibl. de l'Institut, Papiers et correspondance de Hennin, MS 1269, No. 35.

the second year, No. 25, which as originally scheduled would have appeared on April 30, did not come out until August 30. To avoid the subject of Geneva was no part of Mallet's plan, despite the adverse effect on Vergennes of his articles of 1781. On the contrary, No. 25 contained the first installment of his extensive analytical account of the Genevan revolution, the second and concluding installment appearing September 15 in No. 26. His account, which is one of the major contemporary sources, has already been discussed.[144] Suffice it to recall here that the two articles are a denunciation of republican faction, with a particular animus against the Représentant party, and a warning of the foolhardiness of internal faction in a small or weak state bordering a great power. The independence of Geneva, it is evident, according to Mallet, is gone. It was No. 25, just about to appear, with which Mallet Du Pan chose to support his further request to Vergennes for a *tolérance tacite*! His argument no longer emphasized the *décence* and *vérité* of his writing (not that he meant to disregard them), but the nature of his political principles, which valued authority and were devoted to the destruction of "political fanaticism."[145] Again at the same time soliciting Hennin's good offices, he called to the latter's attention the fact that "I have several Sovereigns for subscribers, and the *Annales* are specially protected in their states."[146] Vergennes replied as before, having reexamined earlier issues beside considering the most recent one: "It appeared to me that often you spoke of nations, Princes, and private persons, with a liberty that cannot be tolerated in France."[147] Actually, Vergennes singled out particularly an article on Spain. But Hennin replied, especially mentioning "the great article on Geneva," that indeed it seemed to him that Mallet Du Pan was even less reserved than ever![148]

Mallet was furious. He had stated that he was willing to submit to

144. See above, pp. 94–97.
145. Mallet Du Pan to [Vergennes], Geneva, August 26, 1782, AAE, Correspondance politique de Genève, XCII, fol. 418.
146. Mallet Du Pan to Hennin, Geneva, August 26, 1782, Bibl. de l'Institut, Papiers et correspondance de Hennin, MS 1269, No. 36.
147. Vergennes to Mallet Du Pan, Versailles, October 20, 1782, AAE, Correspondance politique de Genève, XCIII, fol. 420.
148. Hennin to Mallet Du Pan, October 29, 1782, Bibl. de l'Institut, Papiers et correspondance de Hennin, MS 1269, No. 37.

whatever conditions, pecuniary or otherwise, the government might impose[149] (apart, of course, from not discussing *la politique* at all). Now he flung back at the minister a defense of his writing and a sort of veiled defiance: whenever he should be admitted to France, he would be bound by "the expediencies (*les convenances*) of the Kingdom," he would observe the conditions imposed on him. But it was otherwise at present.

> Having lost all hope of surmounting the obstacles that are opposed to me, I believed, Monseigneur, that I was obligated only to the discretion exacted of me by propriety, the respect for sovereigns and the states in which I had obtained free circulation. There is not one, France excepted, where I have been forbidden to come: all have offered me the facilities of the post and encouragements.
>
> Not writing for France from which I am banished, I will make bold to remark to Your Excellency that I am bound only to the general obligations of the impartial, moderate, and scrupulous historian. I will in no way deviate from them, and I thank you, Monseigneur, for having recalled them to me.

Still, in this very letter, Mallet could not resist adding another word on the score of the viewpoint of his journal, which should by rights, he felt, appeal to the minister. "In regard to the degree of fermentation of minds in Europe, and in the anarchy of opinions where we have been cast by the development and the abuse of human knowledge, it is not unprofitable that a work exist where this abuse is pointed out, and where minds are led back to moderation and peoples to tranquillity."[150]

Mallet Du Pan tried yet once more to breach the minister's opposition. It was at the time when Linguet took up again, at London, the publication of his *Annales*, at which point Mallet Du Pan changed the title of his own journal. Whether or not he believed that Vergennes after all was influenced by the idea of his association with Linguet, Mallet saw a possible opening here for another approach. Send-

149. Mallet Du Pan to Hennin, Geneva, August 26, 1782, ibid., No. 36; Mallet Du Pan to Vergennes, August 26, 1782, AAE, Correspondance politique de Genève, XCII, fol. 418.

150. Mallet Du Pan to [Vergennes], Geneva, November 4, 1782, AAE, Correspondance politique de Genève, XCIII, fol. 467.

ing Vergennes a copy of the first issue to bear the title *Mémoires historiques*, he declared that he had absolutely nothing to do with the journal Linguet was now putting out, supporting the assertion by stating that Linguet had recently written an article on Geneva in which he, Mallet Du Pan, had been ill-treated. He reiterated the reasons why he should be given permission to circulate his journal in France—his readiness to accept censorship, his residence in Geneva (this consideration might now possibly carry more weight), his opposition "to the incendiary doctrines and the political satires of modern ranters"; and he referred to "the plan I have adopted of substituting facts for discussions."[151] Actually, the *Mémoires historiques* did not differ from Mallet's *Annales* in the last regard, for in both of them Mallet's work combined fact with interpretation. Conceivably the *Mémoires historiques* might have been different (although this is a dubious conjecture) had Mallet won his point with the minister; but he did not. Vergennes cut the argument short by shifting ground.

> I am indeed persuaded, Monsieur, that wanting to have your new periodical work admitted to the Kingdom, you would take care that it contain nothing to cause you to lose this advantage. It is not then by mistrust of your principles and your prudence that I persist in refusing you the introduction of this work as I had done with the *Annales politiques*. Justice alone, Monsieur, prescribes this conduct to me. We have in France several journals whose authors have acquired privileges, pay pensions or onerous salaries. It matters to them not to have competition, and I must maintain them in their property. For anything else, Monsieur, I will be very glad to find occasions of obliging you. I am, etc.[152]

The clinching argument offered here by Vergennes—the objections of privileged French journals—was one that had come up previously in the discussion. It seems to have been brought up here as a technicality to end Mallet's importunities, since nothing else had succeeded, but the competition offered by a more interesting purveyor of political news than the domestic privileged journals was a

151. Mallet Du Pan to [Vergennes], Geneva, February 25, 1783, ibid., XCIV, fol. 66.

152. [Vergennes] to Mallet Du Pan, Versailles, March 22, 1783, ibid., fol. 97.

serious consideration, if not really, in Vergennes' mind, the primary one. Mallet Du Pan never forgave Vergennes for denying him the greater success he felt he would have achieved, for France no doubt would have given him more subscribers than Switzerland, Italy, Germany, and the Low Countries put together.

How widely and freely Mallet's journal actually did circulate may be inferred from various bits of evidence. The cities listed in the *Annales* where certain designated booksellers were authorized to take subscriptions included Lausanne and Basle for Switzerland; Geneva, of course; the free cities of Frankfort and Hamburg, the latter for "the entire North"; Berlin, for Prussia; Maastricht, for Holland and the Low Countries; Turin, for the kingdom of Sardinia. An Italian translation was published at Florence in the Austrian appanage of Tuscany.[153] "I have several Sovereigns [as well as private citizens of monarchies and republics, of course] for subscribers," Mallet Du Pan had said, "and the *Annales* are specially protected in their States."[154] His terminology in writing to Vergennes came close to an assertion that, except for France, he enjoyed a universal permission.[155] He also proclaimed to subscribers in No. 25 that his work, though forbidden at Paris, was freely received and distributed in the other states of Europe.[156] No doubt there was some exaggeration in his claim (how should the words "received" and "distributed" be construed?) but Mallet Du Pan was not one to make assertions of fact that could not be substantiated. He might falsify his own motives, but not the facts of his circulation. Brissot (no friend to Mallet Du Pan) remarked that Mallet's *Annales* circulated all over Europe.[157]

Mallet Du Pan also distributed his journal anyway in France, as contraband. Without the post the problems of transportation were complicated, and by the threat of interception subscribers always risked the loss of issues. Mallet's *Annales* were successful enough in France, however, to prompt the activity of at least one pirate, at Nantes,[158] but still, when one remembers that Linguet's journal in its palmy days had more than a dozen pirated editions in the king-

153. *Annales*, IV, no. 25 (Aug. 30, 1782), 4.
154. See above, p. 139 and n. 146.
155. See above, p. 140 and n. 150.
156. *Annales*, IV, no. 25 (Aug. 30, 1782), 3.
157. Brissot, *Le Philadelphien à Genève*, p. 4n.
158. *Annales*, IV, no. 25 (Aug. 30, 1782), 3.

dom, one has some measure of the difference. There is another rough index for the conclusion that Mallet's circulation did not approach that of Linguet, in France or anywhere else. Linguet's *Annales* are today generally available (though often enough the examples will be pirated editions), whereas the *Annales* of Mallet Du Pan are extremely scarce, the sets apt, moreover, to be incomplete. The Bibliothèque Nationale possesses only scattered issues.

Still, it was not necessary that Mallet Du Pan should have enjoyed a great circulation in France itself, given all the circumstances, to have impressed that shrewd entrepreneur in the book trade, Charles Panckoucke, proprietor of the *Mercure de France* and other journals, who was looking for talent. At this point it is necessary to take a closer look at Mallet's work.

Mallet Du Pan's *Annales politiques, civiles et littéraires du 18ᵉ siècle*, with the continuation entitled *Mémoires historiques, politiques et litteraire sur l'état présent de l'Europe*, represent his journalistic talent at its full maturity. This is his best work, his most original work, the achievement that entitles him to a high place among the creators of modern political journalism.

The periodical appeared twice monthly, on the 15th and 30th, with great regularity. In two years and four months Mallet Du Pan completed two full subscription years, that is, forty-eight issues, numbered consecutively. These constituted six volumes, also consecutively numbered. He evidently had some help: Bachaumont names Du Rey de Morsan,[159] whom Mallet Du Pan had recommended to Osterwald for the literary part of the *Journal helvétique* at the time he himself contemplated taking over the political part of that periodical. But clearly this was not an extensive collaboration, and the journal was essentially a one-man enterprise in both management and authorship. This is evident not only on the basis of Mallet's correspondence but of the style and content of the publication, which bear the stamp over-all of Mallet Du Pan.

The years of association with Linguet had been a time during which Mallet continually and consciously prepared himself to publish his own journal, and it was probably just as well that the opportunity he coveted was deferred as long as it was. For he learned not

159. Bachaumont, XVII, 336 (Aug. 20, 1781).

only the business of journalism; he learned also how to write. Inclined in his earlier work to a sort of florid exuberance, he learned how to discipline his pen. He came furthermore to a clear conception of the kind of journal he wanted to publish.

On that count, Mallet Du Pan reacted against Linguet's manner. That is, he would not imitate Linguet's incessant self-dramatization. Of course, he would not have succeeded had he tried, for he was no such showman as Linguet, and he had no such fame or notoriety to serve as literary capital. But Mallet had been himself in his twenties something of a show-off, trying to conquer fame quickly by shocking or at least astonishing the public. Although he had got nowhere this way, other than to establish his connection with Linguet, he had at that time admired Linguet's readiness to affront Heaven, and Linguet's success, however specious, in so doing. Then came his personal disillusionment with Linguet and disgust with the tenor of his *Annales,* with their "periodic sorties against all the books, all the systems, all the projects, and all the *corps,*" while at the same time Mallet Du Pan sloughed off something of his own egocentrism. He came to favor the concept of a journal where the author would remain backstage. In sum, it was as part of his personal dissociation from Linguet that Mallet Du Pan consciously defined for himself his own sort of journalism, repudiating Linguet's pyrotechnics and developing a completely different sort of reader appeal, based on the intrinsic interest of serious material attractively presented.

He formulated the concept of a journal that would be, as Linguet's really was not, "a reflective and instructive history of the age," and this concept he described at various times in the journal itself. His preferred designation for his work was contemporary history.

When Mallet Du Pan went to Cassel as Voltaire's protégé to teach literature and history (between which there was then, of course, no demarcation), he went as a disciple. I refer here not so much to Voltaire's general influence over the young man, but to the influence of Voltaire the historian, the historian of the *Siècle de Louis XIV* and the *Essai sur les moeurs.* Voltaire had written to Mallet of his opportunity to present history "in a new way (*dans un goût nouveau*)."[160] The idea of history "dans un goût nouveau," a history of civilization, of *l'esprit du siècle,* intrigued Mallet Du Pan from the

160. See above, chapter 1, p. 23.

start, and it determined in very large measure the content of his journalism. Thus he advertised his *Annales* as "a truly free collection (*recueil*), devoted to developing the general history of the time, in political affairs, legislation, and literature, with reflections. Everything that can characterize the way of life (*les moeurs*), the practices, the spirit, the laws and the events of our epoch will be recorded in it with as much frankness as impartiality."[161] The reader should notice the word *caractériser*, which conveys the concept of *synthèse* (not that Mallet Du Pan used that word). The journal was not to be a miscellaneous compilation. Mallet Du Pan resisted for example certain requests for more book reviews, remarking that there were already plenty of journals that published indiscriminately reviews of all the latest things. Not only was he reluctant to take space for such a purpose from the major articles; his journal had to be selective since it was "devoted to relating . . . the spirit and the history, analytically conceived, of letters, like that of politics and legislation (*consacré à retracer . . . l'esprit et l'histoire raisonnée des lettres, comme celle de la politique et de la legislation*)."[162]

Mallet Du Pan wrote a good deal about historiography in this journal and later in the *Mercure*. To his mind, Voltaire remained the most notable modern historian, with the gift of incomparable style and the power of stimulating ideas along new lines. The impartial critic, he says, "will not refuse him a penetrating insight into the relationships of certain events, a technique, unknown before him, of assembling them without confusion and presenting them from a point of view calculated to interest; usually a quite ample impartiality, a great sobriety in reflection, the art of putting readers on their way and of presenting, with the charms of wit, imagination, and sometimes eloquence, truths and views that one would look for in vain in most modern historians."[163] At the same time, Voltaire as

161. *Annales*, II, no. 13 (Oct. 30, 1781), "Avis" on cover.
162. Ibid., no. 11 (Sept. 30, 1781), pp. 159–60.
163. Ibid., V, no. 36 (Feb. 15, 1783), 208. This is, in French: "un coup d'œil pénétrant sur les rapports de certains événemens, une manière inconnue jusqu'à lui, de les assembler sans confusion et de les présenter sous un point de vue fait pour intéresser; communément une assez grande impartialité, une grande sobriété de réflexions, l'art de mettre les lecteurs sur leur chemin, et celui de présenter avec les charmes de l'esprit, de l'imagination, et quelquefois de l'éloquence, des vériতiés et des vues . . . dont on chercheroit vainement des exemples dans la pluralité des Historiens modernes."

historian was superficial. He was a gifted amateur who did not possess all the qualifications Mallet regarded as necessary in a really professional historian. "He had studied but slightly moral philosophy, legislative enactments, public law, and the political causes of the development, fall, or conservation of empires. Thus his reflections are often inconsequential, likewise his judgments."[164] For Mallet Du Pan, then, it was a question of expanding the Voltairean conception of history, of including within the synthesis the solid matters Voltaire had left out. As a contemporary historian Mallet Du Pan practised what he preached concerning the *études approfondies* that he thought essential to history. An omnivorous reader who did not flinch from serious study, he accumulated a large and solid personal library[165] that was obviously a capital feature of his working professional equipment. He trained himself in the public law of Europe, he studied diplomacy, he developed a shrewd appraisal of the whole rouage of policy that would have been impossible had he relied merely on current information. Financial history, the economic development of states, social questions, religious and ecclesiastical history—he delved into all these subjects, while retaining also the interest in belles lettres and in sciences that he had always had. With all this, Mallet Du Pan's work thus was informed, even erudite in some respects. On the other hand, it was never pedantic. His writing was at the same time both factual and meaningful, a tissue constructed of what he liked to call *faits liés*.

History, for Mallet Du Pan, was analogous to *la physique expérimentale*. It was not philosophy teaching by example, it was science. Over and over again in Mallet's writing occurs the analogy between history and experimental science.[166] History is a kind of companion to or preparation for *la politique expérimentale*.

The historical method properly conceived, he insists, is the reverse of "metaphysical." It begins by the accumulation of facts and the establishment of their authenticity. Mallet Du Pan writes vigorously upon what he terms *la critique*, "the thorough examination of authorities, of the character, of the views, position, trustworthiness of historians, the labor of reconciling them, of verifying conjectures,

164. Ibid., p. 211.
165. Inventories of this exist in the Archives Nationales, F[76] and F[ff].
166. For example: "L'histoire devant servir de physique expérimentale dans l'étude de l'homme. . . ." *Annales*, V, no. 36 (Feb. 15, 1783), 201.

dates, monuments, charters, of separating the true from the probable, of authenticating the latter, and of confronting imposture with reason and actuality; an inexhaustible science, without which the historian is only a chronicler and story-teller."[167] And again one reads: "Separated from *la critique*, History would be the most frivolous of all the sciences, and even one of the most dangerous. Reasoning and reflection are not enough to establish or attack the truth of facts; they can be clarified only by other facts. . . ."[168]

Here Mallet Du Pan passed his severest judgment on Voltaire. For Voltaire's skepticism is "that *scepticisme raisonneur* that dispenses with erudition, and refutes researches with aphorisms. The *Nestor* of *Ferney* rarely discusses authorities; his own is sufficient for him. His opinion about the facts is the proof to which he subjects their verity; he rejects them, he adopts them, according to philosophical arguments. . . . It is a method no less suspect, to evaluate the facts of former times by modern *moeurs*, opinions, characters. Voltaire frequently has recourse to this dialectic, he judges vices and virtues by the primitive dispositions of the human heart, common to all men in all times, without calculating their energy and their changes: because one does not see a Mutius Scaevola in the eighteenth century, he casts doubt on the adventure of this Roman. The *Essai sur l'Histoire générale* is full of this ill-considered pyrrhonism."[169] In other words, for want of proper criteria Voltaire falls back upon a standard of probability in human behavior which is subjective and dogmatic and moreover takes no account of the effects of differences of time and place.

But if Voltaire was to be criticized for deficiencies in historical method, how much more was this the case with the lesser fry who came after him, and particularly all those dealing in contemporary history! "In the reading of so many compilations, that for some time have succeeded the historical works with which France can honor herself, one is right to fear that nothing of this genre remains to us but a library of rumors from gazettes or of fiction (*romans*)."[170] Moreover, some such works, beside raising doubts about the authen-

167. Ibid., p. 205.
168. Letter of Mallet Du Pan to the editor of the *Mercure de France*, Paris, March 14, 1785, *Mercure*, 1785, no. 24 (June 11), p. 73.
169. *Annales*, V, no. 36 (Feb. 15, 1783), 195–97.
170. *Mercure*, 1785, no. 24 (June 11), p. 73.

ticity of the data upon which they draw, are in Mallet's view marred fundamentally by enthusiasm, by fanaticism. Within this category falls, for example, the *Essais historiques et politiques sur la révolution de l'Amérique septentrionale* of Hilliard d'Auberteuil. "The opinions, the maxims, the judgments, the tone, the general character of these Essays are the fruit and the expression of that fanaticism of imagination with which almost all French writers presently are struck, when they speak of laws and liberty,"[171] writes Mallet with distaste. The problem of the bias of the historian, as of *la critique* in general, appeared to him most conspicuously in connection with the "philosophy" and democratic ideology of the period. Mallet Du Pan of course recognized various kinds of bias, but it was *fanatisme philosophique* that he thought most likely in his own time to vitiate the presentation of historical events.

Mallet Du Pan so often refers to his own work as impartial that one needs to pay particular attention to the claim. What it meant chiefly was that Mallet was not the man of a party, or faction, that he stood by himself and would arrive at an independent judgment. The roots of his independency have already been considered in an earlier chapter and will not be discussed again here. It sometimes seemed to contemporaries that he went to considerable trouble to avoid being a party man (I refer to Geneva) and some of them thought that he did not succeed, that he had simply changed about from one party to another. However, he certainly succeeded to the extent of antagonizing every party at one time or another, and he had individual friends and correspondents in all of them. But, to put the matter another way, Mallet Du Pan did not mean, when he said he was impartial, that he would suspend judgment, or treat all parties as equally deserving of praise or blame, or refuse to come to political conclusions with which some people were bound to disagree. In a sense therefore impartiality simply meant that a proper hearing would be accorded. The historian is among other things a judge, but he judges according to principles, not parties. The contemporary historian, having reached his conclusions, is not bound to silence if they are controversial. He is only bound to *la critique* in testing them.

Mallet Du Pan denied that he claimed for what he wrote anything

171. *Annales*, IV, no. 27 (Sept. 30, 1782), 168.

like a definitive quality. Nevertheless, he put a considerable value upon his journalism as being useful both to the labors of future historians and to readers who wanted instruction in the present. "These *Mémoires*," he told readers of his journal, "will be then neither a series of treatises concerning the events of, nor a history of, the age, but the selection of materials for this history; a selection appropriate to forming and explaining the picture of Europe at this moment."[172]

Mallet prided himself upon the critical rigor of his methods for obtaining and interpreting the news. His sources of information were, for one, the gazettes. The gazettes, however, had to be used with utmost caution. He said, when political editor of the *Mercure de France*, that he read twenty English papers every week,[173] but whereas he had some confidence in being able to piece an account together from these, he mistrusted profoundly the Continental publications like the *Gazette de Leyde* and the *Gazette d'Amsterdam*, which were too much subject to government editing in one way or another. Only the *Courier du Bas Rhin*, he declared in 1786, was telling the truth about the revolutionary movement in Holland, and for this it had been barred from France.[174] If one used the gazettes, one had laboriously to sort out the truth from the lies and the half-truths. So Mallet Du Pan resorted, as did other private individuals and business firms who wanted reliable information, to a system of correspondence. He advertised this feature of his enterprise on the cover of his journal: "By reason of the precautions that have been taken, and scrupulous *correspondances* providing selected materials, the truth will in this work find an asylum that is closed to false or doubtful news."[175] As time went on, he enlarged his list of correspondents and his geographical coverage, for the plan of his journal was to cover Europe systematically.[176] He had, he told subscribers at the close of the year 1782, "select *correspondances* in the principal states of Europe."[177] Mallet had begun corresponding with various strategi-

172. *Mémoires historiques*, V, no. 37 (March 15, 1783), 262.
173. Mallet Du Pan to Etienne Dumont, Paris, April 5, 1787, Blondel, "Lettres inédites," p. 106.
174. Mallet Du Pan to Vernes, Paris, September 28, 1786, Bibl. Genève, MS D.O.
175. *Annales*, II, no. 13 (Oct. 30, 1781), "Avis" on cover.
176. *Mémoires historiques*, V, no. 37 (March 15, 1783), 261–62.
177. *Annales*, V, no. 33 (Dec. 30, 1782), "Avis" preceding text, p. 3.

cally located persons in the days following the Cassel episode (there was for example the Prussian nobleman who had commissioned the *Doutes sur l'éloquence*), and he worked to build up his contacts while associated with Linguet. When suggesting to Osterwald in 1779 that he might take over the position of political editor of the *Journal helvétique*, he pointed out: "I have good *correspondances* at the present time."[178]

Mallet Du Pan never divulged in print the names of the individuals who thus supplied him with his information, and he usually hid their identity in letters to third parties, even close friends. It is possible to identify a few, however. There was a certain M. Beauchâteau of Geneva, whose services were solicited in November, 1776, for Geneva,[179] while Mallet was living at Aubonne. For English affairs, at the time of his decision to publish his own journal, he approached his compatriot Samuel Romilly, who was then living in England, through a mutual friend, suggesting a weekly newsletter from him or someone recommended by him.[180] Whether Romilly acceded is not known, but he remained on cordial terms with Mallet Du Pan.[181] Then there was the chevalier Mouradgea d'Ohsson, one-time Swedish chargé at Constantinople, whose relations with Mallet Du Pan in 1788 and 1789 were part of a curious interlude which will be discussed in another connection.[182] Mouradgea d'Ohsson was not precisely a correspondent, but he was a news source. No doubt among these correspondents others beside Romilly were Genevese living abroad for business or professional reasons, or persons of other nationality who were introduced to Mallet Du Pan through some Genevese commercial or financial association. Or the contacts might have developed through the booksellers who were Mallet's agents. The chevalier Mouradgea d'Ohsson was the author of a book on the Ottoman Empire that Mallet reviewed in the *Mercure* with the

178. Mallet Du Pan to Osterwald, Lausanne, March 3, 1779, Bibl. Neuch., MS 1178, fo 22–121.

179. Mallet Du Pan to Beauchâteau, Aubonne, November 14, 1776, Bibl. Genève, MS Supp. 363, Collection Coindet, Autographes Genevois, fol. 69.

180. Cathrine Roget to Samuel Romilly, January 31, 1781, Mallet Papers, London.

181. Etienne Dumont, *Souvenirs sur Mirabeau et sur les deux premières assemblées législatives*, ed. J. Bénétruy (Paris, [c. 1950]), p. 53.

182. See below, chapter 5, pp. 180ff.

highest praise,[183] and here apparently their connection began.

The makeup of the material in the *Annales* of Mallet Du Pan and the *Mémoires historiques* combines short news items with more extensive articles on timely topics. In Mallet's articles there is characteristically some reference, usually just by way of a swift allusion though sometimes more at length, to a historical context. The interpretation is sometimes colored by an obvious didactic purpose, but this never dominates the material as it does in the political dirges composed during the French Revolution that have become the best known of Mallet Du Pan's writings. The material in the *Annales* and *Mémoires historiques* is concrete, factual, it has variety and movement and suggests the multitudinousness of experience. The reader feels that he is confronting actuality.

It was chiefly the superior quality of Mallet Du Pan's reporting that led Panckoucke to seek to employ his services. The occasion was provided by the circumstance that Dubois-Fontanelle, the incumbent editor of the *Journal politique de Bruxelles*, which was the political section of the *Mercure de France*, was in 1783 going to the *Gazette de France*.[184] Panckoucke needed a replacement.

This publisher was, moreover, a monopolizer of journals. His *Journal de politique et de littérature*, founded in 1774 with Linguet as editor, was a merger of two lesser publications.[185] In June, 1778, he took over from the *libraire* Lacombe, who was bankrupt, the ownership of the *Mercure de France* and merged with it the *Journal de politique et de littérature*,[186] from which Linguet had been ousted. The literary portion of the latter was simply fused with the *Mercure*, but the political part, edited by Dubois-Fontanelle[187] and known henceforth as the *Journal politique de Bruxelles*, appeared as a distinct section of the *Mercure*. It took the place of and expanded the hitherto scanty political news carried by the *Mercure* once a month. Both parts of the *Mercure* began appearing three times a month. In

183. *Mercure*, 1788, no. 11 (March 15), pp. 103–19.
184. Bachaumont, XXVI, 71 (June 28, 1784).
185. Advertisement on back cover of the journal in 1774.
186. Bachaumont, XI, 223 (May 14, 1778); ibid., XII, 24 (June 28, 1778); *Journal politique de Bruxelles*, June 25, 1778, p. 73.
187. Louis Trenard, "La presse française des origines à 1778," Part II of *Histoire générale de la presse française*, ed. Claude Bellanger et al. (Paris, 1969), I, 217–18.

July, 1779, the *Mercure* together with its political section began coming out once a week, on Saturday. Panckoucke was the owner also of a political journal known as the *Journal de Genève*, which actually had no connection with Geneva, and which became virtually identical with the *Journal politique de Bruxelles*. It was henceforth simply the name for the political section of the *Mercure* when subscribed for separately from the literary section.[188] Panckoucke's appetite was still unsatisfied. The political propaganda journal, *Affaires de l'Angleterre et de l'Amérique*, was absorbed in 1779.[189] It was even rumored in Paris in 1781 that the famous *Année littéraire*, the principal anti-philosophe organ now that Linguet was out of action, was in danger, since Panckoucke, "that Atlas of the book trade,"[190] backed by the Encyclopedist party, was intriguing to have it "annexed" to his *Mercure*.[191]

It will be remembered that Linguet cherished a bitter grudge against Panckoucke, and Mallet Du Pan had adopted the quarrel as his own. This is clear from his letters to Osterwald, who was, for his part, on friendly terms with the Paris publisher. Mallet complained that Panckoucke had tried vindictively to destroy the *Annales de Linguet*.[192] (The Bachaumont version of the story was that Linguet had attacked Panckoucke's *Mercure* and that Panckoucke had tried, but failed, to get Falconet, one of the editors, to reply in kind.)[193] Osterwald hoped to publish with Panckoucke an edition of Voltaire containing posthumous works.[194] Mallet Du Pan suspected, on the basis of what Voltaire's former secretary, Wagnière, told him of Panckoucke's actions at Ferney, that Panckoucke had other plans,[195] and when Panckoucke and Beaumarchais joined forces to produce

188. *Mercure*, "Avis" attached to the issue of July, 1779; contract between Mallet Du Pan and Panckoucke, March 4, 1784, Mallet Papers, London.

189. George B. Watts, *Charles Joseph Panckoucke, "l'Atlas de la librairie française,"* in Vol. LXVIII of *Studies on Voltaire and the Eighteenth Century*, ed. Theodore Besterman (Geneva, 1969), p. 168.

190. Bachaumont, XVIII, 169 (Dec. 5, 1781).

191. Ibid., XVII, 300 (July 27, 1781).

192. Mallet Du Pan to Osterwald, Lausanne, October 8, 1778, Bibl. Neuch., MS 1178, fo 22–121.

193. Bachaumont, XII, 126 (Oct. 6, 1778).

194. Mallet Du Pan to Osterwald, Lausanne, October 23, 1778, Bibl. Neuch., MS 1178, fo 22–121.

195. Mallet Du Pan to Osterwald, Lausanne, November 21, 1778, ibid.

their famous edition,[196] Mallet wrote to Osterwald: "What you tell me about Panckoucke does not surprise me at all. I predicted to you long ago what has happened to you."[197] Mallet Du Pan the following year advised Osterwald that he himself had taken an interest in another edition of Voltaire to be put out by Cramer of Geneva, who had an inside track with Wagnière for Voltaire's manuscripts. He reported that Beaumarchais' group had made overtures to Cramer through Panckoucke and that Cramer was holding out for publication of a proposed combined edition at Geneva.[198] One wonders whether it was in these negotiations over Voltaire's manuscripts that Mallet Du Pan's first contact with Panckoucke occurred. It should be added at this point that by 1784, after he had entered Panckoucke's employ, Mallet Du Pan was actively soliciting the correspondence of Voltaire from his friends for the Beaumarchais edition, which he said was in every respect worthy of Voltaire's memory.[199] It appears that Osterwald had already himself become a collector of Voltaire-ana for Beaumarchais.[200]

Panckoucke's definite offer to Mallet Du Pan was dated October 16, 1783, but it was preceded by a correspondence that must have begun during the summer before, since Mallet speaks of "all my correspondence with you."[201] A rumor got around during the summer that the *Mémoires historiques* would be discontinued, but Mallet Du Pan denied it.[202] He also informed his readers, however, that he hoped to publish his third year under arrangements that would re-

196. "Préface générale" of Beuchot, in Voltaire, *Œuvres complètes*, ed. Louis Moland, 52 vols. (Paris, 1877–1885), I, xix.

197. Mallet Du Pan to Osterwald, Geneva, November 4, 1780, Bibl. Neuch., MS 1178, fo 22–121.

198. Mallet Du Pan to Osterwald, Geneva, December 17, 1781, ibid.

199. Mallet Du Pan to Rieu, *le père*, Geneva, April 20, 1784, Bibl. Genève, MS Supp. 150.

200. Mallet Du Pan to Osterwald, Geneva, March 20, 1781, Bibl. Neuch., MS 1178, fo 22–121. "Vous voilà donc collecteurs de Beaumarchais," wrote Mallet.

201. Mallet Du Pan to Panckoucke, Geneva, October 29, 1783, in "Deux lettres inédites de Mallet Du Pan," *Mémoires et documents publiés par la Société d'histoire et d'archéologie de Genève*, XXII (1886), 359. All quotations from this letter and those that follow are, when in English, my translation.

202. *Mémoires historiques*, VI, no. 47 (Aug. 15, 1783), 385.

lieve him of business worries—this was apropos of the issue of June 30 being late, owing, he said, to some "annoying complications" (*embarras dégoutans*) in the business side of the enterprise.[203] Was this a reference to pending negotiations with Panckoucke?

Panckoucke's offer was not what Mallet Du Pan wanted. What he wanted, what the announcement to his subscribers suggests, was essentially a continuation of his own journal, written in Geneva but published in France, "enjoying a liberty subordinated to the usages of your [the French] government."[204] It would have been in effect his triumph over Vergennes; but he had rejoiced too soon. Panckoucke already had an understanding with "the Department" that he proposed not to disturb. Before the time of Mallet Du Pan he had thought of a way to increase the political interest of his journals while not running the risk of being charged with embarrassing the government. This was simply to take items extracted verbatim from the foreign journals that were permitted to enter the kingdom and to juxtapose them in the *Journal de Genève* and the *Journal politique de Bruxelles*.[205] The plan attached to the first contact between Mallet Du Pan and Panckoucke incorporated this scheme and was explicit as to its implications: "The *Journal de Genève* is to be only a Gazette of the gazettes, the most complete repertory of all the facts, of all the events that can interest the public curiosity. . . . The historical is to be only an accessory. Never will the Government permit one to expatiate on affairs of state (*la politique*). If the Government were to permit some political discussion, it would still be necessary to be very circumspect, because the ambassadors, the envoys of the various princes, have only too often brought complaints about articles that could hurt them." However, an article of somewhat freer tendency than most could be composed of the statements taken word for word from the foreign gazettes and put in quotation marks.[206] From Mallet's point of view these restrictions, which were obviously made clear at the time of Panckoucke's offer, were vastly disappointing. "From

203. Ibid., VI, no. 44 (June 30, 1783), 256.
204. Mallet Du Pan to Panckoucke, Geneva, October 29, 1783, "Deux lettres inédites de Mallet Du Pan," p. 359.
205. *Mémoire* from Panckoucke to "le Département," n.d., Bibl. Genève, MS D.O.
206. "Plan pour le journal de Genève," dated March 4, 1784, and signed by Mallet Du Pan, ibid. See below, p. 160, for the "Plan."

historian," he protested, "I become gazeteer, and from author, journalist."[207]

This was not all, either. Panckoucke's plan was that Mallet Du Pan establish his domicile in Paris. What, Mallet asked, would that do to his reputation? Writing in Geneva, he was, in the public mind, he said, quite free. True, there was now (since the events of 1782) scarcely more liberty in Geneva than in Paris, but his public was not aware of this; and even though his work if composed in Geneva for a privileged journal published in Paris would be subject to censorship no less than if he resided in the capital, still the public would have more confidence in it. Besides, he had at Geneva "a domestic establishment completely set up," which he dreaded to transplant. Was it Vergennes who had required this? He believed so. One has the feeling, reading between the lines, that the question of the damage to his reputation should he have to write in Paris was not in his own mind the main point, rather that he was somewhat fearful of burning his bridges behind him, fearful, even, for his personal liberty. Mallet proposed in reply that he should remain in Geneva. But he would go to Paris, if need be, asking, for his sacrifices, 3000 livres more of basic salary: 10,000 livres for Paris to 7,000 for Geneva. To bring Panckoucke around to his terms, he said that after all he was distributing the *Mémoires historiques* in France despite its being prohibited there, and moreover he had had another offer from a journalist who wanted to combine the *Mémoires historiques* with a recasting (*refonte*) of the *Mercure*, the product to be published "in a free country." He called Panckoucke's attention also to a new publication being put out at Hamburg entitled *Esprit des gazettes*, which would offer serious competition to the political section of the *Mercure* if the latter were not improved. "Your articles on the North are dry, nothing much, and in general very badly done," declared Mallet Du Pan. "The same is true for Germany. Those on England transgress through an absolute ignorance of the characteristics (*caractères*) and through an appreciation of persons and debates that is almost always false."[208]

Nonetheless, Mallet Du Pan agreed to go to Paris, and for 7,200

207. Mallet Du Pan to Panckoucke, Geneva, October 29, 1783, "Deux lettres inédites de Mallet Du Pan," p. 360.
208. Ibid., pp. 361–63.

livres of basic salary, but with 20 sous additional for each subscription above certain given numbers. In addition, he might earn up to 1,000 livres annually for contributions of a literary nature to the *Mercure*.[209]

What had induced Mallet Du Pan to give up a work that had made his reputation, a publication where his talents had attained their full fruition, in the writing of which he was his own master, his own censor so to speak, what had induced him to become as he said a compiler of gazettes, and that under the eye of the French censor and within the reach of the French police? To this question there is clearly more than one answer. Certainly one major consideration must have been the release from any business responsibilities (printing, subscriptions, distribution both legal and contraband), over which Mallet had always fussed and fumed. The salary, too, though not as much as Panckoucke had given Linguet in 1774 or as Mallet Du Pan had asked, was very likely somewhat better than Mallet's revenue from his *Mémoires historiques* ("I sacrifice profits *almost equivalent* [my italics] to those that await me at Paris"[210]). Then there was the likelihood that Geneva under a reactionary Négatif régime that amounted to a French protectorate offered a future at best uncertain to a journalist so outspoken. And finally, there was the hope that, once he had established himself, he might somehow be permitted to make over the political section of the *Mercure* into something closer to his own ideas. He still clung, as he told Panckoucke, to "the hope of assisting you perhaps some day in a less sterile enterprise."[211] Perhaps this might be when Vergennes should have left the ministry. The opportunity to contribute to the literary section of the *Mercure*, to which the censorship of "the Department" paid relatively little attention, gave him the chance to put one foot in the door. It was above all in the book reviews he wrote for the *Mercure* between 1784 and 1789 that Mallet Du Pan was able to continue the competent analyses of contemporary themes for which his *Annales* and *Mémoires historiques* had been notable.

209. Contract between Panckoucke and Mallet Du Pan, March 4, 1784, Mallet Papers, London. See below, pp. 158–59, for details of this first contractual arrangement between Mallet Du Pan and Panckoucke.
210. Mallet Du Pan to Panckoucke, Geneva, October 29, 1783, "Deux lettres inédites de Mallet Du Pan," p. 359.
211. Ibid., p. 360.

It is quite possible to suppose, even without specific and clear documentary evidence, that some of the opposition at Versailles to the entry Mallet Du Pan had sought into the kingdom for his journal had come from Panckoucke. At any rate, the refusal of Vergennes to allow it, though dictated primarily by political reasons, served the interests of the astute publisher well enough, for it had hampered the rise of a new competitor and delivered him finally into Panckoucke's employ. The *Mercure*, in short, had absorbed another journal.

Five

POLITICAL EDITOR OF THE *MERCURE*: UNDER THE OLD MONARCHY

Panckoucke had acquired a first-rate talent that would, he anticipated (and correctly), assure him a very large share of the expanding market for political journalism. For his part, Mallet Du Pan owed to Panckoucke's management a heightened material prosperity and professional reputation and—a most vital concern—support in his resistance to government interference, political opponents, and competitors. Panckoucke was to be a tower of strength, for which Mallet Du Pan was grateful. The association between publisher and editor developed into one of personal esteem and friendliness, but it was also always, from first to last, businesslike, and no doubt this was one reason why it was so satisfactory.

The political section of the *Mercure de France*, it will be recalled, appeared under two titles. It could be subscribed for separately as the *Journal historique et politique de Genève* (called otherwise *Journal politique de Genève*, or *Journal de Genève*), and it was attached to the *Mercure* as the *Journal politique de Bruxelles*. In Mallet Du Pan's first contract with Panckoucke, dated March 4, 1784, the two publications were treated separately. "M. Mallet Du Pan, citizen of Geneva and presently domiciled in Paris," was charged with composing and editing the *Journal historique et politique de Genève*, according to a certain format. His name would appear at the head of it. Like the *Mercure*, it would appear regularly every Saurday, and M. Panckoucke, the proprietor, would be free to use the material of this journal, in whole or in part, as he had been wont to do previously, to compose from it the *Journal politique de Bruxelles*, attached to the

Mercure. Mallet would have the editorship of the *Journal de Genève* exclusively, while he agreed for his part never to entrust the work to anyone else without the publisher's consent. He also agreed, so long as he remained editor of the *Journal de Genève*, not to work on any other journal, or "gazette de politique." Should he wish to resign, he would give four months' notice in writing, and Panckoucke would be free to choose as a successor whomever he liked. The salary would be 7,200 livres annually, 500 payable each month and the remaining 1,200 each January, Panckoucke defraying the cost of gazettes, correspondence, and other materials used in the composition. Should subscriptions exceed five thousand, "as had happened in time of war," Mallet would receive 20 sous for each subscription above that number. Moreover, should subscriptions to the *Mercure* itself rise "considerably" above the figure anticipated in an agreement made between the publisher and "the Minister" in 1783, as was also to be expected in time of war, Mallet would received 20 sous for each additional subscription in this case, too. Furthermore, the editor of the *Journal de Genève* might compose a certain number of literary articles, for which he would be paid up to 1,000 livres annually. Presumably it was under this stipulation that he wrote the book reviews for the literary section of the *Mercure* that comprise a very solid part of his total contribution to the periodical. Beyond this, Mallet would not be entitled to demand anything from the publisher on the ground that "the composition of the *Journal politique de Genève* will be the composition of the *Journal politique de Bruxelles* attached to the *Mercure.*" It was not stated that Mallet's name would appear at the head of the *Journal politique de Bruxelles,* either.[1] Nor did it in fact appear here or on the title page of the *Mercure.* No names of contributors or editors appeared on the title page of the *Mercure* at this time, nor until December, 1789, at which date the name of "M. Mallet du Pan, Citoyen de Genève," appeared along with those of the literary editors. Nevertheless, it was no secret that the editor of the *Journal politique de Bruxelles* was Mallet Du Pan. More often than not, Mallet and others did not use this title for the journal; they simply spoke of the *Mercure* when they meant its political section.

With the contract, and stated to be a part of it, was a "Plan for the

1. Contract between Mallet Du Pan and Panckoucke, signed by both, March 4, 1784, Mallet Papers, London.

Journal de Genève." The content was to be above all political, since it was political events, according to this instrument, that most interested the public. History (as has already been noted) would be only an accessory. The journal would deal with current events, offering the most complete coverage possible. The articles on France and England were to be done with special care, since it was these, according to the "Plan," that readers turned to first, and the article on France was, it seems, not to be political only, but to include anything that might intrigue the readers' curiosity, without, however, infringing on the rights of other departments of the *Mercure*, i.e., the literary section. Political news was to comprise only factual matter, never discussion, for (as has been noted) "the Government will never permit discussion of policy." Commentary, if any, must be exceedingly circumspect. It was understood, according to the "Plan," that "the Minister" intended the *Journal de Genève* to enjoy the same liberty as the foreign gazettes that were permitted in France, but still one could run afoul of the censorship, even, it seems, when publishing what was simple, factual information. The problem was how to be interesting while remaining safe. Hence Mallet Du Pan was to follow the practice previously adhered to, as we have seen, by the *Mercure*: certain articles dealing with topics of a sensitive nature might be composed of quotations "of a certain liberty," taken verbatim from foreign gazettes with full indication of the source.[2] It remains to be seen how, despite these stipulations, Mallet Du Pan and the Department of Foreign Affairs came to be at loggerheads over the content of the *Journal politique de Bruxelles*.

It was not long before the new editor ran into trouble, but not at first with the government. Other interests beside the state considered that they had a right to interfere. A few months after the contract described above had been negotiated, Panckoucke decided to provide the *Journal de Genève* with a literary supplement which Mallet said increased his total income (*bénéfices*) by about 1,000 écus (3,000 livres). In the first number of this supplement he reviewed disparagingly an *Eloge de Fontenelle* that had been crowned by the Académie. Panckoucke objected to the article and, when Mallet refused to change it, suppressed the number.[3] Outraged, Mallet threat-

2. "Plan pour le Journal de Genève," March 4, 1784, Bibl. Genève, MS D.O.
3. Mallet Du Pan to Vernes, Paris, October 28, 1784, ibid.

ened to resign, for it appeared to him that Panckoucke was simply transmitting orders from the Académie, and this he would not put up with. In coming to Paris he had not agreed, he told Panckoucke, to accept any other censor than the government. "Writing under the laws, I have to respect the censorship [of the government]," he declared, "but I will never stand for the despotism of private individuals." Such a servitude would be all the more dangerous, he said, in that he would have to do with a class of persons inordinately vain and a hundred times more intolerant than theologians, writers who were lip servants of liberty but who would deny it to anyone unwilling to burn incense to the philosophers, so-called. It seems that Panckoucke had accused his editor of behaving in the manner of Fréron and Linguet, those intransigent and none too polite foes of the philosophe literati in earlier decades. "To do me this honor," Mallet retorted, "I think it requisite to wait until I have justified it by my writings. I do not know what idea you have formed, or what you may have been given to think, of my principles and my character; but it is easy for you to see that all the passions that dishonor literature are foreign to me. I dispute nothing with any one: I do not aspire to pensions, or crowns, or Academic seats, or dinners. As I do not live among men of letters, certainly they will not involve me in any party. Whence then comes this mistrust? Only from the suggestions you have been given, and you have been given them because it was justly felt that I would be impartial and truthful." He went on to say that he suspected the marquis de Condorcet in connection with such denigrations—and the reader will remember that Mallet had ridiculed Condorcet's address on the occasion of his reception into the Académie Française.

A work of literary criticism [Mallet went on] cannot be subordinated to these considerations and to these social interests (*ces intérêts de société*). If judgments are given with propriety (*décence*) they should be unfettered. You would be the first bookseller to be made responsible for the opinions, whether flattering or otherwise, of his authors. Where would we be if these gossipings (*commérages*) were to dictate your thoughts to you! As for me, they would cause me to lose, assuredly, what little talent I may have and any sort of desire to excel; I will say more, they would dishonor me in the eyes of the public. It is precisely because I wish to be respected and esteemed that I do not want to become a maker of compliments to people whom it [i.e., the public] neither esteems nor respects. I am then unshakably attached to the resolution of which I have apprised you. Either leave me the most complete liberty in the choice and editing of my articles, without respect to persons, under the sole and strict obligation not to arouse complaints on the part of the government or legitimate reproaches from the public, or we must separate. This displacement will be the misfortune of my whole life. I was shown the precipice: it is inexcusable in me to have closed my eyes to it, and I shall long regret my heedlessness. My confidence in you was unlimited; if it is not reciprocated, if I have to depend on what you hear from persons whose company you frequent, if, in short, my life is to be [a series] of weekly altercations, there is no fate that would not appear to me less frightful.[4]

The cash value of Mallet Du Pan's work was not yet demonstrated, but he must have struck the right notes, for Panckoucke capitulated. Relating the incident to his old confidant Vernes, Mallet Du Pan said he was continuing his work under his own conditions. Still, he was uneasy. Panckoucke's reference to Linguet was clearly a reminder, if veiled, of Linguet's ill-starred career with the *Journal de politique et de littérature.* "My manner," Mallet wrote to Vernes, "displeases the Government, the censors, the philosophes, the Academicians, the journalists; any day P[anckoucke] could be forbidden to employ me; in such a case, no resource or recourse."[5]

Rumors of a difference between the publisher and the political editor of the *Mercure* got around and may have inspired an intrigue against him. Isaac Cornuaud, the one-time Natif chieftain in Geneva, quotes in his memoirs a letter, dated at Paris, December 30,

4. Mallet Du Pan to Panckoucke, Paris, September 12, 1784, Mallet Papers, London.

5. Mallet Du Pan to Vernes, Paris, October 28, 1784, Bibl. Genève, MS D.O. Cf. reference in one of the *nouvelles à la main* to "the abuse that M. Mallet Dupan retails periodically against the defenders of liberty and of philosophy." [Métra, J. Imbert et al.], *Correspondance secrète, politique et littéraire, ou Mémoires pour servir à l'histoire des cours, des sociétés et de la littérature en France, depuis la mort de Louis XV,* 18 vols. (London, 1787–1789), XVII, 172.

1784, purporting to be from Clavière, the Genevan Représentant exile, to Bérenger, Natif exile and friend of Mallet's youth. The letter, says Cornuaud, was picked up on the street where the writer must have dropped it. Although not signed, it was in Clavière's hand and Clavière's efforts subsequently to retrieve it, Cornuaud thought, determined his authorship. It was an inquiry whether Bérenger, whom Clavière would be happy to see join the Genevan exiles in Paris, would be interested in the position of political editor of the *Mercure de France*. The writer said that he was hearing on all sides how Mallet was continually at outs with Panckoucke. His "rage for being singular at all costs *(sa fureur d'être singulier à tous prix)*" was bound to lead to ever mounting disagreements and ultimately a forced resignation. Anticipating this eventuality, Bérenger could put himself in a favorable position to become Mallet's successor. Of course, Clavière went on, it was not a question actually of ousting Mallet, but simply of putting oneself forward against the day when Mallet should have deprived himself, in effect, of his position.[6]

Was Clavière pulling strings at this time to secure Mallet's dismissal? After the débacle of 1782 in Geneva, Clavière had been building a new career, financially and politically. It would be natural for him to want to have a political sympathizer at the *Mercure*, instead of Mallet Du Pan, from whom he could not expect support. A maneuver of this sort would be consonant with Clavière's actions a few years later when he and Brissot de Warville, with whom Mallet had already crossed swords, intrigued against him, together with Mirabeau (as will be related in due course), while publishing their journal, *Analyse des papiers anglais*.[7] Later still, in 1790, there was another attempt, in which Clavière may have been involved, to replace Mallet Du Pan with a sympathizer of the Genevan democrats.[8] It is not known whether Clavière wrote a letter to Bérenger, replacing the one of December, 1784, that had fallen into Cornuaud's hands, or if so, what Bérenger replied.

Mallet himself seems at this time to have been far from suspecting

6. Cornuaud, *Mémoires*, pp. 438–39.
7. See below, p. 168 et sqq.
8. Mallet Du Pan to Mounier, Paris, December 9, [1790], in *Autour d'une Révolution* (1788–1789), ed. Comte [Maurice d'Irisson] d'Hérisson (Paris, 1888), pp. 164–65. See below, chapter 6, pp. 231–32.

Clavière of any skulduggery, but he *was* concerned lest Clavière think him hostile and the author of disparaging remarks. In 1785 there appeared, under the name of Mirabeau, a well-known pamphlet on the Caisse d'Escompte, and there appeared some time later, in the same year, another pamphlet critical of Mirabeau's brochure and uncomplimentary to Clavière. Mallet heard that he was reputed to be the author of the latter work. To set Clavière straight on this he enlisted the help of Salomon Reybaz, another Genevan exile of 1782 and one of Mallet's small circle of friends at Paris. (It is curious how Mallet's closest Genevan friends, at Paris or Geneva or elsewhere, were usually Représentants, not Négatifs—one thinks especially of Jacob Vernes and Etienne Dumont.) It happened that Reybaz had touched Mallet for a loan, which Mallet felt unable to extend, as he was himself pressed for funds, having, he said, just invested what capital he had in some shares in a company for coal mines in the Forez. He suggested Clavière as one of those persons who could most easily come to Reybaz's assistance. In his turn Mallet, assuming that Reybaz would take up the suggestion, requested him to be so kind as to set Clavière right on the matter of the pamphlet.

I was ignorant even of the existence of this pamphlet, [said Mallet], and although I do not dissimulate a very profound scorn for the person of M. de Mirabeau, I am not rash enough to break a lance against a man of that stamp; I understand nothing of the affairs of the Caisse d'Escompte, and moreover, I will never write a line without signing it. I should nevertheless be very sorry if M. Clavière could suspect me for a moment of having had a share in this brochure. He would even commit an injustice to suppose me hostile to him in the least. You will oblige me by giving him this explanation.[9]

Mallet might have felt uneasy on account of Clavière, but at this time his principal anxiety was that caused by his relations with "the

9. Mallet Du Pan to Reybaz, "dimanche soir à 9 heures, 24 8bre" [October 23, 1785], Bibl. Genève, MS fr. 916, Papiers Reybaz, f. 83–84. Mallet seems to have been confused about the date. October 24 was on a Sunday in 1784, but the reference to Mirabeau's pamphlet on the Caisse d'Escompte, and another reference to the arrest of Cardinal Rohan, which occurred in August, 1785, put the letter in the latter year, when October 24 was on a Monday. It is more likely that Mallet was confused about the day of the month than the day of the week, hence I have dated the letter October 23. (To establish the calendar I have used the *Almanach Royal*.)

Department." He complained to Reybaz of being much preoccupied with interference from that quarter. On the question of the revolutionary movement in Holland they had forced him to a determined resistance, he said, and to remonstrances to which they were little accustomed.[10]

By the time Mallet Du Pan came to the *Mercure,* the once aristocratic Dutch opposition to the stadholder, a monarchical type of figure, and to the English alliance for which the House of Orange stood, had changed character radically. It was now primarily a protest movement of the middle class against the oligarchical structure of government in The United Netherlands and the dominance of the mercantile aristocracy, or regents, who now, resentful of these pretensions and worked on by the astute British ambassador, Sir James Harris, began to go over to the House of Orange. The revolutionary party, or Patriots, who invoked the democratic ideology of popular sovereignty, were analogous to the Genevan Représentants. The French Foreign Ministry had refused to support the Genevan Représentants, but it supported the Dutch Patriots despite their ideology, because they were anti-Orange and anti-British.[11] In Mallet's view this policy was most ill-advised, first because it promoted a democratic revolution and secondly because it involved the risk of a confrontation with Britain, Prussia, and Austria. Moreover, the chosen agents of the Foreign Ministry in Holland were "incompetent adventurers" who provided it with a great amount of misinformation, and the publicity promoted by the government was an abuse of the confidence of French subjects. Not that he attempted to publish these views outright in the *Mercure.* He reserved them for confidants like Vernes and Etienne Dumont[12] and for a private notebook that he kept, a collection of miscellaneous jottings,[13] although

10. Ibid.

11. On the diplomacy of the Dutch revolutionary movement see Alfred Cobban, *Ambassadors and Secret Agents: The Diplomacy of the Earl of Malmesbury at The Hague* (London, 1954), passim. The character and history of the movement in its internal aspects during the decade before the French Revolution are analysed in R. R. Palmer, *The Age of the Democratic Revolution. A Political History of Europe and America, 1760–1800,* Vol. I: *The Challenge* (Princeton, N.J., 1959), pp. 323–40.

12. Mallet Du Pan to Vernes, Paris, September 28, 1786, Bibl. Genève, MS D.O.; Mallet Du Pan to Dumont, Paris, April 5, 1787, Blondel, ed., "Lettres inédites," p. 107.

13. "Observations sur Paris," September, 1787, Mallet Papers, London.

he also presumed to argue directly with the foreign minister who succeeded Vergennes, Montmorin.

Mallet's quarrel with "the Department" concerned most specifically their censorship of factual information he considered authenticated and his refusal to repeat in the *Mercure* information carried in
the gazettes favored by the government that he thought was false.
Now Mallet Du Pan was not carrying a torch in the cause of the unlimited freedom of the press. As can be seen in his correspondence
with Vergennes and Hennin at the time he was attempting to secure
permission to distribute his *Annales* in France, he was prepared to
submit to a censor and to what he called the expediencies (*les convenances*) of the kingdom, and he had contracted with Panckoucke
not to discuss policy in the *Mercure*. But he did not consider that his
obligation extended to the suppression of authenticated facts (unless these could be construed as libellous) or to the inclusion of what
he believed to be false information, however august the authority
that desired to use his journal.

The resistance he told Reybaz he had been putting up was only
partially successsful. He was informed by the under-secretary Rayneval in September, 1786, that in the future all articles on France
appearing under foreign datelines (this it will be remembered was
the practice long established at the *Mercure*) would be deleted. Rayneval and the Abbé Aubert had deleted a brief report of a revolt at
Lyon. What would seem to be a sufficiently innocuous piece of foreign news, the announcement of the death of Frederick the Great,
had also been deleted—doubtless, noted Mallet, because the first announcement of it was considered the prerogative of the *Gazette de
France*, a semiofficial journal, and the courier of the court had not yet
arrived with the news! In the world of "privileged" journalism, the
"scoop" was frowned upon. Then an article on Holland, "thoughtful, circumspect, and truthful," was deleted, after which followed
another warning from Rayneval. "The deletion from the *Mercure*
that is practiced at V[ersailles]," Mallet Du Pan exploded to his
private notebook, "proves that they will not tolerate the knowledge
of the least truth on the affair of Holland and that they wish the
public in France to be fed exclusively on the impostures of the *Gazette de Leyde* and that [the Gazette] of Amsterdam."[14] It seems

14. Ibid., September, 1786.

that Mallet tried once to outwit "the Department" by stating in the *Mercure*, in connection with a certain article consisting of extracts from the gazettes, that he denied responsibility for their contents; they were full of falsehoods that it was not his province to single out. The proofs for the *Mercure* only came back with this declaration deleted. Mallet's comment was: "The *Gazette de France* reports all the falsehoods of these gazettes . . . and I was forbidden to destroy them in order not to give the lie to this *Gazette.*"[15]

Mallet advised Vernes about the same time not to believe a word of the Dutch gazettes, which were, he said, filled with lies copied by the *Gazette de France*. Only the *Courier du Bas Rhin*, he said, was telling the truth, and it had therefore been excluded from the kingdom. As for himself, he had recently had nine whole pages on the Dutch affair excised, and since the few remaining paragraphs, taken thus out of context, conveyed a sense contrary to what he had intended, he himself deleted *them*. Never, he swore, would he print a line contrary to the truth or his conscience![16] What he meant, of course, by these somewhat high-sounding words, was that he would not print statements he believed to be untrue or advocate views of which he himself disapproved. Nearly a year later, reporting to Vernes another professional crisis over the Dutch affair wherein his refusal to support French policy almost caused him to lose the *Mercure*, he said that he had adopted as an invariable rule: "To pass over in silence as much as is required; but never a word against my conscience and the truth (*taire tout ce qu'on voudra; mais jamais un mot contre ma conscience et la vérité*)."[17] It was not a principle so much as a *modus vivendi* by which the journalist could preserve his intellectual integrity.

The professional crisis here referred to, which occurred in 1787, is known from an account Mallet Du Pan published of it in the *Mercure historique et politique* late in 1791. The account was written, in part, in order to pay tribute to Montmorin, who had been foreign minister in 1787, and whose conduct in regard to the political editor of the *Mercure* had been, Mallet felt, fair and reasonable. In 1787, when threatened with the loss of his position as editor, he wrote to

15. Ibid.
16. Mallet Du Pan to Vernes, Paris, September 28, 1786, Bibl. Genève, MS D.O.
17. Mallet Du Pan to Vernes, Paris, July 1, 1787, ibid.

Montmorin explaining, in effect, that he could not actively promote
the department's Dutch policy in the *Mercure* because he could not
promote democratic revolution and furthermore he did not think the
department should be doing so either. Montmorin did not take offense either at his resistance to being the department's mouthpiece
or to his observations on policy. Shortly thereafter, some of the
"vagabond Frenchmen," who had been paid in Holland for writing
pamphlets against the Prince and Princess of Orange, and now after
the Prussian intervention had fled back to France, joined forces with
Mirabeau. *They* tried to get Mallet ousted from the *Mercure* in order
to take it over themselves. "They wearied the Department of Foreign
Affairs with horrors and impostures about me," Mallet recollected,
"they painted me, *Mirabeau* in particular, as a *frenzied Anglomaniac*
who was betraying the Government by writing against its views; the
interest of the *Ministers* required that they seize the pen from me and
put it in the faithful hands of *Mirabeau* and his associates."[18] But
Montmorin was too fair-minded to agree, and the plot was foiled.
(Italics are those of Mallet Du Pan.)

Montmorin, however, did grant Mirabeau permission to publish a
journal, *Analyse des papiers anglais*, appearing first in November,
1787. It was, wrote Mallet in his private notebook for January, 1788,
"a periodic libel (*libelle périodique*) . . . where he passes judgment
on the politics of all of Europe. He insults me in it as usual, thinks
that I betray the Government, by which I am [said to be] paid."
(Mallet Du Pan was of course *not* paid by the government, nor was
he writing against its views.) The permission, remarked Mallet, was
a violation of the privilege of the *Mercure*, likewise of another periodical, *Le censeur universel anglais*, and Panckoucke had complained, but to no effect. The ministers, thought Mallet, were afraid
of Mirabeau just as they had been afraid of Linguet.[19] Brissot de
Warville was associated with Mirabeau in this enterprise, and by his
own admission this aspiring philosopher, so full of resentments and
frustrations, was the principal author of the running polemic it maintained for months against Mallet Du Pan.[20] In tone and manner this

18. *Mercure historique et politique*, 1791, no. 49 (Dec. 3), pp. 54–57n.
19. "Observations sur Paris," January, 1788, Mallet Papers, London.
20. Brissot, *Mémoires*, II, 38. On Brissot's personality as a revolutionary,
see Robert C. Darnton, "The Grub Street Style of Revolution: J.-P. Brissot,
Police Spy," *Journal of Modern History*, XL, no. 3 (Sept., 1968), 301–27.

polemic resembled Brissot's *Le Philadelphien à Genève.* Mallet Du
Pan was described here as "a man born in the heart of a republic who
devoted talents worthy of a better use to defending every bad cause
(*toutes les mauvaises causes*) . . . and injuring all free peoples."[21] He
had for example calumniated his Genevan compatriots, the Dutch,
the Americans, and those who in the British Parliament denounced
Warren Hastings.

The *Analyse des papiers anglais* concentrated on Mallet's cham-
pionship of Warren Hastings, which was a prominent theme of the
Journal politique de Bruxelles at this time. For Mallet, Hastings's
impeachment was a manifestation of the nefarious spirit of party, in-
carnate in Edmund Burke, who thus appeared in the *Mercure* as the
villain of the piece. None of the charges against Hastings, Mallet
pointed out, accused him of peculation or of the unjust acquisition
of wealth; mere clerks had come back to England from India wealth-
ier than he. There was no charge against him other than of having
served the state by political maneuvers that were perhaps unjust or
even violent but in no way served also the personal interest of the
accused. Hastings's conduct might well appear to other nations than
the English reprehensible, but only in so far as British policy in India
had itself been reprehensible, "essentially unjust and violent."[22]
Hastings's accusers were a "cabal," but fortunately the procedure in
the House of Lords was entirely judicial.[23] Mallet Du Pan called to
witness French authorities whose testimony was favorable to Hastings. He said that he had written a pamphlet on Hastings for which
he had consulted every Frenchman who had served in India, to find
that not one had failed to speak of Hastings with the highest praise.
He complained of being the object of the wrath of Hastings's critics,[24]
among whom the authors of the *Analyse des papiers anglais* were
conspicuous. The latter not only accused him of siding as usual with
despotism, but suggested that he had been bought by Hastings.[25]
When Mallet asserted in the *Mercure* (according to the *Analyse*)

21. *Analyse des papiers anglais,* I, no. 13 (Jan. 5–9, 1788), 331.
22. *Journal politique de Bruxelles,* 1787, no. 8 (Feb. 24), pp. 172–73.
23. Ibid., 1788, no. 3 (Jan. 19), p. 121, and no. 6 (Feb. 9), p. 87.
24. Mallet Du Pan to Vernes, Paris, August 26, 1788, Bibl. Genève, MS
D.O. The pamphlet to which he refers is unknown to me, and is not listed in
Quérard or in Matteucci's bibliography.
25. *Analyse des papiers anglais,* I, no. 15 (Jan. 15–19, 1788), 389–93, 397.

that certain Continental journals were misrepresenting statements taken from English papers on the subject of the Hastings trial, the *Analyse* retorted that it was only the *Journal politique de Bruxelles* that did this. The charge, it implied, was cowardly. It then went on, in a fine example of the *non sequitur*, to invite the impartial public to decide which one was cowardly, he [Brissot?] "who defends millions of men [the millions of India, presumably] who would never otherwise know their disinterested advocate [Burke]" or he who sided with "a rich and powerful individual known for having bought more than one writer."[26]

Then followed an accusation that Mallet Du Pan was putting French foreign policy in a poor light, not so much, apparently, from what he said as from what he did not say, or what he had said before becoming editor of the *Mercure* (where, in simple truth, he was able to say very little indeed). "It will always appear strange to us," declared the authors of the *Analyse*, "that in a paper devoted to directing, with an almost exclusive right, the opinion of the public in France, the task assumed seems to be to promote (*accréditer*) sentiments contrary to the interests of the French Government." Why? Because (and here the interests of the French government are assimilated by a stroke of the pen to the democratic revolutionary philosophy) the editor possesses a perverse spirit that has never left off calumniating the Republicans of America and the Patriots of Holland and has never written a line against the oppressors of the latter since the misfortune that befell them.[27]

At one point, shortly before these accusations appeared, Mallet Du Pan had written a letter of protest to the editors of the *Analyse*. It concerned the journal's charge, made also by Brissot formerly in *Le Philadelphien à Genève*, and now repeated, that Mallet Du Pan, in his account of the Genevan revolution of 1782, had calumniated "his friends, his brothers, and his benefactors." "Your editor," wrote Mallet to the *Analyse*, may at his ease calumniate my opinions . . . but a personal calumny deserves some attention, were it from the vilest man." It was doubtful, he went on, how capable the editor was of judging what Mallet had written about the last Genevan revolution, but, "well informed as he is," said Mallet sarcastically, "I must

26. Ibid., II, no. 34 (March 7–11, 1788), 138–40.
27. Ibid., p. 140.

tell him that I have never had, in the party he designates [the Repré-
sentants], brothers, relatives, or still less, benefactors. As my memory
may however be at fault, I call on him to name in his paper, without
verbosity or subterfuge, those of my friends, my brothers, and my
benefactors whom I have calumniated. He pretends to (*il annonce*)
so much delicacy and scrupulousness that he will surely not refuse me
the nominal proofs of his assertion, citing the page of my crime."
Mallet dropped what seems to be a veiled hint of a lawsuit: "I shall
await, Monsieur, until Friday, the use which you will judge it proper
to make of this letter, before taking further steps (*avant de passer
outre*)." The letter was printed in the *Analyse*.[28] The only reply was a
footnote, somewhat inconsequential but containing a statement that
the terms "friends," "brothers," and "benefactors" had merely been
meant to designate Mallet Du Pan's fellow citizens[29] in general, that
is, no particular individuals. Thus Brissot wriggled out of a tight
situation.

It was an age of a contentious style in journalism, and while Mallet
Du Pan did as much as any one to make political journalism more
dispassionate and analytical, he too knew how to fight and was a
hard hitter. He was, however, never a character assassin, as Brissot
revealed himself to be in his long feud with Mallet Du Pan. Mallet's
hostile view of revolutionaries was largely of theoretical origin, but it
had a personal component, too, deriving, one suspects, from his own
experience of Brissot and, to a somewhat lesser degree, of Clavière
and Mirabeau.

Embattled as he felt himself to be, Mallet Du Pan had the satisfaction nevertheless of knowing that he enjoyed Panckoucke's support and that an expansion in the circulation of the *Mercure* was attributed in large measure to himself. Panckoucke had been standing
by him all along. After somewhat less than two years at the *Mercure*,
Mallet remarked to Vernes that although the situation with regard
to "the Department" was trying, still there were compensations: "I
write, I let them mutilate my work at will, and I live well enough
(*je touche à bon marché*) on my salary, with which I am satisfied.

28. Mallet Du Pan to the editor of the *Analyse*, January 22, 1788, ibid., I,
no. 15 (Jan. 15–19, 1788), 400. I can explain the fact that the letter postdates the issue only by assuming that the issue was late, yet bore the date
when it should have come out.
29. Ibid.

Panckoucke, whom I cause to run a fever, makes up to me for these mortifications, out of magnanimity; his actions could not be more generous, and more than once I have been obliged to impose limits on them. It is true that the *Mercure* maintains itself at eleven thousand subscribers, despite its weakness. P.[anckoucke] thinks I count for something in this truly inconceivable success."[30] By "weakness" Mallet probably meant that to his mind the *Journal politique de Bruxelles* was, perforce, too much like a gazette, not enough like the substantial journal, the *Mémoires historiques,* that he had formerly published in Geneva.

It must be interjected here that Mallet's figure of eleven thousand subscribers at the close of 1785 is an exaggeration, if one consults the brief periodic statements of his account with Panckoucke in his records.[31] The statement for the year 1786 shows 10,258 subscriptions, an excess of 101 over the norm figure of 10,157 in 1783. For 1787 the excess was 392, bringing the total to 10,549. In 1789 (there is no figure for 1788) the total was 11,055. According to these records, it was not until 1788 or 1789 that the *Mercure's* circulation reached what Mallet reported to Vernes at the close of 1785. The discrepancy between what he told Vernes and what his financial records show is something of a puzzle, for padding figures would not have been in his line, all the more inconceivable here in that the recipient of the information was Vernes. One possible explanation of the difference between 11,000 subscriptions and the 10,258 that his account with Panckoucke for 1786 shows is that he may not have included in the latter figure the subscriptions for the *Journal de Genève.* The trouble with this reasoning is that the basic salary stated to have been paid to Mallet in the records is what he was by the terms of his contract to be paid for composing the *Journal de Genève,* which was to be the substance also of the political section of the *Mercure,* the *Journal politique de Bruxelles.* Possibly the figure 11,000 in December, 1785, was an estimate provided by Panckoucke for the forthcoming year. (It was not Mallet Du Pan but Panckoucke who handled the business end of the enterprise.) Or it might have been simply a mistake.

In any case, however, the trend of subscriptions was up, whatever

30. Mallet Du Pan to Vernes, Paris, December 9, 1785, Bibl. Genève, MS D.O.
31. In the Mallet Papers, London.

the actual figures. This can be in part explained, certainly, by the nature of contemporary events and the public's thirst for news. But at the same time, Mallet Du Pan was a superior reporter and Panckoucke, as Mallet said to Vernes in the letter in question, believed that he was instrumental in the journal's success. Mallet had, it will be remembered, his own individually developed sources of information, his correspondents, in addition to other gazettes; he was brief and to the point; he had a deft touch; he did discuss topics of general interest so far as he was permitted to do so, and his range was extensive. As a weekly news magazine, the *Journal politique de Bruxelles* covered a good deal of ground. Nor was it entirely political, even using the term "political" in a broad sense. Spiritualism and animal magnetism, for example, and M. Blanchard's crossing of the Channel by balloon were included.[32]

Nevertheless, despite his success, of which the very jealousy of Mirabeau and Brissot were continuing indications, a sense of isolation and a feeling of precariousness persisted in Mallet's mind. In October, 1786, he put down in his private notebook that the Abbé Beaudeau [sic] had attacked him in the *Journal de Paris* for writing disparagingly of monarchical states. This was, of course, a gross misreading of his work (it seems indeed rather astonishing) and Mallet Du Pan resented it. He felt that he had been insulted, and was convinced that if he had been someone whose station and influence were to be feared, Beaudeau's criticism would not have been printed; "but I am alone, isolated, a foreigner."[33] No doubt, Mallet's isolation was in part self-imposed. He held himself aloof from the society of other men of letters, professing to despise the whole tribe. His contempt for their acceptance of pensions and gratuities from the government was extreme; they must be toadies, since he who presumed to differ with the government was never offered a pension.[34] In general, he thought men of letters, at least in Paris, avaricious, jealous, and treacherous (and in the case of Mirabeau and Brissot he had indeed some reason to think so). Neither in his personal style nor in his outlook did he feel congenial with any considerable number of them.

32. *Journal politique de Bruxelles*, 1785, no. 24 (June 11), p. 26; ibid., no. 4 (Jan. 22), p. 178.
33. "Observations sur Paris," November, 1786, Mallet Papers, London.
34. Ibid., July and September, [1786], and June, [1788]; Mallet Du Pan to Vernes, Paris, September 28, 1786, Bibl. Genève, MS D.O.

There is no record to my knowledge of his frequenting a salon or a club. He did not even attempt to make contacts that might have smoothed his way at the Department of Foreign Affairs. There was Hennin, for example, an undersecretary, a relative by marriage, and a person to whom Mallet was indebted for having interceded with Vergennes, however unsuccessfully, on behalf of the *Annales . . . pour servir de suite aux Annales de M. Linguet.* Mallet apparently made no attempt to pay his respects. He had been in Paris two years when he received from Hennin a request on behalf of an author, a certain baron de Sainte-Croix, who wanted his new book on the history of English naval power to be reviewed in the *Mercure* by Gaillard and thought Mallet Du Pan might be able to arrange it. (It was of course not Mallet's province to assign reviews for the literary section of the *Mercure*, and as things turned out the review was written by Mallet Du Pan himself,[35] the author's reactions being unknown.) Hennin wrote Mallet that he had told Sainte-Croix that he, Hennin, had little right to make such a request because although he and Mallet were related, he did not recall ever having seen him! "You seem to have shunned Versailles," said Hennin.[36]

Mallet Du Pan may well have been shunning Versailles, simply unable to face anybody in "the Department" with which his relations had been so unsatisfactory, indeed unpleasant, for a number of years. Hennin had been obliging, certainly, but Hennin was part of the organization and shared its viewpoint. Possibly Mallet had even feared—dreadful thought!—that he might have to encounter Vergennes himself.

Sir Bernard Mallet, in his biography of Mallet Du Pan, relates a story of Mallet's relations with Vergennes for which he gives no source and which is patently apocryphal. In 1787, he says, Vergennes refused to accept an article by Mallet on Holland and wrote one in a contrary sense that the editor was asked to insert in its place. Obtaining an audience with Vergennes at Versailles, Mallet told the minister that, rather than do this, he would resign his position. Thereupon Vergennes, seizing his hand, replied: "This must not be; you will give up your article, I shall give up mine, and we will remain

35. *Mercure,* 1786, no. 28 (July 15), pp. 104–21.
36. Hennin to Mallet Du Pan, Versailles, March 28, 1786, Bibl. de l'Institut, Papiers et correspondance de Hennin, MS 1269, No. 38.

friends."[37] This sounds like a garbled version of what passed between Mallet Du Pan and Montmorin in 1787, after the death of Vergennes, which occurred in February of that year. All the evidence about Mallet's relations with Vergennes points to a persistent mistrust on both sides, and no such display of cordiality on the part of the minister.

As for Mallet's feeling, his rancor against Vergennes, in fact, and his contempt, amounted to an obsession. Taking note of Vergennes' death in his private journal, he wrote: "M. de Vergennes used to say: After an author, what I despise most is a book." He then recorded further damaging information, to the effect that Vergennes was said to have left eighteen to twenty million livres, the greatest fortune of any minister since Mazarin, that he and his wife were well known to be extraordinarily avaricious, that the lady's personal history had been so dubious that the minister had only married her through fear of hell-fire, on the occasion of a serious illness.[38] Some of this gossip he repeated to his friend Etienne Dumont, who was in England at the time, adding: "I have assembled important materials on this great man, from which to compose a view (*tableau*) of his ministry. It will assuredly not be a lampoon, but thoughtful men will be able to assess rightly that reputation unfairly acquired (*escamotée*), I know not how, in all Europe. But I adjure you to be silent on this last point; you would not want me to be thrown into the Bastille."[39]

Any hope that the death of Vergennes might bring about some improvement in his relations with "the Department" was soon discarded. He had changed superiors but not his servitude, he said to Vernes, for though Montmorin was a man of very different temperament from Vergennes, the new minister's inexperience led him to depend on his undersecretaries (*premiers commis*). Mallet said he had already offended the one—he was referring to Rayneval—who was carrying on the policy of Vergennes in regard to Holland. He gloated to Vernes, as to Dumont, over "the veritable harvest of materials" on Vergennes with which he had been furnished.[40] (How he had come into possession of them will be considered in another con-

37. B. Mallet, *Mallet du Pan and the French Revolution*, p. 76.
38. "Observations sur Paris," February, [1787], Mallet Papers, London.
39. Mallet Du Pan to Dumont, Paris, April 5, 1787, Blondel, ed., "Lettres inédites," p. 107.
40. Mallet Du Pan to Vernes, Paris, July 1, 1787, Bibl. Genève, MS D.O.

nection.) But his disgust with those who carried on French foreign policy after Vergennes, principally the undersecretaries, mounted to such a point that he was actually writing to Dumont, only a year later: "We have spoken ill, and justly, of M. de Vergennes; he was an eagle in comparison with the barn owls who have succeeded him." [41] At times the department did not even seem to know its own mind. Both the *Gazette de France* and the *Mercure* might be furnished items to publish, only to have them deleted once they were in print. "Uncertainty from weakness and total incapacity," was Mallet's verdict.[42]

The censorship of "the Department" continued to be constant and all-inclusive, in regard to domestic as well as foreign events. On April 17, 1787, Mallet noted in his private journal that his announcement of Necker's *Mémoire justificatif* and of the dismissal of Calonne had been deleted, "doubly," by Rayneval and Aubert. It had been scratched out in the most thorough fashion, lest even a comma escape! These gentlemen had held also that it was forbidden to speak of resignations in any other terms than the *Gazette de France*.[43]

In the weeks following the writing of his letter to Montmorin concerning his position on French policy in Holland, Mallet Du Pan was particularly depressed. He told Etienne Dumont that the "storms" in which he was living were affecting his health and his mind, and he did not know whether he would always have the strength to withstand the governmental vexations that the Dutch affair had aggravated.[44] He was in a mood, it appears, to think of looking elsewhere for employment, and an opportunity seemed to develop through Dumont, to whom Mallet felt close enough to beg Dumont to keep an eye on his son Jean-Louis, a boy of twelve, whom he was sending to England for his education in the care of a young "milord." The boy needed to be got away from an over-protective home environment, and the schools in Paris, Mallet thought, were the worst in Europe, whereas he felt confidence in young Lord Fincastle, who had spent the winter in Paris with them. So it was best that Jean-Louis go to

41. Mallet Du Pan to Dumont, April 28, 1788, Blondel, ed., "Lettres inédites," p. 110.

42. "Observations sur Paris," December, [1787], Mallet Papers, London.

43. Ibid., [April] 17, [1787].

44. Mallet Du Pan to Dumont, June 2, 1787, Blondel, ed., "Lettres inédites," p. 109.

England, but the father would be easier in his mind if he knew Dumont would see his son from time to time, be ready to advise him, and report on his progress.[45]

Now Dumont was at that time frequenting the society of the intellectuals who surrounded Lord Shelburne and was in a position, as he thought, to do his friend and compatriot a service, while at the same time adding to the luster of the Shelburnian circle. The correspondence on the matter dates from 1788. In that year Benjamin Vaughan, Shelburne's secretary, was publishing a journal of opinion, *The Repository*,[46] and an offer was made to Mallet Du Pan, through Dumont, to become associated with this undertaking. It came about the time that Mallet was being assaulted in the *Analyse des papiers anglais*, and he entertained the proposition for some months before turning it down. In view of the fact that Mallet discussed with Dumont as a major consideration the general character of *The Repository*, it would seem that the offer involved Mallet's becoming an editor, perhaps going to England, and this conclusion seems to follow also in view of the terms of his contract with Panckoucke, which specified that he was not to work on any other journal or "gazette de politique" while with the *Mercure*. As he would have had to give up the *Mercure* had he engaged to be a principal contributor to *The Repository*, he would hardly have been able to consider any other terms than a full-time association. He clearly did not consider that his contract with Panckoucke precluded his making occasional contributions to other journals, for he told Dumont that he would send some articles so that the editors of *The Repository* might see whether his views were acceptable to them, and he expected his authorship to be acknowledged unless the tenor of the articles was changed, in which case he should not in any manner be designated as the author.[47] Ultimately, Mallet turned down the *Repository* offer on the ground that the journal was not of a type to which either his ideas or his talents were suited, and was in general a poor sort of publication not likely to succeed. He wrote Dumont:

45. Mallet Du Pan to Dumont, Paris, April 5, 1787, ibid., p. 105.
46. Etienne Dumont, *Souvenirs sur Mirabeau et sur les deux premières assemblées législatives*, ed. J. Bénétruy (Paris, [c. 1950]), pp. 11 (Introduction) and 261.
47. Mallet Du Pan to Dumont, June 19, 1788, Blondel, ed., "Lettres inédites," p. 111.

It belongs to the category of *journaux raisonneurs*, in my opinon the lowest form of journal. I had imagined, on the contrary, that you were thinking of an assembling of factual materials, selected, linked together, examined when doubtful, substantiated when true, assembled with discernment and from reliable sources. . . .

The political part, such as you show it to me, would be extremely difficult to handle and remain often completely sterile: *to single out the errors* [committed] *in regard to commerce, population, the usurpations against peoples, to trace the development of principles, to point out the epoch when a truth begins to penetrate a nation,* etc. . . . all that is the work of centuries and not of a contemporary journalist; he will make of it nothing but wordy twaddle (*bavardage*) like Linguet and other French phrasemakers (*verbiageurs*).[48] [Mallet Du Pan's italics.]

In November of 1788 Mallet Du Pan wrote Dumont a letter from which it is clear that he and the direction of *The Repository* were not coming together, though a small, a very small, opening was still left for the possible resumption of negotiations; "Whatever may be the fate of *The Repository,* I will never refuse to be of service to it when I can, since you and mylord L[ansdowne] are interested in it."[49]

At the same time, there was a corollary offer which Mallet was eager to take up, a correspondence with Shelburne himself. He would be flattered, Mallet said, always assuming, however, that what was wanted was the sort of thing he was able to produce. He must be absolutely free to express his own views. "Without being either *frondeur* or paradoxical, it often happens that I see differently from the articulate public (*la voix publique*)." As for the content, he did not suppose Lord Lansdowne wanted a gazette or expected an infallible report on persons and things. In short, Mallet was proposing an interpretation of the news. As for pecuniary arrangements, this was not a major consideration: "You know me well enough to assure mylord Lansdowne that whatever he does, my desires will be met, if his are by my correspondence."[50]

48. Ibid., pp. 110–11.
49. Mallet Du Pan to Dumont, Paris, November 19, 1788, ibid., pp. 113–14. Shelburne had become marquis of Lansdowne.
50. Ibid.

The matter of *The Repository* was still hanging fire in some form in March of 1789, when, however, it was finally disposed of. "I cannot sacrifice my time and my liberty," wrote Mallet, "to an enterprise that every day appears to be on the point of aborting and that seems to me to have had up to now only a very weak success. I would have sought in it consideration, not money, but it seems that neither one nor the other will be found there." As for the correspondence, he said he would begin it in a few days.[51] (If it exists, I have not seen it.)

There was no note of disappointment in what he wrote Dumont, for meanwhile another, quite different, and more attractive opportunity had seemed to open up. When he rejected the *Repository* offer definitely, he mentioned to Dumont "a long and important labor . . . for a foreign Court" that had been taking all the time he could spare from the *Mercure*,[52] and he was telling Vernes simultaneously that for the past year he had been working harder than ever, strengthening his knowledge of history and public law. For he had been entrusted with a task of a sensitive nature (*une besogne délicate*) for a foreign court and expected this experience to lead to a career "more honorable and more useful than that of letters."[53]

It is evident that what Mallet Du Pan yearned for was "consideration," honor. As political editor of the *Mercure* he was well paid, but he had felt not only threatened but humiliated. Actually, his wishes were more positive than the simple desire not to be interfered with. He wanted what he had to say to be valued by people who controlled policy. He began to think of himself as an analyst whose expertise merited government employment, which in turn would bring with it the "consideration" he did not enjoy as a journalist. Not that Mallet had come to despise his own profession; he simply felt vulnerable and thwarted in it.

The foreign court was that of Sweden, and the story connected with these statements to Dumont and Vernes is curious, concerning as it does an episode in Mallet's career that shows how he could be right royally (in every sense of the word) taken in, despite all his vaunted professional skepticism.

51. Mallet Du Pan to Dumont, Paris, March 11, 1789, ibid., p. 115.
52. Ibid.
53. Mallet Du Pan to Vernes, Paris, March 18, 1789, Bibl. Genève, MS D.O.

The Swedish agent in the business was a certain Mouradgea d'Ohsson, *chevalier* of the Order of Vasa, a Turkish subject (originally at least) of Armenian extraction who had been at one time Swedish chargé d'affaires at Constantinople but who was when Mallet came to know him residing in Paris, where he completed and began to publish in 1787 a comprehensive work on the institutions of the Ottoman Empire, *Tableau général de l'empire ottoman.*[54] Mallet Du Pan, who had high standards, was immensely impressed. In March of 1787 he called the attention of readers of the literary section of the *Mercure* to the *Tableau,* then forthcoming,[55] and reviewed it a year later in the *Mercure* with the highest praise.[56] He also undertook in 1787 to promote the work in England, requesting Dumont to have the prospectus carried by some English periodicals.[57] Mallet's interest in the book was not purely scholarly and literary. It pleased him profoundly that the Ottoman Empire, whose laws, he said, were thought by Europeans to be all comprised in the Koran, should be shown as a civilized polity of European type, and not barbarian. Although it was a theocracy with an identity of the civil and religious authority, and was therefore despotic in the primary sense of the word, it was not, he said, arbitrary, for there was a great body of laws and the prince commanded and was obeyed only according to fixed laws.[58] The work moreover would show up to disadvantage the philosophes, who propagated the Turkish myth to justify the aggressions of their idol, the Tsarina Catherine, against the Ottoman Empire. They would of course try to sabotage it in France, hence all the more should it be advertised in England. Mallet had written Dumont, when sending him the prospectus:

> This work faces another obstacle [the first obstacle was that Frenchmen who could afford to buy so costly a production were not that much interested in learning]: the philosophers of Paris find it very legitimate for an empress who deified Voltaire and who does not believe in the Divine to take over the Ottoman

54. *Biographie universelle, ancienne et moderne* . . . , 85 vols. (Paris, 1811–1862), XXX, 332–34.
55. *Mercure,* 1787, no. 12 (March 24), pp. 186–88.
56. Ibid., 1788, no. 11 (March 15), pp. 103–19.
57. Mallet Du Pan to Dumont, June 2, 1787, Blondel, ed., "Lettres inédites," pp. 107–8.
58. *Mercure,* 1788, no. 11 (March 15), p. 107.

Empire, where the Encyclopedia is not read. They flatter them-selves that under the kindly (*douce*) influence of Catherine II Greece will recover its prosperity and they will be able to go there to form philosophic coteries; they are convinced that learned and enlightened men have the right to drive out the uncivilized and barbarous Turks and that the earth should be-long to the one who pays the best pensions to the Aristippuses and the Epicuruses.[59]

What a chance to kill, or at least maim, two very large birds with one stone, the philosophes and Catherine II! There was, indeed, a third bird whom it would be a satisfaction to hit, though of course he could no longer feel the blow—the late comte de Vergennes, who in Mal-let's view had sold out the Turks to the tsarina.[60]

Mallet must at the outset simply have regarded the chevalier Mouradgea d'Ohsson as a "find" who could provide the political editor of the *Mercure* with first-hand information wherewith to counter the lying gazettes that were the mouthpieces of French policy—information about Russo-Turkish affairs first of all (whence, if not this source, the mass of materials he had accumulated on Ver-gennes?), and then about developments in "the North," i.e., the Baltic. No doubt Mouradgea d'Ohsson was quickly impressed with the intelligence and the potential usefulness of a spirit so congenial in both letters and politics. No doubt also Mouradgea d'Ohsson, or at any rate the Swedish ambassador, the baron de Staël-Holstein, had heard of Mallet's reputation with "the Department" as a "prob-lem child." And they had of course been reading the *Mercure*, espe-cially the political section, along with other journals.

There are signs of the progress of an acquaintance between Mallet and Mouradgea d'Ohsson early in 1787. Mallet noted in his private journal in April of that year that he had dined at the house of the "Chevalier de Mouradgea."[61] In April of 1788, when the chevalier went to London to see Lansdowne on his way to Stockholm, he car-

59. Mallet Du Pan to Dumont, June 2, 1787, Blondel, ed., "Lettres in-édites," p. 108.

60. Mallet Du Pan to Vernes, Paris, September 11, 1787, Bibl. Genève, MS D.O.

61. "Observations sur Paris," April 17 or 18 (it is not clear which from the MS), [1787], Mallet Papers, London.

ried a letter from Mallet to Dumont.[62] When it was that the Swedish ambassador, De Staël, became interested is not clear. Did he act only after cordial relations had been established between Mallet Du Pan and Mouradgea d'Ohsson, or was it he who first conceived of using Mouradgea d'Ohsson to get in touch with a journalist who might be useful to Sweden? In any case, De Staël's diplomatic dispatches in 1789 leave no doubt that it was the skill of the Levantine that carried off the business.

What the ambassador wanted was a good press for the king of Sweden, Gustavus III, and the king's struggle against the tsarina. He was afraid that an alliance might be in the making between France and Russia, since Versailles was not concealing the disfavor with which it regarded the recent rapprochement of Sweden with Britain and Prussia—a relation that must nevertheless be consolidated since Britain and Prussia were the only great powers willing to dispute the field with Russia. France was moreover playing Russia's game in Poland.[63] Having noticed that in "several gazettes" Swedish affairs were done poorly or in a way derogatory to Sweden, the ambassador had made arrangements, he said, with "le sieur Mallet Du Pan, auteur du *Mercure de France*," to present a different picture, both in the *Mercure* and in a brochure where he would examine Russia's policy with regard to Sweden and other European powers. The matter had been arranged completely by "le sieur Mouradgea," since the ambassador could not have appeared without compromising his position. "It is to his pains and his intelligence," wrote De Staël, "that I owe the author's absolute ignorance that it is I who have employed his pen."[64]

Some six months later, De Staël sent to King Gustavus a copy of "the work that I was authorized to have done by M. Mallet du Pan. . . . I cannot congratulate myself sufficiently," he added, "on the warm zeal the Chevalier Mouradgea shows every time it is a question of doing something useful for Your Majesty's service. It is to his

62. Mallet Du Pan to Dumont, April 22, 1788, Blondel, ed., "Lettres inédites," p. 109.

63. Baron de Staël-Holstein, dispatches of January 25 and 29, February 1, March 5 and 12, 1789, *Correspondance diplomatique du baron de Staël-Holstein, ambassadeur de Suède en France. Documents inédits sur la révolution* (1783–1799), ed. L. Léouzon Le Duc (Paris, 1881), pp. 95–98.

64. De Staël, dispatch of April 2, 1789, ibid., pp. 98–99. My translation.

indefatigable efforts and his careful surveillance of M. Mallet that I owe in great part the favorable viewpoint (*bonté*) of this work, as well as the different articles that are inserted from time to time in the *Mercure de France*."[65]

The notices about Sweden in the *Mercure* (that is, the *Journal politique de Bruxelles*) were indeed favorable to Gustavus III, who was acting vigorously to restore royal authority after a long interim of noble dominance in Sweden (the "freedom era"), and to prosecute a strong anti-Russian foreign policy. In his résumé of the political events of the year 1788, published in January, 1789, Mallet Du Pan wrote of the tsarina's successes against the Turks being offset by her political reverses in the North: Sweden, allied with the Porte, had kept in the Baltic the Russian fleet that was about to sail for the Mediterranean. Although Russia had persuaded the Danes to invade Sweden and forced King Gustavus to hasten from Finland, where he was fighting Russia, to defend his lands against Denmark, the Danes had been obliged to withdraw by threats from Britain and Prussia, so that the king of Sweden had found time to arm his people and inspire them with zeal, with the result that he could negotiate from a position of advantage. In Sweden, as in Turkey and in Poland, said Mallet Du Pan, there had been a "political resurrection," operating in all three states against the influence of Russia.[66] Succeeding numbers of the *Mercure* carried on the theme of "political resurrection" in Sweden under the leadership of Gustavus III, with caustic references to attempts of "intriguers" to vilify him and to the credence given in foreign gazettes to the rumors they were circulating. Among these rumors, for instance, was one that the king had actually no intention of working with the Diet and that a force of Dalecarlians devoted to him was on the march to terrorize it. The *Journal politique de Bruxelles* said this was an absurd invention, for only the Diet could give effect to the projects of the government, and moreover, the king was certain of the support of three of the four orders, namely, of the clergy, bourgeoisie, and peasants. Opposition could come only from the nobility.[67] The journal described the enthusiasm manifested for the king by an immsense crowd of people

65. De Staël, dispatch of September 17, 1789, ibid., pp. 226–27. My translation.
67. Ibid., no. 9 (Feb. 28), pp. 145–46.
66. *Journal politique de Bruxelles*, 1789, no. 1 (Jan. 3), pp. 2–5.

at the opening of the Diet,[68] and praised the king's leadership in presenting and securing the adoption of a constitutional enactment, the Act of Union and Security, conferring on him complete authority to conduct foreign policy while leaving to the Diet the power of the purse, and granting commoners the right to acquire noble property and to hold any office in the state.[69] While underlining the importance of royal leadership, it kept insisting that government in Sweden was not about to become an absolute monarchy, as had happened in Denmark in 1660.[70]

The *Mercure* insisted again, also, on the unreliability of the information carried on Sweden, Poland, and Turkey in the "public papers," especially Dutch gazettes, whereas the editor of the *Journal politique de Bruxelles* had taken care to present only authenticated news.[71]

That these articles on Sweden were suffered by "the Department" to be published invites comment. It attests perhaps to a certain impotence felt by authority in the presence of the vast turmoil of opinion that accompanied the elections to the Estates General, then going on. Or just possibly the picture of the vigorous leadership of Gustavus III may have appealed to ministerial authority (to Montmorin, specifically) as the way a king ought to act in such a constitutional crisis as France was then going through, resembling in some respects the Swedish crisis.

There is no reason to think that Mallet Du Pan in these articles was simply taking dictation from Mouradgea d'Ohsson. He could no more have repeated to order what the Swedish agent told him to say than he could have put into the *Mercure* what Rayneval had wanted him to put there, against his judgment, about Holland. Lest this seem too much an argument a priori, we need only turn to Mallet's private correspondence, where we find exactly the same account of things, with the same interpretation. To Vernes, with whom he was always uninhibited, he wrote: "The King of Sweden conducts himself in the most distinguished manner, and people do not know all the dangers he has run and the intrepid spirit he has shown." Describing the way in which the king effectively dealt with incipient treachery in Goth-

68. Ibid., no. 10 (March 7), pp. 1–2.
69. Ibid., no. 13 (March 28), pp. 153–65.
70. Ibid., pp. 191–92.   71. Ibid., p. 148n.

enburg, after which, going out into the streets, he appealed with equal success to the citizenry, and finally clinched his victory by a superb address to the Diet, Mallet concluded: "That's what it is to talk like a man (*Voilà ce qui s'appelle parler en homme*)!" The *Gazette de Leyde*, sold to Russia, had told a thousand falsehoods about these events.[72]

No doubt, the source of Mallet's information was tainted, but he must have realized this, and what he made out of the data was shrewd and informed journalism, while the bias that shows in what he wrote was one that he had come by independently. To destroy faction and achieve a national consensus under royal leadership—the whole drift of Mallet's thinking predisposed him to admire a régime that seemed to be doing these things. That money passed from the Swedish government to Mallet Du Pan is true—more of that presently. But money certainly was not what won him to be an admirer of Gustavus III and pro-Swedish.

The promised brochure could not be sent to King Gustavus until September of 1789, owing to its having had to be printed abroad.[73] Now a pamphlet exists that is almost certainly this work De Staël said he had procured from Mallet Du Pan. It bears the title *Du péril de la balance politique de l'Europe* (London, 1789), and was anonymously published. It is an account of the expansion of Russia under Catherine II and the conclusion is that all states have an interest in stopping Russia, most immediately the Porte, the North, and Germany. There needs to be especially an alliance of the Baltic powers to contain Russia and maintain the balance of power.

The question is, did Mallet Du Pan write this brochure? It has been attributed to him, but also to Claude Charles de Peyssonnel,[74] who has been credited in addition with another anti-Russian work published in 1788.[75] The latter work has never been attributed, so

72. Mallet Du Pan to Vernes, Paris, March 18, 1789, Bibl. Genève, MS D.O.

73. De Staël, dispatches of April 2 and September 17, 1789, *Correspondance diplomatique*, pp. 99, 127.

74. A.-A. Barbier, *Dictionnaire des ouvrages anonymes*, 3rd ed., 4 vols. (Paris, 1872–1879), III, 824, attributes the work to Mallet Du Pan. J. M. Quérard, *La France littéraire*, 12 vols. (Paris, 1827–1864), attributes it to Mallet Du Pan in V, 473; but in VII, 111, he attributes it to Peyssonnel. The *Biographie universelle*, XXXIII, 559, attributes it to Peyssonnel.

75. *Examen du livre institulé: Considérations sur la guerre actuelle des*

far as is known, to Mallet Du Pan, and in the opinion of the present writer the pamphlet *Du péril de la balance politique* did not come from his pen, either. Most certainly Mallet was involved in the preparation of a pamphlet like *Du péril de la balance politique* at the solicitation of the government of Sweden, for there is not only the testimony of De Staël, there are the heretofore noted references in Mallet's own correspondence with Dumont and Vernes to a work in preparation for a foreign court. Moreover, Mallet wrote Vernes in March of 1789, apropos of a discussion of the internal and international affairs of Sweden: "A little work that will be sent to you from I don't know where in a month at the latest [Mallet was optimistic] will make you aware of many things."[76] On the other hand, Mallet did not actually admit his authorship of this "little work." One must take into account furthermore his reluctance in general to publish anonymously. He had assured Reybaz in 1785, when denying authorship of the anonymous pamphlet relating to Mirabeau's brochure on the Caisse d'Escompte, that he would never write a line without signing it.[77] This is no proof of course that he never thereafter did write anonymously but it establishes a presumption. Anonymity did not accord with Mallet's strong sense of literary property, his pride in his work, his willingness to run the risk, if he published at all, in order to have the credit; nor did he want to be criticized for what he had not written. As for the contents of *Du péril de la balance politique*, the general tenor of the brochure was certainly in accord with Mallet's view that the potential objects of Russian aggression should be encouraged to resist. But history in this work is not handled in Mallet's manner. The account is simplistic and one-sided: the tsarina is a wicked woman who began her career of crime by murdering her husband. She, and she alone, was the guilty party in the partition of Poland, the other partitioners acting only in self-defense. The treatment of Tsar Peter III—his admiration for Frederick the Great, his death—is especially sentimentalized. Mallet would have been sar-

---

Turcs, par Volney (Amsterdam, [Paris], 1788). Attributed to Peyssonnel in the *Biographie universelle*, XXXIII, 559.

76. Mallet Du Pan to Vernes, Paris, March 18, 1789, Bibl. Genève, MS D.O.

77. Mallet Du Pan to Reybaz, October 24 [October 23, 1785], Bibl. Genève, MS fr. 916, Papiers Reybaz, f. 83–84.

donic rather than sentimental. As for the style, it lacks his terseness and incisiveness.

If Mallet Du Pan did not write this pamphlet, what then did he do for the Swedish government? Perhaps the problem may be resolved by a phrase in De Staël's dispatch to King Gustavus on sending him the brochure, referring to "the work that I was authorized to have done by M. Mallet Du Pan (*l'ouvrage qu'on m'a autorisé de faire faire par M. Mallet du Pan*)." The implication in the terminology is that Mallet Du Pan was the agent who caused the work to be produced, not necessarily that he was himself the writer. It would seem quite possible that Mallet did a good deal of research, as he said, then farmed out the writing to a competent author whose general position was already known—say Peyssonnel—and with whom he would have discussed the substance of the work.

Whether or not Mallet wanted to be the actual author, and the signs are that he did not, he wanted the credit with the Swedish government for having contributed to carrying out its purposes. Money is mentioned in the correspondence of De Staël. It seems to concern primarily the brochure, although De Staël obviously regards the *Mercure* articles as part of the arrangement. The sum was 3,000 livres,[78] and it apparently was to include the costs of publication, such as the printer's bill and shipping charges, all of which matters were to be handled by Mallet Du Pan, beside the fee of the writer, whoever he was.

Mallet would probably have considered it fair that he himself should receive something as compensation for his time spent on the brochure—but not for what he did in the *Mercure*. For that he was being salaried by Panckoucke and he had no expenses; it was part of his job on the *Journal politique de Bruxelles* to maintain the contacts, by correspondence or otherwise, whence he derived the information from which to compose the *Mercure*, the information that made the journal something more than a gazette of gazettes. The material he got from Mouradgea d'Ohsson was simply a reporter's "haul." Mallet did not have to be paid for using it. As for the interpretation with which the facts he got were clothed, the Swedes were assuredly not buying *that*. They were indeed not buying it in any-

78. De Staël, dispatch of September 17, 1789, *Correspondance diplomatique*, p. 127.

thing he might write for them. (Perhaps this is one reason why Mallet ended by backing away, as is here supposed, from writing *Du péril de la balance politique*—he might well have balked at the whitewashing of the late king of Prussia, for example.) Mallet Du Pan was always very clear in his own mind about what he was being remunerated for. His skills were for hire, but his judgment could not be traded. If a client liked what he had to say, Mallet Du Pan esteemed that he should be paid for the writing. But the money would not determine what he said. Nor, really, would any other form of payment determine it.

In this case, it was not money that was to be the principal reward, not in Mallet's own mind, that is, but the opportunity for a career "more honorable and more useful" than that of journalism. De Staël probably had no idea of this, but Mallet was dealing not with him but with Mouradgea d'Ohsson, who according to De Staël was a subtle man. The intermediary's skill in this matter lay less, perhaps, in successfully concealing the ambassador's role than in handling the political editor of the *Mercure*. One imagines that he quite comprehended the nature of Mallet's dissatisfaction, his pride, and his professional ethics as writer and journalist, besides having formed a pretty accurate impression of Mallet's political views and his intelligence. One imagines also how such an agent might, without actually promising anything, have indicated that a post in a Swedish ministry, that of foreign affairs no doubt, might await the demonstration of Mallet's talents in the matter under discussion.

Of course, no such post materialized. Conceivably Mallet received an offer of employment from Stockholm and turned it down, but if so no trace of it has been found, and it seems improbable. De Staël's correspondence mentions only a monetary compensation, as if nothing else had ever been considered in reality. Not until he became an agent of the Allied powers against revolutionary France did Mallet Du Pan obtain anything like the position he had thought of in 1789. Great must have been his disappointment, and bitter must have been the realization that he had been fooled, misled as much by his own deficiency of skepticism or excess of wishful thinking as by the duplicity of the Swedish agent, Mouradgea d'Ohsson.

So Mallet Du Pan was to remain as political editor of the *Mercure* until his emigration in 1792. There were new and substantial evidences of Panckoucke's appreciation that must have been gratifying. In November of 1789 a new contract was negotiated by which Mallet's salary was advanced from 7,200 livres annually (the base salary in the contract of 1784) to 12,000 livres annually, or 1,000 livres payable each month. In addition, he would receive 20 sous for each subscription above five thousand to the *Journal de Genève,* and for the *Journal politique de Bruxelles,* 20 sous for each subscription above 10,157, which was the figure established by the arrangement signed between Panckoucke and M. de Vergennes in 1783. Panckoucke would continue to defray the cost of gazettes and other materials, and would pay 2,400 livres annually for the assistance of a secretary. There was now added also a pension agreement by which Panckoucke agreed to pay his editor 3,000 livres annually for life in the event he had to give up the *Mercure* because of illness or infirmity, and if he died, to pay his widow 1,500 livres annually. Moreover, Mallet would receive a retirement annuity of 3,000 livres at the end of fifteen years' service as editor, counting from March, 1784. These "fringe benefits" were stated in the contract to be in recognition of the success of the *Journal politique,* "M. Panckoucke recognizing with pleasure that he is obliged to him for the constant success it has had since the year 1784 and continues to have." The name of Mallet Du Pan was to appear at the head of each journal.[79]

With the advent of the Revolution in France, Mallet Du Pan became in some measure again, as formerly in Geneva, an active participant in politics. Until then he was, perforce, passive, unless his altercation with "the Department" over the Dutch business be considered a form of political activity. But as this very altercation indicates, in these last years of the old monarchy he was not intellectually passive. More than that, his political ideas changed significantly, if not radically. He was not the same in 1789 as he had been in 1784.

In part the change was owing to the violently negative reaction he experienced against France, or rather, Paris, from which he gener-

79. Contract between Mallet Du Pan and Charles Panckoucke, Paris, November 3, 1789, Bibl. Genève, MS D.O. A duplicate exists in the Mallet Papers, London.

alized. This in turn had a personal source in his resentment against the conditions of his work, which extended to a revulsion against the government and the society.

In his view the government was at one and the same time despotic and weak, controlled by a selfish aristocracy and by ministers having no fixed principles but living from day to day and hand to mouth, changing their directives with every wind. Within a year of his arrival Mallet recorded a reflection on an imprisonment, a very brief detention, of the dramatist Beaumarchais, for having published an insolent letter to some one or other in the *Journal de Paris*. He noted the intervention of the duc de Chartres and the comte d'Artois, and the laughter of the public. The punishment was too great for an admonition, too little if Beaumarchais had been in the wrong, mused Mallet. "Despotism knows no orderly procedure; it goes always from weakness to tyranny, leaves the fault unpunished or punishes it arbitrarily."[80] The arrest of Cardinal de Rohan in the affair of the diamond necklace led him to reflect that once when the cardinal had laid a "sacrilegious hand" upon the goods of the poor and the Parlement was about to publish a decree against him, the royal court had had the case evoked and protected him. Now, when a great lady (the queen) was involved in the accusation against him, he was seized and thrown into a state prison for a still unproven pickpocket act. Each Frenchman should ask himself, wrote Mallet, "If this can happen to the Grand Almoner of France, how would it be with me?"[81] It seemed to him, moreover, that this aristocratic and despotic government had no feeling for popular suffering. The drought in 1785 had occasioned great suffering and Mallet had had many letters from the provinces, from curés, from noblemen, even from peasant proprietors (*laboureurs*), begging him to inform the king through the *Mercure* of their misery.[82]

In Mallet's appraisal of the struggle of the monarchy with the financial crisis there was no disposition to regard Calonne or even Brienne as the champion of enlightened absolutism against the selfish interests of aristocracy. It was of course Calonne who as controller general, really minister, of finance (1783–1787), revealed the crown's parlous situation, as Necker had failed to do, and who laid

80. "Observations sur Paris," March, 1785, Mallet Papers, London.
81. Ibid., August, [1785].   82. Ibid., June, [1785].

before an Assembly of Notables sweeping proposals for tax reform
and the establishment of provincial assemblies where the influence
of the privileged orders would not be paramount. Yet Calonne had
also begun by spending freely and borrowing heavily, and he undid
the reforms in financial administration of Necker's first ministry
(1776–1781). Necker had taken significant steps to bring revenue
and expenditure under centralized bureaucratic direction and to cur-
tail the liberty of *officiers* in the Department of Finance and other
financiers to manage state funds, which they were accustomed to do
in ways profitable to themselves but costly to the state. Under Calonne the *financiers* (to some of whom incidentally he was closely
related) were back in power, and he used Treasury funds to keep
up stock prices and thus to sustain the credit of *financiers* upon
whom the state depended for loans.[83] The administration of Calonne
seemed to Mallet Du Pan the very summit of despotic irresponsi-
bility. It did not commend him to Mallet, either, that his entourage
included remnants of the Physiocratic sect like Dupont de Nemours,
and Mallet complained that the men of letters were his devotees because he had generously distributed pensions among them.[84] At this
period, and well into 1789, Mallet was a partisan of Necker, because,
it seems, he trusted Necker's fiscal judgment, and perhaps, too, because Necker had been an opponent of the Economists.

Mallet put some value on the stand taken by the nobles in the
Assembly of Notables in 1787 because in his opinion they saw
through Calonne. The clergy, he thought, had enlightened views on
administration. Mallet was for the *parlementaires*, too, because they
were for Necker and "saw through" Calonne.[85]

Still, Mallet was not impressed on the whole by the opposition
to "despotism" (meaning here, to Calonne, Brienne, Lamoignon).
It seemed to him a Fronde. It was not very intelligent, lacked back-
bone, and could be compounded with. Tempers would grow very
warm, but hardly anyone was prepared to make any sacrifice for the
general welfare. All the discontent seemed to evaporate in bold
words. So long as the stupid Parisian could enjoy his customary

83. J. F. Bosher, *French Finances 1770–1795: From Business to Bureaucracy* (Cambridge, 1970), chaps. 8–10 and passim.
84. Mallet Du Pan to Dumont, Paris, April 5, 1787, Blondel, ed., "Lettres inédites," pp. 106–7.
85. Ibid., p. 107.

amusements, he was really indifferent to important political issues. In all the controversy over taxation, the typical Frenchman never gave a thought to the relation between political liberty and the power to tax; all he thought about was the taxes themselves.[86]

In August of 1788, the imminence of a state bankruptcy led Mallet to warn his friends and his brother in Geneva, as he had done indeed already before this, against investing any further in the obligations of the French monarchy. He did not think that the Estates General, if they met, would produce a solution, and all sorts of dangerous political questions would be raised.[87] Toward the close of the year, when the controversy over the organization and procedure of the Estates General (doubling of the representation of the third estate and voting by head instead of by order) had become nationwide, Mallet Du Pan was more than ever convinced that nothing constructive would come from the Estates General, for instead of making common cause against the crown to recover the control of taxation, the orders were fighting each other. The outcome would be simply to restore preponderance to the king.[88] The Third Estate had been stupid. Instead of following the line of demanding that the other orders should pay taxes like itself, it should have demanded to be exempt like them until the fundamental constitutional question had been settled, and a constitution made, that is (Mallet Du Pan meant), until the Estates had secured the power of the purse. For its part, the nobility had not provided the leadership that might have been expected of them in view of their tradition of constitutional opposition; utterly stiff-necked, they would hear of no *rapprochement* with the Third.[89] At the same time, for all his emphasis on the essential importance of a national opposition to the government, Mallet Du Pan was far from falling in with the view, held by many propagandists of the Third Estate, that the king should be subordinate to the Estates General, be their mandatory. He vigorously objected to this idea.[90] There was all the difference in the world between

86. "Observations sur Paris," August, [1787], Mallet Papers, London.
87. Mallet Du Pan to M. Aubert de Tournes, Paris, August 25, 1788, "Deux lettres inédites de Mallet Du Pan," pp. 363–66.
88. Mallet Du Pan to Dumont, Paris, November 19, 1788, Blondel, ed., "Lettres inédites," p. 115.
89. Mallet Du Pan to Dumont, Paris, March 11, 1789, ibid., p. 116.
90. Ibid., p. 117.

an arbitrary and capricious government, as the old monarchy in Mallet's opinion now was, and a royal power which, ruling by the laws and by fixed principles of policy, was at the same time a great force in the state.

Throughout the crisis of the monarchy in France Mallet was much preoccupied with English affairs. His agreement with Panckoucke in 1784 had specified that the article on England in the journal should be prepared with special care, because of the interest readers took in the subject. "A reader of twenty English papers every week," he wrote Dumont, "I assure you I am rather a resident of London than of Paris."[91] The more his disgust with the French increased, the greater became his fascination with events in England.

Mallet Du Pan had been no panegyrist of the English political system. The parliamentary leaders of the seventeenth century he admired as men of high seriousness and political virtue, and the constitutional struggle of that century was in his opinion a great chapter in the history of liberty. But matters were very different in the eighteenth century, beginning with the reign of George I. Mallet's *Annales* and *Mémoires historiques,* written in Geneva during the War of American Independence, had presented a very derogatory view of politics in England, "where opulence and the spirit of party have stifled patriotism in the hearts of the great . . . where today one can count so many party followers (*factieux*) and so few citizens."[92] Political virtue was all but dead. Mallet took issue here with his compatriot Delolme, whose book on the English constitution he was later to promote vigorously, on the subject of the need for political virtue in England: "In a book otherwise profoundly studied, entitled *De la constitution de l'Angleterre,* the author judges it to be unalterable and indestructible, because, he says, it was not founded upon the virtues, it does not need them." This was, Mallet said, an "inconceivable paradox of Anglomania."[93] The eighteenth century parties, Mallet went on, were not the same as the parties born of the seventeenth century struggle between crown and Parliament, a conflict that had contributed to the establishment of the constitution. Under George I, the former constitutional struggle had become merely a

91. Mallet Du Pan to Dumont, April 5, 1787, ibid., p. 106.
92. *Annales,* I, no. 5 (June 30, 1781), 314.
93. Ibid., III, no. 18 (Jan. 30, 1782), 87.

contest for places, a competition for honors and influence. Cabals took form in Parliament and the ministry of the day became the object of attacks such as had formerly been directed against the crown. Mallet Du Pan was especially anti-Whig. He said that since no one sought any longer to overthrow the constitution and since authority was limited by the laws, the Whig party had no *raison d'être*; the Whig Opposition was become but a community of resentments and personal interests, to the point even where Whigs rejoiced at British reverses in the war.[94]

Factions, in short, that is to say, aristocratic cliques, ruled eighteenth century England. "Aristocracy has made progress perceived by all English observers. Elsewhere it is imagined that Parliament is sold to the Crown and that the latter is moving toward tyranny; it is far closer to succumbing to it than attaining it."[95] *Aristocratie* in Mallet Du Pan's lexicon, it should be remembered, was a pejorative term, not synonymous with *noblesse*, which had no disparaging connotation. *Aristocratie* meant an élite of social status and/or money, having political power or influence. The term itself implied faction, and erosion of a political consensus. It is in this sense that Mallet could accuse the Représentant party in Geneva of aristocratic tendencies while at the same time he denounced their doctrine as democratic. For their control of the General Council and the General Council's control of the governing Councils would if achieved amount to aristocracy no less than the regime of the patriciate. During the French Revolution Mallet was to write of factions that were not based on social status or money but arose simply out of demagoguery and a clever manipulation of political opportunities. At that time he reserved *aristocratie* for the extreme Right. But before the Revolution Mallet's "factions" were tied to moneyed or social elites. Factions of all kinds, no matter what other basis they might have, were also characterized to an inordinate degree by love of power, which to Mallet Du Pan was a primary human motivation.

As late as the spring of 1783 Mallet Du Pan was writing on the theme of a faction-ridden government in England. At this time he published two articles in the form of a dialogue between a Frenchman and an Italian, the Frenchman representing the view that

94. Ibid., no. 19 (Feb. 15, 1782), pp. 133–41.
95. Ibid., no. 22 (March 30, 1782), p. 398.

royal despotism in England was increasing, the Italian (the author's mouthpiece) the contrary view that the royal prerogative had all but disappeared, that the crown had been mastered by an "irregular aristocracy." The Commons were its locale, the spirit of party the moving force, and the administration the sanctuary. Twenty or thirty lords, associated with as many "national representatives," could negate the royal counterweight, because they could force the crown to the critical alternative of dissolving Parliament or changing the ministry.[96] Even if the king had a party in the Tories, still they too were a parliamentary faction and the crown was in dependence on them. Mallet at this point said there was really no difference of principle between the parties. The North ministry had not fallen because the king had listened to the authentic voice of the country; it had in fact simply resigned to let the Opposition have the trouble of getting the state out of an impasse, and the new ministry [the Rockingham-Shelburne ministry of March 1782 to February 1783] was none of the king's choosing; the matter was simply a party affair.[97] Then when the king was obliged to dismiss the Shelburne cabinet, there was the North-Fox coalition, which illustrated the fact that party meant the interests of persons, not principles. Although a coalition government might theoretically be considered the most patriotic type, this one was simply a deal between *factieux*.[98]

As for the corruption of members of Parliament alleged against the crown, it was not in itself evidence of a tendency to royal despotism. Rather, it evidenced faction, for it was less the doing of the crown than of the ministry in power, and both parties had profited by it.[99]

Since Parliament in England was so completely in the hands of aristocratic factions, the question was whether it could again become the organ of a national consensus. Mallet Du Pan thought, even in 1783 when he was least Anglophile, that this was possible. The seat of the corruption in politics was London; but in the provinces there was another spirit. There, virtue and political discernment still existed and ministers were appreciated on their merits.[100] Mallet Du

96. *Mémoires historiques*, V, no. 40 (April 30, 1783), 462–63.
97. Ibid., pp. 463–68.
98. Ibid., VI, no. 41 (May 15, 1783), 27–28.
99. Ibid., p. 25.   100. Ibid., p. 33.

Pan did not deplore an obligation in the king to change the ministry
at the behest of Parliament when Parliament represented a truly
national interest: "When a free, impartial, patriot Parliament demands of the King the dismissal of his ministers, that voice of repro-
bation is the voice of the people itself, and the Crown should defer
to it."[101] It was possible that a general election might produce a
salutary change. (Not that Mallet favored the frequent referral of
propositions to a popular referendum, for that would be democracy
—he was thinking rather of crisis situations.)

Then came the general election of 1784, when the prime minister,
the younger Pitt, who was the king's man, was sustained by the
country against a hostile majority in the Commons. Before the dissolution of Parliament Mallet Du Pan, now writing for the *Mercure*,
had said that the government was showing a firmness and constancy
that would end by triumphing over the stubbornness of the opposition.[102] He told his readers at the time of the election that it
was the king's constitutional right to name his ministers. Parliament
might interfere only when misconduct was alleged, not over an issue
of policy. That way led to corruption, for if the prime minister had
to have the support of the House, he would corrupt it to get it.[103]

Announcing that the ministry had secured a majority of over one
hundred forty votes in the Commons, Mallet observed that the most
opulent families and most of the greater names were with the Opposition, that the ministry counted few such among its supporters.
He declared that its victory was "the certain effect of the nation's
wish." "There never has been seen," he asserted, "there perhaps
never will be seen again, this concurrence of the throne and the nation against the influence and the conduct of the representatives of
that nation itself."[104] The king, or rather, royalism, had been for
something in this reversal, Mallet concluded, noting that the address from the throne to the new Parliament had been received with
a tone of respect that was to be contrasted with the attitude of the
previous Parliament.[105] His "Political Survey of Europe in 1784,"
published in the *Mercure* in January of 1785, celebrated again the

101. Ibid., p. 22.
102. *Journal politique de Bruxelles,* 1784, no. 13 (March 27), p. 168.
103. Ibid., no. 14 (April 3), pp. 17–18.
104. Ibid., no. 24 (June 12), p. 60.
105. Ibid., p. 65.

victory of the king and the nation together over aristocracy. "England, whose laws, customs, and liberty, absolutely foreign to the rest of Europe, leave a free development to the passions and to minds their independence—England has presented a drama (*spectacle*) as yet unknown in its annals, the agreement of the People and the Crown against the usurpations of the legislative power, for the maintenance of the balance of this constitution."[106]

The policies of the Pitt ministry during the next few years almost invariably received a favorable mention in the *Mercure*, mingled with numerous references to the financial and economic vitality of England. This was in large measure the result of Pitt's leadership, which, said the *Mercure*, had produced "the phenomenon of a concert of wills, of the silence of the spirit of party."[107]

But the spirit of party was not silenced entirely, and this was the burden of Mallet Du Pan's reporting of the impeachment of Warren Hastings. Hastings was the victim of an Opposition cabal led by Edmund Burke. Mallet much admired Hastings, but characteristically he scorned Burke more.

Then there was the constitutional crisis occasioned by the insanity of King George III. Mallet reported continuously on the progress of this affair, inveighing freely against the Whigs, who appeared again as the champions of aristocracy. It will be recalled that the Whigs maintained that the regency which for a time it seemed necessary to institute belonged automatically and unconditionally to the Prince of Wales, who happened to be their partisan, and that they denied the authority of Parliament to regulate the situation in any way, whereas the ministry, which had a majority in the Commons, stood for the claim of Parliament to establish the regency and the terms under which it should be exercised. Thus the traditional positions of the Whig and Tory parties on the power of Parliament were reversed. Mallet told his readers in his first article on the subject that the decision belonged to Parliament incontestably.[108] He reported at some length the debate on December 16, 1788, when Pitt won victory by a large margin.[109] The sequel, when it was a question as to

106. Ibid., 1785, no. 1 (Jan. 1), p. 4.
107. Ibid., 1788, no. 1 (Jan. 5), p. 4.
108. Ibid., no. 48 (Nov. 29), p. 213.
109. Ibid., no. 52 (Dec. 27), pp. 165–79, 192; ibid., 1789, no. 1 (Jan. 3), pp. 28–29.

what restrictions should be placed upon the regency, he reported in a way derogatory of the Opposition, among whom he said the spirit of party was at its height.[110] The spirit of the constitution and the rights of the nation had been defended by the ministers, he said in summary, the Opposition were but the chiefs of a faction.[111] On the basis of the outcome Mallet Du Pan permitted himself to say that England was the most free and most enlightened state in Europe.[112]

It was in March, 1789, at the time of the elections to the Estates General, when controversy was hot and growing hotter on constitutional issues, that Mallet stated this. Actually, he had been coming to this opinion for some time and this statement of March, 1789, was not his first. In January, 1789, he had contributed to the literary section of the *Mercure* two articles in the form of a commentary on the treatise of the Genevan, J.-L. Delolme, on the English constitution, republished with revisions of detail in 1784, which he now said deserved to be better known in France because it was by all odds the best book on the subject,[113] and the best *cours du droit politique* of free states, infinitely superior to the *Contrat social* of J.-J. Rousseau.[114] Although Mallet insisted that one country, i.e., France, could not possibly copy the constitution of another, i.e., England, in a rubber-stamp sort of way, since any constitution was necessarily the product of a unique historical development,[115] still he clearly thought that Frenchmen could profit from certain lessons to be learned from the constitutional history of England. As he conceived it, this was not an a priori approach to politics; rather, it was "experimental politics (*la politique expérimentale*)," learning from experience, absolutely opposed to the utopianism he detested in so much contemporary political writing.

In his articles on Delolme Mallet developed Delolme's ideas, but in addition he took off occasionally on his own line of thought. He told his readers that the object of Delolme's book was to demonstrate, by reason, experience, and the present example of England, the falsity of an idea that had become prevalent during the previous

110. Ibid., 1789, no. 5 (Jan. 31), p. 233.
111. Ibid., no. 10 (March 7), pp. 16–17.
112. Ibid., p. 17.
113. *Mercure*, 1789, no. 3 (Jan. 17), pp. 109–11.
114. Ibid., no. 4 (Jan. 24), p. 165.
115. Ibid., p. 166.

ten years, namely, that liberty consists exclusively in democracy, that the people is enslaved, or almost so, "wherever it ceases to carry on by itself the functions of sovereignty, wherever it does not present itself as the center, the administration, the supreme judge, the habitual reformer of all powers, wherever, after having created and sanctioned the fundamental laws, it has, by well considered (*sages*) balances, posed limits to its despotism and assured the stability of its own institutions."[116] This seems an accurate enough statement of Delolme's point of view. It was certainly moreover Mallet Du Pan's own object to oppose the democratic doctrine.

In Genevan politics, during the troubles of the 1760's, Delolme had been a theorist of the Représentant party, upholding the view that the General Council, which was not representative but included all persons enjoying the status of bourgeois, was the supreme power in the state, superior to the governing Councils.[117] The constitution of England was, however, subsequently praised by Delolme because, for one thing, the legislative power of the people was not a direct democracy but delegated to representatives. The Commons were more efficient guardians of the people's interests against usurpations of power than the people would have been themselves.[118] Moreover, the people's representatives were checked by an upper house and both found limits set to their ambition in the monarch's position and powers. As king and sole repository of executive power, the monarch posed a final barrier to the ambition of politicians, who could not aspire to attaining an equal eminence, and the king's legislative veto was the guarantee of his position in the constitution.[119] The constitution had built-in guarantees against both aristocracy and anarchy.

Mallet Du Pan's long-standing predilection for a strong authority found corroboration in Delolme and there can be no doubt that it was his rereading of Delolme in conjunction with the constitutional events of the decade of the 1780's in England that turned him into an Anglophile—together with the increasing resentment and disgust inspired in him at the same time by both the French monarchy and many would-be reformers.

116. Ibid., no. 3 (Jan. 17), p. 110.
117. R. R. Palmer, *The Age of the Democratic Revolution*, I, 135 and n.
118. J. L. Delolme, *The Constitution of England, or an Account of the English Government . . .* , 4th ed. (London, 1784), pp. 240–71.
119. Ibid., pp. 218–28 and passim.

In Mallet's commentary on Delolme the English constitution is presented as a historical development. The importance of Parliament was owing in the first place to the centralized monarchy established after the Conquest, for from this resulted a nationally united opposition to royal despotism. England was all along fortunate in that there was but one assembly to which the king could go for funds. Gradually the principles of liberty contained in Magna Carta became fact. However crushing the tyranny of the first Tudors, Parliament never abandoned entirely its claim to a share in power, that is, basically, to the grant of subsidies. The glorious reign of Elizabeth witnessed a national revival which was accelerated in the reign of James I, who provoked a national opposition by his thesis of royal absolutism.[120] Under Charles I the love of liberty was joined in the House of Commons with religious fanaticism and then the storm broke.

But the Puritan Revolution was at its start, Mallet insisted, of an admirable temper. Here Mallet Du Pan went off on his own line. "What is worthy of remark [is that] the first moves of these men, agitated by the two most violent passions of humankind [that is, religious fanaticism and love of liberty], were made with method and reflection. They undertook their work with moderation (*par mesure*) and by constitutional methods. Moderators of the general movement of the nation, they presented to Charles I, not a mob of enthusiasts, but an assembly of statesmen."[121] How was this? It was explained by the composition of the House of Commons, who were the most independent men in England. They were independent by reason of their wealth, which was almost entirely landed. They were independent of places, pensions, and public offices, and belonged only to a single *corps*, the nation. (Political virtue knew of course no attachment to a party apparatus.) The spirit of the times (Mallet Du Pan meant of course the Puritan spirit) guaranteed their sobriety and their freedom from small vanities and ambitions. "They comprised in short an assembly of grave men of severe behavior, strangers to the corruption of cities [one remembers Mallet's characterization of Paris on the eve of the Revolution as a "Babylon"[122]]," men who talked not in order

120. *Mercure*, 1789, no. 3 (Jan. 17), pp. 115–16.
121. Ibid., p. 117.
122. Mallet Du Pan to Dumont, Paris, April 5, 1787, Blondel, ed., "Lettres inédites," p. 105.

to be applauded in the political "circles" and the gazettes, but to bring conviction to virile and serious minds (how different from the shallow and self-seeking phrase-makers constituting the Parisian intelligentsia castigated elsewhere by Mallet Du Pan!). These men eschewed abstract and sophistical theses on natural law and the origins of societies, to adduce positive and historic claims and statutes, as witness the Petition of Right.[123]

Alas, all this changed with the appearance of the fatal virus of democracy, when some ambitious individuals (not named) spoiled the work, feigning to want to substitute a popular liberty for a limited royalty. The constitution was shattered. "The blood of Charles I and ten battles only submitted Parliament and the nation to their own army, which was soon itself enthralled to its cleverest chiefs. Democracy had destroyed the constitution; this democracy led to an oligarchy of generals; the Protectorate beat down everything, Parliament, Army, sects, factions, and Cromwell reigned alone over a people whom frenzy had deprived of its vigor and its reason." But the English recovered their reason to recall Charles II.[124] The Revolution of 1688 reestablished the constitution in all its strength and there were few states as free of political troubles as England since that time.[125]

It was basic to this constitution, said Mallet Du Pan, that the legislative power belonged to Parliament, that is, to king, Lords, and Commons acting concurrently, and to Parliament alone;[126] it was not shared by the people,[127] nor was it shared by the judiciary.[128] At the same time, the independence of the judiciary in its proper sphere was basic, in order that the liberties of individuals be secure, for the features of the constitution that allowed for the influence of the nation to be felt on the government would be a sham without the liberty of individuals. At this point Mallet touched on the forms of judicial procedure.[129] He went on to stress the freedom of the press, which was, however, a freedom for serious and responsible comment (he was thinking of the political press) and not intended for the publication of stupidities and libels and the satisfaction of personal resentments.[130] (In other words, matters were far otherwise in England

123. *Mercure,* 1789, no. 3 (Jan. 17), pp. 118–19.
124. Ibid., p. 119.   127. Ibid., p. 126.
125. Ibid., p. 122.   128. Ibid.
126. Ibid., p. 124.   129. Ibid.
130. Ibid., no. 4 (Jan. 24), pp. 157–58.

than in France, where the political editor of a responsible journal, the *Mercure*, had not been able to write independently, while the authors of the *Analyse des papiers anglais*, who promoted the government line, were free to dispense falsehoods and to libel the journalist whose competition they wanted to destroy.)

Finally, Mallet Du Pan underscored what was Delolme's most distinctive contention, the royal monopoly of the executive power. "The annals of republics, nay of all states, present us with a multitude of useless troubles, of civil wars without effect, of popular convulsions calmed by accords between the parties that divide the state, without the people drawing from them any advantage. . . . But England shows us constantly the opposite result, that is to say, revolutions from which all orders of the people have actually and equally profited. This phenomenon certainly has its cause in there being no possibility of the national representatives appropriating to themselves some branch of the executive power and thus separating their situation from that of the multitude."[131] Mallet rejected any suggestion that an ambition for places at the crown's disposal, and what he termed "the necessary influence of the Crown," might have occasioned in the House of Commons any sacrifice of the general welfare or any subversion of the laws. If you were looking for corruption, the worst form of corruption was the spirit of party.[132]

But even here—and Mallet was off again on a line he did not take from Delolme—how many times had the plurality been seen to recover its independence and rally, not to party, but to "a truly general interest!" This was owing to the fact that landed property determined the composition of the House of Commons. The constitution did not confound the nation with the bourgeois of its cities; its incorruptible guardians were not from the mercantile and municipal aristocracy or middle class. They were the representatives of the counties, who were all rich or well-to-do landed proprietors, living on the land all year except for the duration of the session of Parliament, elected by countrymen who had daily contact with them, and they were men who by reason of the independence their substantial fortunes permitted wanted nothing from public office but the respect and gratitude of their constituents. Even the representatives of the boroughs were restricted by law to persons who had a certain income

131. Ibid., pp. 159–60.   132. Ibid., p. 163.

from land. Mallet, who was quite aware of the movement for parliamentary reform in England, thought it would be mistaken to increase the urban representation; rather, seats should be redistributed
on a county basis, according to "the profound conception" of Pitt.[133]
His idealized picture of the unreformed House of Commons, which
took no account of pocket boroughs or his own earlier judgment that
the king's supporters, too, were a faction, corresponded to his derogatory view of political life in urban polities like Geneva and Holland
and to his contempt for Paris.

The French monarchy, Mallet thought, was obviously headed for
disaster unless it were reformed. French law and custom could not,
he was certain, be disregarded, but on the other hand he had no patience with the parlements' ultraconservative stand on the Estates
General. "The parlements are holding for the old forms," he wrote
Dumont in November of 1788, "and may be regarded as leagued
against the Third or rather against any political innovation of some
importance."[134] The question was not whether there should be any
innovation—of course there should be—but what kind of innovation,
and what tactics should be employed to secure it. Here the experience
of the English suggested guidelines. The three orders ought to present a united front against the crown on the fiscal question, as the
English had done themselves in the seventeenth century, instead of
fighting with each other. Democracy should be avoided as leading
either to aristocracy (faction) or anarchy, both subversive of a truly
national interest or consensus. The executive power should therefore
be strong and single, vested in the crown alone, the crown possessing
a concurrent function in legislation to preserve its own position. The
judiciary should be excluded from the legislative process. The liberties of individuals, including the freedom of responsible writers,
should be established.

Mallet was depressed by the elections to the Estates General, especially those to the Third·Estate. "It is burlesque," he wrote to Dumont, "to see the name of Commons given to some lawyers, public
prosecutors, subaltern judges, together with the bourgeois of their
cities who are among the clientele of these gentlemen (*ces mes-*

133. Ibid., pp. 164–65.
134. Mallet Du Pan to Dumont, Paris, November 19, 1788, Blondel, ed.,
"Lettres inédites," p. 115.

sieurs). This class speaks, acts, determines the electors. In Dauphiné it has caused three-fourths at least of the cultivators to be excluded from them [what part the *noblesse* of Dauphiné may have had in this event Mallet did not consider]." The deputies of this province were all men of the robe (*robins*)—among them not one proprietor of land, he said.[135] Presumably Mallet Du Pan meant those deputies who were members of the Third Estate, for the deputation from Dauphiné included noble proprietors. He was later to change his mind completely about the worth of the deputation from Dauphiné, but not about the importance in general of landed property as a qualification for the people's representatives.

　　Even before he had begun to show his marked bias in favor of the English gentry as a political class which was a part of his conversion to Anglophilism, Mallet Du Pan evinced a somewhat similar disposition to idealize the class of lesser nobility in France. His *Annales* had carried an article on the *noblesse militaire* commenting on the decree of 1781 that restricted acquisition of an officer's commission, except in case of promotion from the ranks, to men who could prove four generations of nobility. Mallet defended this decree on the ground that the purchase of commissions by non-nobles had seriously curtailed the career opportunities open to the lesser nobility, debarred as they were by law and custom from those opportunities that were open to the bourgeoisie in commerce. It was but fair to rectify the balance between birth and money. Moreover, even supposing an equal aptitude in all classes for the profession of arms, the nobility could be presumed to have some superiority owning to war being their traditional vocation. The lesser *noblesse* deserved consideration for their elevation of sentiment and "hereditary courage," their scorn for wealth and distaste for intrigue. Mallet furthermore fulminated in general against *anoblissement* through the sale of offices. It had corrupted *moeurs* and thrown an ever larger burden of taxation on the poor.[136] Mallet was not, at this point, criticizing the tax privilege of the *noblesse de race*, but only of the *anoblis* who were moneyed men. He was inclined to make clear-cut distinctions among the French nobility. Those of the robe, who were originally of course *anoblis*, he had been wont to criticize as mere *frondeurs*, and during

135. Mallet Du Pan to Dumont, Paris, March 11, 1789, ibid., p. 117.
136. *Annales*, II, no. 10 (Sept. 15, 1781), 69–90.

their conflict with Calonne and Brienne over taxes they seemed to him to lack courage. When the Parlement of Paris returned from "exile" in September, 1787, agreeing to accept the vingtième presented (really a defeat for Brienne though Mallet did not so regard the matter), he recorded in his private journal: "People say of the Parlement that they went out like Romans (*Romains*) and came back like *robins*."[137] And a little later he wrote of D'Eprémesnil, one of the most conspicuous members of the parlementary resistance: "D'Eprémesnil has softened; the Court has won him over by caresses and fair words, flattering his vanity. There are your French Brutuses!"[138] In Mallet's lexicon, the parlements were an example of aristocracy rather than *noblesse*. They happened to be on the right side in opposing the despotism of the old monarchy, but they did not do it very well and were none the less a faction. The court nobility he also held in low esteem and mistrusted,[139] much as he considered the Whig peers in England a faction. He did not in his thinking assimilate the lesser nobility to these other two groups. They seemed to him at this time politically more "pure." To be sure, he was soon to lose faith in their political perspicacity, since they were to be instrumental in defeating the constitutional proposal for an upper house in the National Assembly in September, 1789, and persisted later in maintaining what he considered unrealistic views about the possibility of restoring the old regime.[140] But for the present he thought otherwise. It does not appear that, before the year 1789 was well along, Mallet Du Pan had any personal acquaintance in France that would have influenced his ideas about the nobility. He was then as much an outsider in regard to France as to England, albeit a well-informed outsider in both cases.

The censorship in the winter and spring of 1789 seems to have troubled the *Mercure* relatively little. This has already been noted in the case of the articles on Sweden and the North. True, an article on Geneva was deleted. This concerned the Genevan revolution of Janu-

137. "Observations sur Paris," September, 1787, Mallet Papers, London.
138. Ibid., November, [1787].
139. Ibid., April 9 and June, 1787; Mallet Du Pan to Vernes, Paris, March 18, 1789, Bibl. Genève, MS D.O.
140. Mallet Du Pan to Mounier, n.d. [March, 1792], D'Hérisson, ed., *Autour d'une Révolution* (1788–1789), pp. 174–75. In regard to the dating of this letter see below, chapter 6, n. 92.

ary, 1789, which overturned the Négatif régime that had been imposed by France in 1782 and maintained since by French support. A new régime with considerable concessions to the Représentants and also to the Natif population had been set up by a decree of the General Council on February 10. Mallet approved of what had been done, and if he said so in the article in question he would have been writing counter to the policy of "the Department" in an exceedingly sensitive area. Hence, no doubt, the deletion, which he was, however, permitted to announce.[141] But the articles on France were remarkably full. This might possibly have been because Montmorin, who was later to join the party for which the *Mercure* became the organ, approved their tenor and concluded that since very different ideas were freely getting around in print, it would be foolish to forbid the *Mercure* to discuss events at all. In any case, the *Mercure* was able to comment.

Mallet censored himself somewhat, though, and what he said about the Estates General did not accord entirely with his most private thoughts. Whereas he had told Dumont he did not expect anything basically constructive from that body, in the *Mercure* he adopted a posture of optimism. The date of convocation was to be "the solemn day when [the sovereign] will be reunited with all the Orders of the State, to establish public prosperity on the rights of all and on unchangeable institutions."[142] However, his comments in the *Mercure* on the pamphlets that were flooding the country were more indicative of his real sentiments. While some of these productions (which he did not identify) merited praise, a great many, he said, even lacked respect for historical truth. Mallet hastened to protest a statement that Frenchmen under Louis XIV were only slaves, for it was unthinkable that the age of Condé, Catinat, Boufflers, Villars, Colbert, Bossuet, Corneille, Fénelon, Vauban, was an age of degradation![143] To praise the age of Louis XIV in 1789 was indeed to flaunt one's contempt for the present Revolution, and contempt was exactly what Mallet Du Pan felt. Again, complaining that "one is continually being crushed by a hail of pamphlets, ephemeral but

141. *Journal politique de Bruxelles*, 1789, no. 9 (Feb. 28), p. 192. Here Mallet announced the deletion.

142. Ibid., no. 1 (Jan. 3), p. 3.

143. Ibid., no. 3 (Jan. 17), pp. 161–62.

dangerous," Mallet protested the attacks of many of them on "the classes called to govern a multitude for whom, but not by whom, everything ought to be done"—attacks calculated to undermine, he said, all respect for religion, morality, work, deference, and subordination.[144] In April Mallet devoted space to summarizing certain *cahiers*. He singled out, for example, the *cahiers* of the noblesse of the *bailliages* of Nemours and Beauvais, which were for reforms but not to the detriment of the political position or influence of the noblesse or the alteration of their property rights.[145] It is apparent that he was more interested in publicizing any willingness in the nobility to give up their prerogatives than the demands put forth by the Third Estate, although he quoted also from the *cahiers* of the latter.[146] One senses here his hope that French *gentilshommes* might prove to be the equivalent of English country squires.

By the spring of 1789 Mallet Du Pan was completely disillusioned with Necker, whom he considered responsible in large part for the uproar of the pamphleteers and the *bailliage* assemblies, where, so he informed Vernes, the elections were very generally being conducted with money and fisticuffs.[147] Necker was at fault because he had not taken a strong line to settle the controversy over the organization of the Estates General but had, without any concept of leadership, simply played up to the Third Estate. "The conduct of M. Necker," he said to Vernes, "has made me lose half the respect I had for his talents. He has those of an author and a financier, but assuredly not those of a statesman. . . . He has all the pettinesses of an author; one more upset (*coup*), he is only an author: hence his rage to get into print, to sacrifice the State to the opinion [of himself] that he wants to inspire, to please the triflers of Paris who read and become ecstatic over him. Any man so cowardly, so limited, so little informed by experience as to make the popular opinion of the moment his rule of conduct is not worthy to govern. He lacks principles, and without principles, without firmness, one never does anything of merit. His rash promises in the King's name, varnished over with his obscure

144. Ibid., no. 9 (Feb. 28), p. 180.
145. Ibid., no. 14 (April 4), pp. 29–32.
146. For example, the *cahier* of the Third of Toulouse, ibid., no. 15 (April 11), pp. 81–83.
147. Mallet Du Pan to Vernes, Paris, March 18, 1789, Bibl. Genève, MS D.O.

and philanthropic gloss, have made the fire greater, and I doubt that
he will extinguish it."[148] Mallet Du Pan was later to regard Necker as
one of those who in 1789 had done the most to weaken the position
of the king.[149]

About the same time that he was reacting thus negatively to Necker's conduct in regard to the convocation of the Estates General,
Mallet rejected an appeal from Bérenger to approach Necker on
behalf of the Genevan exiles of 1782, who were dissatisfied with
the disposition of their case in the Genevan settlement of February,
1789, that had greatly liberalized the régime imposed in 1782. They
thought the constitutional edict of the General Council enacted
February 10 should have been more democratic than it was, and they
demanded to be restored themselves immediately to their former
public positions. Flournoy and Clavière, for example, hoped to secure what they wanted through the good offices of Necker.[150] "I replied to him [Bérenger]," Mallet said to Dumont, "that he was welcome to take M. Necker for his sovereign, but that, as for me, I
refused, I did not want any republican, become Minister of the King
of France, for our dictator, and that I would submit to the laws freely
made by 1,327 of my fellow-citizens, never to those of a foreign vizier
whoever he might be."[151] He also told Vernes at this time that he had
himself proposed "quite another settlement," but that the terms of
the edict were the best that could be obtained in the circumstances
and he thought all parties should accept them, instead of cherishing
old hatreds. He said he hoped that some day he might return to
Geneva without finding bands of conspirators raging against each
other.[152] From now on Mallet Du Pan was to be more than ever wary
of the Genevan democrats as a threat to the peace and the independence of Geneva.

Once the Estates General had assembled and the issue of voting by
order or by head had been joined, Mallet indicated that he had grave

148. Ibid.

149. Mallet Du Pan to Mounier, October 14, 1790, D'Hérisson, ed.,
Autour d'une Révolution, p. 148.

150. Karmin, *D'Ivernois*, pp. 174–81.

151. Mallet Du Pan to Dumont, Paris, March 11, 1789, Blondel, ed.,
"Lettres inédites," pp. 119–20.

152. Mallet Du Pan to Vernes, Paris, March 18, 1789, Bibl Genève, MS
D.O.

doubts about voting by head, "putting the fate of the State and of the people at the mercy of deliberation in a unicameral assembly."[153] He thought some sort of accommodation was in order, and quoted with approval the *cahier* of the noblesse of Chalons-sur-Marne, which asked that voting be in general by order, but with the proviso that if in each of two orders five-sixths were in favor of a proposal even if in the remaining order no more than one-third were for it, then it should be regarded as the unanimous wish of the three orders.[154]

In view of the fact that voting by order was the shibboleth of all the defenders of privilege, it needs perhaps to be said that this was not quite how Mallet saw the matter. His hostility to the idea of a unicameral assembly, whether it be the Estates General or a new form of legislative body to be created by the Estates General in answer to the general demand for constitutional revision, was based on the conviction he shared with Delolme that aristocracy or anarchy would be the outcome unless built-in constitutional barriers were provided against the rule of demagogues and factions.

A preoccupation with anarchy was evident in the *Mercure*'s reporting of the events of the early summer of 1789. In relating the circumstances that surrounded the attack on the Bastille, Mallet noted the threatening concentration of royal troops about Paris and Versailles which provoked the arming of the Parisians, but he also underscored the threat of anarchy and the success of the Electors of the districts of the city in saving Paris from riotous despoliation. "These first movements [of the search for arms], necessarily irregular, were soon followed by an internal policing, well organized, that saved the capital from the horrors of every sort with which it was threatened."[155] The *jacquerie* was reported with the strongest expression of sympathy for the seigneurs, who were shown as often fleeing in fear from their domains.[156]

In sum, everything in the situation at that time combined with the vigor of the political convictions he had already developed to make Mallet Du Pan the journalistic champion of the party becoming known as the Monarchiens or Anglophiles, who were detaching themselves from the Patriot majority.

153. *Journal politique de Bruxelles*, 1789, no. 19 (May 9), p. 77.
154. Ibid., p. 78.   155. Ibid., no. 30 (July 25), p. 16.
156. Ibid., no. 32 (Aug. 8), p. 141, and no. 33 (Aug. 15), pp. 230–31.

Six

POLITICAL EDITOR OF THE
MERCURE: THE REVOLUTION
(1789-1792)

At the time the censorship was lifted in August, 1789, the *Mercure* announced that more space would be alloted to the *Journal politique de Bruxelles* while the National Assembly was in session, and stated also that "M. Mallet du Pan, Citizen of Geneva, is sole author of the entire political part."[1] This was not exactly news, but since no name of any particular editor appeared as yet on the title page of the *Mercure* or at the head of the political section, the statement both gave credit and laid responsibility where they belonged, which was as Mallet Du Pan always wanted it.

Regarding the debates in the Assembly, his practice, Mallet said, would be to give first a factual summary, then his own reflections.[2] The soul of exactitude, but seldom able himself to be present at sessions, Mallet had trouble finding reporters who could satisfy his requirements. Very few persons, he complained, were capable of seizing a closely reasoned argument (as in constitutional debate), but caught only hyperboles and extravagant sallies. By the middle of September, he told Mounier, he had already changed his correspondents three times.[3] Possibly because of this problem, possibly also to bring more variety into the material (and no doubt because he thought the news warranted the change), he decided in June, 1790, to condense

1. *Mercure*, 1789, no. 32 (Aug. 8), p. 50.
2. *Journal politique de Bruxelles*, 1789, no. 33 (Aug. 15), p. 168.
3. Mallet Du Pan to Mounier, Paris, September 17, 1789, D'Hérisson, ed., *Autour d'une Révolution*, p. 10.

the substance of the debates and to give more attention to foreign policy.[4]

News coverage was of course primary, but from the disappearance of *censure préalable* the *Mercure* was known for Mallet's "reflections." It became conspicuously a journal of opinion. Finding himself in complete agreement with the views of the Anglophiles, or Monarchiens, whose principal theoretician, Mounier, dominated the first Committee on the Constitution, Mallet began vigorously to promote the labors of this group.

The Monarchiens were the party of the "revolution of the notables" of 1788, whose impulse was to unite well-to-do bourgeois with the noblesse in a common front, first of all against "ministerial despotism" and then against any popular agitation whether of countryside or town that threatened property rights. Its primary locus had been the province of Dauphiné, where under the leadership particularly of Jean-Joseph Mounier, lawyer and judge in the Cour Commune of Grenoble, the Estates of Dauphiné, which had been suspended since 1628, were at the close of the year 1788 reconstituted. They were reconstituted, but under new forms worked out in the course of several assemblies of leading Dauphinois of all three orders during the summer and autumn and sanctioned by the crown. The revived Estates, elected by order but deliberating and voting as one body, chose the twenty-four deputies from Dauphiné to the Estates General. The deputies carried an imperative mandate to participate in the acts of the Estates General only under the procedure of vote by head, not by order. It had been Mounier who had brought together bourgeois and *gentilshommes* in the province to promote this injunction, and Mounier was, of course, in the forefront of the struggle in 1789 to transform the Estates General into a unicameral body against the opposition of the majority of the *noblesse* nationally. At the same time, the collaboration of the privileged orders of Dauphiné with the Third Estate had not been achieved without concessions, specifically the imposition of stiff property qualifications for the election of deputies to the Estates of the province and the exclusion therefrom of *anoblis* and *curés congruistes* as representatives of nobles and clergy,

---

4. Notice to readers in the *Mercure historique et politique de Bruxelles* (the title of the political section from December 5, 1789), 1790, no. 26 (June 26), p. 230.

together with an addition to the imperative mandate that would guarantee possessors of any sort of property rights (including, naturally, feudal property rights) against their infringement without compensation.[5] The Monarchiens, including the Dauphinois *noblesse*, participated in the renunciations of privileges, dues, and tithes of the night of August 4, but considered that in the following days, when the decrees embodying the acts of that night were adopted, the majority of the Assembly went beyond the sense of the renunciations made by the *noblesse*.[6]

Mounier, who proposed the Oath of the Tennis Court to prevent the dissolution of the National Assembly by the king, was also early, and in opposition to democratic (that is, anti-aristocratic) publicists, the advocate of a strong royal executive power and a royal veto of legislation in the future constitution that the National Assembly was to write. And in this constitution there should be an upper house which should also have a veto.[7] Mounier, too, had read Delolme and been impressed. Unfortunately for the Monarchiens, the tag of Anglophile, which they accepted frankly, was already a term of opprobrium since the aristocratic conservatives (or reactionaries) in 1788–1789 used the example of the British House of Lords to argue for maintaining the distinction of the orders in the Estates General. While from the summer of 1789 onward the term "Anglophile" designated specifically the Monarchiens, not the extreme aristocratic conservatives, the former were unable to escape the opprobrium that the name carried for the democrats, who contended that Anglophilism was only a front for "aristocracy" (in the word's revolutionary sense).

It was during the course of the constitutional debate in the summer of 1789 that the Monarchien party took palpable form and became separate from the Patriot majority in the Constituent Assembly. At this time occurred the break between Mounier and Barnave, who had been Mounier's close associate in Dauphiné but now accepted the popular revolution in a way that Mounier did not. Among Mounier's principal supporters in the Assembly were the bourgeois deputies P.-V. Malouet and Bergasse, the nobles Clermont-Tonnerre, Lally-Tolendal, and Virieu, and the prelates Champion de

---

5. Jean Egret, *La révolution des notables: Mounier et les Monarchiens, 1789* (Paris, 1950), "Introduction," pp. 1–49, passim.
6. Ibid., pp. 107–9.   7. Ibid., pp. 33–34.

Cicé, archbishop of Bordeaux, Le Franc de Pompignan, archbishop of Vienne, and La Luzerne, bishop of Langres. The latter's brother, who was secretary of state for the navy, was a sympathizer, as was the comte de Montmorin, the foreign minister.[8] Until the October Days of 1789 the party possessed prestige despite its growing alienation from the Patriot majority, several members being successively presidents of the Assembly. Mounier himself was president during the crisis of the October Days.

All this time the *Mercure* praised Mounier as one "whose work is stamped with the quality of sober thoughtfulness (*sagesse*) that accompanies real knowledge, and with the penetration that knows how to distinguish between truth on the one hand and philosophical paradoxes and intellectual conceits on the other."[9] By way of contrast, there was the abbé Sieyès, also a member of the committee, who had produced "an abstract treatise on the primitive principles of civil society,"[10] such as Mallet believed had no justifiable place in politics. Presumably he was referring to Sieyès's draft of a Declaration of Rights.

On the question of a Declaration of the Rights of Man and the Citizen, Mallet Du Pan was more conservative than Mounier, who was influential in writing the Declaration in its final form;[11] for Mallet pronounced himself from the beginning opposed to the very principle of any such preamble to the work of the constitution. The rights of men in society were derived from convention, not the law of nature; a declaration of rights in the abstract would but open the way to anarchy. The Bill of Rights written by the English, he pointed out, was limited to considerations of constitutional law. The Americans had not followed this precedent; but future generations of Americans would find the principles and the safeguard of their liberty in their constitutional laws, not in their declarations of rights.[12]

The debate on the declaration was interrupted by the sessions of the Assembly that produced the August Decrees, which abolished the "feudal system" and privilege as a legal concept, along with much

8. Ibid., chaps. 2 and 3, passim.
9. *Journal politique de Bruxelles*, 1789, no. 32 (Aug. 8), p. 99.
10. Ibid., p. 100.
11. Egret, *La révolution des notables*, pp. 133–36.
12. *Journal politique de Bruxelles*, 1789, no. 33 (Aug. 15), pp. 172–73, and no. 35 (Aug. 29), pp. 328–31.

else in the old régime. In his précis of the first of these sessions, the
dramatic night of August 4, Mallet Du Pan was reserved. He said that
it was an epochal event in the history of Europe and "the human
heart." He presented the renunciations of seigneurial rights and of
privileges in the Assembly as acts of generosity beyond the demands
of justice,[13] and did not speculate on the political aspects of the situation. He had always thought the seigneurial system anywhere in Europe full of abuses, hence by so much he could commend what had
occurred. But on the other hand there was the frightening presence
of popular violence, and he had given ample indication of his sympathy with the seigneurs during the *jacquerie* that preceded the
drama in the Assembly. Still, he did not at this point lament a triumph of anarchy, as he almost certainly would have done at a later
time. One has the feeling that he did not wish to seem to be speaking
out of turn.

During the latter part of August and the first weeks of September
the great controversy concerned the Monarchiens' proposals for a
second legislative chamber and a royal veto, and here the *Mercure*
was far from reserved. Not only did it support these proposals, it denounced the popular democratic agitation in Paris that their foes on
the Left encouraged. "The discussion at Versailles on the royal sanction having heated many heads here," Mallet wrote in his issue of
September 5, "on Sunday evening the Palais Royal deliberated on the
matter. The expulsion of several deputies of every Order was called
for, particularly some of those from Dauphiné, to whose zeal and
talents, incidentally, the beginnings of French liberty were owing.
The bringing of the King and the Dauphin to Paris was talked of, and
all virtuous citizens, all incorruptible patriots, were exhorted to
transport themselves immediately to Versailles. M. de la Fayette
[this was one of the very few occasions when Mallet Du Pan found
Lafayette to be *bien pensant* politically and on hand when needed]
took measures to prevent the execution of this project, and happily
the persons who had conceived it gave it up for the moment."[14] In
his issue of September 12 he said the tenor of the debates in the Assembly, showing the majority to be hostile to the royal veto, inspired
him with terror: liberty, public security, and the respect necessary to

13. Ibid., no. 33 (Aug. 15), pp. 193–95.
14. Ibid., no. 36 (Sept. 5), pp. 83–84.

a great monarchy were at stake.[15] By the time this was in print, the royal veto had been defeated, and Mallet's article might well have appeared a defiance of the Assembly. Perhaps it was shortly after this that he himself received a warning from the Palais-Royal. Perhaps it was earlier, for he had some time previously announced in the *Mercure* that he would review a book by Mounier, the *Considérations* [Mallet wrote "Observations"] *sur les gouvernements, et principalement sur celui qui convient à la France,* which had been published about August 15 as a sort of manifesto of the Monarchien party,[16] and it may have been this specifically about which he was warned.

In any case, Mallet wrote Mounier, who was still, of course, at Versailles, that he had not published the promised review because he had been visited by four "madmen" (*forcenés*) from the Palais Royal, who advised him to refrain from writing about Mounier or his works, on pain of the public being prevented from buying and reading the *Mercure.* Outraged, Mallet told his friend that, having resisted the ministry for five years at the peril of his liberty and his fortune, he hoped he would show no less independence in the face of "the philosophers of the [Place] de la Grève (*les philosophes de la Grève*), the Hotel des Monnaies, and the Palais Royal." However, he had an obligation to the proprietor of the *Mercure,* who had been visited with the same threats, and he could not therefore invite dangers that were not his alone.[17]

Although Mallet gave up reviewing Mounier's *Considérations* at this point, he did not desist from referring to the Monarchiens in laudatory terms and from promoting their program as the *sine qua non* of a free government in France. He nailed this flag to the masthead of the political section of the *Mercure,* and there it stayed for two and a half years, so long as he was the political editor. He was singularly uncompromising, in regard either to Left or to Right. His constancy, or stubbornness, however one chooses to regard it, may have been materially responsible for giving the party what vitality it retained (which was very little indeed) throughout the Revolution.

15. Ibid., no. 37 (Sept. 12), p. 109.
16. Egret, *La révolution des notables,* p. 122.
17. Mallet Du Pan to Mounier, Paris, September 17, 1789, D'Hérisson, ed., *Autour d'une Révolution,* pp. 10–11. All quotations from the correspondence published by D'Hérisson are, when given in English, my translation.

Mallet's association with the Monarchiens in 1789 had made him, for the first time in his life, genuinely a member of a party, with a feeling of commitment to a political group. One senses that he found this not unpleasant after so many years of isolation, particularly isolation in Paris. There is a tell-tale expression in his letter to Mounier about the visitation from the Palais-Royal: what had brought this upon him, he said, was, beside his announcement of a forthcoming discussion of Mounier's brochure, his praise for "our" first constitutional plan.[18] And it must also have been a satisfaction to think that the foreign minister, Montmorin, his old antagonist, was also in the party with the right principles, abjuring the rationale of his former silly position as a promoter of democratic revolution in Holland. Mallet did not of course say that Montmorin had repudiated his own former policy as foreign minister. He speculated however that Mounier might already have learned from Montmorin the reason for the nonappearance of the article on Mounier's *Considérations*, as though they were all confreres among whom news would travel fast.

Mallet Du Pan had always boasted of his independence of party, but as we have already seen, he had meant simply that he was not bound, that no party apparatus controlled his movements or the expression of his opinions. He would have said likewise that if he now worked for a party, he was no less independent. The thing was that he and the party happened to subscribe to the same views. In truth, he had been in no sense converted by the Monarchiens. He had held these views before he knew them or even before they existed as a party. When he declared a year later: "As for my political principles, they are mine and I owe them to no one (*ils sont à moi et à moi seul*); anterior to the Revolution, the latter has given them in my mind a new degree of force"[19]—when he said this, he was simply stating the fact.

Mallet Du Pan had no feeling at all that, as a citizen of Geneva and not a French subject, his political activity in France was out of place. He was a Genevan doing business abroad like many other Genevans. His business happened to be journalism, which dealt in pub-

18. Ibid., p. 10.
19. *Mercure historique et politique*, 1790, no. 48 (Nov. 27), p. 296. (From November 6, 1790, "Bruxelles" was dropped from the title.)

lic affairs; but if his commodity were in demand, if the law of the host country did not exclude it, if he did not violate the laws, where was the objection? Moreover, the Revolution in France, like the revolutions in Geneva or in Holland, appeared to him supra-national, and for this reason, too, it was not at all incongruous to him that he should be involved. The cause of the régime in France was also the cause of Europe. Here his attitude corresponded to that of the revolutionaries themselves. It was an attitude that seems in both cases less akin to nineteenth and twentieth century concepts concerning world revolution than to the cosmopolitanism of the old Europe.

Mallet Du Pan, however, by no means discounted the sense of nationality and feeling of patriotism. Feeling strongly himself about the independence of Geneva, he expected Frenchmen to react in the same way about their own country, and the time was not yet come when he would begin to think in terms of armed foreign intervention in French affairs. The matter was still ideological, and on this ground he had in 1789 no doubt of the propriety of his actions.

Mallet was subjected to a second domiciliary visit shortly after the October Days,[20] of which the *Mercure* had given an account that was not relished. Mallet dealt with the subject in two successive numbers, those of October 10 and 17, the first presenting a rather summary account of what happened, the second enlarging on this and probing into causes.[21] His horror of anarchic violence shows in every line. "The whole day long," he writes, "Paris thus spewed forth on Versailles a prodigious number of women and armed men," a mob whose violent acts, such as the killing of certain members of the Garde du Corps at Versailles, he relates graphically. His explanation of the causes of the uprising turns on the shortage of bread—a peculiar shortage, however, he says, for there was always bread to be had but only after people had had to queue up for it for hours at the bakers' shops. Of course, this was the doing of the Palais-Royal, which in this way roused popular indignation and mobilized popular action to intimidate the Assembly and to force the king's acceptance "pure and simple" of the constitutional measures already enacted, i.e., the Declaration of the Rights of Man and the Citizen, and the August De-

20. Ibid., p. 285.
21. Ibid., 1789, no. 41 (Oct. 10), pp. 164–68; and no. 42 (Oct. 17), pp. 221–31.

crees. Mallet claims that one would have to go back to the sixteenth century in France for anything analogous to the October Days, that is (he means to say), for any events so fraught with civil insecurity, treachery, and bloody action perpetrated by a fanatical populace under the direction of no less fanatical political chieftains.

In the course of this account, Mallet took occasion to praise the courage and the principles of Mounier and other Monarchiens, notably the comte de Virieu, and affirmed their right to dissent from the political views of the majority.

As for the visitation he himself suffered in consequence of his articles about the October Days, Mallet's view of the Revolution throughout its course was deeply colored by such experiences of personal harassment—and this was not the last—at the hands of the demonstrators. He resented in these episodes the violation of his liberty to speak his mind more than he had resented formerly the interference of the Department of Foreign Affairs, for it did not even have the law behind it. It was extra-legal, the despotism of opinion, and the work of a "faction." "All the legislative activity of France is entirely within a club," he wrote Mounier early in 1790, "that is directed by a secret committee. There all resolutions are prepared in advance. There, a small minority has sworn to submit itself to the majority, which rallies even the most timorous souls to the leaders of the faction. This tactic (*politique*) came to them from Geneva, where it has long been used. Debate at the Tuileries is only for form's sake." [22] Mallet told Mounier he had been right to leave the Assembly after the October Days, when Mounier had returned to Dauphiné, there to attempt to organize a provincial opposition to the constitutional decrees of the Assembly. Mallet had at first regretted Mounier's departure, but it now seemed to him the only sort of protest the Minority, as he usually called the Right, could effectively make. Some of the Monarchiens, he went on, had organized a club named the Impartials, to which Mallet belonged, but in the utility of which he had little faith. The name itself betokened a weakness. When you had to fight strong parties, he said, your own colors must arrest attention; otherwise you would do better not to form an association at all. Unfortunately, as Mounier's failure in Dauphiné had demon-

22. Mallet Du Pan to Mounier, March 14, 1790, D'Hérisson, ed., *Autour d'une Révolution*, p. 96.

strated, little was to be hoped for from the country at large.[23]

In April of 1790 Mallet journeyed to Geneva to put his son Jean-Louis in his brother's business.[24] He also hoped to find refreshment in the quieter atmosphere of the city he had not seen for six years but of which he thought fondly, and in the renewal of old acquaintances. In particular he looked forward to seeing Vernes, though his old friend's political views were to the left of his own. "Although you have taken the Jacobin cowl," he wrote Vernes, "I trust that you will receive me with the *Pax tecum*, instead of hanging me from the street-lamp (*réverbère*)."[25] He also planned, he wrote Mounier, to finish in Geneva a work he had under way on constitutional principles. As this description does not fit any known published work of Mallet's, presumably it never saw the light in the form intended at that time. It is possible that in or near Geneva he also saw Mounier, who was in any case there not long afterward.[26]

During Mallet's absence, the *Mercure historique et politique de Bruxelles*, as the political section had been named since December 5, 1789, continued to appear. The interim editor was very possibly Jacques Peuchet, who was to substitute for Mallet Du Pan during the summer of 1791 after the king's flight, when Mallet went into hiding. It was announced on Mallet's return that he had been in Geneva and had not participated in the *rédaction* since April 8. The announcement was as follows: "A sojourn of two months at Geneva, his own country (*sa Patrie*), has prevented M. Mallet du Pan from participating in any way in the editing of this journal, since 8 April last. Unchangeably devoted to the principles as well as to the tone that he has adopted, he would, should the liberty to write be threatened by any sort of tyranny whatsoever, abandon to more flexible hands a labor which, in his, will never be dishonored."[27] It has been deduced

23. Ibid., pp. 96–101.

24. B. Mallet, *Mallet du Pan and the French Revolution*, p. 107, quoting the reminiscences of Mallet's son, John Lewis Mallet.

25. Mallet Du Pan to Vernes, Geneva, May 15, 1790, Bibl. Genève, MS D.O.

26. Mallet Du Pan to Mounier, Paris, March 14, 1790, D'Hérisson, ed., *Autour d'une Révolution*, p. 101; L. de Lanzac de Laborie, *Un royaliste libéral en 1789: Jean-Joseph Mounier. Sa vie politique et ses écrits* (Paris, 1887), p. 246.

27. *Mercure historique et politique de Bruxelles*, 1790, no. 26 (June 26), p. 229.

from this that Mallet left Paris at this time because of threats from the Left, and that he is saying here that he had abandoned the editorship to some one more flexible than himself, since he would never dishonor his task by submitting to any sort of tyranny.[28] Such a construction does not seem to the present writer warranted. What is true is that the substitution of another editor had been perceived, and Mallet told Mounier he had been overwhelmed with communications from people who thought him permanently withdrawn.[29] In the announcement he is obviously telling his readers that he was away simply because he was visiting his *patrie*, but he adds that if in the future he is prevented from writing freely, he will not stay. Characteristically, he makes this declaration in a high moral tone, but he is not saying that the interim editor in the present case was more flexible than he on the score of principles—which would have been to insult a colleague who had been pinch-hitting for him. As for Mallet's situation in Paris, it was far from being bad enough in the spring of 1790 to force his withdrawal, even temporarily. What evidence there is for Mallet's motives for going to Geneva at this time points simply to the need for a vacation (he had been working on the journal steadily, and under pressure, for six years) and the desire to renew family ties and old acquaintances.

Readers were also apprised in the issue of June 26 that the résumé of the events of the year 1789, which had not appeared in January, 1790 (a résumé of the events of the preceding year being a regular feature of the *Mercure* every January), would be forthcoming.[30] It appeared July 10. The article had been deferred in January, the author explained, in the hope that the Revolution would soon be over, but alas, the ferment was only increasing. "Over" in what sense? It is difficult to see here anything more than a plausible excuse for the writer's having wanted more time to deal with a topic so overwhelming as the Revolution. Actually, the résumé when written did not provide a summary of the events of the Revolution of 1789. It did not

28. George B. Watts, *Charles Joseph Panckoucke, "l'Atlas de la librairie française,"* in vol. LXVIII of *Studies on Voltaire and the Eighteenth Century,* ed. Theodore Besterman (Geneva, 1969), p. 176.

29. Mallet Du Pan to Mounier, June 24, 1790, D'Hérisson, ed., *Autour d'une Révolution,* p. 113.

30. *Mercure historique et politique de Bruxelles,* 1790, no. 26 (June 26), pp. 229–30.

deal specifically with France but took a European view. The crisis was
European, and it was described as the gravest imaginable. Only at
the epoch of the dissolution of the Roman Empire had there been a
comparable disturbance. "All states are experiencing or await the
shock. Thoughtful patriots, impatient with long abuses, demand of
it their reformation; the men of factions hope for disorder from it;
political sects, the fulfillment of their theories; and crime, impunity."
Changes were being promoted whose long-term effects populations
conscious only of their present abuses could not foresee. And all this
was going on in a climate of democracy. In the past, great political
changes benefiting the people without however invoking their collaboration had been accomplished; but now the people were being
involved. And the tendency to take men back, as Mallet put it, to the
day of creation, i.e., to invoke the social contract, natural rights, and
other such antihistorical concepts, was destroying the work of centuries—customary rights, usages, habits, conventions in general, along
with, it must be admitted, the "usurpations" also coming down from
the past. Mallet Du Pan predicted an interval of utopianism: "The
moment prepares us for the indefinite renovation of the social system." (One need not dwell on the horror of such thoughts to a
prophet of *la politique·expérimentale*.) Some states, like England,
Mallet went on, presented the example of "a happy alliance between
liberty and subordination," but their experience counted for nothing
against "present-minded theorizing" (*le raisonnement d'un jour*).
Peoples that had long been free would be able to resist the corruption, but those who had been oppressed and ignorant, or were just
emerging from despotism (e.g., the French) would not, and if the
indigent classes were to gain the upper hand, Mallet warned, no
citizen would be secure six months in his business, his fortune, or
his very life. Great states would dissolve in social warfare. At the
beginning of the Revolution, the French people, called by their king
himself, had come together with a unanimous will to be free, but
this memorable event had been succeeded by a "Revolutionary
tyranny."[31]

Actually, of course, in 1788 and 1789 Mallet Du Pan had been
pretty contemptuous of the political behavior of the French, but it
would never have done to say this in 1790, and even in his conscience

31. Ibid., no. 28 (July 10), pp. 73–78.

as historian Mallet might have argued that, however he had felt in 1789, a real contrast existed between 1789 and 1790, which was the point to be made.

At this critical moment in the history of Europe, he went on, certain sovereigns had complicated the situation by undertaking ruinous wars—Mallet meant the tsarina and the late Holy Roman Emperor Joseph II. Even the king of Prussia appeared to have designs upon the Netherlands, risen in revolt against the emperor. But happily steps had been taken to preserve the balance of power in the North and Germany, and the accession of Leopold II had been favorable to the cause of peace.[32]

The modern reader's reaction to this so-called résumé is a feeling of regret that the historian seems to have disappeared in the propagandist. Mallet had shown a greater objectivity in writing about the revolution in Geneva, his own country, than he was showing in dealing with revolution in France. He was beginning to lose his touch for realism, his sense of the variety of human experience, of manifold factors. His analytical and descriptive talents were, as is foreshadowed here, more and more to be devoted to the elaboration of a theme, the incompatibility of liberty with democracy.

Mallet had returned from Geneva just in time to witness the preparations for the most spectacular event of the year 1790, the Festival of the Federation, which he believed to have had the purpose of turning the hereditary monarchy proclaimed by the Constituent Assembly into an elective one. You would not have doubted this, he wrote to Mounier at Geneva, if you could have seen the session in the Assembly when nobility was abolished, if you could have seen Lafayette having all the princes of the blood, the Dauphin included, reduced to the simple status of active citizen.[33] In Mallet's view, Lafayette had been consistently a "republican," a popularity-seeker building a faction on the destruction of the principle of monarchical authority, of an authority functioning in its own right apart from the commands of the legislative body.

In the *Mercure* Mallet entertained his readers with a colorful account of how all kinds of people had pitched in to help prepare the

32. Ibid., pp. 79–93.
33. Mallet Du Pan to Mounier, June 24, 1790, D'Hérisson, ed., *Autour d'une Révolution*, p. 114.

Champ de Mars for the great Festival of July 14. His tone was not sympathetic but detached and ironical.[34] This story was matched by a sardonic account of the meeting of the Revolution Society in London on July 14, when the "Club de la Révolution" (i.e., the Revolution of 1688) celebrated the anniversary of the fall of the Bastille. "Mr. Price harangued the guests in his turn," wrote Mallet, "calling to their attention the *union of philosophy and politics* in the system of the new governments; especially, he hoped that each citizen would cease to love his country the better to worship the human race. The Doctor ended by predicting a holy league among France, America, Holland, and a regenerated England to make the *world happy*. So be it!"[35]

But the Festival of the Federation, Mallet Du Pan concluded with pleasure, had boomeranged on its "republican" promoters, for the *Fédérés* had shown themselves remarkably royalist. Demonstrations for the king, queen, and royal family had been enthusiastic, he reported to Mounier, and the provincials had resisted the attempts of Parisian crowds to change their sentiments. They were even disillusioned with the Assembly, having seen it in session.[36] In the *Mercure* Mallet reported that the Fédérés had gone home full of loyalty to the laws establishing "monarchical liberty" and to the king, despite the efforts of Parisian democrats (Mallet's term) to corrupt them.[37]

To say that the laws established "monarchical liberty" was, for Mallet Du Pan, to stretch the truth, but it was important to put as good a face on things as possible. And at this point in time, actually, he was feeling that there was, despite the decree abolishing nobility, no reason to despair utterly. Quite apart from the hopeful signs among the Fédérés from the provinces, the situation seemed to him rather fluid. He wrote Mounier that the Jacobins and Lafayette's Club de 1789 were at odds, the former moving vigorously toward a republic, the latter holding back. Sieyès was working to reconcile the two factions, but if he succeeded, he would destroy thirty or forty

34. *Mercure historique et politique de Bruxelles*, 1790, no. 29 (July 17), pp. 214–15.

35. Ibid., no. 31 (July 31), pp. 323–25.

36. Mallet Du Pan to Mounier, July 21, [1790], D'Hérisson, ed., *Autour d'une Révolution*, p. 133.

37. *Mercure historique et politique de Bruxelles*, 1790, no. 31 (July 31), pp. 366–67.

present members of 1789, who had made overtures to the Impartials. Mallet rejoiced that *that* project had come to nothing (so little confidence did he feel in the Fayettists), but still, "in the midst of this complicated state of things, I see glimmerings, conjunctures that are in the offing." Perhaps the worst of the situation for the party of monarchical liberty was the senseless conduct of a part of the Right, "which listens only to its own resentments. And then this King! If he had only half the courage and the resolution of his wife!"[38] If only, Mallet Du Pan must have been thinking, Louis XVI had been Gustavus III, whom he described in the *Mercure* about this same time as "this prince always equal to his difficulties, full of courage, sense, and personal fearlessness, enterprising in his conceptions, bold in their execution, never daunted by reverses, knowing how to compensate for them."[39] Had Louis XVI been Gustavus III, the propaganda of monarchical liberty would not have been such uphill work.

Mallet continued to advertise the views of his and Mounier's party despite its weakness in the Assembly. He corresponded continually with Mounier, now living in Geneva, encouraging him to publish his ideas and a defense of his conduct, and undertaking to see Mounier's work through the press in Paris whenever he should be ready to publish it. He gave space to Mounier in the *Mercure* and attempted to secure space for Mounier's statements in other journals, beside writing himself in the *Mercure* in defense of Mounier against his enemies.[40]

His mood of optimism, however, rapidly evaporated as he noted that Jacobin Clubs were mushrooming all over the country. "There are established in the Kingdom nearly sixty societies called Friends of the Constitution, corresponding with that of Paris," he reported in the *Mercure* late in August. "In some places, these Clubs perform the function of Search Committees, of Inspectors of Municipalities,

38. Mallet Du Pan to Mounier, July 21, [1790], D'Hérisson, ed., *Autour d'une Révolution*, pp. 134–35.

39. *Mercure historique et politique de Bruxelles*, 1790, no. 28 (July 10), pp. 93–94.

40. Mallet Du Pan to Mounier, July 21, [1790], D'Hérisson, ed., *Autour d'une Révolution*, pp. 129–30; August 8, 1790, ibid., pp. 137–38; October 14, 1790, ibid., pp. 147–50; December 4, 1790, ibid., p. 150; December 9, 1790, ibid., p. 164. See also *Mercure historique et politique de Bruxelles*, 1790, no. 31 (July 31), pp. 371–80; ibid., no. 33 (Aug. 14), pp. 185–87, publishing a letter of Mounier to Mallet Du Pan, July 31, 1790.

of inquisitors into the sentiments of the citizens. Several municipalities have judged them to be incompatible with the Constitution."[41] The Constitution was in Mallet's opinion a weak reed, but if it could be employed against the Jacobins, well enough.

A climactic point in Mallet's professional affairs was reached late in November, when yet a third attempt was made to intimidate him. It had been preceded by attacks in the Patriot press, particularly by Brissot, to whom Mallet referred, when writing to Mounier, as "cet infame Brissot."[42] In his *Patriote français*, Brissot referred to the *Mercure* as

> a journal that is the delight of expiring aristocracy, whose author does not love the Search Committee, doubtless for the same reason that neither thieves nor their champions love the light.

In a certain article, Brissot went on, he had counted eighteen lies in twenty-four lines, exclaiming:

> And there is the man who gives certificates of probity and patriotism to MM. Mounier and Lally-Tollendal; there is the man who makes himself the Don Quixote of all the conspiracies. . . . And there is the man, again, who has the rascality to soil what is most sacred, to ridicule the so fraternal festival of July 13 celebrated at London by the friends of the revolution . . . to ridicule one of those philanthropists who have grown old in the practice of the virtues, in combats for liberty, Doctor Price.[43]

Mallet Du Pan complained in the *Mercure* that the freedom of the press, proclaimed in the Declaration of the Rights of Man and of the Citizen, had not been defined in the law, that the responsibility of authors had not been determined. Dissidents were continually defamed by self-appointed spokesmen of the majority. Instead of liberty, there was a despotism of opinion. In Mallet's view, a law on the liberty of the press should establish penalties both for the defama-

41. *Mercure historique et politique de Bruxelles*, 1790, no. 35 (Aug. 28), p. 340.

42. Mallet Du Pan to Mounier, July 21, [1790], D'Hérisson, ed., *Autour d'une Révolution*, p. 130.

43. Quoted in Sayous, I, 202n., from the *Patriote français* for August 6, 1790. My translation.

tion of other writers and for incitement to disobedience of the laws.[44]

Mallet's third visitation, of November, 1790, occurred not long after the sacking of the town house of the maréchal de Castries. A deputation of some fifteen individuals, calling themselves representatives of the patriotic societies of the Palais-Royal, demanded that he change his political line in the *Mercure*, where they said he was attacking the Constitution and the Assembly. Mallet argued with them. He pointed out that the Constitution proclaimed liberty of thought and the press, that if he had attacked the Constitution, he was ready to answer the charge in a court of law. But he did not recognize the authority of private persons like themselves. They replied, Mallet reported, that the Constitution was the general will, law the will of the strongest, that they were expressing to him the will of the nation, to which he should accede on pain of the people's justice and should write in support of the dominant opinion. Mallet answered them much as he had once answered Montmorin and Rayneval, that they might silence him but that he would never write contrary to his convictions, he would never become an "apostate."

Reporting this unnerving experience at length in the *Mercure*,[45] Mallet took the opportunity to defend his position and once more to publish his principles. The article was a statement which would, he no doubt hoped, conciliate those at least who had no personal cause to wish him ill.

Mallet fell back upon the assertion of freedom of speech and of the press in the Declaration of the Rights of Man and the Citizen: either this article was a notable fraud, or no private person could deprive him of the liberty thereby guaranteed without committing a criminal offense. "If each partial society," he said, meaning no doubt the Jacobins, "attributing to itself the power of the nation and of public authority, is able to silence the law, to oppose the wish of the people to the sacred privileges of the citizens, [the whole] society is dissolved, innocence no longer has an asylum, and the constitution is nothing but the absence of all government."[46]

But he went beyond this. His visitors had reproached him with

44. *Mercure historique et politique de Bruxelles*, 1790, no. 5 (Jan. 30), pp. 347–51, 379–91; ibid., no. 28 (July 10), p. 74.

45. Ibid., no. 48 (Nov. 27), pp. 283–306. Extensive excerpts are given in Sayous, I, 212–33.

46. Sayous, I, 217. My translation.

favoring the old régime, to which he had replied (and said again here in the *Mercure*) that the old régime had no more decided enemy than himself. He had been accused of being an "enemy of the Revolution." This was, he said, a "sacramental and mystic term which serves as the signal for murderers, as that of Huguenot served them in the sixteenth century." He was a friend of the Revolution in so far as it meant "change as a consequence of which an absolute monarchy, gangrened with abuses, dissolved already before its fall," gave place to a constitutional monarchy. His political principles had been independently arrived at and were formed before the Revolution, which had only strengthened them. He persisted in regarding the principles of the British constitution as the only ones proper to a large state, where monarchy ought to be preserved, the only ones that could reconcile liberty and authority, the influence of the people with the supremacy of the law. Unless the legislative power were divided, and the executive power single, there were bound to be factions.[47]

Mallet then went on to make an assertion that is rather surprising in view of what has been shown to be his political development. "Ever since I have had the sentiment of reason, and since twenty years of dwelling in the midst of popular disturbances have ripened my judgment, mixed governments have appeared to me the only ones compatible with human nature ... the only ones ... that can succeed given the moral degeneracy at which modern peoples have arrived."[48] The time element in this assertion is not quite clear: just how far back was Mallet reaching in his experience? It seems however that he was attempting to avow a long-time preference for constitutional monarchy over, especially, absolute monarchy. He had already made a similar assertion earlier that year when describing himself as a victim of ministerial despotism in the last years of the old regime: "I have all my life professed my horror of absolute monarchy."[49]

Actually, of course, Mallet Du Pan was a latecomer to a theoretical preference for mixed government, though to be sure his conversion preceded by two or three years the assembling of the Estates General. Conceivably, his former defense of the powers of the governing Councils at Geneva could be regarded as a defense of mixed govern-

47. *Mercure historique et politique,* 1790, no. 48 (Nov. 27), pp. 294–96.
48. Ibid., p. 297.
49. Ibid., no. 13 (March 27), pp. 18–19n.

ment—in this case, against not monarchy but democracy; but the impression his statements would leave in the minds of Frenchmen in 1790 would be that of a derogation of absolute monarchy. To say that he had had a lifetime horror of it would have stated the case only if "absolute" were equated with "despotic." He had, indeed, preferred the term *monarchie simplifiée* to *monarchie absolue*, but the monarchs he praised at length—Joseph II, Leopold II, Frederick II— were in the parlance of the time "absolute." Mallet Du Pan himself, referring to the Prussian monarchy in his résumé of the events of 1789, used the term *monarchie absolue* for it.[50] Mallet, who could be an expert casuist (as already noted), no doubt would have defended himself here if challenged. But the biographer is interested in why he should have been moved to edit the record. He was, it seems, willing to stretch the truth for the sake of the cause of monarchical liberty, for he set store upon a reputation for consistency and may have felt that both as party spokesman and as pundit his position would be damaged if he admitted to having changed his mind. One remembers his sensitivity to the charge of having gone from party to party during his career in Geneva. No doubt the motive involved also a realization of the perils of his position. He was incurring danger simply by promoting "monarchical liberty," which involved a criticism of the Patriot majority and the Jacobin Club, but he could at least deny having approved the French monarchy of the old régime. Mallet was certainly alarmed, partly by the threat of physical violence to his person or his property, partly by the possibility of losing the *Mercure*, which could be boycotted. At the same time, he was convinced that he could always win a respectable livelihood abroad as a journalist, and he was a fighter, more angered by the attack upon his liberty than alarmed by the threat against his professional position.

In regard to his position, moreover, he was assured of Panckoucke's continuing support. This extraordinary individual was determined that politics should not impair the prosperity of the publishing business. Circulation was what counted, and this was Mallet's great card. Panckoucke was moreover the proprietor also of the *Moniteur*, which he founded in 1789 and which represented the opinion of the Patriot majority, while in the reporting of parliamentary debate its function paralleled that of the *Mercure*. Because of the difference in view-

50. Ibid., no. 28 (July 10), p. 85.

point of the two journals Panckoucke was the object of witticisms, like the remark of Camille Desmoulins: "When M. Panckoucke leaves the workshops where his *Moniteur universel* is printed, he is the very devil of a patriot; when he sets foot in the precincts of his *Mercure de France, dédie au roi,* a sudden metamorphosis takes place in him and he is observed to become the rabid *aristocrat.*"[51] But the question for Panckoucke was not completely one of profits, which necessitated getting on with both the régime and the reading public of various opinions. It was a matter also of a free press and of loyalty to his authors and editors, whom he stood behind and whom he rewarded financially without reservations as to their political acceptability. Such at any rate was the case with Mallet Du Pan, whose terms improved as his position became politically more precarious. Mallet's contract of November, 1789, which raised his base salary to 12,000 livres, with additional pay depending on circulation and with a pension agreement,[52] was negotiated following the second threat from the Palais Royal. Panckoucke had been threatened, too, by other journalists, who called him an enemy of the Revolution and even a partisan of the censorship! Panckoucke answered the charges. A notice appeared in the *Mercure* on November 21 affirming that, as for his sentiments about the Revolution, he had been an advocate of vote by head even before the meeting of the Estates General; and as for the censorship, he had always found it intolerable and had never had any dealings with the ministry to the injury of the public. He added, however, that he deprecated scurrilous and incendiary writings that had no public utility and were injurious to individuals.[53] The new contract in both its financial arrangements and its complimentary language recognized the political editor as a principal reason for the journal's success, and it was shortly after this, in the issue of

51. Quoted in Léonard Gallois, *Histoire des journaux et des journalistes de la Révolution française* (1789–1796), 2 vols. (Paris, 1845–1846), II, 395. My translation.

52. Contract between Mallet Du Pan and Panckoucke, Paris, November 3, 1789, Mallet Papers, London. A copy of this document exists in the Bibliothèque Publique et Universitaire de Genève, MS D.O. The pension was to be 3,000 livres annually on retirement after fifteen years' service, counting from 1784, or on retirement because of disability. In the event of his death, his widow would receive 1,500 livres annually.

53. "Observations de M. Panckoucke, *Mercure,* 1789, no. 47 (Nov. 21), pp. 80–84.

December 5, 1789, that the names of the editors of the *Mercure*, including Mallet Du Pan, began to be placed on the title-page, which now read:

> Mercure de France, dédié au roi, composé et rédigé, quant à la partie littéraire, par MM. Marmontel, de la Harpe & Champfort, tous trois de l'Académie Françoise: & par M. Imbert, ancien Editeur: quant à la partie historique et politique, par M. Mallet du Pan, Citoyen de Genève.

This accorded with the terms of the new contract, which stated that Mallet Du Pan was sole editor of both the *Journal de Genève* and the *Journal de Bruxelles*, there being no difference between them, whereas the first contract, that of 1784, had given Mallet exclusive editorial rights only in the *Journal de Genève*, his name appearing then at the head of that journal only.

The title of the political section was changed with the issue of December 5, 1789, from *Journal historique et politique de Bruxelles* to *Mercure historique et politique de Bruxelles*. On November 6, 1790, it became simply *Mercure historique et politique*. Why *Bruxelles* was dropped from the title is not known. Possibly it was because of the association of the city with the emigration, or possibly, simply because of the irrelevance of the name for a generation for whom the internal history of the *Mercure de France* would have no significance.

In 1790 the number of subscriptions increased to the point where Panckoucke, on August 1, accorded a new agreement. The document stated that whereas on November 3, 1789, a decline in subscriptions had been feared, owing to "competition," they had on the contrary mounted. Beginning January 1, 1791, Mallet's salary would be 2,000 livres for every 1,000 subscriptions. Now Mallet's records show that in 1789 the number of subscriptions had reached or was expected to reach a figure in excess of 11,000,[54] and by the evidence of the contracts it was continuing to rise. Say that there were 12,000 subscriptions for 1791, Mallet's salary, exclusive of what he might be paid for

54. Account of Panckoucke with Mallet for 1789, dated at Paris, February 9, 1790, Mallet Papers, London. This document states: "L'arrêté de compte avec M^r le comte de Montmorin, signé le 8 8bre 1789, porte ce nombre à 11,055." It is not entirely clear whether this was the figure for the *Mercure* alone, or included the *Journal de Genève*.

contributions, if any, to the literary part of the *Mercure*, would be 24,000 livres. The agreement stated that out of this Mallet would pay for his secretary (whose duties included reporting the debates in the Assembly) and the journals and gazettes he needed, whereas Panckoucke had paid for them before: but, if subscriptions should decline considerably for any reason, Mallet's salary would not be *less* than the 12,000 livres agreed on in 1789, and Panckoucke would again provide the secretary and the materials. The pension arrangements of 1789 were confirmed.[55]

The political editor was doing very well indeed, provided he did not encounter a boycott. As for the publisher, a simple calculation will indicate his take. A subscription to the *Mercure* cost 32 livres until December, 1789, when it was raised to 33 livres.[56] In 1790, assuming 11,500 subscriptions, the gross receipts would have been 379,500 livres. Aside from Mallet's salary, there would be the costs of printing and distribution, an unknown figure. Whatever one guesses for this, the profit must have been very considerable and the *Mercure* was of course only a part of Panckoucke's business. By Mallet's testimony, Panckoucke was the opposite of miserly, but his very liberality was that of a rich man.

Mallet Du Pan reported to Mounier that after the third visitation, in November 1790, to which he referred as his "excommunication," various colleagues on the *Mercure* (i.e., the literary section), in addition to various deputies, hoped that he would resign or be dismissed. They had got together to select his successor and had fixed first on Volney, then on Du Roveray, the Genevese democrat. Panckoucke had also been threatened again and was, said Mallet, frightened. He made various proposals to his political editor, not specified by Mallet in his letter to Mounier but unacceptable. Mallet stood firm for either of two alternatives: his immediate withdrawal or confirmation of all existing arrangements and complete liberty in the editorship. Panckoucke recovered from his fright. Both his interest and his goodwill, said Mallet, brought him around to his editor's point of view, and an agreement was reached upon which the editor could sleep

---

55. "Addition to the instrument agreed on between MM. Panckoucke and Mallet November 3, 1789, relative to the editorship and composition of the political journals," August 1, 1790, Mallet Papers, London.
56. Announcement in the *Mercure*, 1789, no. 49 (Dec. 5), p. 26.

with some sense of security. In the case of new threats and dangers, the *Mercure historique et politique* would be transported to a foreign location. Where? Geneva Mallet would not consider, for communication with Paris was slow and difficult, and the likelihood of a democratic revolution in Geneva under French auspices would make the city impossible for him. Both he and Panckoucke favored Brussels. That city was now free and quiet, they would have the protection of the government, Brussels was only two days from Paris and communications were prompt and easy, living conditions were agreeable and less expensive than at Geneva, printing and paper costs were reasonable. Mallet suggested that Mounier become associated with him in the event of the *Mercure historique et politique* being moved abroad.[57]

The details of this plan were set forth in a contract with Panckoucke dated November 20, 1790. According to this instrument, it would be, strictly speaking, only the *Journal de Genève* that would be taken abroad, but it would bear the title *Mercure historique et politique* and Mallet's name would be put at the head of it. Panckoucke would be free to appoint someone else, whomever he chose, to edit the political journal attached to the *Mercure de France*. Mallet would be furnished the register of subscribers to the *Journal de Genève* and the names of all subscribers who might leave the *Mercure de France*. The enterprise would be owned by Mallet and Panckoucke jointly, in equal shares. The journal would be expected to pay Mallet's salary of 1,000 livres monthly, together with the costs of production, except for the cost of the initial establishment of the enterprise, which Panckoucke would bear. Mallet agreed not to work on any other journal or "papier politique," and he also promised to conceal Panckoucke's identity if it should be deemed dangerous for the publisher-*libraire* to be known as having any share in the foreign-produced *Mercure historique et politique*. There was more business risk for Mallet in this contract than in the preceding ones, but the project involved additional expense and risk for Panckoucke, too, while at the same time he agreed to continue the pension and retirement plans of 1789, provided he were still publishing the journals. There was, in addition, an advantageous agreement for the termina-

57. Mallet Du Pan to Mounier, December 9, 1790, D'Hérisson, ed., *Autour d'une Révolution*, pp. 164–66.

tion of his employment with Panckoucke. Should Mallet have to give up editing the journals at Paris and *not* take the *Journal de Genève* elsewhere, Panckoucke would pay him 1,000 livres monthly for six months, after which he and Mallet would be free of all engagements. If after the six months Mallet should decide not to continue with the *Mercure*, or with any other journal at all, Panckoucke would give him an annuity of 2,000 livres and one of 1,200 to his widow in the event of his death.[58]

As things turned out, Mallet remained with the *Mercure* in Paris for nearly a year and a half longer. He simply stiffened as the political milieu grew more and more inhospitable, and, confident that Panckoucke would not let him down, pursued a course of personal "brinkmanship."

The year 1791 opened in the midst of furor over the clerical oath. The National Assembly having determined to break clerical opposition to the Civil Constitution of the Clergy by the requirement of the civic oath from all incumbents of clerical office, a deadline was set in January. Mallet Du Pan was on the side of the nonjurors. The *Mercure* told its readers that the number of nonjurors in the Assembly was higher than the Patriot journalists had allowed, being a good majority, and said of the juring bishops of Autun (Talleyrand) and Lydda (Gobel) that their conscience had happily found itself in accord with their temporal interest,[59] thus suggesting that the religious position of the nonjuring clergy was the only tenable one, if not inferentially impugning the motives of all the jurors. The correctness of the nonjuring position was exactly the view Mallet took in an article written some three months later, after the Papal condemnation of the Civil Constitution. Any of the truly useful reforms of the Civil Constitution would have had the support of the clergy, Mallet said, but no Christian church had ever admitted that the political sovereign could impose reforms upon it without at least being consulted. Admission of the contrary would be a profession of atheism.[60]

It should be noted that Mallet did not, however, here ascribe the Civil Constitution and the clerical oath to the malevolent influence

58. Contract between Panckoucke and Mallet Du Pan, Paris, November 20, 1790, Mallet Papers, London.
59. *Mercure historique et politique*, 1791, no. 3 (Jan. 15), pp. 209–10.
60. Ibid., no. 17 (April 23), pp. 282–83.

of "philosophy." He said rather that the action of the Assembly was a derivation from the religious controversies that had troubled the reign of Louis XV: the oath resembled "a vengeance of Jansenism, abetted by popular fanaticism and the pride of absolute sovereignty."[61] The Jansenism he was referring to, of course, was the political Jansenism of the parlements, which had fought the hierarchy and the Jesuits in the interest of the superiority of the secular power in matters of ecclesiastical government and discipline. It is rather curious to find Mallet Du Pan siding with Rome rather than the state over the Civil Constitution, since the tenor of his views heretofore in regard to the regulation of religion by the state had favored the interest of the latter. So he had thought in respect to the governments of the old régime, and when the Protestant deputy Rabaut-Saint-Etienne had wanted to have freedom of worship for non-Catholics proclaimed by the National Assembly as one of the basic liberties of men and citizens, not simply a toleration to be accorded on sufferance, Mallet Du Pan had objected, on the ground that not all religions were useful to the state.[62]

It seems that in the last analysis it depended on what the nature of the state was. The Jacobin state, the rule of a faction built upon democracy, was the subversion of law and a national consensus, a bad thing. The Church of Rome, beside being entitled to respect as having been the state church for centuries, appeared now in Mallet's eyes as a tactical ally, at the least.

Mallet's view of the relations between Catholics and Protestants in France was likewise affected by the controversy over the Civil Constitution. It seemed to him that French Protestantism was become Jacobinical, and it was therefore suspect. He despised Rabaut-Saint-Etienne for adopting the principles of revolutionary democracy and blamed him and other Jacobin Protestants for the religious disorders that broke out in the Midi in 1790, notably the massacre of Catholics at Nîmes. Historical scholarship in recent decades has pointed up the responsibility of Catholic counter-revolutionaries like François Froment, working for the émigré princes, in stirring up the antagonisms that produced this terrible event.[63] Mallet Du Pan, who was in-

61. Ibid., p. 286.
62. *Journal politique de Bruxelles*, 1789, no. 36 (Sept. 5), pp. 66–79.
63. Emmanuel Vingtrinier, *La contre-révolution: premiére période, 1789–*

clined to see the Catholic and anti-Jacobin leadership in the Midi only in terms of the moderation of a man like the baron de Marguerittes, the Catholic mayor of Nîmes, from whom he got an account of the affair, wrote positively to Mounier of his conviction that those really responsible for the Nîmes massacre were Rabaut and his friends in a "Patriot club," using religion as a pretext to win a party. If all Languedoc were set ablaze, he said, it would be because such persons were using the Protestants in order to rule with their support and destroy all resistance to democracy.[64] He did not attribute the political aggressiveness of the Protestant community at Nîmes to the persistence of a sense of being beleaguered[65] and a consequent desire to make the most of the opportunity offered by the Revolution to be a political force. Mallet said in the *Mercure* that before the recent horrors at Nîmes Protestants and Catholics had been living together fraternally in the Midi, and suggested that it was not the Catholics who had caused tension to increase.[66]

Mallet drew a parallel in the *Mercure* between the position of the Protestants before the Edict of Toleration of 1787 and that of the nonjuring clergy in 1791. He claimed that the overwhelming number of Catholic clergy had accepted the Edict of Toleration. Now *they* were being persecuted. It was conceivable that future generations would regard as justifiable the expropriation of the Catholic clergy, the abolition of their privileges, and the changes in discipline, but there would only be indignation at their persecution by the requirement of the clerical oath and the threats to which the nonjurors were being in many cases subjected.[67]

Mallet Du Pan, it might be recalled in this connection, was and always had been particularly inclined to crusading for the underdog, especially when the overdog was a "faction." So it had been with

---

1791, 2 vols. (Paris, 1924), I, 186–230; Burdette C. Poland, *French Protestantism and the French Revolution: A Study in Church and State, Thought and Religion, 1685–1815* (Princeton, N.J., 1957), pp. 122–24.

64. Mallet Du Pan to Mounier, June 24, 1790, D'Hérisson, ed., *Autour d'une Révolution,* pp. 116–17.

65. James N. Hood, "Protestant-Catholic Relations and the Roots of the First Popular Counterrrevolutionary Movement in France," *Journal of Modern History,* XLIII, no. 2 (June, 1971), 245–75, passim.

66. *Mercure historique et politique,* 1790, no. 50 (Dec. 11), p. 139.

67. Ibid., 1791, no. 3 (Jan. 15), pp. 212–15.

him in the case of Rousseau (the faction here being the philosophes), the Natifs of Geneva, Warren Hastings, Mounier. He viewed
himself as an underdog, too, in the struggle against the Jacobins, and
the Catholic clergy now seemed to him such.

About this time—early 1791—Mallet welcomed also to the good
cause, even more surprisingly, Hastings's adversary, Edmund Burke,
toward whom he had felt for years an almost personal animosity. It
took him some time to adjust his thinking to a new evaluation
brought about by Burke's denunciations of the French Revolution,
and at first, reporting Burke's sentiments as expressed in parliamentary debates, he said Burke was too extravagant.[68] But in December,
1790, the *Mercure* signalled the appearance of Burke's pamphlet, *Reflections on the French Revolution*, which it said was now in its
fourth edition. Such a book as this, opined the political editor, could
not be turned off by invectives and bad jokes; it demanded a serious
and extended consideration.[69] In February of 1791 the *Mercure* said
Burke's work had been translated into German and claimed that
everybody of note in Germany agreed with it.[70] These favorable notices drew fire from Mallet's critics, who contrasted them with his
former denunciations of Burke in regard to the Hastings affair. Net-
tled, Mallet made the obvious retort that one need not be expected to
regard all a man's actions in the same light.[71]

Mallet did not, so far as is known, leave a critique of Burke, but
even without this the resemblances and differences between them
are clear enough. Burke's romanticism, the mysticism in which he
enveloped the concept of tradition, was foreign to Mallet's outlook,
which was much more rationalist; but in Burke's rejection of the
political philosophy of the rights of man and the sovereignty of the
people and his insistence on the primacy of convention and historical
development, the advocate of *la politique expérimentale* would find
assumptions like his own. Unlike Burke, Mallet Du Pan did not
idealize the old régime, and he would have said the old monarchy in
France had received its just deserts, yet he experienced much the
same recoil as did Burke from the revolutionary developments—from
the ecclesiastical work of the Constituent Assembly, including even

68. Ibid., 1790, no. 8 (Feb. 20), pp. 244–45.
69. Ibid., no. 50 (Dec. 11), p. 96.
70. Ibid., 1791, no. 8 (Feb. 19), pp. 167–70.
71. Ibid., no. 9 (Feb. 26), p. 251n.

the secularization of Church property, from such levelling legislation as the abolition of nobility, from "anarchy." Although Mallet was to criticize severely the French die-hards who insisted on having nothing but the restoration of the old régime, those people whose view of the past and aristocracy corresponded the most closely to that of Burke in the *Reflections*, Mallet nevertheless in 1791 welcomed this apostle of conservatism as another tactical ally. Perhaps the publishing success of Burke's *Reflections* was one reason for Mallet's growing emphasis on the importance of propaganda for the counter-revolution.

Mallet Du Pan remained uninhibited in his direct criticism of the Jacobins. These Friends of the Constitution, who had sworn so many times to maintain it, were now talking openly of a republic, he charged in the *Mercure* in January of 1791, naming particularly Robert and Brissot, "the patriot Brissot, great swearer of oaths, elector, inquisitor, informer, and the greatest servant of liberty when it is a question of interfering with that of someone else."[72] (If Brissot wanted a duel in this fashion, Mallet could take him on! Mallet would of course have claimed that his invective was based on fact, whereas Brissot's had been pure slander.)

During the spring of 1791 Mallet became genuinely alarmed about his own safety. When the son of Pastor Vernes reminded him of a "small sum"—the phrase is Mallet's—the journalist had borrowed from his father, Mallet wrote to Vernes with embarrassment and contrition, but begged to postpone payment. "You find me in the most critical situation," he declared. "My position and the continually increasing danger of the circumstances have obliged me to put a considerable part of my savings in security abroad; I cannot draw on them before the end of the year. What remains to me I keep as a means of saving myself in case I am forced to precipitate flight, or to ransom my life. I hope to keep it to the last from the scoundrels who have established the rule of crime here in the name of liberty, but we are rapidly approaching scenes of too great violence for one not to neglect the precautions prudence counsels. I beg you then to wait until the autumn for this repayment. However, if it becomes necessary to you, I would make every effort at the moment you required it."[73]

72. Ibid., no. 1 (Jan. 1), p. 69.
73. Mallet Du Pan to Vernes, Paris, May 28, 1791, Bibl. Genève, MS 1923/81, Lettres et billets écrits à Jacob Vernes ... Album d'autographes.

The extreme emergency envisaged in this letter did not eventuate that year, but on June 21, the day after Louis XVI and his family had fled the Tuileries for the border of the kingdom, Mallet experienced a fourth domiciliary visit without legal formalities, this time from the Section of the Luxembourg. Happening not to be at home and being warned, he and his wife did not return. Although he did not leave Paris, for fifteen days (or thirteen, as he told Mounier), he kept his whereabouts secret, while the Comité des Recherches of the Municipality conducted a sort of investigation of his affairs, appropriating certain papers, including a recent letter from Mounier. Meantime, there was a rumor that he was dead, another that he was in prison, and still another that he was an émigré at Brussels with Monsieur. After the two weeks had elapsed his house was free and he returned to it,[74] but not yet to the *Mercure*. From June 21 until the writing of No. 36, the issue of September 3, he contributed nothing to the journal, it was announced, but two pieces, a paragraph on Switzerland and a recital of the misfortunes of a certain family named Guillin. It was announced further that the political editor of the *Mercure* during that interval of more than two months was Peuchet.[75] Peuchet composed it absolutely in the spirit of Mallet Du Pan. Peuchet claimed, for example, that it would have been only natural for the king to attempt escape from what amounted to captivity. He thought the majority in the Assembly had reacted too severely in suspending the king from his functions but said with approval that the "odious charge" of betraying the country to the foreigner had not come from them.[76] He rejoiced at the schism of the Jacobins from which arose the Feuillant party,[77] and approved actions taken by the Municipality against such "incendiary" papers as the *Ami du Peuple*.[78] As for the external situation, nothing presently indicated an intervention by the powers, he thought, although they might be provoked to it by an "outrage" against the king or by revolutionary propaganda in

74. Mallet Du Pan to Mounier, July 11, 1791, D'Hérisson, ed., *Autour d'une Révolution*, p. 194.

75. *Mercure historique et politique*, 1791, no. 36 (Sept. 3), pp. 54 and 58–61. Mallet here explains the nature of the search of his house and the fact that he was in hiding in Paris.

76. Ibid., no. 28 (July 9), pp. 152–54.

77. Ibid., no. 31 (July 30), p. 400.

78. Ibid., no. 32 (Aug. 6), p. 82.

their territories or by the policy of France in such a case as the dispute over the feudal rights of the German princes in Alsace.[79] One wonders if Peuchet might not have been discussing with Mallet Du Pan the content of the *Mercure* during these weeks.

In any case, Mallet's own views about the Varennes crisis, while he was away from the *Mercure*, are clear from his letters to Mounier. For the first time, Mallet appears as a proponent of foreign intervention. He did not think France could long avoid it and was prepared to welcome it inasmuch as, regretfully, he saw no possibility of mastering the "factions" by an appeal to reason and experience; for the factions were supported by popular sentiment and would, if necessary, sacrifice even property to the multitude in order to keep their power. Should there be a war the émigrés would not be the major factor, since by themselves they could count on very little support in France. But, said Mallet, the force that would oppose the factions, wherever it came from, should limit itself to restoring a voice to those (and they were millions, Mallet said) who now did not dare declare themselves. If on the other hand, it should presume to dictate a form of government too far removed from the now dominant ideas, if it were despotic and vengeful, merely substituting a different faction for the one now ruling, the results would be calamitous. In some ways the situation in France was, thought Mallet, "propitious for us." He was writing shortly before the schism of the Jacobins and he noted the divisions there. He classed together as republicans who wanted "the democracy of the rabble" Robespierre, Pétion, Buzot, Clavière, Brissot. Then there was the party of Duport, Barnave, and the Lameths, who, attempting to move toward the Right, had approached Malouet (Mallet's close friend) and Cazalès with proposals very close to "ours," and had not been repulsed. Mallet thought Lafayette, whose own following he said had declined and who hated the popular leaders, might go so far as to fight them—even Lafayette, unreliable as he had always been, was a possible ally. The worst of the situation was the disunity among the Right, together with the extremism of many of them. The proposals of Duport and the Lameths were certain to be opposed not only by the republicans and a part of "1789" (Lafayette's club originally), including Condorcet, but also by "our *aristo-*

79. Ibid., no. 29 (July 16), pp. 254–55; no. 34 (Aug. 20), pp. 195–96.

crates enragés." D'Eprémesnil, for instance, would have nothing if not the three orders and the parlements. And the spirit of intrigue and personal ambition was still rife among them.[80] From this time Mallet's criticism did not spare the extreme Right, and he was soon to express it openly. He said to Mounier that he was in no mood to sacrifice himself "for ingrates as despicable as their adversaries are."[81]

The approaching dissolution of the Constituent Assembly in September led Mallet to publish in the *Mercure*[82] an essay, reprinted subsequently as a pamphlet, entitled *Du principe des factions, et de celles qui divisent la France.* It was, he said, a time for stock-taking on the achievements of the old Assembly before the new one came in. The essay is not, however, a résumé and critique of legislative enactments. Again the historian tends to disappear in the propagandist: the essay is a tract for the times. It is of some interest as a statement of Mallet's concept of the dynamic of revolution. With the substantive causes of revolution he deals here only incidentally. He begins by making a distinction between types of revolutions, or rather revolutionaries, because it is really they in whom he is interested: "There is a great difference between legislators who set up a government to create harmony among all the social classes, and founders of sects or factions." The Revolution in France is one of factions. It is violent, and all violent revolutions give birth to factions. It is democratic, and "democracy is their element." Political and legal equality (this is what Mallet means, though his term is *égalité sociale*) do not destroy the other sorts of inequality *ipso facto,* but are the means of reducing to a common level all those whom society has raised above their fellows. Here enter the demagogues as heads of factions corresponding to social interests in conflict, for there is nothing to stop them in a régime without counterforces. Since the dogma of popular sovereignty lends itself to all possible extensions, society tears itself apart in the progression from a constitution like that of 1791 to complete anarchy.

Beyond this, the essay comprises a description of the various fac-

80. Mallet Du Pan to Mounier, Paris, June 26, 1791, D'Hérisson, ed., *Autour d'une Révolution,* pp. 178–89.

81. Mallet Du Pan to Mounier, July 11, 1791, ibid., p. 195.

82. *Mercure historique et politique,* 1791, no. 38 (Sept. 17), pp. 229–39; ibid., no. 40 (Oct. 1), pp. 49–69; ibid., no. 41 (Oct. 8), pp. 125–40.

tions in the Constituent Assembly, from Right (the Minority) to
Left (the Majority). The first subgroup on the Right consists of men
who want to restore the *status quo ante* 1789 in every detail. At this
point Mallet produces such a horrendous description of the old monarchy and its would-be restorers as no ardent revolutionary could
quarrel with and such as was calculated to win him the most intense
dislike in the entourage of the émigré princes. Then comes what he
called the "party of the primitive constitution," who wanted a monarchy in which Estates General and parlements and the privileged
orders should predominate. Then there is the monarchical party that
grew out of the revolt of Dauphiné, and Mallet takes the opportunity
of setting forth again, devotedly, its political tenets and point of
view. A fourth faction rose briefly on the Right under the name of
Friends of the Monarchical Constitution, willing to accept the Constitution of 1791 except for the destruction of monarchical authority,
but it soon perished, being detested by the rest of the Right and out-
lawed by the Jacobins. The party of monarchical liberty (the party
of Mounier and the Monarchiens) had virtually perished, too,
crushed by the October Days, and its members, while holding to
their opinions, had merged into the other parties of the Right, notably the party of the primitive constitution. In a way, the essay is a
dirge for the Monarchiens. In Mallet's mind they did not really con-
form to his definition of a faction, since they (and they alone, really)
were the party (he thought) of a national consensus and stood for
the liberty of individuals against not only a despotic government but
the despotism of "partial societies" (i.e., the Jacobins). But as they
were obviously an identifiable group in the Constituent Assembly,
they had to be included in the enumeration along with the factions.
Mallet notes a tendency to polarization as an obstacle to the success
of this party. While they and their supporters themselves had generally moved to the party of the primitive constitution, the party of
the extreme Right was every day strengthened by the adherence of
other persons revolted by the excesses of the Revolution, by the insecurity of persons and property, the tyranny of the clubs, the weakness of the police, the vexations experienced by all who had a rank or
considerable property while employments were given to mediocrities
and zealots without regard to qualifications for service to the state.

As for the party of the primitive constitution, their inflexibility was in proportion to the blows and the defamation they in particular (clergy, magistracy, noblesse) had suffered, and he thought it was probably impossible to convert people who had been so deeply offended.

The subgroups of the Left were, of course, all divisions of the Jacobins, of whom Mallet was to say elsewhere that they alone were a faction—the rest merely cabals. In general his characterization of the Left is less nuanced than that of the Right. All had originally played to the multitude, all had originally conspired to leave the king no authority in his own right, to make him merely the servant of the legislature. The first group among the Majority are a rather heterogeneous collection of opportunists and of theoreticians influenced by Rousseau, not republicans in a formal sense but antimonarchical. The center of this group was, to begin with, the Club de 1789, a rival to the Jacobin Club, which however had recovered an ascendancy.

The Feuillants are the second principal group among the Left. Coming out now for monarchy and a strong executive power where they had once dogmatized the principles that would perpetuate the Revolution, demanding now the repression of the clubs they had once founded, both they and the Assembly they dominated had lost popularity to the out-and-out republicans, the third subgroup of the Left. Including both sincere enthusiasts and agitators who were making a career out of revolution, the republicans were uncompromising because they above all others meant to found a democracy in France. This faction had struck deep roots, deriving its sustenance from the decay of all the moral bonds of society—of religion, of marital obligations, the duties of children, of servants, of youth. Without any pronounced advantage in number, the republicans had the advantage of greater agreement in opinion and zeal in conduct. The moment will come, Mallet predicts, when all France will be divided between the republicans and the extreme royalists. Polarization notwithstanding, Mallet Du Pan for one stuck to his own line.

The topic of principal interest during the last months of 1791 and the first of 1792 was, of course, the possibility of war. In September Mallet had dealt in the *Mercure* with the Declaration of Pillnitz, in which the emperor and the king of Prussia had declared (August 27,

1791) that the position of the king of France concerned all the sovereigns of Europe, who were invited to collaborate in the restoration of a true monarchical government in France, and proclaimed that in such case the emperor and the king of Prussia would act promptly with the necessary force to attain the desired end. Mallet insisted that the Declaration was basically moderate and foreshadowed no precipitate action,[83] notwithstanding the belief of the émigrés who were pouring out of France. If other powers than Prussia and Austria had acceded to the Declaration of Pillnitz, thus fulfilling the essential condition for an attack on France, this, he said, was not known.[84] Such a move was moreover not consonant with Leopold's character as so far understood, and Mallet's information from Berlin gave no hint of it there.[85]

Mallet said in January that civil and foreign war were scourges to be avoided if it were possible, but he also remarked that in any case a foreign armed mediation would be the only means of saving the French monarchy. At the same time he published a warning, not to the Left but to the Right and to the Powers. If the Powers and the émigrés were defeated, the interests of the émigrés would be forever lost to the vengeance of the revolutionaries. What of the effects of such a war on Europe? The sovereigns would probably be unable to win it, said Mallet, by arms alone. Against the propaganda of the *Rights of Man*, by which the revolutionaries were attempting to subvert their subjects, they would have to oppose a *Charter of the Peoples*, counter-propaganda showing the interest of all their subjects in the conservation of order and of legitimate governments. Mallet also called upon the émigré princes to break their stubborn silence and to imitate Henri IV, who by manifestoes frequently proclaimed identified his own griefs with those of the nation.[86] For, as every one knew, Henri IV won a throne and popularity. For his pains, Mallet was denounced by the extreme Right, which affected to see him as no better than a Jacobin.[87]

The *Mercure* presented the relations of France and Europe at this

83. Ibid., no. 39 (Sept. 24), p. 264.
84. Ibid., no. 41 (Oct. 8), pp. 123–24.
85. Ibid., no. 42 (Oct. 15), p. 157.
86. Ibid., 1792, no. 1 (Jan. 7), pp. 21–22, 64–69.
87. Ibid., no. 9 (March 3), pp. 57–58 and 58n.

juncture not only as a question of the interest of the ruling houses in saving the French monarchy, and of their preventing the subversion of their own people, but as a question furthermore of resisting the unilateral repudiation of treaties by revolutionary France and her annexation of adjacent territories under the theory of national self-determination. Mallet had been quick to indicate hostility to this theory when it appeared in a debate in the National Assembly early in 1790 over the incorporation of Corsica into the French monarchy, Genoa having protested this as a violation of the treaty of cession of 1768.[88] The annexation of the papal territory of Avignon on the ground simply that this was the will of the Avignonese had been, when proposed, objected to by the political editor of the *Mercure*, who indicated that he considered it to be the harbinger of a predatory foreign policy. "There, then, is the fate with which, it is rumored, Geneva, Savoy, the Pays de Vaud are threatened."[89]

Mallet was, in fact, much alarmed about Geneva, mentioning the matter in a letter to Mounier about the same time. When he rejected Geneva as a possible location for the *Mercure* if he had to leave Paris, he wrote: "Geneva will be pulled into this vortex. Don't think the plan has been given up. I am certain that they are working on it industriously."[90] Who were working on it? The Genevese democrats at Paris, naturally. They had been dissatisfied with the outcome of the Genevan revolution of 1789, as Mallet, who was on the inside at that time, well knew. It was one of the Genevan democrats, Duroveray, who had been proposed as Mallet's successor on the *Mercure* in 1790,[91] and another, Clavière, was high in the councils of the Brissotins, the principal revolutionary expansionists. In February of 1791 Mallet published an article of some length on Genevan affairs. Here he explained the grievances of the Natifs, then said that the greater part of their fiscal and mercantile disabilities had by degrees disappeared since 1768. Periodically moreover a certain number had been admitted to the bourgeoisie, thus gaining the right to sit in the General Council, without, however, the distinction between Natifs and Bourgeois being destroyed. (In other words, those who remained

88. Ibid., 1790, no. 5 (Jan. 30), p. 361.
89. Ibid., no. 29 (July 17), p. 224.
90. Mallet Du Pan to Mounier, December 9, 1790, D'Hérisson, ed., *Autour d'une Révolution*, p. 166.
91. Ibid., pp. 165–66.

Natifs still had no political rights.) It was this distinction that, in 1789, "intriguers" undertook to abolish entirely. Mallet was referring to what transpired following the enactment of the constitutional Decree of February 10, 1789, which was unsatisfactory to the Natifs as well as to the exiles like Clavière. Mallet pointed out to his French readers that to destroy the distinction between Natifs and Bourgeois would make the Genevan government far more a popular democracy than that of France, where the legislative body was representative and the franchise restricted to active citizens. The leaders in Geneva were being "astutely directed," said the *Mercure*, from Paris. Those who were promoting the admission of the Natifs to the General Council were, by the admission even of the Patriot journalists of the capital, working for the annexation of Geneva to France.[92] During the fall of 1791, the *Mercure* called attention to Jacobin-inspired agitation in the Pays de Vaud and Savoy as well as Geneva, with the object of uniting these lands to France.[93]

But the spotlight was on the actions of the emperor and the king of Prussia. On March 1, 1792, Leopold II died, having in his reign of two years pacified Hungary and the Netherlands, which his brother's reforms had driven to revolt, concluded peace with the Turks, and formed an alliance with his rival Prussia, in the face of the French Revolution. In his obituary notice,[94] expressing the greatest admiration for the late emperor in all respects, Mallet remarked on these accomplishments as well as Leopold's earlier achievements when grand duke of Tuscany, and then added: "A course of new enterprises opened before the Emperor. The greatest role was reserved for him; he died while Europe remained uncertain whether he was convinced of it and determined to play it."[95] What role? To be the leader, surely, of a European coalition against the French Revolution. Mallet had no confidence that Francis II could supply such leadership. It was probably at this time that he wrote to Mounier in discouragement:

We shall be a republic in four months, without fail, unless the foreigner, or civil war, comes to check and destroy the Jacobins, absolutely preponderant.

92. *Mercure historique et politique*, 1791, no. 9 (Feb. 26), pp. 236–43.
93. Ibid., no. 39 (Sept. 24), p. 268, and no. 42 (Oct. 15), pp. 150–51.
94. Ibid., 1792, no. 12 (March 24), pp. 219–20.
95. Ibid., p. 220.

Now I foresee that the Emperor [Francis II, clearly], on whom our fate depends, will move just after his brother-in-law has been dethroned and the Monarchy destroyed.

I sense that it can be agreeable to him to see France become bankrupt, our finances ruined, our resources destroyed, our properties divided up, and the state dissolved; but no public-spirited Frenchman will enter into this infamous calculation, and the imperial prudence will only be seen as the certain way of filling the kingdom's calamities to the brim.

I believe neither in the lamentations (*les pleurs*), nor the interest, nor the talents, nor the sincerity of the cabinet of Vienna, the most deceitful in Europe.

I have absolutely no esteem for the Emperor in any respect; I have absolutely no regard for his counsellors in Paris or Brussels, regarding our affairs. . . .[96]

If external affairs were depressing to contemplate, the internal situation was worse. Scoundrels were masters of the kingdom and of

96. Mallet Du Pan to Mounier, [early March, 1792], D'Hérisson, ed., *Autour d'une Révolution*, p. 176. This letter is undated. The editor, D'Hérisson, has placed it at some time between the letters of December 9, 1790, and June 26, 1791, but in my opinion it must have been written after the death of Leopold (March 1, 1792) became known and shortly before the appointment of the Girondin ministry on March 10. Mallet's opinion of "the Emperor" here is completely at variance with his eulogy of Leopold II published in the *Mercure* for March 24. It is impossible to think of Mallet Du Pan writing two such disparate opinions, or such a poor opinion at all of Leopold, whom he had always admired, as is expressed in the letter. The emperor referred to must be Francis II, hence the letter postdates March 1, 1792. There are other indications that the letter was written not in 1791 but in 1792. One of them is a reference to a work by Mounier that was still unpublished and that, from the indications in this and other earlier letters, must have been the *Recherches*, which was to appear in July. There is also Mallet's presentiment that a republican revolution is imminent, which is not apparent in documents undoubtedly dating from 1791. Finally, there is his opinion, expressed in the letter, that it is useless for him to keep harping on "the two chambers" and that he should concentrate on the appeal to proprietors, an attitude that does not fit the pattern of his writing before the end of 1791, but becomes conspicuous thereafter. As for the other terminal date, it seems to be indicated by the following sentence in the letter; "Dans peu de jours vous verrez les ministres chassés, ou démis, et le gouvernement passer à l'Assemblée nationale qui nommera les ministres." This is what did happen on March 10, 1792.

a nation "totally brutalized"; and on the other side there were only intriguers—not any element of party leadership or well-considered planning. Mallet said that he himself had given up writing about the constitution, preaching the two chambers, to which the hostility of both the democrats and the aristocrats, among the latter the *petite noblesse* in particular, was insurmountable. "It is an army and not a constitution (*code*) that will save us." [97] At the same time, he hoped Mounier would persist in the publication of his work on the French Revolution—he was referring it appears to the *Recherches sur les causes qui ont empeché les Français de devenir libres*, which came out in July, 1792. [98] Mounier's stature, he thought, would give it interest, however unpopular the subject.

Meanwhile, the strategy that would seem to promise most, certainly the strategy for him in the *Mercure*, was to confine one's propaganda to very general ideas, such as the necessity of basing liberty on monarchy and monarchy on liberty, and to stress the points on which palpable interests might combine, particularly the defense of property. "The coalition of proprietors, the interest and the power of property—let us confine ourselves to this base for the moment and reserve our philosophical discussions for the study." [99]

The common interest of all proprietors in containing the Revolution was a theme to which Mallet was devoting ever more emphasis. The attack on property had of course begun with the Revolution, and one of his charges against the Jacobins was that from the beginning they had not scrupled to win power by appealing to the hatreds and cupidities of the multitude, both rural and urban. Even those who in 1791 became the Feuillants had in 1789 appealed to or condoned its intervention. But by the time of the king's flight it was obvious that the sans-culotte movement was a force that had divided the Jacobins. Those who remained Jacobins Mallet thought wanted to establish the "democracy of the rabble" (*démocratie de la canaille*). They included among others such as Robespierre, the Brissotins, [100] and they all wanted to overthrow the monarchy. He had sometimes

97. Ibid., pp. 174–75.
98. Lanzac de Laborie, *Un royaliste libéral*, pp. 259–60.
99. Mallet Du Pan to Mounier, [early March, 1792], D'Hérisson, ed., *Autour d'une Révolution*, p. 176.
100. Mallet Du Pan to Mounier, Paris, June 26, 1791, ibid., p. 184.

called all the Jacobins of 1789 and 1790 republicans, but the term he later preferred for their doctrine was "royal democracy,"[101] in his view a bastard conception, to be sure, but still distinguishing them from later out-and-out republicans.

The Revolution had first attacked property in the form of feudal property rights, property in office, and the corporate holdings of the Church, but from the middle of 1791 what Mallet had in mind was the possibility, nay probability, of a much more generalized attack. At the beginning of the year 1792 he published in the _Mercure_, in his review of the events of 1791, a warning on the direction of revolutionary democracy. Here he reverted again to an analogy between the present and the period of the dissolution of the Roman Empire, of the barbarian invasions. "The Roman Empire and its riches were taken over," he wrote, "not by the ordinary right of war, but . . . by the right of the multitude, avid for possessions, [to rule] over the few who possess everything. Indigent peasant nations appropriated for themselves, like herds of cattle, nations that were rich and lacking energy." This was what was threatening Europe now, though with a certain difference. "The Huns and the Herulians, the Vandals and the Goths will come neither from the North nor from the Black Sea; they are in the midst of us."[102] In his issue of March 10, 1792, Mallet said, in effect: Proprietors, unite!

> The day has come [he declared] when the proprietors of all classes must finally feel that they will in their turn fall under the axe of anarchy; they will pay for the fact that a great many of them stupidly concurred in the first pillage because the brigands then were Patriots in their eyes.[103]

Mallet Du Pan had also conceived of a quite different tactic which he was for trying. He would have the Royalists address propaganda to the sans-culottes themselves, attempt a popular counter-revolution. This is the testimony of Isaac Cornuaud, the Genevan politician who had formerly endeavored to keep the Natifs from joining with the

101. _Mercure historique et politique_, 1791, no. 41 (Oct. 8), pp. 125–26. In no. 38 (Sept. 17), p. 238, Mallet Du Pan uses the term "monarchical democracy."

102. Ibid., 1792, no. 2 (Jan. 14), p. 77.

103. Ibid., no. 10 (March 10), pp. 138–39.

Représentants and to attract them to the Négatifs instead. Cornuaud, who had become a lamp manufacturer, says that on a business
trip to Paris in September, 1791, he frequently saw Mallet Du Pan
and at his house talked with Royalists about political tactics. He and
Mallet agreed on the idea of distributing throughout even the inner-
most recesses of the city a multitude of writings calculated to excite
"the mass of honest citizens" against "the horrible faction of Jacobins." Back at Versoix, where his lamp-manufacturing firm was located, Cornuaud shortly received from Mallet, through the latter's
brother in Geneva, a letter authorized by "a Minister," proposing
that he, Cornuaud, pass the winter at Paris helping to compose, for a
fee, some popular writings, of which no one knew the secret better
than he. Cornuaud accepted, returning to Paris in November. But
the project did not go well. Malouet had already composed some
pieces which Cornuaud rejected as not simple enough for the *petit
peuple,* or varied enough in their appeal. He was then given the task
of editing the compositions of "certain writers," in which he would
interpolate material. By the first of January he had published nineteen brochures of eight pages each. Mallet and his friends were
pleased, he recorded, but Cornuaud himself was not optimistic, for
there was too much competition from haranguers in the political
cafés and clubs. He therefore proposed that his pamphlets be ped-
dled by a large number of hawkers and also distributed by partisans
of the "moderate monarchists" themselves. He furthermore wanted
clubs to be established in all parts of Paris and boldly attended, in
order to influence the action of other clubs. According to Cornuaud,
Mallet agreed with him, but none of his suggestions was acted on,
not even the manner of distributing his pamphlets.[104]

No doubt the failure of his own party to carry the war into the
enemy's territory, so to speak, contributed to Mallet's increasing
pessimism. As for the extreme Royalists, he had already said publicly
that they were unrealistic and now said so again. One of Mallet's last
contributions to the *Mercure,* written shortly before the declaration
of war on April 20, was an article warning that the Revolution would
be exceedingly hard to combat. The most fatuous ideas prevailed, he
complained, among the émigrés. No sooner did they leave French

104. Cornuaud, *Mémoires,* pp. 488–92.

soil than, notwithstanding their present hardships, their confidence in the future returned. Either the Powers would recover their homes and titles for them, they thought, or the people, disabused by the Revolution, would hasten to give them back. Their illusions were maintained by catchwords: "Disorder leads to order," "the Frenchman will never be satisfied without a King," "democracy dies of itself," and so on. The statements might be true in the long run, said Mallet, but not in the short. Disorder only bred disorder. Frenchmen were undergoing a process of continuous social displacement, power now passing from proprietors to the proletarians (*prolétaires*) and "their flatterers."[105] The national character itself would tend to make the people tenacious of the consideration they had secured, for France was a nation with whom "the rage to be something" (*la fureur d'être quelque chose*) was the dominant passion.[106]

At the same time, Mallet made an effort, directed rather at the Left than the Right, to interpret the coming war with Austria (which he of course did not know would be declared by the French themselves) as a war not against the French nation, but only against the Jacobins. The cause of the Powers was not only the cause of the *aristocrates* but of the entire *saine partie de la nation*, of everyone but the Jacobins.[107]

At last the moment came when Mallet Du Pan concluded that Paris was too dangerous for him. Sayous says, without citing his source, that some time in April Mallet was warned by several members of the National Assembly that his arrest was imminent.[108] Since war was at hand, and since his own image with the Patriots was that of a member of the so-called "Austrian committee," he might well have reached the decision to emigrate without the stimulus of a particular incident.

What his plans were at the moment of decision is not known. Presumably he intended to take the *Mercure historique et politique* to Brussels, as provided for in his most recent contract with Panckoucke, that of November, 1790. But almost immediately there developed another alternative of a sort to make the strongest kind of

---

105. *Mercure historique et politique*, 1792, no. 14 (April 7), pp. 46–52.
106. Ibid., p. 54.
107. Ibid., pp. 65–66.   108. Sayous, I, 269.

appeal. Through Malouet and Montmorin, he was offered the role of a special emissary of the king of France to the courts of Vienna and Berlin and to the émigré French princes at Coblentz. It would be his task to secure from Austria and Prussia a manifesto assuring the French that no partition of their country was contemplated, that the Powers were making war not on the French nation but on a "faction antisociale" (the Jacobins), in the interest both of the legitimate sovereigns and of the peoples of all Europe; that their objective in France was solely to restore the authority of the king such as His Majesty understood it, after which a general settlement would be negotiated between the king and the Powers.[109] Mallet had, of course, already, in the *Mercure*, said that such was the policy of Austria and Prussia, and he had already exhorted the émigré princes to identify their grievances with those of the French nation. He could believe the mission offered him was of the first importance, and doubtless he was gratified by the confidence shown in his judgment. Here at last was an opportunity to enter upon a role, if not a career, "more honorable than that of letters."

There may have been another factor in his calculations. The profits of the *Mercure* had declined greatly during the summer and fall of 1791. Peuchet had complained, during the weeks when he was the political editor, following the king's attempted flight, that the distribution of the journal was being interfered with widely.[110] Evidently subscriptions fell off. During the fall Mallet and Panckoucke reviewed the situation and the prospects for 1792, and Panckoucke told Mallet he could count on 18,000 livres, 6,000 more than the minimum specified by the contract of August, 1790, which in this respect had not been superseded by the November contract. Mallet must have let fall some doubt about the figure of 18,000, for he received a written confirmation from Panckoucke, in a typical vein:

> You will always, my dear friend, find me disposed to be just and to do everything that is acceptable to you. What I told you, what I repeated to your wife, I will stand by. I will give you next year 18,000 livres. . . . Cut out the supplements; let us retrench, never separate our interests and . . . all will go well. . . .

109. Instructions carried by Mallet Du Pan, quoted in Sayous, I, 286–87.
110. *Mercure historique et politique*, 1791, no. 32 (Aug. 6), p. 87.

> You are mistaken if you think I have made up on *Genève* what I have lost on the *Mercure*. The actual loss is on both journals.[111]

On December 17, 1791, the *Mercure de France* appeared under a new title, *Mercure français, politique, historique et littéraire,* and was no longer "dédié au roi." The inference is, given the other circumstances, that this was an attempt on Panckoucke's part to update the format with some concession to revolutionary terminology. But at the same time it was explicitly stated on the title page that "M. Mallet du Pan, Citoyen de Genève," was solely responsible for the political part.

In the spring of 1792 Mallet Du Pan may well have wondered, however, if a monarchist journal, counting on a French readership for the bulk of its subscriptions, could now possibly have the kind of success that would justify it to Panckoucke as a business proposition. It might be just as well to try a different terrain. There was the termination-of-contract agreement (1,000 livres monthly for six months) to fall back on, too, should the venture be abortive. So Mallet Du Pan set out for Frankfort, where the emperor and the king of Prussia would be found together for the imperial coronation.

---

111. Panckoucke to Mallet Du Pan, Paris, November 11, 1791, Mallet Papers, London.

Seven

THE JOURNALIST IN EXILE

Mallet travelled to Frankfort by way of Geneva, since a visit to his *patrie* provided a plausible reason for the journey and going directly to Germany would have increased his risks.[1]

At Frankfort, he was accorded conferences with the Austrian and Prussian ministers, who questioned him upon the state of opinion in France, and he recorded his impression that they accepted the draft manifesto substantially as he presented it.[2] He wrote Mounier that he believed his mission had had complete success.[3] As is well known, the cabinets of Austria and Prussia ended by sanctioning the very different, more hostile and threatening manifesto approved by Fersen, Marie Antionette's spokesman,[4] and appearing over the signature of the duke of Brunswick.

This must have been a severe shock, despite the fact that only a few months earlier Mallet had expressed a very low opinion of the Austrian chancellery. A natural reaction would have been to wash his hands of Allied policy, but he felt too much involved, and moreover he needed employment. Geneva, where he had taken up residence on leaving Frankfort and whither his family had made their way to join him, was expensive as always, and his resources were dwindling. Panckoucke owed him salary and Mallet wrote asking for it. However, the year 1792 had been terrible for the *Mercure*. Mallet's name was not

1. Sayous, I, 290.
2. Notes of Mallet Du Pan quoted in Sayous, I, 306–9.
3. Mallet Du Pan to Mounier, Frankfort, July 20, 1792, D'Hérisson, ed., *Autour d'une Révolution*, pp. 218–19.
4. R. R. Palmer, *The Age of the Democratic Revolution*, II, 36–37; Georges Lefebvre, *La Révolution française* (["Peuples et civilisations," ed. Louis Halphen and Philippe Sagnac, Vol. XIII], 3rd ed.; Paris, 1951), p. 264. Lefebvre says that it is not clearly known why the version approved by Fersen was chosen.

dropped from the title-page until after the Revolution of August 10, so that his departure for Frankfort was to that degree covered. It seems that Peuchet had again become political editor on Mallet's departure, hence the substance of the political section remained monarchist. Peuchet was briefly imprisoned following the August revolution and withdrew from the journal,[5] after which it was announced that the principles found in the political section would be very different from what they had been heretofore.[6] The *Mercure* next appeared under the title *Mercure français, par une société de patriotes,* and the editorial roster underwent a reorganization accordingly.[7] Panckoucke told Mallet that his own political position had been dangerous. "The sansculotte Panckoucke," he wrote with wry humor, "embraces the Citizen Williams [the letter is addressed to "Williams"]. If he [Panckoucke] had not always burned with the purest flame of patriotism, the guillotine and the 20 pike thrusts of September 3rd would have recalled him to reason." And his financial position was comparably precarious. The *Mercure* had lost almost two thousand subscriptions during the months of August, September, and October. While he acknowledged the debt owing to "his friend Williams," and would do what he could from time to time as his situation permitted, it was absolutely impossible to make any payment at the present moment,[8] which was the beginning of the year 1793.

Subsequently, Mallet hoped to recover certain assets he had left in Paris on deposit with various persons. In December of 1796 his brother, who was obliged to make a trip to that city, undertook to get possession for him, but everything was gone—plate, jewelry, claims to debts (*créances*). Only his muff, confided to his furrier, was recovered! Whether the other depositaries had been afraid [of being accused of aiding an émigré], or were merely faithless, they had

5. MS note of John Lewis Mallet with Peuchet's correspondence in the Mallet Papers, London; *Nouvelle biographie générale, depuis les temps les plus reculés jusqu'à nos nours* . . . , 46 vols. (Paris, 1853–1866), XXXIX, 770.
6. *Mercure français, journal historique et politique,* 1792, nos. 34 and 35 (Aug. 31), p. 169.
7. Ibid., no. 51 (Dec. 15), title page.
8. Panckoucke to Williams [Mallet Du Pan], Paris, January 2, 1793, and February 9 (or February 26?), [1793], Mallet Papers, London.

excused themselves, he said, on "the most shameful pretexts."[9]

Mallet was convinced that he had an essential service to offer in the procurement and interpretation of intelligence about revolutionary France, in which the Allied Powers were woefully deficient and too much influenced by the émigrés in the entourage of the princes. So in the spring of 1793 he left Lausanne, where he had recently taken refuge from the increasingly Jacobin climate in Geneva, and proceeded to Brussels, the diplomatic center of the Coalition. Here he succeeded in becoming personally known to the representatives of the Powers, particularly Lord Elgin.[10] He had already drawn up a memorandum which was presented in April to the kings of Prussia and Sardinia, describing the opposition in the Convention between the Gironde and the Mountain and calling for the prosecution of the war with unrelenting vigor.[11] Early in August he published, at Brussels, his *Considérations sur la nature de la Révolution de France, et sur les causes qui en prolongent la durée*. Although it was a further bid for his recognition as an expert on the Revolution and the war, it was, characteristically, sharply critical of the governments with which the author sought employment, as well as of the émigré milieux. The Powers were, he said, fighting a slow, unimaginative kind of war, not appreciating the nature of French military strength; and they had failed to give any effective aid to internal insurrection.[12] But not only this, they were fighting the war without regard to the opinions of any Frenchmen but the émigrés. The war alone, said Mallet, could not defeat the Revolution. The struggle would have to be carried into the sphere of opinion by a vigorous propaganda.[13] Mallet said that the Revolution was moving fast into the phase of a *sans-culotte* republic of the poor against all the propertied. He tended to identify *sans-culottes* with *prolétaires*, workers without property. The Montagnards of '93, whom he usually called *Maratistes*, were their leaders or demagogues.[14] The propaganda of the Coalition must present goals acceptable to the majority of Frenchmen, at least to all those

9. Mallet Du Pan to the comte de Sainte-Aldegonde, February 7, 1796, Sayous, II, 209.

10. Sayous, I, 331, 335–36, 355–60, 391.

11. Quoted in Sayous, I, 347–53.

12. *Considérations sur la nature de la Révolution de France, et sur les causes qui en prolongent la durée* (London, Brussels, 1793), pp. 48, 66.

13. Ibid., pp. 2, 68–69.   14. Ibid., pp. 22–42, 61.

Frenchmen who were hostile to or afraid of the *Maratiste* republic
but supported the Convention because they mistrusted the objectives
of the Powers. It must be made clear, first, that the object of the war
was not the partition of France but the end of the Revolution, and
second, that the end of the Revolution was not to be equated with
the restoration of the old régime. The thought of returning to the
old régime was intolerable not only to the *sans-culottes* but to all
those who, now hostile to or afraid of the *sans-culotte* republic, had
been revolutionaries earlier. Too many people of different classes had
already benefited from the Revolution for it to be possible to put the
clock back to 1788. For this reason, the word "counter-revolution"
was unfortunate as a term in propaganda. It should be declared that
the powers were at war with France just because they could not permit the existence of a state in their midst where persons and property
were not held inviolable and where a continuing social revolution was
in progress.[15] Mallet was saying, in short, that the property rights that
had vanished with "feudalism," with venality of office, and with the
corporate endowment of the Church could not be insisted on, at
least to all their former extent, but that a wide and profound appeal
could be made upon the score of all remaining property rights and
the security of individuals against the terror wielded by one or another agency or group.

The question naturally arises how far the governments of the old
régime in central and eastern Europe could accept this point of view
on property, although it was presented to them only as a matter of
wartime strategy, not on the basis of an inherently justifiable distinction between "feudal" and other forms of property. But although the
émigré colony at Brussels did not fail to proclaim its detestation of
the author, Mallet was satisfied with the reception of the *Considérations* by the representatives of the Allied Powers.[16] He next undertook to communicate to Lord Grenville, British foreign secretary,
information that he had currently about the situation in France and
Switzerland.[17] The sequel to this was the composition of a series of
mémoires addressed to Lord Elgin, the British representative at
Brussels, toward the close of 1793 and in 1794. They were written

15. Ibid., pp. 50–52, 70–78.
16. Sayous, I, 371–72.
17. Ibid., pp. 382–90, quoting Mallet's memorandum.

from Berne, whither Mallet had gone to reside under an old agreement between Berne and Geneva that granted the right of *bourgeoisie* in the one to the *bourgeois* of the other[18] (and as *citoyen*, Mallet Du Pan was of course also *bourgeois de Genève*). Berne was as yet far from being Jacobin and was an ideal location for the center of the intelligence network that Mallet Du Pan created. He remained there four years, until his expulsion in the fall of 1797 on the demand of the French.

The first of these communications aforesaid, dated November 20, 1793, and sent not only to Elgin but also to Mercy-Argenteau, the emperor's representative, began with general observations on the nature of the Revolution, which was not one but successive revolutions, each limiting further than the one preceding it the concept of "people," until it now appeared that the people, the sovereign power, were "the famished, the indigent, the sans-culottes."[19] Mallet reviewed the failure of successive efforts to arrest this progression, including the quite inadequate policies of the Coalition. The strength of revolutionary France was at the moment greater than ever, both in the military sense and in the control of opinion within the country. It was now to be a fight to the death between the Powers and the Revolution,[20] and the former must take far more effective action than they had done hitherto. They must somehow convince the French, Mallet said once more, that it was not a war of kings against the rights of peoples. They must furthermore employ the services of men familiar with revolutionary movements to make use of popular opposition to the Revolution, without, however, attempting to take over the internal insurrections they promoted. They should follow up their military successes by forming a widespread volunteer counter-revolutionary organization. In short, the counter-revolution must somehow be popularized.[21]

Elgin was impressed, decided to employ Mallet's services upon a regular basis,[22] and in the first six months of 1794 received the series

18. Ibid., II, 308.
19. Mallet Du Pan to Lord Elgin and the comte de Mercy-Argenteau, then governor-general of the Austrian Netherlands, Sayous, I, 394–99.
20. Ibid., pp. 401–15. 21. Ibid., pp. 417–18.
22. Elgin to Lord Grenville, Brussels, February 14, 1794, *The Despatches of Earl Gower*, ed. Oscar Browning (Cambridge, 1885), Appendix, pp. 312–13.

of intelligence reports[23] above mentioned. These dealt particularly with the dictatorship of the Committee of Public Safety and the means by which it governed France and managed to wage the war. Mallet provided not only the data but interpreted them, as he conceived he was especially qualified to do. The reports were vivid, concrete, cogent, composed with all the skill of the professional journalist. Although the historian today may find errors of fact in them,[24] and they were of course slanted, they were on the whole and have been recognized as a remarkably informed and intelligent reconstruction of the situation.

The correspondence with Elgin was succeeded by a similar correspondence with Don Rodrigo de Souza-Coutinho, the Portuguese diplomatic representative at Turin, extending from the beginning of 1795 through 1797. This Lisbon correspondence was set up on British initiative as a way of maintaining communication with Mallet at Berne: Lisbon was a "letter box."[25] Because it has been published in extenso, the best known correspondence of this type by Mallet Du Pan is that with the Court of Vienna, from the end of 1794 until the close of February, 1798.[26] There was also a much less extensive correspondence with Berlin, through Hardenberg, between 1795 and 1799.[27]

The identity of Mallet's sources of information has long intrigued the curiosity of scholars, particularly the French sources. While he listened gladly to émigrés of various descriptions, he also had his regular correspondents within the country, who got the communications out one way or another. He dealt with people he knew, whose veracity he could count on. One of these, certainly, and probably the

23. They may be found in *The Despatches of Earl Gower*, Appendix, pp. 314–71, and in Historical Manuscripts Commission, *Report on the Manuscripts of J. B. Fortescue, Esq., Preserved at Dropmore* (London, 1899), III, 491–508. Pp. 489–91 reproduce a report of February 16, 1794, that is also published in *The Despatches of Earl Gower*, pp. 340–43.

24. For example, in Mallet Du Pan to Lord Elgin, [March 1794], Fortescue Manuscripts III, 491, Fabre d'Eglantine is said to be a member of the Committee of Public Safety.

25. J. de Pins, "La correspondance de Mallet du Pan avec la Cour de Lisbonne," *Annales historiques de la Révolution française*, no. 178 (Oct.– Dec., 1964), pp. 472–73.

26. Published as *Correspondance inédite de Mallet du Pan avec la cour de Vienne (1794–1798)*, ed. André Michel, 2 vols. (Paris, 1884).

27. Copies of this exist in the Mallet Papers, London.

principal informant for the capital, was Peuchet, his old associate on the *Mercure*. The papers in London left by Mallet Du Pan to his descendants include a file of letters, almost indecipherable, signed with pseudonyms such as "St. Julien, négociant," but endorsed in another hand "Peuchet" and accompanied by a note of John Lewis Mallet, Mallet Du Pan's son, to the effect that Peuchet became, after the Revolution of August 10, his father's assiduous correspondent, much valued by the former editor of the *Mercure* for his shrewd observation and his knowledge. Peuchet, who must have been quite intrepid, appears to have lived by his wits. Attainted of royalism after August 10, he nevertheless became during the Terror an administrator of the district of Gonesse (Seine-et-Oise). He had formerly been an official in the department of police in the municipal administration of Paris, and under the Directory he went to the Ministry of Police where he was in charge of the bureau dealing with litigation concerning émigrés, priests, and conspirators. This was the post in which he was able to be such a knowledgeable informant for Mallet Du Pan. However, his royalist sympathies betrayed him, and after the coup d'état of 18 Fructidor (September 4, 1797), when the Councils were purged of newly elected royalists, he was obliged to flee.[28] If other informants had Peuchet's knowledge and perspicacity, and there is reason to think some of them did, then the Berne intelligence office was well served indeed.

Mallet used his simultaneous connections with the several courts to try to influence policy. Especially, the Pretender Louis XVIII must be brought to see that he could establish no profitable relation with the monarchist movement in France if he continued to support the demands of the most reactionary émigrés. What then should be the monarchists' objective? On the one hand, Mallet seems almost to have abandoned the Monarchien program as a viable one for France and to have reverted to absolutism as the optimum solution. With his characteristic tendency to insist that he had been constant in his ideas, he wrote to Souza Coutinho:

> Since well before the Revolution, and still more since 1789, it has been made clear to me that so numerous, inconstant, and vain a nation [as the French], with whom each individual has a

28. *Nouvelle biographie générale*, XXXIX, 771.

craze for doing anything with impunity, will never tolerate for long a mixed monarchy, or great political assemblies, or the division of powers. The new order of this kind that will succeed in getting established will unfailingly be the start of innovations, disputes, reviving troubles.[29]

However, to gather the widest support possible for a monarchical restoration it would be necessary to start with a régime of large political liberty, reforming it as circumstances would allow in a monarchical direction. It would be necessary to begin even further to the Left than the Monarchiens. Much as he mistrusted the Constitutionnels and disapproved of the Constitution of 1791, Mallet thought that document had the advantage of having been a political reality and of being closest to the views of the moderate republicans whom the monarchist movement might attract. The Constitutionnels, moreover, he thought more royalist than formerly; they could be won over to a strong monarchy by assurances that there would be no reprisals against them or denial of places and favors.[30] The great thing, the necessary thing now was for all monarchists to come together, and of them all the émigré court would have to make the greatest initial concessions since their insistence on the political and social system that had obtained in 1788 was the principal stumbling block to the acceptance of Louis XVIII in France.[31] Mallet himself still held the monarchy of 1788 in contempt, not only its "ministerial despotism" but "those insolent courts of justice usurping the veto over the King and annually fomenting disturbances by their decrees." One could, he thought, establish the plenitude of royal authority while at the same time moderating its exercise by institutions conformable with the national character and customs.[32] But this would

29. Mallet Du Pan to Souza-Coutinho, February 15, 1796, in De Pins, "Correspondance de Mallet du Pan avec la Cour de Lisbonne," *Annales historiques de la Révolution française*, no. 183 (Jan.–March, 1966), p. 86. My translation.

30. Mallet Du Pan to Souza-Coutinho, March 28, 1795, ibid., no. 182 (Oct.–Dec., 1965), pp. 480–84.

31. Mallet Du Pan to Souza-Coutinho, February 16, 1796, ibid., no. 183 (Jan.–March, 1966), pp. 85–86; Mallet Du Pan, various letters to the Court of Vienna, *Correspondance . . . avec la cour de Vienne*, January 8, 1795, I, 47–48; November 28, 1795, I, 372–73; March 6, 1796, II, 22; March 17, 1796, II, 35; April 19, 1797, II, 265; May 10, 1797, II, 276.

32. Mallet Du Pan to Saladin-Egerton, Berne, December 6, 1795, in

be after *a* monarchy, one probably somewhat like that of 1791, had been restored. He said these things also to the émigré court itself, when Louis XVIII and the count of Artois solicited his opinion on the chances of a Bourbon restoration.[33]

In the spring of 1796 Mallet published in support of the monarchist movement against the republican Directory a pamphlet entitled *Correspondance politique pour servir à l'histoire du républicanisme français,* which he was informed went through three editions in Paris within a few months although it was not cheaply priced.[34] Here he gave vehement expression to the disappointment he felt in consequence of the setbacks to the counter-revolution within the year just elapsed. For one thing, the Coalition was breaking up. First Prussia, then Spain, had made peace separately with republican France. Had the powers held together and had there been a general peace, he wrote to friends, the Coalition might have come off with advantage, but now the defeat of the Revolution, which France was carrying abroad, was further away than ever.[35] Within France, the situation was equally gloomy, owing to the failure of the insurrection of the monarchist sections of Paris on 13 Vendémiaire, year IV against the Convention and the decree that required two-thirds of the legislature chosen under the Constitution of 1795 to have been members of the Convention. Again privately, Mallet said the uprising had been premature, precipitated by ill-considered urging from émigré sources close to Louis XVIII and the count of Artois.[36]

In the *Correspondance politique* Mallet vented his rage at the conduct of the Powers, which had refused "to have also their Committee of Public Safety" and had pursued separate policies leading to the dissolution of their coalition, and which, moreover, had never made clear to Frenchmen, as they should, that their object was to

Victor van Berchem, ed., *Lettres de Mallet-Du Pan à Saladin-Egerton, 1794–1800* (Geneva, 1896), p. 26.

33. Memoranda for Louis XVIII, written in July, 1795, quoted in Sayous, II, 150–66.

34. Mallet Du Pan to the Court of Vienna, 6, 1796, *Correspondance . . . avec la cour de Vienne,* II, 126.

35. Mallet Du Pan to the abbé de Pradt, April 19, 1795, Sayous, II, 143–44; Mallet Du Pan to the comte de Sainte-Aldegonde, August 1, 1795, ibid., p. 176.

36. Mallet Du Pan to the comte de Sainte-Aldegonde, November 4, 1795, ibid., pp. 189–91.

defeat the Revolution, not to subjugate France, with the result that
they had worsted neither the one nor the other.³⁷ The criticism was
similar to that contained in the *Considérations* of 1793. "The moment is approaching," Mallet declared, "[for recognizing] that alternative foreseen two years ago, of an eternal war with an uncon-
querable foe (*ennemi indompté*), or of a disastrous peace with an
enemy without faith."³⁸

However, he had written the *Correspondance politique* more for
France than for foreign consumption, he said,³⁹ though his appeal
was directed to moderates everywhere, in France and in Europe
generally, persons who "combined rectitude of heart with that of
ideas"⁴⁰—in short, potential if not actual monarchists. The work resembles the *Considérations* not only by its strictures upon the Allied
governments and the reactionary émigré milieux, but in its general
view of the revolutionary dynamic and its emphatic contention that
the Revolution endangers *all* forms of property. But the time is
1796, not 1793, and Mallet's message is above all a warning that the
so-called constitutional Republic, the Directorial government, is
merely the Revolution in another costume. The Revolution is, of
course, democracy, that is, the sovereignty of the people—and all that
Mallet Du Pan ever had to say against democracy and democratic
factions is here recapitulated with a certain violence. The power of
all the successive republican regimes has been founded, it is said, on
the concept of a "*revolutionary* government," that is, on the nega-
tion of the rule of law, without which there is no liberty.⁴¹ For this is
what the sovereignty of the people (Mallet also uses the term "general will") means. When that concept is applied to a society that
already exists, then it invariably amounts to the oppression of the
minority by the majority, in respect to anything but especially to the
rights of property.⁴² One should not be misled by the aspect of con-
stitutionality in France, for that is only an appearance; French repub-

37. *Correspondance politique pour servir à l'histoire du républicanisme
français* (En Suisse [Hamburg], 1796), Avant-propos, pp. III–IV, and Introduction, pp. xxxix–liii.

38. Ibid., Introduction, p. liv.

39. Mallet Du Pan to the abbé de Pradt, quoted in Sayous, II, 232, without
date.

40. *Correspondance politique*, Avant-propos, p. IV.

41. Ibid., Introduction, p. iv.   42. Ibid., pp. xx–xxii.

licanism has been, still is, and always will be a regime of "limitless submission to a tyranny without restraint."[43] Many persons, more abroad actually than in France, persuade themselves that under the Directory the rule of law is returning, simply because the mass executions and spoliations of the Jacobin Terror have ceased; but the *principle* of terrorism remains[44] and is as it were established. This is the lesson, for example, of Vendémiaire, which Parisians are taking so lightly. "It was reserved for our age," Mallet exclaims ironically, "to see the ways (*moeurs*) of Asiatics [he means the acceptance of violence as something ordinary] constituting the cement and the representation of this strange republicanism."[45]

Mallet declares that the Terror was above all the means to widespread depredations upon property. The same was, and is, true of the war being waged by the revolutionaries.[46]

Constitutions have proliferated, but one cannot look forward to the French republicans producing a truly constitutional regime. On the whole, viable constitutions are the work of generations. No body of men in any case, Mallet asserts, ever produced, *de novo*, such a thing. Only a sole Legislator ever successfully formulated a "legislative code." But even such a possibility is scarcely to be thought of in the circumstances, for neither France nor Europe would tolerate a "Legislator," so greatly had society become corrupted in the present century. Nay, even a reformer would not be tolerated. If ever a "Liberator" does rescue France from the clutches of its constitution-makers, Mallet asserts, the height of his success will be to reconcile old and new prejudices, the interests that preceded the Revolution and those that have followed it. This he sees as the task of a monarchical restoration.[47] However, what actually will happen in France if the democratic revolution is left to run its course is that power will be seized by a single tyrant, in place of the present multiple tyrants, for this is the pattern of such revolutions.[48] When and how the desired liberation will occur, if it does, is not made clear: Mallet does not venture to prophesy.

The coup d'état of 18 Fructidor, year V (September 4, 1797), led

43. Ibid., p. viii.
44. Ibid., pp. v–vi.
45. Ibid., p. vi.
46. Ibid., Lettre première, pp. 13–35.
47. Ibid., Introduction, pp. xii–xiv, xxiv–xxviii, xxx–xxxii, and xliii.
48. Ibid., p. xviii.

Mallet to observations about the Directory that followed along the lines of those contained in the pamphlet of 1796. This purge of deputies suspected of royalist sympathies after the elections of 1797 introduced a regime, wrote Mallet to the Court of Vienna, which could not be described as anything but thoroughly dictatorial. Though dictatorial it was not, however, stable: the government of the French Republic, said Mallet, was and ever would be only a passing mode, a transition from one revolution to another. The governing elite contained two principal types: Thermidorians who thought only of their own personal security and ambition, and others who, more dangerous, were revolutionaries by principle and wanted to revolutionize Europe. Mallet foresaw furthermore the revival of "democratic and anarchic" institutions accompanied by terror—though the present regime had its own brand of terror, too.[49] The Revolution here is still a juggernaut, moving by its own law.

At one juncture, Mallet essayed a more active political role than that of propagandist or of adviser to the courts to which he furnished intelligence. In 1794, the Constitutionnel Théodore de Lameth had appeared near Freiburg seeking Mallet's assistance as intermediary with the Allied Powers in connection with a conspiracy to cause the fall of the Committee of Public Safety, and Mallet undertook to present his proposal to the British. Grenville sent William Wickham to Berne to deal there with British interests, and Wickham was not impressed. The matter came to nothing, there was even some suspicion of the nature of Mallet's contacts in France, and he felt he had been put in the wrong by both sides.[50] Subsequently, however, his relations with Wickham became cordial, with the result that Wickham was to assist with the launching of the *Mercure britainnique*.

About this time (late 1794 or early 1795) Mallet Du Pan encountered also Madame de Staël, another émigré in Switzerland, who in 1792 had been conspicuously associated with the constitutional monarchists. Or rather, it is more correct to say that Mallet declined the encounter, finding a pretext to refuse her request to see him. "At any time, certainly," she wrote him in a brief *riposte*, "a mind as superior as that of M. Mallet Du Pan would have excited my curi-

49. Sequence of dispatches to the Court of Vienna between September 26, 1797, and January 13, 1798, *Correspondance . . . avec la cour de Vienne*, II, 338–97, passim.
50. Sayous, II, 93–110.

osity; but nowadays I experience an almost insane need to hear someone speak of France with reason and justice. Extreme opinions, the
resource of those who can only take in one idea at a time, fatigue my
mind by their monotonous absurdity, and my heart is withered by all
these calumniating and murderous hatreds which, according to their
several degrees of force, prevail in the universe. I separate myself
therefore with a lively regret from an hour of real pleasure."[51]

Sayous opines that what seems on the face of it (though the circumstances are not really known) a somewhat churlish denial on
Mallet's part was owing principally to his agitation over the suspicion
of his being hand in glove with the Constitutionnels, in disregard of
London's views, and his unwillingness to court further criticism
along the same lines.[52] However this may be—and Sayous suggests
also some measure of personal prejudice—Mallet Du Pan was never
one to pursue his ends by joining a clientele, and certainly not the
clientele of such a person as Madame de Staël. Salon politics in
short were never in his line (as by now it must be clear), and moreover he had no esteem whatsoever for Germaine, baronne de Staël,
herself. Indeed, he went so far as to mention her disparagingly in his
correspondence of 1795 with the Court of Vienna, referring to her
"impudence" and "immorality."[53]

The Berne intelligence service was forced out of existence by the
consequences of the coup d'état of 18 Fructidor (September 4, 1797),
which dried up important sources of information among monarchists
in France, and by the demand of the Directory for Mallet's expulsion
from Berne. Quite apart from the fact that his monarchist position
was unacceptable to the Directory, Mallet Du Pan had more specifically antagonized both it and Bonaparte, recently victorious in
Italy, by several blasts against French territorial aggressions. These
publications concerned the question of the neutrality of the secondary states. In his *Lettre à un ministre d'état* (March, 1797), Mallet
declared that their neutrality would not save them.[54] This brochure
was followed by two letters to a member of the Council of Five Hundred, a certain Dumoulard, and communicated to the *Quotidienne*

51. Ibid., pp. 109–110. My translation.
52. Ibid., p. 109.
53. Mallet Du Pan to the Court of Vienna, June 21 and August 23, 1795,
Correspondance . . . avec la cour de Vienne, I, 233, 290.
54. Sayous, II, 293. Sayous gives the title as *Lettre à un homme d'état*. . . .

in Paris, where they were published over Mallet's name in May, 1797. The subject of the one was the declaration of war against Venice and of the other the imminent revolutionizing of Genoa.[55]

Since it was necessary to move out of French-controlled territory, Mallet thought of Neuchâtel, where he had once lived with Osterwald, but the Court of Prussia, whose policy since the Peace of Basel in 1795 was French-oriented, did not assent.[56] He thought also of Austrian territory, and possibly of service with the emperor, and received permission to sojourn, at least temporarily, at Freiburg-in-Breisgau, where an émigré colony of congenial views collected and where he spent the winter.[57]

At one juncture much earlier, at the close of the year 1793, it seems that his friend the comte de Montlosier had suggested to Mallet Du Pan, in a moment of profound discouragement for both, that they emigrate together to the Crimea and there found an agricultural colony.[58] A year later Malouet twitted Mallet Du Pan about preferring Russia to America, where he was himself, he said, planning to settle. He thought Mallet unduly prejudiced by the expectation of disorders arising in the United States when Washington should die.[59] It seems extremely unlikely, however, that Mallet ever really considered the Crimea. Sayous says that his health was too poor for him to entertain this project.[60] Beyond that, Mallet Du Pan was at least as prejudiced against Russia as against the United States, though on different grounds. There is no reason to suppose he thought any better of Catherine II (who was still alive when Malouet wrote, in 1795), than he had before the Revolution, or that he supposed Russia to be any less primitive and despotic than he had understood it to be formerly. For him seriously to consider Russia, there would have had to be no refuge in western Europe.

The duchy of Brunswick was a possibility,[61] but in the end Mallet Du Pan went to England, of which he had been thinking all along, encouraged by Wickham and others to anticipate that a journal

55. Ibid., pp. 302–10.
56. Ibid., p. 332.
57. Ibid., pp. 332–34.
58. Ibid., I, 392.
59. Malouet to Mallet Du Pan, February 17, 1795, in *Mémoires de Malouet*, ed. Baron Malouet, 2nd ed., 2 vols. (Paris, 1874), II, 422–23.
60. Sayous, I, 392.
61. Ibid., II, 332, 361.

something like the old *Mercure historique et politique* would be sufficiently well received to give him a livelihood.[62]

Thus came into existence, in August or September, 1798 (Mallet had arrived in May),[63] the *Mercure britannique: ou Notices historiques et critiques sur les affaires du tems*, published in London and appearing twice a month in both French and English versions, with the English version, the *British Mercury*, coming out five days later than the French. It ran for two and one-half years, terminating with No. 36, which Mallet said was almost entirely the work of his friends, since he was too ill then to go on. He died of consumption on May 10, 1800, at the Richmond residence of one of them, the émigré Lally-Tolendal.[64]

The *Mercure britannique* was a shoestring enterprise dependent entirely on subscriptions, receiving no government subsidy except a subscription for twenty-five copies destined for the conquered French colonies.[65] Mallet had also to bear the considerable cost of the gazettes and journals he used in the composition of his work.[66]

What the Foreign Office was most interested in was, of course, intelligence, but the communications Mallet received from the Continent were spotty and irregular. He wrote Wickham in December of 1798 that it would be difficult to supply Canning with information the latter had requested about Switzerland, for there "everyone is mute," and his correspondents were begging him not to write to them since all their letters were opened.[67] Still, he did receive some information from Switzerland and Germany that he passed on to the ministry, evaluating it as was his wont.[68] As for France, he had some correspondents there, too, on whose reports he formed, for example, his view of the strength of Bonaparte's régime at the beginning of the Consulate. On this subject he told his friend the chevalier de Galla-

62. Ibid., pp. 357–60.
63. Ibid., p. 361.
64. Ibid., pp. 447–48.
65. Ibid., p. 367.
66. Mallet Du Pan to Wickham, December 11, 1798, Public Record Office, London, F.O. 27, vol. 53.
67. Ibid.
68. Letter from Mallet Du Pan, February 26, 1798, communicated to [Lord Grenville?] by "Mr. Huskisson," ibid.; Mallet Du Pan to "My lord" [Grenville?], July 15, 1799, ibid., vol. 54; Mallet Du Pan to "Monsieur" [Wickham?], September 13, 1799, ibid.

tin in February, 1800, that the testimony about Bonaparte by the
many French merchants who were coming to London to buy colonial
goods agreed absolutely with that of "all my letters."[69] That was
during a lull in the war, however, and for the most part the intelligence available to the Foreign Office from Mallet's sources was relatively sparse,[70] while by the same token the coverage of the *Mercure*

69. Mallet Du Pan to the chevalier de Gallatin, February 28, 1800, Sayous,
II, 439.
70. The ministry itself did have some sort of spy network in France and
it involved a certain "M. Mallet," by and concerning whom there are a number of documents in the Public Record Office, F.O. 27, vols. 53 and 54. This
individual repeatedly requested payment from Canning for bulletins obtained
by him from a correspondent in Paris who used the name "Julie Caron." In
Jacques Godechot, "Le Directoire vu de Londres," *Annales historiques de
la Révolution française*, XXI (1949), 319–20, "M. Mallet" is identified with
Mallet Du Pan, who is thus described, both here and in the same author's
La Contre-révolution 1789–1804 (Paris, 1961), p. 90, as an espionage agent
employed by the British government, the head of an organization, in 1798
and 1799. Now in the view of the present writer there can be no doubt that
Mallet Du Pan would have been happy to be at this time in the regular
employ of the British government, instead of being treated as a kind of
incidental partner in the exchange of intelligence, for services in which role
the somewhat meager assistance given the *Mercure britannique* was considered sufficient compensation. But it also seems to the present writer that,
for several reasons, "M. Mallet" could not have been Mallet Du Pan. He
is identified in a letter of the adventurous Channel raider, Sir Sidney Smith,
dated on his ship the *Tigre* at Spithead, August 26, 1798, as "the Rouen chief
M. Mallet," and attached to one of the latter's letters is a note reading: "This
M. Mallet is an agent Sir S. S. left here for the arrangement of the correspondence with Paris." Now Mallet Du Pan as an intelligence agent before
coming to England never worked out of Rouen and had never at any time
lived there. He customarily used the name Mallet Du Pan, which would
distinguish him from other persons named Mallet. These were very possibly
numerous around Rouen, whence Mallet's own ancestors had emigrated to
Geneva in the sixteenth century. He was known to the public as Mallet Du
Pan, and furthermore, having achieved a certain celebrity as a journalist
and publicist, he would probably have been sufficiently well known to Sir
Sidney Smith and even to minor officials in the Foreign Office not to have
been identified merely as "the Rouen chief" or as "an agent Sir S. S. left
here." The handwriting of the letters signed by "M. Mallet" is not that of
Mallet Du Pan. The kind of intelligence work the "Rouen chief" was engaged in—simply the procurement and transmittal of packets of bulletins—
was not what Mallet Du Pan considered appropriate to his qualifications as
an interpreter of intelligence and adviser to governments (though, to be
sure, he did sometimes transmit raw data along with his interpretations).
And finally, the correspondents of Mallet Du Pan, so far as we can form an
idea of them, were not the sort of people to threaten the discontinuance of

britannique was by no means equal to that of the former *Mercure historique et politique.*

The new journal nevertheless justified itself financially, although not on anything like the scale of Panckoucke's *Mercure.*[71] It also obtained an international reputation, for it appears to have sold widely on the Continent, even being pirated. Expurgated versions were appearing in Paris at the time of the coup d'état of 18 Brumaire. Mallet published a disavowal of these, saying that the only authentic editions were those printed in London and sold by the agents named on the cover or distributed on the Continent by the Imperial posts or the house of Fauche in Hamburg.[72]

The journal made its debut with the long article comprising the first three numbers, entitled "An Historical Essay upon the Destruction of the Helvetic League and Liberty."[73] This came out of Mallet Du Pan's immediate experience and the subject touched him closely. Running through the essay is a note of denunciation of the Directorial policy of territorial expansion that Mallet saw as a revival of Girondism.[74] His contempt and intense hostility for the Directory are indeed reminiscent of his earlier animus against the Gironde. Mallet had dreaded the Mountain but in a way respected it; the Gironde he had not only dreaded but hated and despised.

Among other principal articles were those that discussed, at some length, Bonaparte's accession to power. Mallet's reaction was very definite. Although he did not write precisely in the terms of his prediction of 1796, in the *Correspondance politique*, about the Revolution ending with a "single tyrant,"[75] he was thinking in those terms. Here, clearly, was the single tyrant, not the Liberator, let alone a Legislator. What he said was that, while it was impossible to disapprove the principle of a revolution (i.e., Bonaparte's advent to

their services if their pay were not immediately forthcoming, as "M. Mallet" implied his were. In sum, the head of the "apparatus" indicated in the Record Office documents concerning "M. Mallet" must, I think, be some one other than Mallet Du Pan. (From the documents, it would appear that the "M." means "Monsieur," not a name. If it meant a name, the identification with Jacques Mallet Du Pan would have been of course still less plausible.)

71. Sayous, II, 442.
72. *British Mercury*, IV, no. 29 (Nov. 30, 1799), 255.
73. Ibid., I, nos. 1–3 (late Aug. and Sept., 1798), i–xii, 1–270.
74. Ibid., pp. 98, 102–6.
75. *Correspondance politique*, pp. xviii–xix.

power) that ended the progress of disorder and anarchy, still one could not be happy about the means by which this one had been accomplished.⁷⁶ Now Mallet was not one to deplore the use of military force per se; it seems that what he really deplored was the elevation of a military chieftain just because he disposed of the force; and in particular he mistrusted this chieftain. Mallet was not unaware of the collaboration of Sieyès in the Constitution of the Year VIII, which would not have recommended it to him for that matter, but he saw in the business, from first to last, mainly Bonaparte. The constitution represented only the despotic ambition of this personage. "I have never heard of any free republic," he wrote of that document, "in which the People were so stripped of their privileges and of their influence; not [nor?] any aristocratic state in which the chief magistrate was invested with so monstrous a power as that of the Chief Consul."⁷⁷ Very shortly, however, he expressed privately the opinion that Bonaparte was acting with great skill in securing widespread support for his régime, and said that he thought the time when Louis XVIII would be restored appeared to him very remote.⁷⁸

Had Mallet Du Pan lived to see the Civil Code and the Concordat, would he have come to regard Bonaparte as the Liberator France required? It is conceivable. His friends Mounier and Malouet came over to Bonaparte. But again, had Mallet lived and been permitted to return to France, where he had been denied citizenship by the treaty of annexation of Geneva,⁷⁹ would the régime not have seemed to him as despotic as that which he had lived and worked under in France before the Revolution? He would probably have had to turn to journalism, and it is somehow impossible to imagine Mallet Du Pan putting out a journal that would have been tolerated by the First Consul, let alone the French Emperor. He would have found himself after all in the company of Madame de Staël, whom Bonaparte exiled, not to mention those continuators of the philosophe tradition, the members of the Division of Moral and Political Sciences of the Institut de France, which Bonaparte suppressed.

76. *British Mercury*, IV, no. 30 (Dec. 16, 1799), 333.
77. Ibid., IV, no. 32 (Jan. 15, 1800), 464.
78. Mallet Du Pan to the comte de Sainte-Aldegonde, February 27, 1800, Sayous, II, 435–36; Mallet Du Pan to the chevalier de Gallatin, February 28, 1800, ibid., p. 439.
79. Sayous, II, 356 and n. 2, p. 356.

It was to compensate for the thinness of the news, suggests Sayous,[80] that Mallet published in the *Mercure britannique* a number of articles more retrospective or purely historical than those he had been wont to write for the *Mercure historique et politique*.

Such an inference is no doubt partly justified, but only partly, for Mallet Du Pan already possessed a developed historical view of the Revolution and had committed much of his thought to paper before he was faced by the dearth of intelligence. The tendency back to history in his work seems rather to have been produced by the overthrow of monarchy in France and the impossibility of his continuing to play a role directly in the constitutional struggle.

Under the first impact of the French Revolution the historian in Mallet Du Pan had permitted himself to be elbowed aside by the advocate. During the years of exile, however, the historian recovered his place. Not that the advocate disappeared, or that Mallet attempted a narrative history of the Revolution. The only extended treatment of events that appeared over his signature was the "Historical Essay upon the Destruction of the Helvetic League and Liberty," and this too was rather more a tract for the times than a history. But, both in his contemporaneously published writings (especially the *Mercure britannique*) and in the correspondence that he composed in 1793 and 1794 for the British Foreign Office are reflections on the causal factors and the dynamic of the French and European Revolution that for historiographical interest go beyond anything he had published earlier, while they are also partly an extension of ideas he had adumbrated before 1789. Even then, he had regarded himself as the historian of a society in transition. He was fascinated by questions of reform and revolution in society at large. As a journalist, he had denied that his work could be in any sense historically definitive, but his journalism was historically oriented. Fate permitted him to witness the Revolution in France, and therefore to mature and complete his conceptions, even while at the same time becoming emotionally more involved in what was occurring, playing the role of advocate.

Mallet Du Pan thought that one of the stumbling blocks in the way of effective opposition to the Revolution was that people generally had very simplistic ideas about its causes. Contemporaries, he remarked, instead of looking at the historical process broadly and in

80. Ibid., p. 442.

depth, were wont to see only accidental events produced by transient causes, because for one thing this was more consoling—it was possible thus to believe that the hated events could be overmastered by superior force. But on the contrary, such climacteric calamities as the European revolution of the close of the eighteenth century were the product of social factors developing over a long period of time and there was nothing accidental about them.[81]

To explain the origins of the eighteenth century revolution one had to begin with the era of the Reformation, which was another such convulsion with consequences of like magnitude. The consequences here were not only spiritual but political, for by the time of the peace of Westphalia the power of the secular rulers, the monarchs, was vastly increased. In France, Louis XIV carried the tendency further, completing the political humbling of the nobility. At the same time, he raised two new powers, the one that of the merchant-manufacturers (*négociants*) and men of capital (*capitalistes*) the other that of the men of letters. The first power battened on the war needs of the state, and the second, which had been intended simply to embellish the life of the court, became fifty years later the regulators of public opinion. Under Louis XV the levelling process in the society continued, and soon the old system of orders failed to correspond to the newer economic and social realities. Commerce, travel, a cosmopolitan spirit, and the press, which made the opinions of one person the property of millions, together with the equalizing effect of the diffusion of wealth upon "the influence, education, and capacity of citizens"—all this culminated in a "terrible struggle" between the system of the preexisting distinctions and that of the new distinctions.[82] "It is on this conflict," said Mallet Du Pan, "infinitely more than on liberty, forever unintelligible to the French, that the Revolution has been founded and will rest until the end. Its republicanism ends by reconstituting the powers it had overthrown, for it is to their displacement, not their destruction, that its founders, its file leaders, its legislators, have aspired."[83] Here, laying stress on broad social and political factors in the historical process, Mallet developed a conception of social evolution as historical cause that was only occasionally foreshadowed in his earlier writings. For example,

81. *Mercure britannique*, IV, no. 32 (Jan. 10, 1800), 455–56.
82. Ibid., pp. 456–61.   83. Ibid., p. 462.

he had always associated the political discontent of the Genevan Représentants with the increasing prosperity of the city in the eighteenth century (the implication being that money corrupts, especially new money); but the idea of the growing disparity in France between the wealth of the middle classes and their position in the hierarchy of orders, which he saw as a fundamental issue of the French Revolution, is more sophisticated as sociological analysis.

But it was not this social conflict that brought about the first act of the Revolution in France. A purely political factor was also involved, and at the start it was primary. "A revolution," said Mallet Du Pan, "is essentially a displacement of power, which occurs necessarily whenever the former power no longer has the force to defend the public interest or the courage to protect itself."[84] This happened at the moment when the king, in monarchist theory the sole ruler and administrator, was forced to convoke the Estates General. This, the "disastrous innovation" of the Estates General, derived from the disorder of the finances and the ill-considered policies of successive ministers, together with the conflicts they engendered between the sovereign and "the great corporations of the state [i.e., the parlements]."[85]

In Mallet's analysis the nobility do not appear as a dynamic social element. The conflict of the parlements with the crown throughout the eighteenth century is not seen as an aspect of a "resurgence of the *noblesse*," but simply as the actions of certain "great corporations of the state." The social dynamism, and therefore more of the responsibility, lies with the middle classes.

The French Revolution was in reality a series of revolutions. A second displacement of power, called by Mallet the Revolution of July 14, occurred with the reunion of the orders in a single assembly. It was here that the social antagonism above described produced its effects. A third revolution, that of October 6, consolidated the second, putting the king into the hands of the city of Paris. A fourth, that of August 10, 1792, caused power to pass from the monarchists of the Constitution of 1791, the *constitutionnaires* (Mallet writes now *constitutionnaires*, now *constitutionnels*), to the republicans.

84. Mallet Du Pan to Lord Elgin and the comte de Mercy-Argenteau, November 30, 1793, Sayous, I, 395.
85. Ibid., pp. 395–96.

In the fifth, that of May 31, 1793, power passed from the Girondins to the *sans-culottes*.

Each revolution was made in the name of the people, but the sense of the word changed nearly every time. At the first revolution, it meant all classes of the population (as when the parlements opposed the crown in the name of the people or nation). At the second, the *factieux*, notably the abbé Sieyès, limited the meaning to the third estate. At the Revolution of August 10, the republicans were divided as to whether the term should include the proprietors, and the upshot, in the Revolution of May 31, was that it did not. It meant only "the famished, the indigent, the *sans-culottes*," who were of course the most numerous and therefore the strongest part of the nation. (One observes again how the word *sans-culottes* in Mallet's vocabulary tends to be synonymous with "the poor" and with *prolétaires*.) Each revolution furthermore was followed by a displacement of property rights: the revolution of the Estates General by the abolition of pecuniary privileges; that of July 14 by the suppression of tithes, corvées, and part of the feudal dues; that of October 6, by the confiscation of the property of the clergy; and that of May 31, by the enactment of the Maximum, which Mallet referred to as the first of the "agrarian laws."[86] Mallet held that under the Jacobin dictatorship, the rule of the *Maratistes* as he termed it, the Revolution was proceeding toward the principle that property was common to the whole society.[87] Among the resources of the revolutionary government in 1794 he counted heavily its ability to command "all the properties of the realm, capital and income."[88]

Mallet explained the proletarian character that he saw the Revolution assuming by the misery of the poor. Nor did he regard this as being merely a product of the disturbed conditions of the Revolution. He said that a disproportion between wages and the cost of the necessities of life (*subsistances*) had long been increasing in almost all the great states of Europe, and claimed that this had been demonstrated by statistics drawn up in England by "the Committee of Commerce and Colonies." The country most affected was France.[89]

86. Ibid., pp. 397–99.
87. Ibid., pp. 399–401.
88. Mallet Du Pan to Lord Elgin, January 24, 1794, *Despatches of Earl Gower*, Appendix, p. 323.
89. *Considérations sur la nature de la Révolution de France*, pp. 22–23.

The *sans-culottes*, unlike the bourgeoisie, had had a real, i.e., an economic, grievance. They were not merely jealous, and their basic aims were more economic than political. But being men they, too, were not immune to jealousy and to being corrupted by the love of power, that great and universal human vice. And although their own actions were anarchistic, they were ultimately led by a revolutionary government that understood the organization of power incomparably well. Mallet Du Pan became aware that the dictatorship of the Committee of Public Safety offended the anarchism of the *sans-culottes*, whose leaders became in turn a faction, the Hébertists, whom the Committee destroyed, but none the less the Revolution that the Committee led was in his thinking the revolution of "the poor" against the propertied.[90] The war itself took on this character, involving the spoliation of conquered territory.[91] Following the episodes of Germinal and Prairial, Year III, wherein the erstwhile *sans-culotte* régime was given the coup de grace, there was established, as Mallet related it, a neo-Girondin one,[92] but sans-culottism was not absolutely dead.[93] It was moreover a logical possibility in any republican régime of the time and Europe must dread it since the Directory's policy was to republicanize Europe.[94]

The *sans-culotte* revolution was the culmination of terrorism and of attacks on property, but it had been implicit in Jacobinism from the start, and the advocates of "royal democracy," the men of 1789–1791, had done much to be forgiven, though in the interests of monarchy they must be reconciled. To forgive the Girondins, the sophistical republicans and ideologists *par excellence*, revolutionaries such as Brissot and Condorcet, was impossible. Both these subfactions were in their heyday demagogues and but for them there would have been no *sans-culotte* revolution. It was in France as it had been earlier in Geneva: the political virus had spread from the well-to-do to the lower classes.

90. Mallet Du Pan to Lord Elgin, [March] 1794, *Fortescue Manuscripts*, III, 491–508; [Mallet Du Pan to Elgin], Berne, June 8, 1794, *Despatches of Earl Gower*, Appendix, pp. 367–70.

91. *Considérations sur la nature de la Révolution de France*, pp. 26–27.

92. Mallet Du Pan to the Court of Vienna, June 3 and 13, 1795, *Correspondance . . . avec la cour de Vienne*, I, 219 and 225.

93. Mallet Du Pan to the Court of Vienna, December 27, 1795, ibid., p. 401.

94. Mallet Du Pan to the Court of Vienna, May 25, 1796, ibid., II, 77.

It was to be expected that the *sans-culotte* revolution would be stopped everywhere, at least for the present. But the feudal nobility had been shaken to its foundations throughout Europe, except in states where hereditary distinctions had been invested with a political character and had thus been "tied to the public interest and even to that of liberty." The Catholic clergy, Mallet added, had been threatened with an analogous loss of their property rights and prerogatives.[95] These were the principal social results of the Revolution, as he saw them in 1800.

Mallet Du Pan's view of the causes of the Revolution, while stressing socio-economic and political factors, extended also to the influence of ideas, and he discussed this subject at length in more than one connection. Now the contemporary preoccupation with philosophy as a revolutionary influence seemed to him (as it seemed to his friend Mounier)[96] to have produced a great deal of silliness. With the obscurantism of such people as the abbé Barruel he had absolutely no patience,[97] and complained that a league of "counter-revolutionary fools and fanatics" in Europe would, if they could, forbid men to observe and think, and by so much were really discrediting the counter-revolution.[98] In 1793, writing to Lord Elgin on the causes of the Revolution, he went so far as to say: "It is an error to think that the French Revolution draws its origin, as is commonly said, from the spirit of philosophy, of depravity, and of irreligion that has long reigned in France. . . . The immoderate (*mal réglé*) spirit of philosophy, like the immoderate spirit of religion, like the dogmatic spirit of whatever sort it may be, uses or takes over revolutions, but does not make them."[99] The origin of the Revolution was political, as he went on to explain, thence proceeding to describe its successive phases in terms of the socio-economic and political factors that have already been described. But it is impossible to think, in view of every-

95. *Mercure britannique*, IV, no. 32 (Jan. 10, 1800), 462–63.
96. J.-J. Mounier, *De l'influence attribuée aux philosophes, aux francs-maçons et aux illuminés sur la révolution de France* . . . (Tubingen, 1801), passim.
97. Lanzac de Laborie, *Un royaliste libéral*, p. 302, quoting from the *Mercure britannique*, I, 549.
98. *Correspondance politique pour servir à l'histoire du républicanisme français*, p. vi.
99. Mallet Du Pan to Lord Elgin and the comte de Mercy-Argenteau, November 20, 1793, Sayous, I, 394–95. My translation.

thing else he had to say on the subject, that Mallet Du Pan was here simply dismissing philosophy as an element in the causal pattern of the Revolution. Rather, he was making the point that ignorance generally prevailed as to what had actually happened in France, and was perhaps suggesting that the statesmen and intelligent persons of the Coalition states should resist the distracting temptation to witch-hunting and devote their efforts to coping more effectively with the political and material phenomena that confronted them.

For what, then, *was* philosophy responsible?

A decade and more before the Revolution, Mallet Du Pan had believed he was witness to a widespread decline of morality, and his own early anti-philosophism was related to this conviction.[100] In the Revolution he claimed to see overwhelming evidence of such a decline, carried even further. He thought the appeal of the republicans was based on "the corruption (*dépravation*) of *moeurs* . . . the destruction of all the restraints of morality, of honor, of religion . . . the loosening of the bonds of husbands and wives, of sons, of servants, of youth, of all social relationships."[101] The revolutionary individualism, in short, was but the culmination of that hedonism in the Enlightenment that Mallet Du Pan had always deplored. Against the philosophes, against not only the atheists but also Voltaire and his like, must be laid the charge of teaching men to substitute sophistical reasoning for the rules imposed by conscience and tradition, of calling into question everything hitherto learned from religion, experience, and "sound" philosophy, and of "having thus prepared the public anarchy by an anarchy of mind."[102]

As for the contributions of the philosophes to the Revolution in its specifically political sense, that is, to democracy and republicanism (since this was what the Revolution meant to Mallet Du Pan), one must make distinctions, for the philosophes were by no means all alike. Mallet exonerated Voltaire completely, although he did so in an uncharitable way that suggests a revival of the old animus: Voltaire was actually a flatterer of kings, not their enemy.[103] Moreover, Voltaire's appeal as a writer was limited to the upper classes,

100. See above, chapter 2, passim.

101. "Du principe des factions, et de celles qui divisent la France," *Mercure historique et politique*, 1791, No. 41 (Oct. 8), pp. 135–36.

102. *British Mercury*, II, no. 14 (March 15, 1799), 358–59.

103. Ibid., pp. 343–45.

and even there to the more frivolous elements.[104] (What would Mallet have replied if one had at this point objected to him his own early admiration, and that of many in Calvinist Geneva, for the sage of Ferney?)

If Voltaire was politically innocuous, not so Rousseau, who "seduced honesty itself" and who had a far larger public among the middling and lower classes. Mallet Du Pan now (that is, in 1799) described Rousseau in terms whose hostility contrasts sharply with the praise he had formerly accorded him as a powerful defender of morality against the hedonists and atheists. Rousseau now wore a thoroughly antisocial appearance. His jealous independence, said Mallet Du Pan, his poverty and the wandering life in which his youth was passed, and his aversion for every kind of "civil superiority," dictated all his theories. "He revived the Levellers' and Anabaptists' dogmas of equality; his hatred for the distinctions of rank shows itself in every one of his works. . . . He it was alone who introduced among the French the doctrine of the sovereignty of the people. . . . I could hardly mention a single Revolutionist who was not transported by his anarchical theorems. . . ."[105]

It was not that Mallet Du Pan had waited until the French Revolution to discover that the *Contrat social* was a dangerously democratic book, for such was not the case. But where he had once been able to write dispassionately of it, and seems earlier to have regarded Rousseau as but the most eloquent spokesman for the Genevan democrats, he now singled out his late compatriot for special opprobrium. Yet it must also be noted that he did insist that Rousseau, no less than Voltaire, would have recoiled from "the theoretical and practical system of Jacobinism" as developed in the Revolution: Rousseau would not have considered democracy as a form of government or a republic viable in France, or sanctioned the *sans-culotte* revolution.[106]

Of more immediate influence than Rousseau in the formation of the "theoretical and practical system of Jacobinism" (by which Mallet no doubt had in mind the unicameral assembly, the minimization of the royal prerogative, the clubs—above all the clubs) were, in

104. Ibid., pp. 353–54.
105. Ibid., pp. 354–55.   106. Ibid., p. 338.

Mallet's opinion, two other philosophes. One was Condorcet, whom he had criticized before the Revolution for *esprit de système* and whom he continued to despise as a leading Girondin ideologist. The other was Diderot, singled out particularly for his collaboration in the later and more seditious editions of Raynal's *Philosophical and Political History of the Establishments and the Commerce of the Europeans in the Two Indies.* Mallet did not wish to denounce Raynal himself, who had publicly retracted his errors, but Diderot was fair game. What these two (Condorcet and Diderot-Raynal) had done was to "form" a new generation, the revolutionary generation of philosophes.[107] For as Mallet saw it, the relation between philosophy and the Revolution was to be understood only if one realized that philosophy itself had become denatured, so to speak, even since the death of Voltaire and Rousseau. It no longer had intellectual substance. The philosophes of the Revolution were a "crowd of petty reasoners without genius and without principles . . . pretenders to the dignity of philosophers." They were in short trouble-makers, slogan-mouthers, demagogues, who suddenly appeared from everywhere with the convocation of the Estates General.[108] When, on the eve of the French Revolution, Mallet had complained that the culture of the Enlightenment was degenerating into a sort of nihilism, he was thinking chiefly of moral and intellectual manifestations of such a decline, but much political writing had also appeared to him to have an unrealistic if not downright anti-intellectual tenor. Now that the French Revolution had occurred, he read the nihilist development fully as much in political terms. This was the "immoderate spirit of philosophy" that had, as he said to Elgin, not caused but taken over the Revolution and that had given it its fanatical character. Mallet's latter-day thought about the direction of "philosophy," both moral and political, drew upon his earlier conceptions, but the tone of his utterance was harsher and more strident—even toward the earlier masters, Voltaire and especially Rousseau. The worthy Mably also appeared in retrospect much too republican.[109] For Mallet had been embittered by the French Revolution. He had adventured his career in France and had lost, and with the subjec-

107. Ibid., pp. 357–58.
108. Ibid., pp. 352–53, 358–61.   109. Ibid., p. 356.

tion of Geneva and all Switzerland he had also lost, as he said, "a country, relations, and friends."[110] Still, he was himself the child of the Enlightenment, and to make philosophy responsible without reservation for all the sins of the revolutionaries, to repudiate reason and take refuge in obscurantism, a counter-revolutionary anti-intellectualism, was unthinkable.

A representative of the developing eighteenth century interest in the history of society and social change, and a notable practitioner of the historian's craft in relation to his journalism, Mallet Du Pan adhered firmly, it thus appears, to a pluralistic view of historical causation. He would have regarded any sort of monism as *esprit de système*, a fanatic disregard of the multiplicity of phenomena. By the same token, there was nothing teleological about his conception of the direction of social change. Patterns might be discerned, it is true, but what had happened in France and seemed to be happening elsewhere (because Europe was a single civilization) was the outcome simply of the interplay of many sorts of phenomena. It did not reveal God's Providence, or the advance of Reason, or a movement toward any particular form or ideal of ultimate society. In so far as Mallet Du Pan thought in deterministic terms, he had adhered to a cyclical view of culture prior to the French Revolution and probably continued to do so, since the revolutionary epoch could be regarded as a degenerative phase; but such a conception did not intrude itself into his analysis of what was taking place.

Nor was Mallet Du Pan a deterministic thinker in a more primitive way. To be sure, quotations may be adduced purporting to show that Mallet, at least as an émigré, succumbed to fatalism, and his tendency to melancholia seems to support such an interpretation. He wrote, for example, of "the imperative nature of things, that is to say, that force independent of men and governments, which ties them to the consequences of their own works and ends by winning the mastery over them after having ceased to obey them."[111] Still, what does this say, if it says anything, but that the consequences of one's actions may be harder to escape than one had supposed? Then there is also

110. Ibid., I, nos. 1–3 (Aug. and Sept., 1798), viii.
111. Quoted in Fernand Baldensperger, *Le mouvement des idées dans l'émigration française* (1789–1815), 2 vols. (c. 1924), II, 81, citing the *Mercure britannique*, May 10, 1799.

the assertion: "Two despotic sovereigns soar above (*planent sur*) our wills, necessity and the imperious course of events." Now the context in which these words appear is a complaint that the opponents of the Revolution never see any alternatives but the best or the worst, all or nothing, whereas it is well to be more realistic.[112] The figure of speech would seem only to signify that in a world where one must act the choices are limited, and one must often settle for less than the most desired outcome. Mallet Du Pan would have agreed that conscious volition in human action where the object was to alter the trend of a whole society was up against tremendous odds. And yet, social change was the outcome of human choices, great or small. The important thing in political action, like anything else, was to know how to choose one's course. This knowledge, this method, lay in *la saine philosophie,* wisdom gleaned from the best thought of the past, and in *la politique expérimentale,* for the practice of which history, in particular contemporary history, afforded a mine of experiential data. Both the historian (including in the genre the political journalist) and the statesman needed to be empiricists.

112. *Considérations sur la nature de la Révolution de France,* p. 77.

Bibliography

Manuscript Collections

Switzerland

Bibliothèque Publique et Universitaire de Genève. Correspondence, with some related papers, in MS Supp. 150; D.O.; Collection Coindet, MS Supp. 363; Collection Eynard; Archives Tronchin 219; Papiers Reybaz, "Lettres de principaux correspondants"; MS Bonnet 40 and 77.
Bibliothèque Publique de la Ville de Neuchâtel. Lettres de Mallet Du Pan à la Société Typographique de Neuchâtel, MS 1178, fo 22–121.

France

Archives Nationales, Paris. Catalogue of the library of Mallet Du Pan, émigré, in F^{76} and F^{ff}.
Archives du Ministère des Affaires Etrangères, Paris. Correspondance politique de Genève, vols. 84, 87, 88, 90, 92, 93, 94.
Bibliothèque de l'Institut de France, Paris. Papiers et correspondance de Pierre-Michel Hennin, MS 1269.
Bibliothèque de la Ville de Reims. MS 1916, Lettre 183.

England

Public Record Office, London. Correspondence in F. O. 27, vols. 53 and 54.
Mallet Papers, London. Private archives of the Mallet family, descendants of Mallet Du Pan, under the custodianship of Lady Mallet, widow of the late Sir Victor Mallet, of Wittersham House, Tenterden, Kent. Correspondence and other papers of Mallet Du Pan, the greater number postdating 1791. Many have been published in Sayous and in the *Mémoires de Malouet* (q.v.).

Published Sources

Correspondence

Brissot, J.-P. *Correspondance et papiers.* Ed. Claude Perroud. Paris, [1912].

Mallet Du Pan. Blondel, Aug., ed. "Lettres inédites de Mallet du Pan à Etienne Dumont (1787–1789)." *Revue historique,* XCVII (Jan.–April, 1908), 95–121.

———. Descostes, François, ed. *La Révolution française vue de l'étranger* (1789–1799). *Mallet du Pan à Berne et à Londres d'après une correspondance inédite.* Tours, 1897. (Includes extensive quotations from what De Pins says were copies, now lost, of the correspondence addressed to Souza Coutinho.)

———. "Deux lettres inédites de Mallet du Pan." *Mémoires et documents publiés par la Société d'histoire et d'archéologie de Genève,* XXII (1886), 357–66.

———. Dufour-Vernes, Louis. *Recherches sur J.-J. Rousseau et sa parenté, accompagnés de lettres inédites de Mallet-Du Pan, J.-J. Rousseau et Jacob Vernes.* Geneva, 1878.

———. Gower, George Granville Leveson, Earl. *The Despatches of Earl Gower, English Ambassador at Paris from June 1790 to August 1792 . . .* [with Appendix], Ed. Oscar Browning. Cambridge, 1885. (The Appendix contains dispatches of Mallet Du Pan to Lord Elgin in 1794, together with a letter of Elgin to Lord Grenville on the subject of Mallet Du Pan's services.)

———. Hérisson, Comte [Maurice d'Irisson] d', ed. *Autour d'une Révolution* (1788–1799). Paris, 1888.

———. Historical Manuscripts Commission. *Report on the Manuscripts of J. B. Fortesque, Esq., Preserved at Dropmore,* vol. III. London, 1899. (This volume contains a dispatch of Mallet Du Pan to Lord Elgin of March, 1794.)

———. Michel, André, ed. *Correspondance inédite de Mallet du Pan avec la cour de Vienne* (1794–1798), *publiée d'après les manuscrits conservés aux archives de Vienne. . . .* 2 vols. Paris, 1884.

———. Pins, J. de. "La correspondance de Mallet du Pan avec la cour de Lisbonne," *Annales historiques de la Révolution française,* no. 178 (Oct.–Dec., 1964), pp. 469–77; no. 182 (Oct.–Dec., 1965), pp. 468–84; no. 183 (Jan.–March, 1966), pp. 84–94. (The series of articles consists of an introduction followed by selections from the archival correspondence.)

———. Sayous, A. *Mémoires et correspondance de Mallet du Pan, pour servir à l'histoire de la Révolution française. . . .* 2 vols. Paris, 1851. (The title is misleading, for the work contains no memoirs of Mallet in the usual sense. It is a collection of letters, with some material from a personal journal or diary kept at times by Mallet and some selections from his contemporary publications, all strung together in a biographical framework written by Sayous. Some letters addressed to Mallet Du Pan are included.)

————. Van Berchem, Victor, ed. *Lettres de Mallet-DuPan à Saladin-Egerton 1794–1800*. Geneva, 1896.

Malouet. *Mémoires de Malouet publiés par son petit-fils le baron Malouet. Deuxième édition, augmentée de lettres inédites.* 2 vols. Paris, 1874. (The correspondence, which is in vol. II, consists principally but not entirely of letters from Malouet to Mallet Du Pan.)

Staël-Holstein, baron de. *Correspondance diplomatique du baron de Staël-Holstein, ambassadeur de Suède en France.... Documents inédits sur la révolution (1783–1799) recueillis aux Archives royales de Suède. ...* Ed. L. Léouzon Le Duc. Paris, 1881.

Voltaire. *Voltaire's Correspondence.* Ed. Theodore Besterman. 107 vols. Geneva, 1953–1965.

Memoirs

Brissot, J.-P. *Mémoires (1754–1793).* Ed. Claude Perroud. 2 vols. Paris, [1910].

Cornuaud, Isaac. *Mémoires de Isaac Cornuaud sur Genève et la Révolution de 1770 à 1795.* Ed. Emilie Cherbuliez with an introduction by Gaspard Vallette. Geneva, 1912.

Dumont, Etienne. *Souvenirs sur Mirabeau et sur les deux premières assemblées législatives.* Ed. J. Bénétruy. Paris, [1950].

Garat, D. J. *Mémoires historiques sur le XVIIIe siècle.* Second edition. 2 vols. N.p., 1821.

Mallet Du Pan. See under *Correspondence.*

Peuchet, Jacques. *Mémoires sur Mirabeau et son époque.* 4 vols. Paris, 1824.

Journals

Mallet Du Pan, author and editor. *Annales politiques, civiles et littéraires du dix-huitième siècle; ouvrage périodique, pour servir de suite aux Annales de M. Linguet.* Title changing March 15, 1783, to *Mémoires historiques, politiques et littéraires sur l'état présent de l'Europe.* 6 vols. London [Geneva], 1781–1783.

————. *Journal historique et politique de Genève.* Paris, 1784*–1792.

————. *Mercure de France,* political section, successively entitled *Journal politique de Bruxelles* (Paris, 1784* et sqq.); *Mercure historique et*

* 1784 is the date when Mallet Du Pan became editor. The journals themselves antedated his editorship.

politique de Bruxelles (Dec. 5, 1789 et sqq.); *Mercure historique et politique* (Nov. 6, 1790 et sqq.)

———. *Mercure britannique.* 5 vols. London, 1798–1800.

———. *The British Mercury.* 5 vols. London, 1798–1800. (The English version of the preceding title.)

Analyse des papiers anglais. Paris, Nov. 14, 1787–Nov. 19, 1789.

Annales politiques, civiles et littéraires du dix-huitième siècle; ouvrage périodique, par M. Linguet. London, Brussels, Paris, 1777–1792.

Journal de politique et de littérature, contenant les principaux évènemens de toutes les cours; les nouvelles de la république des lettres, &. Brussels [Paris], 1774–1778. (1778 was the date when Panckoucke merged the journal with the *Mercure,* of which it became the political section.)

Journal helvétique, ou Annales littéraires et politiques de l'Europe, et principalement de la Suisse. Neuchâtel, 1733–1782.

Mercure de France, dédié au roi, par une société de gens de lettres. Paris, 1672 et sqq. under various titles. (The title here given is the one it had under Panckoucke from 1778 to Dec. 17, 1791, when it became *Mercure français, politique, historique et littéraire.*)

Nouvelles à la main

Bachaumont, Louis Petit de, and continuators. *Mémoires secrets, pour servir à l'histoire de la république des lettres en France, depuis MDCC-LXII jusqu'à nos jours; ou Journal d'un observateur.* . . . 36 vols. London, 1780–1789.

Grimm, [F.-M, baron de] et al. *Correspondance littéraire, philosophique et critique par Grimm, Diderot, Raynal, Meister, etc.* Ed. Maurice Tourneux. 16 vols. Paris, 1877–1882.

Lescure, M.-F.-A. de, ed. *Correspondance secrète, inédite, sur Louis XVI, Marie Antoinette, la cour et la ville de 1777 à 1792.* 2 vols. Paris, 1866.

Collected Works

Condorcet, Marquis de. *Oeuvres de Condorcet.* Ed. A. Condorcet O'Connor and M. F. Arago. 12 vols. Paris, 1847–1849.

Linguet, S.-N. *Oeuvres de M. Linguet.* 6 vols. London, 1774.

Voltaire. *Oeuvres complètes de Voltaire.* Ed. Louis Moland. 52 vols. Paris, 1877–1885.

Pamphlets by Mallet Du Pan[1]

Compte rendu de la défense des citoyens-bourgeois de Genève, adressé

1. These, listed in chronological order, are not a complete list of Mallet

aux Commissaires des Représentants, par un citoyen natif. [1771].

Quelle est l'influence de la philosophie sur les belles-lettres? Discours inaugural prononcé à Cassel le 8 avril 1772, par Mr. Mallet, Professeur en Histoire et Belles Lettres-Françaises. Cassel, [1772].

*Doutes sur l'éloquence et les systêmes politiques, adressés à M. le baron de B * * * *; chambellan de S. A. R. le prince H. de P. Par M. M., citoyen de Genève.* London, [Neuchâtel], 1775.

Idées soumises à l'examen de tous les conciliateurs par un médiateur sans conséquence. [1780.]

Supplément nécessaire à un ouvrage intitulé: Le Philadelphien à Genève. . . . 1783. (Taken from *Mémoires historiques*, no. 45, July 15, 1783.)

Du principe des factions en général, et de celles qui divisent la France. Paris, 1791. (Taken from *Mercure historique et politique*, Sept.–Oct., 1791, nos, 38, 40, and 41.

Lettre de M. Mallet du Pan à M. d. B. sur les événemens de Paris du 10 Août. [1792.]

Considérations sur la nature de la Révolution de France, et sur les causes qui en prolongent la durée. London, Brussels, 1793.

Correspondance politique pour servir à l'histoire du républicanisme français. Hamburg [and London], 1796.

Books and Pamphlets by Others than Mallet Du Pan

Argenson, Marquis d'. *Considérations sur le gouvernement ancien et présent de la France, comparé avec celui des autres états; suivies d'un nouveau plan d'administration.* Amsterdam, 1784 [first edition published in 1764].

Brissot, J.-P. *Le Philadelphien à Genève, ou Lettres d'un Américain sur la dernière révolution de Genève, sa constitution nouvelle, l'émigration en Irlande, etc., pouvant servir de tableau politique de Genève jusqu'en 1784 [sic].* Dublin, 1783.

DeLolme, J.-L. *The Constitution of England, or an Account of the English Government: In which it is compared, both with the Republican Form of Government, and the other Monarchies in Europe.* Fourth edition. London, 1784.

[Ivernois, Sir Francis d'.] *Tableau historique et politique des deux dernières révolutions de Genève* [1768–1789]. London, 1789.

―――――. *Un mémoire inédit de Francis d'Ivernois sur la situation politi-*

Du Pan's miscellaneous publications. Not all the reprints from his journals have been included, or the book reviews and other articles he occasionally contributed to other journals, or pamphlets the writer knows only by report.

que à Genève au début de 1791 et sur les moyens d'y établir un gou-vernement stable. Ed. Otto Karmin. Geneva, 1915.

Mounier, Jean-Joseph. *De l'influence attribuée aux philosophes, aux francs-maçons et aux illuminés, sur la Révolution de France*. . . . Tübingen, 1901.

Special Studies[2]

Acomb, Frances. *Anglophobia in France 1763–1789: An Essay in the History of Constitutionalism and Nationalism*. Durham, N.C., 1950.

Baldensperger, Fernand. *Le mouvement des idées dans l'émigration française* (1789–1815). 2 vols. Paris [c. 1924].

Bosher, J. F. *French Finances 1770–1795: From Business to Bureaucracy*. Cambridge, 1970.

Ceitac, Jane. *Voltaire et l'affaire des Natifs*. Geneva, 1956.

Chaponnière, Paul, *Voltaire chez les Calvinistes*. Paris, 1936.

Chapuisat, Edouard. "Voltaire et Mallet Du Pan." *Revue des travaux de l'Académie des Sciences morales et politiques et comptes rendus de ses séances*, 4ᵉ Série, 1952 (1ᵉʳ trimestre), pp. 152–64.

Choisy, Albert. *Notice généalogique et historique sur la famille Mallet de Genève, originaire de Rouen*. Geneva, 1930.

Cobban, Alfred. *Ambassadors and Secret Agents: The Diplomacy of the First Earl of Malmesbury at The Hague*. London, 1954.

Crue, François de. "Necker, Mirabeau at les Genevois de la Révolution." *Bibliothèque universelle et Revue suisse*, CXI (July–Sept., 1923), 1–17.

Cruppi, Jean. *Un avocat journaliste au XVIIIᵉ siècle: Linguet*. Paris, 1895.

Darnton, Robert C. "The Grub Street Style of Revolution: J.-P. Brissot, Police Spy." *Journal of Modern History*, XL, no. 3 (Sept., 1968), 301–27.

Darnton, Robert. *Mesmerism and the End of the Enlightenment in France*. Cambridge, Mass., 1968.

Desnoiresterres, Gustave. *Voltaire et la société française au XVIIIᵉ siècle*. 8 vols. Paris, 1867–1876.

Egret, Jean. *La Révolution des notables: Mounier et les Monarchiens, 1789*. Paris, 1950.

Entrèves, Alessandro Passerin d'. *Mallet Du Pan*. Reprinted from *Occidente*, no. 5 (Sept.–Oct., 1951).

2. In general, the following is a list of works cited; but a few of the titles, without having been specifically cited, have nevertheless been included because of their particular usefulness in certain respects.

————. "Mallet du Pan: A Swiss Critic of Democracy." *The Cambridge Journal*, I, no. 2 (Nov., 1947), 99–108.

Fazy, Henri. *Les constitutions de la République de Genève. Etude historique.* Geneva and Basel, 1890.

Gallois, Léonard. *Histoire des journaux et des journalistes de la Révolution française* (1789–1796). 2 vols. Paris, 1845–1846.

Gay, Peter. *Voltaire's Politics. The Poet as Realist.* Princeton, N.J., 1959.

Godechot, Jacques. *La Contre-révolution. Doctrine et action 1789–1804.* Paris, 1961.

————. "Le Directoire vu de Londres." *Annales historiques de la Révolution française*, XXI (1949), 311–36; XXII (1950), 1–27.

Grimsley, Ronald. *Jean D'Alembert* (1717–83). Oxford, 1963.

Hermann-Mascard, Nicole. *Le censure des livres à Paris à la fin de l'ancien régime* (1750–1789). Travaux et recherches de la Faculté de Droit et des Sciences économiques de Paris, Série "Sciences historiques," no. 13. Paris, 1968.

Hood, James N. "Protestant-Catholic Relations and the Roots of the First Popular Counterrevolutionary Movement in France." *Journal of Modern History*, XLIII, no. 2 (June, 1971), 245–75.

Karmin, Otto. *Sir Francis d'Ivernois* (1757–1842). *Sa vie, son oeuvre et son temps.* Geneva, 1920.

Lanzac de Laborie, L. de. *Un royaliste libéral en 1789: Jean-Joseph Mounier. Sa vie politique et ses écrits.* Paris, 1887.

Lüthy, Herbert. *La banque protestante en France de la révocation de l'Edit de Nantes à la Révolution.* Vol. II: *De la banque aux finances.* Paris, 1961.

Mallet, Bernard. *Mallet du Pan and the French Revolution.* London, 1902.

Martin, Henri. "Etude sur Linguet." *Travaux de l'Académie Impériale de Reims*, XXX (1859), 341–425; XXXI (1860), 81–149.

Matteucci, Nicola. *Jacques Mallet-Du Pan.* Naples: Instituto Italiano per gli Studi Storici, 1957.

————. "Mallet du Pan, genevois et européen." *Bulletin de la Société d'histoire et d'archéologie de Genève*, XI (1957), 153–68.

Moeckli-Cellier, Maurice. *La Révolution française et les écrivains suisses-romands* (1789–1815). Neuchâtel, Paris, 1931.

Palmer, R. R. *The Age of the Democratic Revolution. A Political History of Europe and America, 1760–1800.* 2 vols. Princeton, 1959–1964.

Pappas, John N. "Rousseau and D'Alembert." *Publications of the Modern Language Association*, LXXV, no. 1 (March, 1960), 46–60.

————. *Voltaire and D'Alembert*. Indiana University Humanities Series, no. 50. Bloomington, Ind., 1962.

Paris, Henri. "Rapport sur les concours." *Travaux de l'Académie Impériale de Reims*, XXX (1859), 484–503.

Pins, J. de. "La correspondance de Mallet du Pan avec la cour de Lisbonne." *Annales historiques de la Révolution française*, no. 178 (Oct.–Dec., 1964), pp. 469–77.

Poland, Burdette C. *French Protestantism and the French Revolution: A Study in Church and State, Thought and Religion, 1685–1815*. Princeton, 1957.

Société d'Histoire et d'Archéologie de Genève. *Histoire de Genève des origines à 1798*. Geneva, 1951.

Sordet, Louis. *Histoire des résidents de France à Genève*. Geneva, 1854.

Tate, Robert S., Jr. *Petit de Bachaumont: His Circle and the Mémoires secrets. Studies on Voltaire and the Eighteenth Century*, ed. Theodore Besterman, vol. LXV. Geneva, 1968.

Taylor, George V. "The Paris Bourse on the Eve of the Revolution, 1781–1789." *American Historical Review*, LXVII, no. 4 (July, 1962), 951–77.

Trenard, Louis. "La presse française des origines à 1788." Part II of *Histoire générale de la presse française*, vol. I, edited by Claude Bellanger et al. Paris, 1969.

Vingtrinier, Emmanuel. *La contre-révolution: première période, 1789–1791*. 2 vols. Paris, 1924.

Watts, George B. *Charles Joseph Panckoucke, "l'Atlas de la librairie française." Studies on Voltaire and the Eighteenth Century*, ed. Theodore Besterman, vol. LXVIII, 67–205. Geneva, 1969.

Works of Reference

Almanach royal.

Barbier, A.-A. *Dictionnaire des ouvrages anonymes*. Third edition. 4 vols. Paris, 1872–1879.

Biographie universelle, ancienne et moderne. ... 85 vols. Paris, 1811–1862.

Choisy, Albert. *Généalogies genevoises. Familles admises à la bourgeoisie avant la Réformation*. Geneva, 1947.

Dictionnaire historique et biographique de la Suisse. ... 7 vols. and *Supplément*. Neuchâtel, [1920–].

Galiffe, J.-A., et al. *Notices généalogiques sur les familles genevoises depuis les premiers temps jusqu'à nos jours*. 7 vols. Geneva, 1829–1895.

Geisendorf, Paul-F. *Bibliographie raisonnée de l'histoire de Genève des origines à 1798.* Vol. XLIII of *Mémoires et documents publiés par la Société d'histoire et d'archéologie de Genève.* Paris, 1966.

Haag, Eugène. *La France protestante: ou, Vie des protestants français qui se sont fait un nom dans l'histoire. . . .* 10 vols. Paris, Geneva, 1846–1859.

Hatin, Eugène. *Bibliographie historique et critique de la presse périodique française. . . .* Paris, 1866.

Montet, Albert de. *Dictionnaire biographique des Genevois et des Vaudois.* 2 vols. Lausanne, 1877–1878.

Nouvelle biographie générale depuis les temps les plus reculés jusqu'à nos jours. . . . 46 vols. Paris, 1853–1866.

Quérard, J.-M. *La France littéraire, ou dictionnaire bibliographique des savants, historiens et gens de lettres de la France, ainsi que les littérateurs étrangers qui ont écrit en français, plus particulièrement pendant les XVIIIe et XIXe siècles.* 12 vols. Paris, 1829–1864.

Rivoire, Emile. *Bibliographie historique de Genève au XVIIIe siècle.* Vols. XXVI–XXVII of *Mémoires et documents publiés par la Société d'histoire et d'archéologie de Genève.* Geneva, 1897.

Senebier, Jean. *Histoire littéraire de Genève.* 3 vols. Geneva, 1786.

Index